British Civilization

An introduction

Seventh edition

John Oakland

Routledge
Taylor & Francis Group

LONDON AND NEW YORK

First published 1989
Second edition 1991
Third edition 1995
Fourth edition 1998
Fifth edition 2002
Sixth edition 2006

This seventh edition published 2011
by Routledge
2 Park Square, Milton Park, Abingdon, Oxon OX14 4RN

Simultaneously published in the USA and Canada
by Routledge
711 Third Avenue, New York, NY 10017 (8th Floor)

Routledge is an imprint of the Taylor & Francis Group, an informa business

Designed and typeset in Berling by
Keystroke, Station Road, Codsall, Wolverhampton

British Library Cataloguing in Publication Data
A catalogue record for this book is available from the British Library

Library of Congress Cataloging in Publication Data
Oakland, John.
   British civilization : an introduction / John Oakland. — 7th ed.
      p. cm.
   Includes bibliographical references and index.
   1. Great Britain—Civilization—Textbooks. I. Title.
   DA110.O25 2010
   941—dc22   2010023761

ISBN 13: 978–0–415–58327–5 (hbk)
ISBN 13: 978–0–415–58328–2 (pbk)
ISBN 13: 978–0–203–83581–4 (ebk)

Contents

British Civilization

The seventh edition of this highly praised textbook has been substantially updated and revised to provide students of British studies with the perfect introduction to Britain, the country and its people, politics and government, education, economy, media, arts and religion. It includes:

- discussion of recent developments and areas of topical interest in British society such as immigration, the recession, devolution and Britain's relationships with the US and the EU, and coverage of the 2010 election
- new full-colour illustrations
- exercises and questions to stimulate class discussion
- insights into the attitudes of British people today towards important issues
- updated suggestions for further reading and useful websites
- a fully updated companion website featuring links to relevant articles and videos online, filmographies, quiz questions and instructors' resources.

British Civilization is a vital introduction to the crucial and complex identities of Britain.

For supplementary exercises, questions and tutor guidance, go to **www.routledge. com/textbooks/oakland**

John Oakland is former Senior Lecturer in English at the Norwegian University of Science and Technology and the author (with David Mauk) of *American Civilization* (now in its fifth edition), *Contemporary Britain*, and *British Civilization: A Student's Dictionary* (now in its second edition).

Reviews of this edition:

'This is an excellent core course book, suitable for both native and non-native speakers of English alike.'

Howard Jopp, *University of Hull*

'John Oakland covers a wide range of topics without becoming bogged down in details and while preserving the complexities of British civilization issues and debates.'

Ane Vikaune, *NTNU*

'For those who are fascinated by Britain, this is a book not to be missed; for those who aren't, this book will certainly change your mind.'

Li-Jiuan Lilie Tsay, *Ming-Chuan University*

'A highly readable exploration of British culture, media and the arts. This would be a valuable addition to the bookshelf for all undergraduates of the field.'

Russell Clark, *Keele University*

Reviews of the previous editions:

'John Oakland is the doyen of civilization studies.'

British Studies Now

'This is a first rate, lucidly written text.'

G.E.C. Paton, *Aston University*

'Suitable above all because it covers so many areas of contemporary institutions . . . a useful reference work.'

Patrick Leech, *University of Bologna*

'Strikes a balance between providing up-to-date information and being a source of general reference.'

Anne K. Bjørge, *Norwegian School of Economics and Business Administration*

'An excellent presentation of the British economic and political/institutional system.'

J. Condriou, *Université de Provence*

'A perfect tool and source for class activities.'

Borek Sousedik, *Tobos ELTR, Czech Republic*

Plates

Figures

Tables

Preface and acknowledgements

This book examines central structural features of British society, such as politics and government, international relations, the law, the economy, social services, the media, education and religion. Chapters on the country, the people, arts, sports and leisure are also included to illustrate the geographical, human and cultural diversity of British civilization. Opinion polls are used throughout to indicate the attitudes of British people to the social conditions in which they live and operate.

The book tries to apply description and analysis to its evaluation of the UK. Each chapter refers to relevant historical and policy contexts and provides information on current developments in Britain. The book allows students to organize their own responses to British society and encourages critical discussion. Essay and term exercises at the end of each chapter direct readers to central issues and can be adequately approached from material contained in the text. Further information may be found in suggested further reading and relevant websites. Recommended introductory dictionaries for terms are Crowther, J. (2005) *Oxford Guide to British and American Culture*, Oxford: Oxford University Press and Oakland, J. (2003) *British Civilization : A Student's Dictionary*, London: Routledge.

A book of this type is necessarily indebted for many of its facts, ideas and statistics, to a range of reference sources, which cannot all be mentioned here, but to which general acknowledgement is gratefully made (see also Further Reading at the end of each chapter). Particular thanks are due to the annual publications of the Office for National Statistics (especially *Regional Trends, Social Trends, Annual Abstract of Statistics, Family Spending* and *Key Population and Vital Statistics*), London: Palgrave Macmillan; the annual *British Social Attitudes*, National Centre for Social Research, London: Sage Publications; newspapers of record such as *The Times* (London); and public opinion poll sources, such as Market and Opinion Research International (Mori); IPSOS Mori;Gallup; ICM; Populus; and YouGov.

The websites included in this book are mainly those of public organizations. Although these may present official and standard views, they are often more permanent, up to date and informative than many independent websites, which can quickly change their addresses and content or simply disappear.

The term 'billion' in this book refers to 'a thousand million'.

Companion website

A range of student and instructor resources accompanying this book can be found online at **www.routledge.com/textbooks/oakland**. Instructor resources are available in a password-protected area of the site, and these include guidance on using the book in teaching and additional short essay questions similar to those that appear at the end of chapters. For those short essay questions marked in this book with an asterisk (*), there are suggestions for instructors on what to look for in student responses. Passwords are available to instructors through the website.

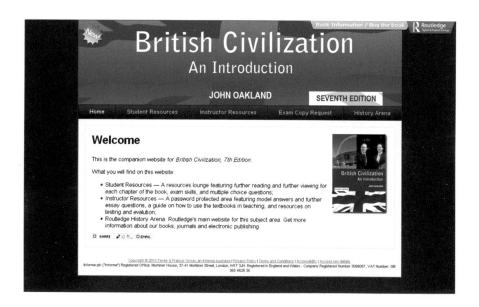

Chronology of significant dates in British history

Early history

Prehistory:	British Isles and Ireland originally part of European land mass: warmer conditions alternated with severe Ice Ages
700,000 BC:	butchered animal bones and stone artefacts indicate hominid activity
500,000 BC:	earliest human bones found in southern England (Boxgrove Man)
c. 250,000 BC:	nomadic Old Stone Age (Paleolithic) peoples arrived
50,000 BC:	warmer climate encouraged arrival of ancestors of modern populations
10,000 BC:	end of Ice Ages. Population consisted of hunter-gatherers and fishers
5,000 BC:	contemporary islands gradually separated from Continental Europe
c. 3,000 BC:	New Stone Age (Neolithic) peoples populated the western parts of the islands. Farming introduced; stone and earth monuments built
c. 1,800 BC:	Bronze Age settlers (Beaker Folk) in southeast and eastern England; traded in gold, copper and tin
600 BC:	settlement of the Celts (Iron Age) from western and central Europe began
c. 200 BC:	invasions by Belgic tribes, mainly in eastern England
55–54 BC:	Julius Caesar's exploratory expeditions
AD 43:	Roman conquest of England, Wales and (temporarily) lowland Scotland by Claudius began. Christian influences
122–38:	Hadrian's Wall built between Scotland and England
400:	Gaelic Scots (Scotti) from Ireland colonized western Scotland
c. 409:	Roman army withdrew from Britain; wars between the Celts
c. 410:	Germanic (Anglo-Saxon) invasions began
c. 450–600:	eight Anglo-Saxon kingdoms (the Heptarchy) gradually created in England. Mainly Celtic peoples in Wales, Ireland, Scotland and Cornwall
430:	existing Celtic Christianity in Ireland later spread by St Patrick (from 432) and other missionaries in Ireland, Scotland, Wales and northern England

597:	St Augustine preached Christianity (Roman Catholic Church model) to Anglo-Saxons of southern England. Creation of ecclesiastical capital in Canterbury, Kent
664:	Synod of Whitby chose Roman Catholic Church model for British Christianity
789–95:	Scandinavian (Viking) raids began
800:	Cornwall conquered by Anglo-Saxons
820:	Anglo-Saxon kingdoms dominated by Wessex; union of the Heptarchy
832–60:	union of Scots and Picts in Scotland under Kenneth Macalpin to form most of the eventual kingdom of Scotland
860s:	Scandinavians controlled much of northern and eastern England (East Anglia, Northumbria and eastern Mercia – the Danelaw)
871–99:	reign of Alfred the Great of Wessex
878:	Scandinavians defeated in England by King Alfred of Wessex and confined to the Danelaw
954:	the Kingdom of England formed; recovery of the Danelaw
1013–4:	Sven of Norway/Denmark conquered England
1014:	Scandinavians defeated in Ireland
1018:	Scotland came under English rule

The early Middle Ages

1066:	September; King Harold defeated Norwegian army at Stamford Bridge, October; William I (the Conqueror) defeated King Harold at Hastings and ascended the English throne. The Norman Conquest; feudalism introduced
1072:	William I invaded Scotland
1086:	Domesday Book (tax and land records) compiled for England by Normans
1169:	Henry II invaded and controlled the east coast of Ireland
1200s:	first Oxford and Cambridge colleges founded
1215:	King John signed Magna Carta at Runnymede, near Windsor, which protected English feudal (aristocratic) rights against royal abuse
1258 and 1264:	first English parliamentary structures
1282:	much of Wales controlled by England under Edward I
1295:	the Model Parliament (first regular English Parliament)
1296:	the Scots defeated by Edward I
1297:	first Irish Parliament
1301:	Edward of Caernarvon (later Edward II) named as first Prince of Wales
1314:	Scottish victory at battle of Bannockburn regained Scottish independence
1326:	first Scottish Parliament

The late Middle Ages

1337:	Hundred Years War between England and France began
1348–9:	plague (Black Death) destroyed a third of the islands' population

1362:	English replaced French as the official language
1381:	Peasants' Revolt (popular rebellion) in England
c. 1387–c. 1394:	Geoffrey Chaucer wrote *The Canterbury Tales*
1400–10:	Failed Welsh revolt by Owain Glyndwr against English rule
1406:	Earl of Derby bought Isle of Man from Scotland
1407:	House of Commons became responsible for taxation
1411:	first university in Scotland founded (St Andrews)
1415:	Battle of Agincourt; England defeated France
1455–87:	Wars of the Roses between Yorkists and Lancastrians
1469:	Orkney and Shetland transferred to Scotland by Norway
1477:	first book printed in England, by William Caxton

Towards the nation state (Britain)

1509:	accession of Henry VIII
1513:	Henry VIII defeated the Scots at Flodden
1534–40:	Henry VIII broke with the Papacy and became head of the English Church (Roman Catholic); beginning of the English Reformation
1536–42:	Acts of Union led to legal and administrative integration of England and Wales
1547–53:	Protestantism became official religion in England under Edward VI
1553–58:	Catholic reaction under Mary I; Roman Catholicism restored
1558–1603:	Elizabeth I; Protestantism confirmed
1558:	Calais, England's last possession in France, lost
1560:	creation of Protestant Church of Scotland by John Knox; the Scottish Reformation
1585–90:	first English colonial ventures in North America
1587:	Mary Stuart, Queen of Scots, executed in London
1588:	defeat of Spanish Armada
c. 1590–c. 1613:	plays of William Shakespeare written
1600:	East India (trading) Company founded
1603:	dynastic union of England and Scotland under James VI of Scotland (James I of England); Union of the Two Crowns
1607:	Plantation of Ulster (Northern Ireland) with Scottish and English Protestant settlers; establishment of first permanent English colony in North America at Jamestown (Virginia)
1611:	the Authorized (King James) Version of the Bible issued
1628:	monarch's power restricted by the Petition of Right
1641:	rebellion in Ireland
1642–48:	Civil Wars between King Charles 1 and Parliament
1649:	execution of Charles I; monarchy abolished
1653–58:	Oliver Cromwell ruled England as Lord Protector
1660:	monarchy restored under Charles II (the Restoration)
1665:	the Great Plague in England
1666:	the Great Fire of London
1679:	Habeas Corpus Act passed. Party political system gradually initiated
1686:	Isaac Newton proposed laws of motion and gravitation
1688:	The Glorious Revolution; accession of William III and Mary II to the throne

1689:	the Declaration of Rights
1690:	Irish defeated by William III at the Battle of the Boyne

The eighteenth century

1707:	Acts of Union joined England/Wales and Scotland (Great Britain); unification of Scottish and English Parliaments
1715:	Scottish Jacobite rebellions crushed
1721:	Robert Walpole became Britain's first prime minister
1739:	War with Spain
1742:	War with France
1745:	Failed Scottish rebellion under Bonnie Prince Charlie to restore the British throne to the Stuarts
1756:	the Seven Years War
1750s–1830s:	Industrial Revolutions
1759:	war with France; Canada won from French
1761:	opening of the Bridgewater Canal began the Canal Age
1765:	Isle of Man purchased by British Crown
1769:	the steam engine and the spinning machine invented
1775–83:	American War of Independence; loss of the Thirteen Colonies
1793–1815:	Revolutionary and Napoleonic Wars

The nineteenth century

1801:	Act of Union joined Great Britain and Ireland (United Kingdom)
1805:	Battle of Trafalgar: Nelson defeated the French navy
1807:	abolition of the slave trade in the British Empire; ending of slavery in 1833
1815:	Napoleon defeated by Wellington at Waterloo
1825:	opening of the Stockton and Darlington Railway, the world's first public passenger railway
1829:	Catholic emancipation (freedom of religious worship)
1832:	First Reform Act extended the male franchise (vote) by 50 per cent
1837–1901:	reign of Queen Victoria
1838:	the People's Charter and the beginning of trade unions
1839:	The Durham Report on dominion status for some colonies, such as Canada
1845:	disastrous harvest failure in Ireland
1851:	first organized trade unions appeared
1853–6:	The Crimean War
1868:	Trade Union Congress (TUC) established
1870:	compulsory elementary state school education introduced in England. Canada became first dominion state
1871:	legal recognition of trade unions
1899:	The Boer War (South Africa)

The twentieth century

1901:   death of Queen Victoria
1904:   Entente Cordiale with France
1910–36:   the British Empire reached its global territorial peak
1911:   political veto power of the House of Lords restricted
1914–18:   First World War
1916:   Easter Rising against Britain in Dublin
1918:   all men over 21 and women over 30 receive the vote
1919:   League of Nations created
1921–2:   Irish Free State established by Anglo-Irish Treaty; Northern Ireland remained
            part of the United Kingdom with its own devolved parliament
1924:   first Labour government
1926:   the General Strike
1928:   votes for all women over 21
1930s: economic depression, poverty and high unemployment; Jarrow March 1936
1931:   British Commonwealth of Nations emerges
1936:   abdication of King Edward VIII
1939–45:   Second World War (Winston Churchill, Prime Minister, 1940)
1940:   the Battle of Britain
1941:   Anglo-American alliance sealed with the Atlantic Charter
1942:   Beveridge Report laid the foundations for the Welfare State; American troops
            arrived in Europe (Belfast)
1944:   Butler Education Act: state secondary education free and compulsory to 15;
            allied troops landed in Normandy on D-Day (liberation of France)
1945:   United Nations formed with Britain as a founder member; Labour won
            landslide general election with Clement Attlee as prime minister
1947:   the Yalta Conference shaped post-war Europe; independence for India and
            Pakistan, beginning of large-scale decolonialization; coal industry nationalized
1948:   National Health Service created, free medical care for all: postwar
            immigration from the Commonwealth began: Olympic Games, London
1949:   Irish Free State became the Republic of Ireland; NATO created; the modern
            Commonwealth emerged
1950:   British troops supported US forces in Korean War:
1951:   Conservatives under Winston Churchill won general election; Festival of
            Britain
1952:   accession of Elizabeth II
1953:   Watson and Crick published discovery of DNA
1955:   Conservatives won general election with Sir Anthony Eden as prime minister:
            commercial television started
1956:   the Suez Canal Crisis; Britain's first nuclear power station became operative
1957:   Ghana became first British colony in Africa to gain independence; Britain
            tested its first hydrogen bomb; Clean Air Act; Eden resigned as prime
            minister, replaced by Harold Macmillan
1958:   first phase of motorway system opened
1959:   Conservatives under Harold Macmillan won general election
1960:   Britain joined European Free Trade Association (EFTA)
1963:   Conservative Sir Alec Douglas-Home became prime minister; new
            universities opened; France vetoed Britain's entry to European Economic
            Community (EEC), now EU

1964:   the rise of supermarkets: Labour won general election with Harold Wilson as prime minister

1965:   death penalty (by hanging) for serious crimes abolished; comprehensive education system initiated

1965–9:   oil and gas discoveries in the North Sea

1966:   England won football World Cup

1967:   abortion and homosexuality legalized

1968:   protest and violence erupted in Northern Ireland

1969:   vote extended to all persons over 18; Concorde, the world's first supersonic airliner, made its first flight

1970:   Conservatives won general election with Edward Heath as prime minister

1971:   decimal currency introduced; first British soldier killed in Northern Ireland's 'Troubles'; North Sea oil concessions auctioned

1972:   direct rule from Westminster in Northern Ireland; 14 killed on Bloody Sunday, Londonderry, Northern Ireland; Asians expelled from Uganda with many settling in Britain

1973:   Britain left EFTA and entered EEC (now EU)

1974:   (February) General election resulted in 'hung Parliament' with Harold Wilson as prime minister; (October) Labour won small majority in general election with Harold Wilson as prime minister

1975:   referendum affirmed Britain's continued membership of EEC

1976:   Britain forced to borrow money from International Monetary Fund; Harold Wilson resigned as prime minister and was replaced by James Callaghan

1978–79: Strikes paralysed Britain during 'Winter of Discontent'

1978:   world's first test tube baby born in Oldham

1979:   Margaret Thatcher: Britain's first woman prime minister; Lord Mountbatten killed by IRA; Wales and Scotland rejected devolution

1981:   Social Democratic Party (SDP) formed; hunger strikes by Republican prisoners ended after 10 deaths; Humber Bridge opened; race riots in Brixton

1982:   the Falklands War with Argentina; economic recession

1983:   Conservative Prime Minister Margaret Thatcher re-elected in landslide victory

1984:   Miners' strike over pit closures; IRA bombers attacked Conservative Party Conference in Brighton

1985:   Anglo-Irish Agreement gave Irish Republic a part in the organization of Northern Ireland

1986:   Major national industries privatized

1987:   Conservative Prime Minister Margaret Thatcher won third general election

1988:   SDP merged with Liberal Party; party became the Liberal Democrats

1989:   Tim Berners-Lee invented the World Wide Web

1990:   introduction of 'poll tax' provoked riots in London; Thatcher resigned; replaced by John Major

1991:   Liberation of Kuwait; Operation Desert Storm

1992:   Conservatives won general election with John Major as prime minister: withdrawal of pound sterling from ERM on 'Black Wednesday'

1994:   Channel Rail Tunnel between France and Britain opened; first women priests ordained in Church of England

1997:   Referendums on devolution for Scotland and Wales; sovereignty of Hong Kong transferred to China; Labour won general election with Tony Blair as prime minister

1998:   Belfast (Good Friday) Agreement; endorsed by referendums in both parts of
             Ireland; election of devolved Northern Ireland Assembly
1999:   devolution structures in Scotland (a Parliament) and Wales (an Assembly)

The twenty-first century

2000:   number of hereditary peers entitled to sit and vote in the House of Lords
             reduced from 750 to 92; global stock markets fell as 'dotcom bubble' burst
2001:   Labour won general election with Tony Blair as prime minister; foot and
             mouth disease in rural Britain; Northern Ireland Assembly suspended until
             2007
2003:   gains for Democratic Unionist Party and Sinn Féin in Northern Ireland
             Assembly elections: Britain and coalition forces invaded Iraq
2004:   10 new states joined the EU
2005:   Labour Party achieved third successive victory in general election, with Tony
             Blair as prime minister; Northern Ireland Assembly remained suspended;
             IRA ordered members to cease 'military operations'; international
             decommissioning body reported that IRA weapons had been 'put beyond
             use'; some Unionist paramilitaries moved to disarm; Kyoto Protocol on
             climate change came into force; suicide bombers killed 52 people on
             London's transport systems
2006:   Northern Ireland Assembly met between May and November for the first
             time since suspension in 2002; thwarted attempts to blow up planes between
             UK and USA using liquid explosives
2007:   in Northern Ireland, Assembly restored and Ian Paisley led a new power-
             sharing government as First Minister, with Sinn Féin's Martin McGuinness as
             his deputy; Gordon Brown became prime minister and Labour Party leader
             following the resignation of Tony Blair; failed car bomb attacks in London
             and Glasgow; severe floods in central England caused great damage
2007–09:   credit crunch: financial and banking problems; international recession
2008:   Labour Party suffered worst local election results in 40 years, finishing behind
             the Conservatives and Liberal Democrats with 24 per cent of the national
             vote 2009; in European elections, on a low turnout of 33 per cent, Labour
             polled 15.7 per cent of the vote and finished third behind the Conservatives
             (27.7 per cent) and United Kingdom Independence Party (16.5 per cent); in
             local elections Labour polled its worst ever local result with 23 per cent after
             the Conservatives on 38 per cent and Lib Dems on 28 per cent
2010:   British general election resulted in a hung Parliament and coalition
             government between Conservatives and Liberal Democrats

1

The British context

This chapter examines four aspects of British civilization (historical growth, structural or institutional change, contemporary conditions and British attitudes to the country). These will be later treated in more specific detail according to chapter topics (such as government, education or religion). Each is placed within a historical perspective in order to show how Britain has evolved to its contemporary position.

The historical context is an important tool for understanding British society, whether for Britons or overseas observers. However, the search for historical 'truth' inevitably involves contested interpretations of the same assumed facts. Surveys also regularly suggest that many British people of all ages are in fact ignorant of much of their country's past and current history. For example, a poll by student accommodation provider UNITE in February 2010 (shortly before the May general election) found that 33 per cent of students did not know that Gordon Brown led the Labour Party, while 34 per cent could not name David Cameron as Conservative leader; and fewer than 50 per cent knew that Nick Clegg was leader of the Liberal Democrats.

On the other hand, international respondents to questionnaires often reveal stereotypical perceptions of Britain and its people. They tend, confusingly, to see the British as either fair-minded, outward-looking and tolerant or as closed-minded, insular, conventional and backward-looking with an exaggerated and outdated respect for their history and traditions. The country is often perceived from abroad only through images of monarchy, castles, aristocracy, quaint behaviour, class conflict, a stagnating, risk-averse economy, unimaginative food and old-fashioned institutions. Such stereotypes do not accurately convey the complex and diverse reality of contemporary Britain with its contradictions, strengths and weaknesses.

In order to combat ignorance of the country, British critics call for the comprehensive teaching of British history in schools and a general improvement in educational standards. The previous Labour government introduced what many see as inadequate courses on citizenship into the school curriculum in the hope that pupils will learn what constitutes a British civic culture and social structure. Official bodies also attempt to counter negative overseas images. It remains to be seen whether these efforts at consciousness raising will be successful.

Historical growth

Britain's constitutional title today is the United Kingdom of Great Britain and Northern Ireland or UK. The nation comprises large and smaller islands off the north-western European mainland, which at various points are touched by the North Sea, the English Channel, the Irish Sea or the Atlantic Ocean. The biggest island, Great Britain, is divided into England, Scotland and Wales, and Northern Ireland shares the second-largest island with the Republic of Ireland, with which it has a land border.

In prehistory, these areas were visited by Old, Middle and New Stone Age nomads, some of whom later settled permanently. From about 600 BC–AD 1066, the islands experienced successive settlement and invasion patterns from peoples who originated in mainland Europe, such as so-called Celts, Belgic tribes, Romans, Germanic tribes (Anglo-Saxons), Scandinavians and Normans. In conventional accounts of British history, these immigrants over time collectively created a multi-ethnic British population with mixed identities and different origins.

The early settlers and invaders contributed haphazardly between the ninth and twelfth centuries AD to the building blocks on which were gradually established the separate nations of England, Wales, Scotland and Ireland (with England and Scotland gaining strong early individual identities by the tenth century). They experienced very different internal situations, abrupt political changes and a degree of violence as well as external conflicts both with one another and other countries in their historical growth to nationhood. There are still substantial differences between these peoples and competing allegiances within the four countries themselves.

Later developments within the islands were greatly influenced first by the expansionist, military aims of English monarchs and second by a series of political unions. Ireland and Wales had been effectively under English control since the twelfth and thirteenth centuries respectively, while Scotland was joined dynastically to England in 1603. Movement towards a British state (with its Parliament power base in London) was achieved by political unions between England, Wales and Scotland (Great Britain) in 1707 and between Great Britain and Ireland in 1801. In 1921, southern Ireland left the union to eventually become the independent Republic of Ireland while Northern Ireland remained part of the United Kingdom.

These historical developments involved political deals, manipulation and constitutional struggles and encouraged the gradual creation of a centralized British state, the UK, which owed much to English models and dominance. State structures such as the monarchy, government, Parliament and the law developed slowly and unevenly, rather than by planned change, to provide an umbrella organization for the four component countries. But there were also periods of violent upheaval and ideological conflict (such as royalist and tribal battles, civil wars, nationalist revolts by the Scots, Welsh and Irish against the English, struggles with European powers, religious ferment and social dissension).

Despite a confused and haphazard history full of unforeseen events, some historians have argued that the modern British state developed in an evolutionary and pragmatic manner. This process has been attributed to the supposed insular and conservative mentalities of island peoples, with their preference for traditional habits and institutions, orderly progress and distrust of sudden change. Some influences have come from abroad during the long historical process. However the absence of any successful external military invasion of the islands since the Norman Conquest of AD 1066 has allowed the nations of England, Scotland, Wales and Ireland to develop internally in distinctive ways, despite frequent and violent struggles among and within them.

The social organizations and constitutional principles of the British state, such as parliamentary democracy, government, the law, economic systems, a welfare state and religious faiths, have developed slowly. They have been forged by disputes, conflict, self-interest, consensus, compromise and conquest. The eventual structures and philosophies of British statehood have been imitated by other countries, or exported abroad through the creation of a global empire from the sixteenth century and a commercial need to build world markets for British goods.

The developed British Empire was an extension of earlier English monarchs' internal military expansionism within the islands and in mainland Europe. Following initial reversals in Europe, they sought raw materials, possessions, trade

PLATE 1.1 The eleventh- or twelfth-century Bayeux Tapestry in Bayeux, France, depicts the Battle of Hastings, 1066, and the Norman Conquest of England.
(Roger-Viollet/Rex Features)

PLATE 1.2 Oliver Cromwell (1599–1658), English general, politician and puritan who led the Parliamentary army against King Charles I in the English Civil War (1642–51). He became Lord Protector of England (1653–58) after the king's defeat and execution in 1649. The period 1649–1600 constitutes the only break in the English monarchy's otherwise continuous history. *(Rex Features)*

and power overseas. This colonialism was aided by increasing military might (achieved by later victories over European and other nations) into the twentieth century.

Internally, successive agricultural revolutions in Britain from the New Stone Age and Anglo-Saxon period added appreciably to the country's wealth, exports, prestige and international trade. Britain also developed an early manufacturing and financial base. It became an industrial and largely urban country from the late eighteenth century because of a series of industrial revolutions and inventions. Throughout its history, Britain has been responsible for major and influential scientific, medical and technological advances.

The historical development of the British state and its empire was aided by increasing economic and military strength, so that by the nineteenth century the country had become a dominant industrial and political world power. It was a main player in developing Western ideas and principles of law, property, business, liberty, capitalism, parliamentary democracy and civil society.

Political union within Britain, despite continuing tensions, had also gradually encouraged the idea of a British identity (Britishness), in which all the component countries of the UK could share. This was tied to Britain's imperial position in the world and an identification with the powerful institutions of the state, such as the monarchy, law, Parliament, the military and Protestant religion. But national

PLATE 1.3 Cecil Rhodes (1853–1902) was a British-born South African politician who epitomized expansive British colonialism in the nineteenth century. He founded Rhodesia, now Zimbabwe. This *Punch* cartoon links British imperialism with the Colossus of Rhodes (a statue of Apollo on the Greek island of Rhodes which was one of the Seven Wonders of the World until destroyed by an earthquake).
(Punch Cartoon Library)

THE RHODES COLOSSUS
STRIDING FROM CAPE TOWN TO CAIRO.

identities in the four countries of the union persisted and became stronger as competing forces arose in the twentieth century. Pressure for constitutional change eventually resulted first in the partition of Ireland in 1921 and second in devolution (transfer of some political power from the London Parliament to elected bodies in Scotland, Wales and Northern Ireland) by 1998–9. These changes encouraged fierce debate about such issues as the nature of Britishness, national identities within the union and the future constitutional and political structure of the United Kingdom (including the possibility of complete independence for Scotland), which are still being addressed in contemporary Britain.

The British state has seen many other political reforms over time, such as the extension of the vote in the nineteenth and twentieth centuries, the diminishing power of the aristocratic House of Lords, the increasing authority of the elected House of Commons and the decline of executive monarchy in the parliamentary structure. Britain underwent substantial collectivist social changes in the twentieth century, such as nationalization (with the state becoming the owner of public industries and services) and the creation of a welfare state. These emphases later changed as government economic policies shifted British society, collectively and individually, along more free market lines.

The country experienced significant change, as well as relative decline, in the twentieth century. Its social and economic strength was seriously reduced by the effects of two world wars in the first half of the century and by the dismantling of its imperial global power in the second half. Its ethnic composition, state structures, social policies, religious beliefs and economic institutions have all been affected by profound domestic developments and external pressures. Traditional notions of Britain's place in the world, the nature of its society and hopes for its future have been subjected to debates, re-evaluation and pressures on many levels. These continued as the country entered the twenty-first century.

Since the Second World War (1939–45), Britain has had to adjust with difficulty to the results of a withdrawal from empire, which was inevitable in the face of rising nationalism and self-determination in the colonies; a reduction in world political status; global economic recessions; a relative decline in economic power; increased foreign competition; internal social change; a geopolitical world order of superpowers (the United States and the Soviet Union); international fluctuations and new tensions after the break-up of the Soviet Union in the 1990s,

PLATE 1.4 Edward Heath (1916–2005), who, as British Conservative prime minister (1970–74), led Britain into the then European Economic Community (now European Union) by signing the EEC agreement in 1972.
(PUBLI PRESS/Rex Features)

PLATE 1.5 Bomb attack on London bus, Tavistock Square, 7 July 2005. Suicide bombers attacked the London transport system, including the Underground, destroying a double-decker bus and killing fifty-six people (including thirteen on the bus).
(*Balkanpix.com/Rex Features*)

with the USA becoming the dominant force; the emergence of Far Eastern powers such as China and India; and a changing Europe following the destruction wrought by two world wars.

The nation has been forced into a reluctant search for a new identity and direction, both internationally and nationally, which some critics argue it has not yet achieved. While maintaining many of its traditional worldwide commercial, cultural and political links, such as the increasingly criticized 'special relationship' with the United States of America, it has nevertheless moved from empire and the successor Commonwealth towards an avowed economic and political commitment to Europe, mainly through membership of what is now the European Union (EU).

In recent centuries, Britain has rarely seen itself as an integral part of mainland Europe. It has sheltered behind the sea barrier of the English Channel and its outlook has been westwards and worldwide. Yet today the psychological and physical isolation from Europe is slowly changing, as illustrated by increased cooperation between Britain and other European countries and by the opening in 1994 of a Channel rail tunnel between England and France. However, the relationship between Britain and Europe continues to be problematic and new associations have been forced by events and circumstances rather than wholeheartedly sought. A scepticism about Europe and the historical impulses to national independence and isolationism still appear to condition many British people in their dealings with and attitudes to the outside world, despite their reliance on global trade and international relationships.

British politicians argue that isolationism is not a viable option in a globalized world. Britain has been involved, not without continuing public protest, in recent overseas military action in Bosnia, Kosovo, two Iraq wars, Afghanistan and other trouble spots worldwide as a coalition partner in the North Atlantic Treaty Organization (NATO) and American-led military action. Britain has attracted terrorist threats itself (arguably for some critics as a result of such commitments), culminating in suicide bombings against the London public transport system by British-born Islamists on 7 July 2005 and further failed attempts on 21 July. These terrorist attacks have raised debates about the nature and loyalty of the country's multi-ethnic population and about government policies on asylum seekers and immigration as the country seeks to protect itself in a changing world. Britain has become intimately involved in the globalized debates of the twenty-first century, from which it cannot isolate itself as it did at periods in its earlier history.

Structural change

Contemporary Britain is facing a variety of structural or institutional issues, the outcome of which will determine how the society develops. Historically, structural change has been inevitably conditioned by social, economic, legal, religious and political developments. Some were abrupt and often violent, while others occurred in a slower, more pragmatic fashion. The resulting structural features have taken different forms and sizes, operate on national and local levels, and condition cultural identities, values and attitudes.

The major formal features, such as Parliament, law and government, are concerned with state or public business and initiate policies in 'top-down' form. Decisions are decided by centralized and multi-level bodies (whether elected or appointed) in the power hierarchy and then imposed on lower levels. Some of these processes are criticized in Britain because they allegedly distance decision-makers from the general public, undercut accountability and result in a 'democratic deficit'.

British people frequently complain that they should be consulted more about institutional changes in society and have a greater say in local and national affairs. Elites and bureaucrats at various levels may lack competence, waste taxpayers' money on dubious projects and produce inadequate policies. This situation has led to a disenchantment with and withdrawal from political processes by many people, a distrust of politicians and angry demands that public officials should be more accountable.

However, there are many other structures on both public and private levels of social activity, such as sports activities, families, leisure activities, neighbour-hoods, youth culture, faith groups, local communities, interest groups, ethnic fellowships and habitual ways of life which have their own particular value systems and organizations. They often have a 'bottom-up' form in which policies and behaviour are said to be linked closely to the concerns of society's grassroots. They may illustrate more localized, informal and democratic characteristics than the top-down model. But these communities, including local government, can also be dominated by elites, which may be in conflict with other individuals who object to being controlled by the leadership. This situation at both local and national levels may provoke a sense of alienation and powerlessness in the excluded groups.

The 'British way of life' and British identities are determined by how people function within and react, whether positively, negatively or apathetically, to social structures. These are not remote abstractions but affect individuals directly and immediately in their daily lives. For example, government policies impinge upon citizens and their families; commercial organizations influence choices in food, music, clothes and fashion; the media may try to shape news values and agendas, or seek more profits; sponsorship and advertising may determine the nature of sports, the media and other activities; devolved government bodies in Scotland, Wales and Northern Ireland initiate policies for their own regions; local govern-ment throughout the UK conditions communal activities; and community life is subject to small-scale (and sometimes eccentric) influences.

These structural features reflect a range of practices on both high and popular cultural levels in Britain. High cultural forms may often appeal to a minority and be connected to wealth and class concerns, although the blurring of class barriers, expanded education and a decline in deference have now opened these up to more widespread participation. Yet popular cultural activities have always been present in British society. They have become more numerous and diverse since the 1960s because of greater affluence, more varied life opportunities and new accessible forms. Such a mass popular culture (reflected in for example sport, television, music and fashion) is now significant and influences social patterns, behaviour, economic consumption and the adoption of very diverse lifestyles. For some critics, however, it has resulted in a trivializing and superficial element of British life.

The number and variety of top-down and bottom-up structures mean that there are many different and often conflicting 'ways of life' in contemporary Britain, which contribute to the pluralistic nature of the society. Some critics argue that the main defining features of British life are a healthy diversity and change at all levels. Others maintain that these phenomena, particularly since the 1960s, have led to social fragmentation and antisocial behaviour, a weakened sense of community and civic responsibility, a decline in nationally accepted values and identities, confusion and uncertainty. Yet others suggest that the emphasis upon 'pluralism' and 'diversity' is inaccurate. They stress instead those normative and traditional behaviour patterns or values which arguably still exist for most people in Britain.

It has historically been argued that national and local behaviour in Britain has often reflected a strong individualistic streak in the British mentality, which views 'authority' with suspicion and has often led to nonconformity in many areas of society. Debate in the 2010 general election campaign frequently focused on whether the country was an entrepreneurial, a cooperative or a centralized state. The discussion also posed the question of whether traditional notions of community, engagement and commitment are failing in Britain and whether the country has become a 'broken society' without fixed social or familial points.

Traditionally it has been assumed that organizational structures must adapt to new situations if they are to survive, and their present roles may therefore be very different from their original functions. Pressures are consequently placed on them to more adequately reflect and respond to current public worries and concerns. The performances of British national and local institutions are vigorously debated and many are found wanting. It is questioned whether they are able to cope with and reflect the needs and demands of a complex contemporary life; whether (and how) they might be reformed in order to operate more efficiently and responsively; or whether they are in fact capable of operating in today's Britain.

Such questioning is also linked to very varied arguments about how the country should be organized socially, politically and economically. It is often debated whether this soul-searching actually results in appropriate action or merely promotes divisive, fashionable and temporary programmes, which quickly fail. Arguably, the inconclusive result of the 2010 general election, in which no party won a majority of the votes, reflects these doubts and concerns.

Contemporary conditions

The 'state of Britain' debate and the anxieties of the British about the direction of the society have been widely discussed in recent years. A leader in *The Times* (London, 2 November 2005) argued that:

> Britons have long prided themselves on pragmatism and common sense. The British way of life, an accretion of centuries of experience in these islands, has largely been based on what works: the social structures, economic relationships and the framework of justice. There was never a need for a formal constitution; the law, evolving in response to changing circumstances, was based on shared values, general tolerance and a common understanding of rights and duties.
>
> But in the last thirty years, this complacency has been shaken. A multicultural Britain can no longer rely for its cohesion on a common background. Devolution, regional nationalism, ethnic division and religious extremism have so widened the divisions that the old certainties no longer prevail. What now passes for common sense? What is the glue holding this disparate society together? What is Britishness?
>
> Five years ago the question was academic. Now it is as acute as it is sensitive. Immigration has enhanced and enlivened the country, but has brought to Britain people with beliefs, values and backgrounds far removed and sometimes at odds, with the prevailing culture. A misunderstood multiculturalism has led to social and cultural fragmentation at the expense of a common core. And the shock of the 7/7 [2005] bombings has raised the question: what does it mean to be British?

Britain today is a complex society in which diversity and change have created problems as well as advantages. While the country may give an impression of homogeneous or uniform behaviour in certain respects, there are divisions caused by such factors as the influence of London on the rest of the country; the cultural distinctiveness of Wales, Scotland, Northern Ireland and England; demands for greater autonomy in local government and less centralized control from London as well as for greater democracy and accountability in local government itself; disparities between affluent and economically depressed areas throughout the country (including the crime, decay and social deprivation to be found in many inner-city and rural locations); alleged cultural and economic gaps between areas in the north and south; political variety (reflected in support for different political parties in different areas of the country); continuing debates on the positions of women, special-interest groups and minority ethnic communities (the latter involving tensions between British national identity and ethnicity); campaigns or demands for a variety of individual and collective rights (with the conflict between rights and responsibilities); a gulf between rich and poor, with a growing under-class of disadvantaged, alienated or rootless people; tensions between the cities and the countryside; and increasing generational differences between young and old in all ethnic groups (associated with the increasing longevity and numbers of the elderly and criticism of youth behaviour).

Such features illustrate some, if not all, of the present divisions in British society. They also suggest a decline in the allegedly traditional deference to author-ity, consensus views and support for national institutions such as the monarchy, the professions, schools, churches and Parliament. Britons are now more noncon-formist, multi-ethnic, secular and individualistic than in the past. Opinion polls suggest that they themselves feel they have become more aggressive, more selfish, less tolerant, less kind, less moral, less honest and less polite. Their society has been portrayed in research surveys as one riddled with mistrust, coarseness and cynicism in which materialism, egotism, relativistic values, celebrity worship, personal entitlement, vulgarity, public emotionalism and sensationalism constitute the new modes of behaviour.

On some levels, such developments have led to an increase in antisocial behaviour, yobbishness, public scruffiness, vandalism, serious alcohol and drug abuse, 'binge drinking', disputes between neighbours, violent crime and assaults, public disorder, the growth of criminal gangs and gun and knife attacks, which many British people find disturbing. The tolerant civic image of individual liberty, social cohesion, identity and community which foreigners and Britons often have of the country has suffered. For some critics, this has been replaced by dysfunctional families, social fragmentation, instability, isolation and community disintegration.

A Populus poll for *The Times* in February 2010 found that a large majority (70 per cent of respondents) believed British society was broken and 73 per cent believed British politics were broken; 64 per cent thought Britain was going in the wrong direction; 56 per cent stated that they hardly recognized the country they were living in any more; and a considerable 82 per cent felt it was time for a change. On a 0–10 scale of dissatisfaction to satisfaction, the political system rates lowest at 4.32. The performance of national government was rated at 4.42, while the National Health Service (NHS) was at 6.51. Other responses suggested a general dissatisfaction with the state of Britain, with 42 per cent saying that they would emigrate if they could. According to a quality of life index published by *International Living* magazine in January 2010, Britain had dropped to twenty-fifth place on a list of the best countries in the world to live in. The UK's climate, crime rate, congested roads and long working hours were apparently to blame for its low position on the list.

However, the Populus poll above did indicate some relatively positive and optimistic results. Many respondents (50 per cent) said they felt Britain's best years were still to come; 48 per cent were happier than ten years ago; 60 per cent looked forward to the future with optimism; and 55 per cent thought that their children's lives would be better than their own.

Critics, politicians and a majority of respondents in public opinion polls want a return to civic responsibility, consensus or inclusive politics and a caring society in which individuals feel that they have a place. Yet these hopes may conflict with the changes which have affected Britain over the past sixty years and produced a society with diverse experiences and expectations. The essential question remains whether negative images of contemporary Britain are widespread and representative of the whole society or the result of occasional 'moral panics' often generated by an intrusive media and social commentators. Opinion polls seem to indicate that many British do feel that the negatives have increased, are now more apparent in everyday life and are symptomatic of real social breakdown.

Contemporary society is often measured against an assumed earlier history. However, research demonstrates that the past in Britain was not as idyllic as is sometimes imagined and that there were periods when the levels of crime, aggression, violence, poverty and deprivation were far greater than they are now, both in the cities and countryside. Yet the myth of a golden age and older patterns of positive behaviour still hold considerable romantic attraction for many British people. There is consequently a tension between presumed tradition and attempts at modernization or change; a pervasive sense of hopelessness in the face of problems; a frustration that institutional structures or the 'authorities' are unable to rectify difficulties; and a feeling that the individual is powerless to influence reform.

Nevertheless, despite major domestic social changes, international pressures and greater internal diversity, there is still a conservatism in British life which regards change with suspicion. This may lead to tension between the need for reform and a nostalgia for an assumed ideal past, causing difficulties for progress, the evolution of social structures and the solving of the nation's problems.

Fundamental change does not come easily to old cultures such as Britain, and social structures – or the human beings who operate them – are often resistant to major alteration. It is argued that since the 1960s the country has been unwilling to face large-scale reassessment of its social, political, economic and institutional structures and is now being overwhelmed by events beyond its control and its capacity to alleviate. A relative economic decline since the late nineteenth century was joined to a political system and national mentality unable to cope with the reality or needs of the post-industrial and culturally diverse society that Britain had become. Much of this decline was supposedly due to long-term and global events which were not reversible. Despite this inevitability, the country arguably still suffers from structural defects, which could respond to radical rethinking. Pragmatic evolution and a complacent attachment to past habits are, in this view, no longer sufficient. Yet people have lost their faith in the political process since recent expenses scandals in Parliament (2008–09).

Britain does have its problems, which some critics argue are made worse by an alleged lack of governmental competence and vision. Yet despite the often lurid picture of social decay painted by many commentators, the essential fabric of British society is not necessarily falling apart. Biased ideological views and a British capacity for self-denigration and complaint can encourage unbalanced, sensational views and extreme media reporting, with the result that events may be exaggerated beyond their national importance or representative value.

Britain has changed over the past sixty years, with most of its people now enjoying greater prosperity and opportunities than in the past, so that poverty today is a relative, rather than an absolute, concept. Many parts of the economy had experienced strong growth relative to other European countries after 2001, but Britain was seriously affected by the global economic downturn and recession of 2007–09, from which it is emerging more slowly than its competitors. Opinion polls have suggested that greater relative prosperity has not brought greater happiness for many Britons. Consumerism, increased ethnic diversity, feminism and an expanded role for women (particularly in a mobile workforce), greater individual freedom and increasing (if not complete) tolerance for alternative lifestyles (such as the increased acceptance of gays), technological advances and new economic policies have done much to transform Britain, sometimes for the better, sometimes for the worse. However, continuing structural and social problems, as well as very varying life chances and opportunities for its people, warn against undue complacency.

Assumptions about the alleged traditional certainties of British life have in fact been strongly questioned in recent decades by all political interests. Conservative governments under Margaret Thatcher (1979–90) tried to reform social structures and promote new economic attitudes. They attempted to reduce the state's role in public affairs and replace it with 'market forces'. The focus was upon economic growth; competition; privatization (the ownership of state concerns transferred to the private sector often by the sale of shares in new companies); the creation of choice and standards in public services such as education and health; and the reform of bodies such as the trade unions, some professions and local government. People were encouraged to be more responsible for their own affairs without automatic reliance on the state for support (the 'dependency culture') and to adopt more individual competitiveness and efficiency (the 'enterprise culture').

Such policies were partly successful on some economic and political levels, but there was resistance to the alleged accompanying selfishness and social divisiveness. While some people applauded the freedoms of an enterprise culture, others strongly wished for more intervention and funding in public social services. This suggests that it is difficult to change Britons' attitudes and that many still look to the state for support in areas such as health, education and social security. Nevertheless, free market or neo-liberal economic programmes continued under the Conservative Prime Minister John Major (1990–7) and Labour Prime Ministers Tony Blair (1997–2007) and Gordon Brown (2007–10)

Meanwhile, the Labour Party modernized its internal structures and policies and moved to the political centre in an attempt to change its public image and appeal to middle Britain. Since gaining power in 1997 (repeated in 2001 and 2005), the Labour government followed the Conservative economic approach, while initially pursuing cautious fiscal and monetary policies, in an appeal to the electoral middle ground. In its early years in government, it also attempted, not without opposition, to modernize Britain by supposedly creating a 'new, young and inclusive' society.

Labour claimed it was addressing social and economic realities, emphasizing personal initiative and responsibility while stressing that hard choices had to be made. It spent large amounts of public money on education, health, transport, social security and the police service in order to prevent their decline, raising fears of personal income tax rises to pay for them. But a majority of respondents to opinion polls felt they had not seen great improvements in public services under the Labour government and many lost their trust in the Labour leadership after 2007. The difficulties involved in balancing the free market and social welfare models of society continued. It seemed that budget deficits and reduced growth indicated that the government was losing its grip on the economy and services. Prior to the general election of 2010, there was a growing disbelief by voters in the Labour government's ability to steer the country through the recession, to pay off the budget deficit, to avoid tax increases, to maintain public services and to avoid greater costs.

Opposition to some government policies under all political parties and acceptance of others demonstrate that social change can occur in various, often interconnected, ways. Some social structures wither away because they are no longer used, while others are reformed internally as new situations arise. Additional forces for change are opposition political parties with their alternative programmes; interest or pressure groups exerting influence upon decision-makers; grassroots movements protesting at some action or lack of action; rebellion by members of Parliament (MPs) of all parties against proposed government legislation; campaigns by the media to promote reform or uncover scandals; and the weight of public opinion for or against official plans. However, central government initiatives in London (and those of devolved government in Scotland, Wales and Northern Ireland) are the single most important factors in determining structural change at national and local level as politicians implement policies or respond to events.

The British traditionally allow their governments a great deal of power in the running of the country. However there is a limit to their tolerance, and their disquiet may be shown in public opinion polls (such as those revealing a declining trust in government and its policies); demonstrations (such as street protests about the Iraq war, British involvement in Afghanistan, international capitalism, climate change and the banning of fox hunting); and general election results (such as the 2010 election, when Labour lost ninety-one seats in the House of Commons). Most politicians have been traditionally sensitive to the views of the people since their hold upon political power is dependent upon the electorate. Governments usually govern with one eye on public opinion and generally attempt to gain acceptance for their policies. They have to move cautiously, even with overall majorities in the House of Commons, and can suffer setbacks in some of their programmes.

The British assume, rightly or wrongly, that they have an individual independence and liberty within the framework of social institutions and are quick to voice their disapproval if their interests are threatened. Protest is a traditional reaction, as well as being a safety valve against more serious social and political disruption. Yet dissent may be neutralized by the promise of reform, or simply ignored by government, politicians and bureaucrats. Adequate responses may not come from the authorities and there is always the danger of more serious conflict, apathy and public alienation as the gap between the voters and elected politicians grows.

The British today are confronting different cultural and economic realities than in the past when they had a more clearly defined world role and a greater sense of national identity. They do not enjoy the benefits of earlier industrial revolutions, such as cheap raw materials, cheap labour and an uncompetitive world market, but have moved to a post-industrial economy in which the service sector and job flexibility dominate. The society has seen a decline in traditional certainties and become more mobile, stressful and conflict-ridden. Critics argue that the old pragmatic methods of innovation, which illustrate the British tendency to muddle through difficulties without long-term planning or fundamental reform, are no longer sufficient for an era in which specialized education and training, high-technology competence and a need to respond to international competition are the main determinants.

British attitudes to Britain

A quotation from *British Social Attitudes*: 1988–9 (pp. 121–2) suggested that:

> The [British] public's trust in the pillars of the British establishment is at best highly qualified . . . [They] seem intuitively to have discovered that the surest protection against disillusionment with their public figures and powerful institutions is to avoid developing illusions about them in the first place.

This observation has become more relevant in recent years as opinion polls indicate increasing dissatisfaction with politicians and authority figures; scepticism at the performance of institutions and their bureaucracies; disengagement from formal political engagement reflected in low election turnout and reduced membership of political parties; but a trend towards political action represented by public protests, demonstrations, petitions, media campaigns and membership of single-issue or special-interest groups. These attitudes partly reflect an individualistic, independent and dissenting British tradition that has been historically cynical, irreverent and critical about state structures and powerful individuals. Institutions such as the monarchy, Parliament, law and the Church have had to earn the approval and support of the British people, which could also be taken back.

In recent years, however, the powerful state has intruded further into people's lives, micro-managing more and more of their work and leisure. Britain has the highest number of CCTVs of any European country and, in the view of critics, interferes increasingly in the lives of its citizens and monitors their activities, whether innocent or criminal.

Opinion polls and research surveys frequently report on central areas of British life which affect people on a personal everyday level and are of concern to many of them. They very often give a more accurate picture of what is happening at a grassroots level in society than policies promoted by political parties and comments from politicians. However, while the polls valuably reveal respondents' views, they do have to be approached with a certain caution. They may only deal with topical rather than long-term concerns and responses to particular questions may change considerably within a short period of time. Questions may be posed to influence the answers given. Unprompted questions ask respondents to suggest concerns of their own choosing. Prompted questions ask them to choose from a list of issues shown or read to them. Contradictory answers to questions on the same topic may be given in different polls. Nevertheless, polls can be significant and accurate indications of how people are reacting to the state of British society. In spite of their denials, politicians do in fact seem to take the results of polls, surveys and focus groups seriously. Their eventual policies may amount to a response to public concerns.

An Ipsos MORI poll in April 2010 (see Table 1.1) prior to the May general election found that respondents were concerned about many areas of British society. The economy remained among the most important issues facing the country for 55 per cent of respondents at a time when Britain was slowly, but unsurely, pulling out of recession. Race relations/immigration had moved into second place with 33 per cent of respondents. This marked a 4 per cent increase since February 2010 and indicated an increasing concern on the part of the public. Crime was in third place at 25 per cent of respondents, and 21 per cent placed worries about unemployment, factory closures and the lack of industry in fourth place. In fifth place was the National Health Service (NHS), hospitals and health care at 20 per cent and in sixth place at 19 per cent were education and schools. The placing of these concerns have fluctuated over the past decade, but all have appeared consistently near the head of the list.

TABLE 1.1 The 23 most important issues facing Britain today (%), 2010

Economy/economic situation	(55)
Race relations/immigration/immigrants	(33)
Crime/law and order/violence/vandalism/anti-social behaviour	(25)
Unemployment/factory closure/lack of industry	(21)
National Health Service/hospitals/health care	(20)
Education/schools	(19)
Defence/foreign affairs/international terrorism	(14)
Morality/individual behaviour/lifestyle	(8)
Inflation/prices	(8)
Drug abuse	(8)
Poverty/inequality	(7)
Pensions/social security/benefits	(7)
Pollution/environment	(6)
Housing	(5)
Low pay/minimum wage/fair wages	(5)
Taxation	(5)
Public services in general	(4)
Population levels/overpopulation	(4)
Local government/council (property) tax	(4)
Petrol prices/fuel	(4)
EU/Europe/Euro	(4)
Transport/public transport	(3)
Pound/exchange rate	(2)

Source: Adapted from Ipsos MORI April, 2010
Note: Some respondents have given multiple answers

At a time when Britain was withdrawing the last of its troops from Iraq, 14 per cent of the public saw defence/foreign affairs/international terrorism as an important issue, with rising concern about the war in Afghanistan, the losses of military personnel and alleged insufficient military equipment for the forces.

A YouGov poll in December 2009 (see Table 1.2) interestingly revealed respondents' opinions about many of the issues discussed in this chapter with reactions over a longer time span. It showed how Britons had responded to events in the first decade of the twenty-first century in cultural, economic and political terms. This period saw Britain move economically from bust to boom before suffering severely in the global recession of 2007–10. The decade had left the British feeling less secure and less trustful of their leaders, but also less outspoken.

The above polls continued a trend in which the economy, crime (law and order, violence and vandalism), health (the National Health Service) and education have consistently been very prominent concerns in recent years. Race relations

---

TABLE 1.2 British attitudes in the first decade of the twenty-first century, 2009

1. 53 per cent worried about UK terrorism harming them or their family.
2. 53 per cent thought the British were as class-ridden as ever; 41 per cent believed the class divide was getting smaller.
3. 62 per cent had made small lifestyle changes to fight global warming.
4. 65 per cent thought that life was better for them than it had been for their parents at the same age.
5. 68 per cent said that women's position had improved – but not as much as men's.
6. 88 per cent believed that the cult of celebrity had helped to make Britain a coarser, cruder society.
7. 41 per cent thought that having troops in Afghanistan increased the risk of terrorism in Britain.
8. 48 per cent have never trusted politicians. Of those who used to trust them, 33 per cent no longer did so.
9. 60 per cent were concerned that Muslims in Britain often live in totally separate communities.
10. 62 per cent believed that political correctness meant that they dared not say what they really meant.
11. 64 per cent said that mobile phones and the Internet had made life better.

Source: adapted from YouGov for *The Sunday Times*, 27 December 2009

(including immigration and asylum seekers) have varied in importance as have defence, foreign affairs and international terrorism after the 11 September 2001 terrorist attacks on New York, the Islamist bombing of the London transport infrastructure on 7 July 2005, the wars in Iraq and Afghanistan and the continuing threat of terrorism in Britain. The issues of pensions and social security have advanced because of the crisis facing pension provision in Britain, people's fears about their finances in old age and concern about an ageing population.

However, previous primary concerns such as the euro, the European Union, devolution, trade unions and Northern Ireland had lost their immediacy. Many worries are 'bread and butter' economic issues such as housing, wages and prices, while others, such as morality and individual behaviour, drug abuse, environmental concerns and pollution, reflect the inner state of the nation. Other opinion polls in 2009–10 confirmed these findings in the run-up to the 2010 general election and suggested that personal 'bread and butter' issues were more likely to influence how most people actually cast their vote on polling day.

Other elements also influence public opinion as witnessed by the daily news coming out of Afghanistan. Nevertheless, in the event, the 2010 election had an inconclusive result; no one party was regarded as the winner or had a majority of the votes; the electorate was not convinced by the arguments in the election campaign; and a continuing frustration and disillusionment with politicians was clearly expressed. A hung Parliament led, inevitably perhaps, to a coalition government.

The rankings in the opinion polls above do not imply that other issues are unimportant. The polls show a wide range of concerns from the economy to nuclear weapons and include many structural features or institutions which are of immediate daily concern to the British public and condition their attitudes to their society. They collectively suggest a picture of contemporary Britain which will be examined in closer detail in later chapters. They also allow commentators to range widely in their opinions of Britain from those indicating a country in terminal decline to others who suggest more positive outcomes despite the problems. The latter would suggest the traditional self-image of an evolutionary society which is coping with pressures.

Exercises

Explain and examine the following terms:

insular	grassroots	pragmatic	sponsorship
deference	conservatism	inner-city	diversity
consensus	euro	pluralism	ethnic
nostalgia	autonomy	post-industrial	modernization
myth	dependency	nonconformist	evolutionary
enterprise	Thatcher	yobbishness	community
hierarchies	homogeneous	inclusive	apathetic
dissent	micro-managing	celebrity	CCTVs
vandalism	'bottom-up'	property tax	globalized

Write short essays on the following topics:

1   Examine the view that Britain is an old-fashioned, backward-looking and conventional society with a political and institutional framework that is unable to cope with the demands of the contemporary world.

2   What do the polls and quotations in this chapter tell us about British people and their society?

3* Examine the idea of structural and social change in society. Consider the forces which might bring it about.

Visit **www.routledge.com/textbooks/oakland** for multiple-choice questions, links to related YouTube clips, tips on approaching essay questions, and much, much more.

Further reading

1   Abercrombie, N., Deem, R., Penna, S, Soothill, K., Urry, J., Walby, S. and Warde, A. (2000) *Contemporary British Society*, Oxford: Blackwell Publishers
2   *Annual Abstract of Statistics*, London: Office for National Statistics and Palgrave Macmillan
3   Black, J. (2002) *A History of the British Isles*, London: Palgrave Macmillan
4   Black, J. (2004) *Britain since the Seventies: Politics and Society in the Consumer Age*, London: Reaktion Books Ltd
5   English, R. and Kenny, M. (eds) (1999) *Rethinking British Decline*, London: Macmillan
6   Ferguson, N. (2004) *Empire: How Britain Made the Modern World*, London: Penguin Books
7   Halsey, A.H. and Webb, J. (2000) *Twentieth-Century British Social Trends*, London: Palgrave/Macmillan
8   Lynch, M. (2008) *Britain 1945–2007*, London: Hodder Education
9   Marr, A. (2010) *A History of Modern Britain*, London: Pan
10 Marr, A. (2009) *The Making of Modern Britain*, London: Macmillan
11 Marwick, A. (2000) *A History of the Modern British Isles 1914–1999*, Oxford: Blackwell Publishers
12 Sampson, A. (2004) *Who Runs This Place?:The Anatomy of Britain in the 21st Century*, London: John Murray (Publishers)
13 Savage, S.P. and Atkinson, R. (2001) *Public Policy Under Blair*, London: Palgrave/Macmillan
14 Office for National Statistics (annual) *Social Trends*, London: Palgrave Macmillan

Websites

Central Office of Information: www.coi.gov.uk
Prime Minister's Office: www.number-10.gov.uk
British Tourist Authority: www.visitbritain.com
British Council: www.mori.com/polls/1999/britcoun.shtml
The MORI Organization: www.mori.com
Office for National Statistics: www.ons.gov.uk
The National Archives: www.nationalarchives.gov.uk
Website of UK Government: www.direct.gov.uk
Ipsos MORI polls: www.ipsos-mori.com
The *Guardian* newspaper: www.guardian.co.uk

2

The country

Many British people say that they are concerned about the effects of human and natural activity on the country's environment. However, an Ipsos MORI poll in March 2010 found that the economy, race relations, unemployment, crime, health care and education were of greater concern to respondents than the environment and pollution (6 per cent) or rural life and the countryside (1 per cent). Furthermore, respondents to a MORI Social Research Institute poll in May 2004 felt that environmental problems could be tackled only through international agreement and not by individual nations. But global attempts to avert environmental damage from the Kyoto Convention in 1973 to the Copenhagen Conference on climate change in 2009 have not been encouraging. Meanwhile, scepticism about the scientific data on climate change has grown.

It also seems that British people differ in their knowledge of environmental matters and have varying views about how personally active and consistent they should be in helping to combat pollution. In practice, individuals, companies, public authorities and government departments continue to harm the environment in different ways, despite maintaining their concerns about it.

The Department for the Environment, Food and Rural Affairs (Defra) has formal responsibility for agriculture, fisheries, environmental protection and rural communities in the UK. It develops land policy and regulations, although there are frequent complaints about its performance. It cooperates with the Scottish Government and the National Assemblies of Wales and Northern Ireland, which have devolved environmental responsibilities for their own countries. European Union and United Nations policies also influence British rural and urban landscapes.

Geographical identities

The country's full title for constitutional and political purposes is the United Kingdom of Great Britain and Northern Ireland, with the short forms 'UK' and 'Britain' being used for convenience. Britain comprises a number of islands lying off the north-west coast of continental Europe which are often known geographically (if inaccurately for some people, on political grounds) as the British Isles. The mainland of England, Scotland and Wales forms the largest island with the political title of Great Britain. Northern Ireland shares the second-largest island with the Republic of Ireland, which has been politically independent since 1921. Smaller islands, like Anglesey, the Isle of Wight, the Orkneys, Shetlands, Hebrides and Scillies, are also part of the British political union.

However, the Isle of Man in the Irish Sea and the Channel Islands off the north coast of France are not part of the United Kingdom. They each have their own identities, legal systems, legislatures and administrative structures and are self-governing Crown dependencies which have a historical relationship with the British Crown. However, the British government is responsible for their defence and foreign relations and can intervene if good administration is not maintained.

Many people in the islands may identify themselves at one level with the larger British national unit and respond to a sense of Britishness, although this feeling appears to be weakening among white Britons and strengthening among non-white and mixed ethnic groups. On a smaller level of geographical identification, the peoples of Scotland, Wales, England and Northern Ireland have historically been conscious of their diverse original identities and the gradual growth of larger collective identities. Such awareness appears to have increased in Scotland, Wales and (arguably) Northern Ireland since the transferring of some political power from the London Parliament (1998–9) by the establishment of a Parliament in Edinburgh and Assemblies in Cardiff and Belfast. England was not included in this devolution process, but the reform seems to have provoked a greater awareness among some English people of their separate identity.

Britain has often been divided up into geographic 'regions'. These may reflect a specific identity, although opinions differ on how strong this actually is. Regions are not the same as modern local government structures (see Chapter 4) and are physically larger. In the past, they have served as assistance and development areas; service locations for supplies of gas, water and electricity; or as economic planning regions. Following devolution, Scotland, Wales and Northern Ireland became self-governing 'national' units rather than 'regions' and nine regions were created in England, which took the form of Regional Development Agencies (RDAs – see Figure 2.3). They were unelected politico-economic structures, which were appointed by government to organize and maximise regional development. It was intended that they would develop into elected regional government assemblies in England analogous to the devolved structures in Wales, Scotland and Northern Ireland. This did not happen outside London, and English people tended not to identify with the RDAs, which were often regarded as remote, government-controlled, artificial, expensive and unaccountable to their regional constituents. The Conservative/Liberal Democrat government intended to replace them in 2010 with Local Economic Partnerships (LEPs) in an attempt to cut costs, decentralize power and encourage 'localism'.

On a smaller level, 'localism' is considered to be more significant than 'regionalism' in British life as a cultural, identifying force. It illustrates a sense of belonging, which becomes more evident with increasing distance from London and the UK government. It reflects a determination by local populations to assert their individual identities and is often based on ancient county structures (such as Yorkshire and Kent in England); cities and towns (such as Manchester,

Liverpool, Newcastle, Birmingham, Glasgow, Edinburgh, Belfast, London, Swansea and Cardiff); villages; and, to a lesser extent, on local government areas.

Identification with local areas was more significant when the British were a rural people living in villages or small communities and were less mobile. Today, such an identity continues, possibly with reduced effect. Although new local government authorities have replaced some old city and county labels, the former geographical identities often persist for people living in these areas.

Physical features and climate

Physical features

Historically, Britain's physical features have influenced human settlement, population movements, military conquest and political union. They have also conditioned the location and exploitation of industry, transport systems, agriculture, fisheries, forestry and energy supplies. Today they continue to influence such activities and are tied to public concerns about pollution, climate change, the state of the environment and the quality of food products. Some have been affected by government policies and European Union directives on agriculture, fisheries and carbon emissions. Since many Britons live in heavily populated areas, they are directly affected by these issues and by the activities of public and private bodies upon the environment.

In recent years, the countryside has become a fierce political issue. Rural inhabitants, campaigning groups such as the Countryside Alliance, conservationists and farmers feel neglected by the UK central government and local politicians. They object to the destruction and pollution of the physical environment; the concreting of rural land for house building, airports and roads; the decrease in rural services such as shops, post offices, local hospitals and pubs; and the supposed ignorance of country life on the part of central and local government planners. There has historically been a tension between urban and rural cultures. Some people are averse to rural life while many feel a traditional (if romanticized) nostalgia for and identity with the countryside, and some ten million people live in rural areas.

Britain's geographical position is marked by latitude 50°N in southern England and latitude 60°N across the Shetlands. It lies within 10° of latitude and has a small and compact size when compared with other major European countries. Yet it also possesses a great diversity of physical features, which surprises those visitors who may expect a mainly urban and industrialized country. The many beauty spots and recreation areas, such as the fifteen National Parks in England (for example, the Lake District), Wales (for example, Snowdonia) and Scotland (for example, the Cairngorms), and other areas of natural beauty may be easily reached without much expenditure of time or effort.

Britain's physical area covers 93,025 square miles (242,842 square kilometres). Most is land, with the rest comprising inland water such as lakes and rivers. England has 50,052 square miles (129,634 sq km), Wales has 7,968 (20,637), Scotland has 29,799 (77,179) and Northern Ireland has 5,206 (13,438). England is larger than the other countries and has the biggest population (51, 446,000 or 84 per cent) in an estimated UK total of 61, 383,000 in mid-2008, up by 408,000 since 2007. These factors partly explain the English dominance in British history and the often hostile attitudes of Scotland, Ireland and Wales towards their neighbour.

FIGURE 2.1
The British Isles and the Republic of Ireland

The distance from the south coast of England to the most northerly tip of the Scottish mainland is 600 miles (955 km), and the English east coast and the Welsh west coast are 300 miles (483 km) apart. These relatively small distances have aided the development of political union and communications and contributed to largely standardized social, economic and institutional norms throughout Britain. But, prior to the eighteenth century, there were considerable obstacles to this progress, such as difficult terrain, inadequate transportation, local customs and political conflict.

Britain's varied physical characteristics, such as the Giant's Causeway and Antrim coast of Northern Ireland, the White Cliffs of Dover in southern England, the Highlands of Scotland and the Welsh valleys and mountains, are a source of identification for many. These result from a long geological and climatic history. Earth movements forced mountains to rise from the seabed to form the oldest parts of Britain. Warmer, subtropical periods then resulted in large swamp forests which covered lowland zones. These in turn were buried by sand, soil and mud, and the forests' fossil remains became coal deposits. Later, the climate alternated between warmth and Arctic temperatures. During the latter Ice Age periods, glaciers moved southwards over the islands, with only southern England remaining free from their effects.

Highland areas were slowly worn away by weathering agents such as wind, ice and water. This process rounded off the mountain peaks and moved waste materials into lowland zones, where they were pressed into new rocks and where the scenery became softer and less folded. The geological and weathering changes shaped valleys and plains and dictated the siting of Britain's major rivers, such as the Clyde in Scotland; the Tyne, Trent, Severn and Thames in England and Wales; and the Bann and Lagan in Northern Ireland.

Natural forces have also affected the coastlines as seas have moved backwards and forwards over time. Parts of the coastal area have either sunk under the sea or risen above it. These processes continue today, particularly on the English coasts. Geological tilting from north to south, rising sea levels and erosion have resulted in the loss of land, houses and farms, while the sea's retreat has created either chalk and limestone uplands or sand beaches along some coasts.

Britain was originally part of the European mainland. However, the melting of the glaciers in the last Ice Age raised sea levels. The country became separated from the continent by the North Sea at its widest point and by the English Channel at its narrowest. The shortest stretch of water between the two land masses is the Strait of Dover between Dover in southern England and Calais in France (24 miles, 38 km).

There are many bays, inlets, peninsulas and estuaries along the coasts and most places in Britain are less than 75 miles (120 km) from some kind of tidal water. Tides on the coasts and in inland rivers, in addition to heavy rainfall, can cause flooding in many parts of the country. Local and national authorities must choose between losing land to the sea through managed retreat plans or providing substantial finance to construct defences against this threat. For example, a London flood barrier was completed in 1984 across the river Thames and there are proposals for more protection of the capital. Flooding, which is now connected with climate change, has become more frequent and seriously affects many low-lying inland areas throughout the country, with people suffering property and financial loss.

The coastal seas are not deep and are often less than 300 feet (90 metres) because they lie on the Continental Shelf, or raised seabed adjacent to the mainland. The warm North Atlantic Current (Gulf Stream) heats the sea and air as it travels from the Atlantic Ocean across the Shelf. This gives the country a more temperate climate than would otherwise be the case, given its northerly position, although there are fears that a melting of the Arctic ice packs may upset this balance and result in colder weather conditions. The Gulf Stream also influences

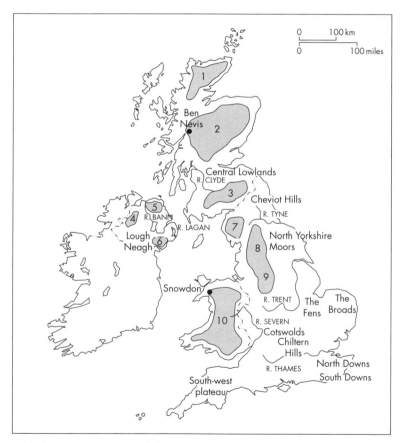

1 North-West Highlands	4 Sperrin Mountains	8 Pennines
2 Central Highlands	5 Antrim Mountains	9 Peak District
(Grampians)	6 Mourne Mountains	10 Welsh Massif (Cambrians)
3 Southern Uplands	7 Cumbrian Mountains	

FIGURE 2.2

Highland and lowland Britain

the coastal fish breeding grounds, on which the national fishing industry is considerably dependent.

Britain's physical relief is divided into highland and lowland Britain (see Figure 2.2). The highest ground is mainly in the north and west. Most of the lowland zones, except for the Scottish Lowlands and central areas of Northern Ireland, are in the south and east of the country, where only a few points reach 1,000 feet (305 metres) above sea level.

The north and west consist of older, harder rocks created by ancient earth movements, which are generally unsuitable for cultivation. The south and east comprise younger, softer materials formed by weathering processes, which have produced fertile soils and good agricultural conditions. Much of the lowland area, except for urban and industrial regions, is cultivated and farmed. It largely comprises fields, which are divided by fences or hedges. Animal grazing land in upland zones is separated either by moorland or stone walls.

England

England covers two-thirds of the island of Great Britain. It consists mainly of undulating or flat lowland countryside, with highland areas in the north and south-

PLATE 2.1 The White Cliffs of Dover, high chalk cliffs on the south-east coast of England which are subject to sea erosion in places.
(David Lomax/Rex Features)

west. Eastern England has the low-lying flat lands of the Norfolk Broads, the Cambridgeshire and Lincolnshire Fens and the Suffolk Marshes. Low hill ranges stretch over much of the country, such as the North Yorkshire Moors, the Cotswolds, the Kent and Sussex Downs and the Chiltern Hills.

Highland zones are marked by the Cheviot Hills between England and Scotland; the north-western mountain region of the Lake District and the Cumbrian Mountains; the northern plateau belt of the Pennines forming a backbone across north-west England; the Peak District of Derbyshire at the southern reaches of the Pennines; and the south-western plateau of Devon and Cornwall.

The heaviest population concentrations centre on the largest (historically industrial and manufacturing) towns and cities, such as London and in south-east England generally; the West Midlands region around Birmingham; the Yorkshire cities of Leeds, Bradford and Sheffield; the north-western area around Liverpool and Manchester; and the north-east region comprising Newcastle and Sunderland.

Wales

Wales is a highland country, with moorland plateau, hills and mountains which are often interspersed with deep river valleys. This upland mass contains the Cambrian Mountains and descends eastwards into England. The highest mountains are in the National Park area of Snowdonia in the north-west, where the dominant peak is that of Snowdon (3,560 feet, 1,085 metres).

PLATE 2.2 Valleys, fields and rolling hills in Powys, a county in central Wales. *(Andrew Drysdale/Rex Features)*

Lowland zones are restricted to the narrow coastal belts and lower parts of the river valleys in south Wales, where two thirds of the Welsh population live. The chief urban concentrations of people and industry are around the bigger southern cities, such as the capital Cardiff, Swansea and Newport. In the past, the highland nature of Wales hindered conquest, agriculture and the settlement of people.

Scotland

Scotland may be divided into three areas. The first is the North-West and Central Highlands (Grampians), together with a number of islands off the west and north-east coasts. These areas are thinly populated, but comprise half the country's land mass. The second is the Central Lowlands, which contain one-fifth of the land area but three-quarters of the Scottish population, most of the industrial and commercial centres and much of the cultivated land. The third is the Southern Uplands, which cover a number of hill ranges stretching towards the border with England.

PLATE 2.3 Ben Nevis, the highest mountain in the UK, and the characteristic Loch Linnhe in the Scottish Highlands
(The Travel Library/ Rex Features)

The Highlands, with their lochs and fiord coastlines, and the Southern Uplands are now smooth, rounded areas since the original jagged mountains have been worn down by weathering forces. The highest point in the Central Highlands is Ben Nevis (4,406 feet, 1,343 metres), which is also the highest place in Britain.

The main population concentrations are around the administrative centre and capital of Edinburgh, the commercial and formerly heavily industrial area of Glasgow, and the regional centres of Aberdeen (an oil industry city) and Dundee. The climate, isolation and harsh physical conditions in much of Scotland have made conquest, settlement and agriculture difficult.

Northern Ireland

Northern Ireland shares an island with the Republic of Ireland and since 1921–2 has had a 303-mile (488-km) border in the south and west with the Republic. It has a north-eastern tip which is only 13 miles (21 km) from the Scottish coast, a fact that has encouraged both Irish and Scottish migration.

PLATE 2.4 The Giant's Causeway in Antrim, on the northern coast of Northern Ireland, was created 60 million years ago when a field of volcanic lava cooled and formed hexagonal blocks of basalt.

(Eye Ubiquitous/Rex Features)

Northern Ireland has a rocky northern coastline, a south-central fertile plain and mountainous areas in the west, north-east and south-east. The south-eastern Mourne Mountains include the highest peak, Slieve Donard, which is 2,796 feet high (853 metres). Lough Neagh (153 square miles, 396 sq km) is Britain's largest freshwater lake and lies at the centre of the country.

Most of the large towns, like the capital Belfast, are situated in valleys which lead from the lough. Belfast lies at the mouth of the river Lagan and has the biggest population concentration. However, Northern Ireland generally has a sparse and scattered population and is a largely rural country.

Climate

The relative smallness of the country and the influences of a warm sea and westerly winds mean that there are no extreme contrasts in temperature throughout Britain. The climate is mainly temperate, but with variations between coolness and mildness. Altitude modifies temperatures, so that much of Scotland and highland areas of Wales and England are cool in summer and cold in winter compared with most of England. Temperatures are lower in the north than in the south and national average temperatures rarely reach 32°C (90°F) in summer or fall below –10°C (14°F) in winter. Yet the ten warmest years since 1861 occurred from the early 1990s, with 1998, 2002 and 2003 being the hottest, indicating for some critics the effects of man-made global warming from carbon emissions rather than natural change. On the other hand, 2009–10 was the coldest winter in thirty years in many areas, with temperatures continuously below 0° C and the heaviest snowfalls in a generation.

The main factors affecting rainfall in Britain are depressions (low-pressure areas) which travel eastwards across the Atlantic Ocean; prevailing south-westerly winds throughout much of the year; exposure of western coasts to the Atlantic Ocean; and the fact that most high ground lies in the west.

The heaviest annual rainfalls are in the west and north (a 60-inch, 1,600-millimetre average covering all heights), with an autumn or winter maximum. The high ground in the west protects the lowlands of the south and east, so that annual rainfall here is moderate (30 inches, 800mm). The months March to June tend to be the driest ones; September to January the wettest; and drought conditions are infrequent, although they have occurred more frequently in recent years and can cause problems for farmers, water companies and consumers.

Low-pressure systems normally pass over northern areas and can produce windy, wet and unstable conditions. In recent years, they have moved south and Britain has had more frequent storms, heavier rainfall and flooding, with suggestions that these are linked to climate change. However, high-pressure systems, which occur throughout the year, are stable and slow-moving, resulting in light winds and settled weather. These can give fine and dry effects, both in winter and summer.

Sunshine in Britain decreases from south to north, inland from the coastal belts and with altitude. In summer, average daily sunshine varies from five hours in northern Scotland to eight hours on the Isle of Wight. In winter, it averages one hour in northern Scotland and two hours on the English south coast.

These statistics show that Britain is not a particularly sunny country, although there are periods of relief from the general greyness. The frequent cloud cover over the islands means that even on a hot summer's day there may be little sunshine breaking through, giving rise to humid, sticky conditions. Sunshine can frequently mix with pollutants to give poor air quality both in the cities and rural areas, which may adversely affect those with respiratory and other illnesses.

Such climatic features give the British weather its changeability and what some regard as its stimulating variety. Discrepancies between weather forecasts and actual results often occur and words such as 'changeable' and 'unsettled' are generously employed. The weather is a national institution, a topic of daily conversation and for some a conditioning factor in the national character. Britons tend to think that they live in a more temperate climate than is the case. However, it is argued that in future Britain can expect wetter autumns and winters with more storms; warmer springs and summers; and periods throughout the year with unpredictable weather and temperatures. These developments are linked to global warming, whether created naturally or from human sources (e.g. carbon emissions).

Agriculture, fisheries and forestry

Agriculture

Soils vary in quality from the thin, poor ones of highland Britain to the rich, fertile land of low-lying areas in eastern and southern England. The climate usually allows a long, productive growing season without extremes. But farmers can sometimes have problems because of droughts or too much rain and too little sunshine at ripening and harvest times.

Britain's long agricultural history includes a series of farming revolutions from Neolithic times. Today, there are some 300,000 active farms, ranging from small units to huge business concerns and two-thirds are owner-occupied. They use about 75 per cent of the total land area, although there is concern that farmland is being increasingly used for building and recreational purposes. Some 477,000 people (1.4 per cent of the workforce) are engaged in farming as full-time, part-time and casual workers. Its share of the Gross Domestic Product (GDP) was an estimated 1.2 per cent in 2009. Although its exports are important, Britain imports some 70 per cent of its food requirements, largely because of seasonal demand.

Many farms in Scotland, Northern Ireland, Wales and northern and south-western England specialize in dairy farming, beef cattle and sheep. Some farms in eastern and northern England and Northern Ireland concentrate on pig production. Poultry meat and egg industries are widespread, with intensive 'factory farming'. Most of the other farms in southern and eastern England and in eastern Scotland grow arable crops such as wheat, barley, oats, potatoes, oilseed rape and sugar beet. Horticultural products such as apples, berries and flowers are also widely grown.

Agriculture is still a significant industry and organized interest group. It is productive, intensive, mechanized and specialized. But, after a profitable period in the early 1990s, farming experienced a difficult period due to the high value of the pound, a fall in farm prices and a series of diseases such as BSE (Bovine Spongiform Encephalopathy) in cows (1996), its link to CJD (Creutzfeldt-Jakob disease) in humans, swine fever and foot and mouth disease (2001). Animals were lost, income was reduced, especially for small farmers, and many left the industry or turned their land to non-farming activities. Some parts of agriculture are profitable but smaller farmers have difficulties, despite government and EU subsidies.

The Common Agricultural Policy (CAP) of the European Union (EU), which accounts for 46.7 per cent of the EU's budget, has also affected British farmers. Its original protectionist aims were to increase productivity and efficiency; stabilize the market; ensure regular supplies of food; give farmers reasonable rewards by providing them with subsidies; set minimum guaranteed prices for food products through price support; and standardize the quality and size of produce.

British governments have argued that the CAP is unwieldy, costly for consumers, bureaucratic, restrictive for producers, open to fraud and leads to surplus food. They maintain that British farming should reflect the needs of the market, meet consumers' demands, reduce subsidies and emphasize better land management. Developing countries have also objected to EU subsidies undercutting their farmers and home markets. They and the USA react to restrictions on foreign foodstuffs entering the EU, which have now been somewhat liberalized.

EU reform and simplification of the CAP from 2004–5 coincided with the entry of Eastern European nations into the EU and continuing negotiations with the World Trade Organization (WTO) over tariff barriers. Farm subsidies are being reduced and are now more dependent upon environmental protection, competition, a market orientation, cuts in overproduction, food safety and animal health. But there is still conflict within the EU over cuts in subsidies and the CAP itself.

Fisheries

Britain is one of Europe's leading fishing nations and operates in the North Sea, the Irish Sea and the Atlantic. The fishing industry is important to the national economy and is centred on ports around the coasts. The most important fish catches are cod, haddock, whiting, herring, mackerel, plaice and sole, which are caught by the 7,271 registered vessels of the fishing fleet. The fish-farming industry (salmon, trout and shellfish) is a large and expanding business, particularly in Scotland.

However, employment in and income from fishing have declined substantially. This is partly due to changes in fish breeding patterns and a reduction in fish stocks because of overfishing. Many fishermen have become unemployed and fishing towns on the English and Scottish coasts have suffered, but the industry still accounts for 73 per cent of Britain's fish consumption. Fishermen number 11,774, with some two jobs in associated occupations (such as fish processing) for every one fisherman. The British government believes that the industry can be profitable and sustainable if it modernizes to cope with the pressure of global competition.

The industry has also been affected by the EU's Common Fisheries Policy (CFP) and British government policies, which have affected the fishermen's old freedom of operation. The need to conserve fish resources and prevent overfishing is stressed. Zones have been created in which fishermen may operate and quota systems operate inside and beyond the zones to restrict fish catches. Measures to limit the amount of time fishing vessels spend at sea and to decommission (take out of operation) fishing boats have further restricted employment and the fishing fleet. Fishermen are angry with British government and EU policies and their loss of livelihood, yet without fish conservation there will be reduced supplies in future. Additionally cod, which has long been a staple fish catch, may disappear from the North Sea because of the threat from climate change and a rise in sea temperatures.

The CFP is criticized for poor management and failure to prevent dwindling fish stocks. It is argued that the policy, which is due to be reformed by 2012, should emphasize environmental sustainability of the seas; devolve the management of fisheries from an EU level to regional and local areas; and ensure that the size of the EU fleet matches the available fish stocks. Significant changes are arguably needed to avoid the further decline of the British (and European) fishing industry.

Forestry

Woodlands cover 6.6 million acres (2.7 million hectares) of Britain and comprise 9 per cent of England, 17 per cent of Scotland, 14 per cent of Wales and 6 per cent of Northern Ireland. These figures represent 12 per cent of the total UK land area and amount to a doubling of trees since 1947, yet Britain is still the least forested country in Europe. Some 35 per cent of productive national forests are managed by the state Forestry Commission or government departments and the rest by private owners. About 35,000 people are employed in the state and private forestry industries and 10,000 are engaged in timber processing.

However, these activities contribute only 15 per cent to the national consumption of wood and associated timber products, which means that the country is heavily dependent upon wood imports. The government has encouraged tree-planting programmes in Scotland, Wales and the English Midlands, and allowed the sale of state woodlands to private owners in order to reduce public expenditure and to increase productivity. New plantings, controlled felling, the expansion of timber industries and a profitable private sector may reduce Britain's present dependence upon imports and benefit the environment.

Forestry policy is supposed to take conservation factors into account in the development of timber facilities. But such aims are not always achieved and there is disquiet about some government programmes. Environmentalists campaign against the destruction of woodlands for road building and airport expansion, advocate increased fast-growth tree planting to combat carbon emissions and try to preserve the quality of the existing woodlands. These in recent years have been badly affected by disease, unreasonable felling and storm damage in 1987, 1990 and the 2000s.

Energy resources

Primary energy sources are oil, gas, nuclear power, hydroelectric power and coal. The most important secondary source generated from these is electricity. About 200,000 people work in energy production; three of Britain's largest companies (Shell, BP and British Gas) are in this sector; and the energy industries accounted for some 3.3 per cent of GDP in 2008 as part of industry and manufacturing (23 per cent). However, there are problems with energy sources and concerns about pollution and environmental damage arising from their exploitation. Most energy industries have now been privatized, but there is still criticism about their services and regulation.

Electricity is mainly provided by coal-, gas- and oil-fired power stations, hydroelectric power, eight nuclear power stations and renewable sources. Gas amounted in 2009 to 45 per cent of the total electricity supply, coal 32 per cent, nuclear 13 per cent, renewable sources 6 per cent and oil one per cent. It is estimated that electricity demand will increase by 50 per cent over the next twenty to forty years because of an increase in the number of electrically powered vehicles and electric heating.

Since 1980, Britain has produced most of its own energy needs. This was due to the growth in offshore oil and gas supplies, which made a crucial contribution to the economy and to the balance of payments through the export of crude oil, oil products and gas. Multinational companies operate under government licence and extract these fuels from the North Sea and Atlantic fields.

However, because governments have encouraged high extraction rates, supplies of oil and gas will continue only into the early twenty-first century. There is already a heavy dependence on imported foreign gas and oil as British supplies diminish, and in the winter of 2009–10 Britain relied on imports for half its gas supplies. The development of existing resources and the search for alternative forms of energy are crucial for Britain and its economy. The positions of coal and nuclear power need to be more adequately debated and further research is required into renewable energy such as biomass, solar, wind, wave and tidal power.

Coal is an important natural energy resource, but there are objections to its use on pollution grounds. After a reduction in the workforce and the closure of uneconomic pits in the 1980s, the coal industry was privatized. But coal is expensive and there is a lack of demand from big consumers, such as electricity power stations, which use gas, oil and cheap coal imports. There have been more pit closures and the future of the industry is uncertain although some pits have reopened in the Midlands. Modified (and cleaner) coal-burning power stations could be viable alternatives for the future, although higher electricity bills will be needed to fund the technology designed to capture the carbon from such stations. Nevertheless, more fossil-burning power stations may have to be built in the next fifteen years to meet a third of Britain's electricity needs.

The expansion of nuclear power, partially privatized in 1996, to satisfy energy needs has been uncertain. But the previous Labour government in 2005 indicated in a change of policy that it wanted to replace ageing reactors and possibly build more nuclear stations to cope with the problems caused by global warming, a decrease in oil and gas supplies and obligations to reduce carbon emissions. However, positive support for nuclear power has been low and concerns about nuclear waste and safety continue. A MORI survey in December 2007 found that 35 per cent of respondents were favourable to nuclear power on balance while 26 per cent were unfavourable, suggesting that public opposition has declined slightly. The building of new stations was acceptable to 54 per cent of respondents if it would help to tackle climate change, with 48 per cent agreeing that nuclear power was needed because renewable sources of energy alone are unable to supply electricity requirements. Some 63 per cent of respondents believed that Britain needed a mixture of energy sources, including nuclear and renewables, to ensure a reliable supply of electricity. However, the election of a coalition government in 2010 may result in a re-evaluation of nuclear policies.

Alternative forms of renewable energy are becoming more important. Electricity generation by wind power is already operative on land and at sea, although there is opposition to wind turbines in the countryside as well as doubts about their economic viability and the reliability of wind as a power source. The use of tidal and wave power is being implemented on some coasts and estuaries and solar energy is already provided, with plans for more research. These and other forms of renewable energy such as biomass and the excavation of heat from rocks and the Earth's core are important for Britain's future energy needs, particularly as environmental concerns grow, but their capacity is limited at present to 5 per cent of all energy and electricity production. The previous Labour government wished to increase this to 10 per cent by 2010, 15 per cent by 2015,

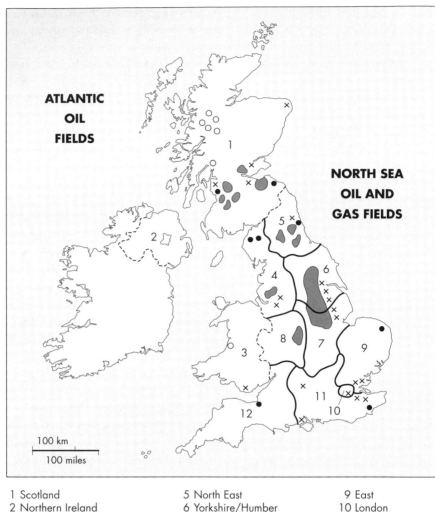

FIGURE 2.3 English RDAs (4–12), devolved areas (1–3) and energy sources

20 per cent by 2020 and eventually to 30 per cent, largely from wind farms. If nuclear power were phased out and replaced by wind power alone, this would still leave three-quarters of the nation's electricity to be generated by fossil fuels. Renewable sources of energy such as wind and solar power were supported by 78 per cent of the people according to a MORI poll in January 2006, although such plans could be opposed if sited in unacceptable areas.

Critics argue that insufficient research and funds are being devoted to alternative supplies; that the potential of nuclear power has not been sufficiently investigated; that oil and gas have been wasted rather than extracted more slowly; that not enough consideration has been given to a cleaner coal sector; and that industry is reluctant to use more environmentally friendly technology which would cut harmful emissions. Britain's domestic and industrial energy users are extravagant compared to those of other European countries, although their consumption is lower than those of emerging industrial nations such as India and China. The provision of cheap and environmentally suitable energy for both domestic and industrial use is a considerable problem for Britain, and energy prices have risen steeply in recent years.

Transport and communications

Transport and communications are divided between the public and private sectors of the economy, although most former state businesses have now been privatized. Roads, railways, shipping and civil aviation form the country's transport system. British Telecom, competing telecommunications companies, the Royal Mail, the Post Office and private postal delivery firms supply most communications needs.

Transport

Central agencies and local government are responsible for different types of road in the *road network*. Motorways and trunk roads are the largest elements and carry most of the passenger traffic and heavy goods vehicles. Yet many roads are in bad condition, do not meet the top safety rating and are unable to handle the number of vehicles on them, resulting in Britain having the heaviest road traffic congestion in Europe. Expansion, modernization and repair of roads are environmentally damaging, expensive and usually inadequate to meet the estimated future number of vehicles. While the previous Labour government cancelled some controversial road-building programmes in an attempt to cut the demand for road space and to persuade drivers to adopt alternative methods of transport, new road building is still carried out to satisfy infrastructure needs and traffic flows. However, new policies may move finance from roads into a major upgrading of the rail network.

In 2009, there were 34.4 million licensed vehicles. These included 28.5 million private cars, 507,900 heavy goods vehicles, 3.2 million light goods vehicles, 1.3 million motorcycles, 180,100 buses and coaches and 607,200 other vehicles. Car transport is the most popular and accounts for 80 per cent of passenger mileage, while buses and coaches take 2 per cent. Despite Britain's very high road density, it also has a relatively good safety record in which road accidents and casualties have decreased as an average over time. However, attempts to further curb accidents, congestion and speeding by introducing more road taxes

PLATE 2.5 Bendy bus negotiating New Oxford Street, London. This type of bus started to replace most of the popular double-decker Routemaster buses in 2001. It has proved controversial and will be replaced by a new type of Routemaster in autumn 2010.
(Alisdair, Macdonald/Rex Features)

and speed cameras to control aggressive drivers are controversial and opposed by motorists.

Private road haulage has a dominant position in the movement of inland freight. Lorries have become larger and account for 80 per cent of this market. Campaigners argue for the transfer of road haulage to the railways and the publicly owned inland waterways (canals). Yet the waterways are used only for a small amount of freight transportation because of expense, although they are popular for recreational purposes. The use of rail freight, however, is increasing for bulk commodities.

Public bus services have declined, particularly in rural areas, because of the increased cost of providing the services, which has led to increased private car usage. Conservative governments deregulated bus operations and most local bus companies have now been privatized, with local government subsidies. There has been a considerable expansion in private long-distance express coach services, which are cheaper than the railways, but bus services generally in Britain are underfunded and inadequate for potential demand. There is a lack of healthy competition outside London and little effective regulation of the bus industry. Critics argue that taxpayers who pay for bus subsidies and passengers who use the service receive poor value for money.

The world's first public passenger steam *railway* opened in 1825 between Stockton and Darlington in north-east England. After 100 years of private operation, the railways became state-owned in 1947 before being privatized in 1997. One company (Network Rail) now owns the railway lines and infrastructure while the trains and stations are leased to and operated by private regional companies (such as Stagecoach, National Express and Arriva). The government subsidizes and ultimately controls the railways. There are frequent calls for the railway system to be renationalized and constant criticism of its performance

Rail services account for 5 per cent of all passenger mileage and consist of a fast inter-city network linking all the main British centres, local trains which supply regional needs, and commuter services in and around the large areas of population, particularly London and south-east England. Increased electrification of lines and the introduction of diesel trains such as the Inter-City 125s travelling at a maximum speed of 125 mph (201 km/h), have improved rail journeys considerably. However, such speeds and facilities are still inferior to those in other countries and current railway tracks in Britain do not permit the greater speeds available to newer trains.

Many railway lines and trains are old and need replacing, and privatization has not solved problems of financing and lack of adequate services. A number of fatal crashes in recent years and the resulting repair of large sections of track caused chaos in the railway network and drew attention to the shortcomings of the system. The situation has slowly returned to normal and passenger totals are increasing, although suffering a slowdown in 2009; newer trains are being introduced on West and East Coast services; and there are plans for the updating of fast-train railways on northern routes from London. But there is still much criticism about the performances of the rail companies, fare increases, overcrowding, cancellations, delays, unpunctuality, late arrivals, staffing and poor services. Similar complaints are also made about the London Underground system (the Tube), which covers 254 miles (408 km) of railway line in the capital and has been partly privatized. It is argued that the inadequate state of Britain's railways is due to underfunding, at a time of increasing demand, with expenditure and state subsidies being below European averages, despite profits for the railway companies.

The *Channel Tunnel*, run by a French/British private company, Eurotunnel, opened for commercial use in 1994 under the English Channel with two terminals, Folkestone (near Dover) and Coquelles (near Calais), being 31 miles (50 km) apart. It was meant to improve passenger and freight rail travel between Britain and mainland Europe and has taken business from sea/ferry services. It provides a drive-on, drive-off shuttle service for cars, coaches and freight vehicles, as well as passenger trains (Eurostar) from the renovated (2007) St Pancras International Station in London. A high-speed rail connection between Ashford and London has been completed and there are plans to bring domestic trains from the rest of Britain into the European hub at St Pancras. The Channel Tunnel services are relatively efficient although serious breakdowns and delays occurred in the winter of 2009.

There are over 300 *ports* in Britain, but most are small concerns. The bigger ports, like Clyde, Dover, Hull, Grimsby, Southampton, Felixstowe and Cardiff, service most of the trade and passenger travel requirements. However, the shipping fleet has declined since the peak year of 1975, with the cargo market now dominated by a small number of large private sector groups and container ports. Yet 75 per cent of Britain's overseas trade (by value) is still carried by sea. Most of the passenger ports have been privatized. Although passenger mileage has been reduced, the Port of Dover is Europe's busiest ferry port. Cargo and passenger traffic may decline further due to competition with the Channel Tunnel and aviation.

Britain's *civil aviation* system accounts for 1 per cent of passenger mileage and is in the private sector following the privatization of the former state-owned airline, British Airways, in 1987. There are other carriers, such as British Midland International and Virgin Atlantic, which run scheduled and charter passenger services on domestic and international routes, as well as air freight services. There has also been a recent increase in low-cost airlines, such as EasyJet and Ryanair (which carries the most passengers in Europe). All are controlled by the Civil Aviation Authority (CAA), an independent, partially privatized body which regulates the industry and air traffic control.

There are 142 licensed civil aerodromes in Britain, of varying size. Heathrow and Gatwick Airports outside London are the largest and busiest in terms of aircraft movements. These airports, together with Stansted in south-east England and Glasgow, Edinburgh and Aberdeen in Scotland, were owned by the private-sector BAA. They handled 73 per cent of air passenger traffic and 84 per cent of air cargo movements. In 2009, Britain's independent Competition Commission ordered BAA to sell three airports (Gatwick – now sold –, Stansted and one Scottish airport) within two years to promote competition. Many of the regional airports, such as Luton, Manchester, Birmingham, Belfast, Newcastle and East Midlands, are controlled by local authorities and provide the country's remaining passenger and cargo needs. Competition for passengers and freight is fierce at all airports.

It is argued that the expansion of existing airports (particularly regional facilities) and the provision of new ones will be necessary if Britain is to cope with increased consumer demand and competition from Europe. However, such projects are very expensive, controversial and frequently opposed for environmental reasons because of the construction work, noise, pollution and traffic they would involve. There is also disquiet about plane congestion in the skies over Britain and the carbon emissions caused by aircraft. Campaigners also protest against the construction of new runways at airports, such as a third Heathrow runway, and the lengthening of existing runways.

The inadequacy of the British transport system stems from the lack of an integrated infrastructure of roads, railways and airports catering for passengers and freight. This could arguably ease road congestion, satisfy demand and improve the environment, but such developments involve considerable expense and Britain invests less in transport than any other European country. Governments are reluctant to spend more public money, although the Labour government formed partnerships with the private sector to allow the latter to invest in the state transport infrastructure.

Communications

Communications systems in Britain are also divided between the public and private sectors. The main suppliers are private telecommunications companies such as *British Telecom (BT)* and the publicly owned *Royal Mail*, which includes the *Post Office*.

Telecommunications is one of the most competitive and rapidly expanding sectors of the economy. British Telecom (BT) was originally in public ownership, but was privatized in 1984, has some 71 per cent of market share and provides domestic and international telephone and telecommunications systems, with 20 million domestic and 8.5 million business subscribers. There was much criticism of BT's performance following privatization. Although some service problems were solved, and it became an influential world force, it has again experienced problems with its funding and expansion programmes, as well as with customer relations.

Private companies compete fiercely with British Telecom in a volatile, entrepreneurial market in which companies emerge, merge and disappear. The successful ones grow rapidly and are licensed to provide telecommunications facilities and develop broadband services.

The strongest and most competitive growth in recent years has been in mobile telephones and services provided over the Internet. According to the Office for National Statistics, the number of mobile phone users had risen to over 79 per cent of households by 2009 (85 per cent of all individuals) with network suppliers such as Orange, O_2, Vodaphone, T-Mobile, Carphone Warehouse and 3. By 2008 the proportion of households owning a home computer had risen to 72 per cent and access to the Internet and e-mail covered 66 per cent. However, Internet usage is greater in companies, libraries and schools.

The General Post Office was established in 1635 as a government department, which included the Royal Mail delivery service. Today, the Royal Mail is a public limited company which owns Parcelforce and the Post Office counter service. Responsible for the collection, handling and delivery of some 80 million letters and parcels every day, it has sorting offices throughout the country which employ a sophisticated handling system based on the postcodes allotted to every address in Britain. Local post offices (counter services) throughout the country (some of which have been controversially closed in both rural and urban areas) provide postal and other services, and the large Parcelforce Worldwide operates domestically and overseas. The Royal Mail's international connections and customer base are expanding, but the growth of electronic communications such as e-mail and the Internet has now made serious inroads into its markets and it is losing profits. The Royal Mail does not have a monopoly on the collection and delivery of letters. Licensed competition by private sector couriers and express operators, although limited at present, is likely to increase, and there are proposals to split the service into two or partly privatize it.

Attitudes to the environment

A wider British awareness of environmental issues coincided with the rise of the Green movement in the 1980s and mainstream political parties eventually adopted 'green' policies with varying degrees of commitment. An Environment Agency was created within Defra; Acts of Parliament were passed to safeguard the environment, reduce pollution and penalize polluters; EU legislation imposes regulations upon member states; and international action tries to resolve environmental problems.

Britain, the European Union and signatories to the 1997 Kyoto Protocol (in force in 2005) see global warming as the greatest danger facing the world community. Yet participants at the 2009 Copenhagen Conference on climate change could not agree on appropriate and coordinated action.

Polls suggest that a majority of British people are uncertain about global warming; ignorant of its potential consequences; and unwilling to embrace costly action which may be personally inconvenient, such as giving up driving, flying and plasma television sets. Scepticism about global warming and claims about its man-made origins has increased since 2009. In a BBC/Populus poll in February 2010, 25 per cent of respondents said they did not think global warming was happening while 75 per cent said that it was a reality. A *Sunday Times*/YouGov poll in December 2009 found that 41 per cent of respondents trusted climate scientists to tell the truth about global warming while 44 per cent did not.

Despite these attitudes, the reality of a changing climate is already evident in Britain, whether man-made or not, and does cause public concern. Summer droughts and winter and summer floods have become frequent. The UK is vulnerable to rising seas on its east and south coasts, and wildlife and the countryside are being affected. Heatwaves are expected to become common, and Britain's climate will arguably become like that of Mediterranean Africa.

Some, though by no means all, of the general public are concerned about vehicle and aircraft pollution, traffic congestion, the lack of an adequate public transport system, the exploitation of natural habitats, the use of energy resources, the safety of agricultural products, the effects of greenhouse gas emissions and the damage caused to personal health by environmental problems. Statistics reveal that UK carbon emissions by source in 2009 were energy industries (33 per cent); transport (21 per cent); residential (12 per cent); manufacturing and construction (13 per cent); agriculture (7 per cent); industrial processes (4 per cent); waste treatment and disposal (4 per cent); and commercial and institutional (3 per cent).

Critics argue that British government policy on carbon emissions trading does not address the basic causes of pollution. Trading allows a country to avoid some penalties for its pollution by trading emissions with other countries or by storing carbon gas. The government has sometimes seemed to argue that the development of cleaner, more efficient technology in cars, aircraft, factories and power stations is the solution to emissions, since reductions in industrial production will allegedly harm the economy. Although Britain reduced carbon emissions by 13 per cent in 2010, it missed its 20 per cent target. The previous government planned a 34 per cent reduction by 2020 and 80 per cent by 2050. But emissions will grow unless practical savings plans are in place rather than a reliance on carbon trading.

Earlier polls showed that respondents believed that environmental protection should rate higher than economic growth or the interests of companies; that the government should protect the environment; that environmental problems should be tackled; and that people were prepared to make sacrifices to clean up the environment and conserve wildlife. Yet such views do not always lead to sensitive or effective behaviour and there is still widespread environmental damage in rural and urban areas.

Preventive action to protect the environment is often insufficient. Controls and planning rules may lack force; polluters evade regulations and taxes or suffer only minor fines; insufficient pressure is put on companies to modernize their facilities, adopt cleaner technology and file environmental reports on their activities; and there are disputes over protection costs between local and central government, as well as internationally. Polls in *The Ecologist* magazine in 2001 found that 65 per cent of respondents thought that the previous Labour government had not improved the environment since coming to power in 1997 and was spending too little on it. This view was reflected in a MORI research poll in 2004 where 63 per cent of respondents wanted to see more urgent action taken by government.

Some people in Britain are apparently willing to take specific measures themselves, such as buying unleaded petrol, using energy-saving light bulbs, cutting down on the use of plastic bags and recycling household rubbish to reduce domestic energy use. Recycling (35 per cent in 2009) has proved relatively successful, though higher targets have to be set. The practice of using landfill for household waste (54 per cent) needs to be cut. London has one of the highest rates of rubbish dumping among European cities. Some 11 per cent of waste is in fact used to produce energy by incineration and composting. But polls suggest there still remains a strong need to raise public understanding of global warming and Britain's role in tackling it.

Two specific areas, vehicle and aircraft usage, are large contributors to carbon emissions. These will increase as the deterioration in public transport persuades more people to use private vehicles and government accepts an expansion of cheap air travel. Britons are overly dependent on the car (with families owning more and bigger polluting vehicles) and alternatives have been neglected. The car is now seen as a major environmental problem and the government has made attempts to curb its unnecessary use, reduce speed limits, punish aggressive speedsters, introduce payment or tolls for road usage, ration road space in favour of buses, increase taxes or charges on car usage in cities and give funding to local schemes which improve public transport. A congestion charge was introduced in London, whereby owners are charged for driving into central areas. This initially reduced traffic by some 25 per cent. But its effect has been reduced and polls suggest that Britons are divided about using congestion charging to reduce traffic. Opposition to charges in 2005 forced local government outside London to drop the scheme.

These findings suggest that people refuse to give up their cars easily (or at all) and are unwilling to surrender their 'right' to drive. While polls consistently show that a majority of respondents wish for better public transport, cuts in traffic pollution, a reduction in congestion and the removal of freight from the roads, they are less keen on restricting car use or banning cars completely. They seem to accept motor taxes, charges or tolls as an inevitable part of their dependence upon the car.

Critics, on the other hand, have alleged that the government is blocking public transport schemes designed to reduce car usage, congestion and emissions because it is reluctant to lose income from road and fuel taxes. It is felt that the government is relying on the faster introduction of greener and technologically improved cars rather than attempting to cut vehicle numbers.

Other critics maintain that governments always want increased revenue and have allegedly encouraged the growth of air travel through low-cost airlines. However polls suggest that people now realize that air travel does damage the environment and has a serious effect on climate change. *British Social Attitudes* in 2009 found that respondents were willing to accept big rises in air fares to reduce the environmental damage caused by flying. They agreed that people should pay more for tickets to offset such damage even if this makes air travel much more expensive (49 per cent agreed and 28 per cent disagreed).

However, they were ambivalent about whether there should be stronger limits on flying. They seem willing to pay charges but are unwilling to curb usage. Offsetting damage by higher fares echoes the practice of emissions trading, but does not solve the problem. It is also argued that a reduction in vehicle and aircraft passenger numbers in 2008 was caused not by a desire to restrict travel for environ-mental reasons, but by the effects of higher fuel prices in the economic downturn.

British governments have studied integrated transport systems (roads, rail and air) designed to relieve environmental pressures, but have not produced a satisfactory model. Problems arise because of Britain's varied geography and the disputed role of local authorities. It is difficult to implement one overall plan and to agree on who will pay the costs. A 2001 poll in *The Ecologist* showed that 61 per cent of respondents did not want more roads to relieve traffic congestion, with resulting pollution, noise and damage to existing roads and property. They preferred money to be spent on alternatives and a large majority in a 2001 MORI poll wanted to see more goods carried by rail. But this solution requires an upgraded, more efficient railway infrastructure and increased funding.

Land usage is also a connected and contentious issue in Britain. Agricultural, woodland and greenfield land is being increasingly used for building and recreational purposes. There has been an increase in suburban sprawl as house building encroaches on rural areas. The previous Labour government wanted to build three million new homes nationwide to counter housing shortages, the lack of affordable housing and demographic change. It pressed for 640,000 of these houses to be built in south-east England and the Midlands. Giant supermarkets and shopping centres are also being built in the countryside to service consumer demand.

Research surveys and opinion polls regularly report that people are worried about the future of the countryside and want to stop housing development, building work and road/airport schemes which damage the environment. Government policies are supposed to force local planning authorities to build homes on available brownfield land within towns before granting permission to develop greenfield sites. Yet the latter is increasingly being allowed, and brownfield house building leads to much smaller and more crowded housing plots, as well as building speculation.

Serious air pollution in Britain is caused by factories, power stations, cars, buses, aircraft, lorries and domestic homes discharging carbon emissions into the air. It affects both urban and rural areas, is a threat to people's health (particularly the elderly, asthmatics and those with respiratory problems) and was linked for the first time in 1997 to heart attacks. Although pollution was reduced by Clean Air Acts in the 1950s and 1960s, it still reaches harmful levels, particularly in summer when pollutants mix with sunshine and humid conditions to produce high ozone levels.

Other forms of environmental damage, such as sea and beach pollution, are allegedly caused when untreated sewage and toxic industrial waste are pumped into the sea by commercial companies and local councils. Britain has reduced discharge levels, but pollution levels on some beaches still exceed safety limits. Rivers are also polluted by industrial waste, toxic fertilizers, pesticides and farm silage. This has caused public concern about the safety of drinking water from reservoirs and the water companies have been pressurized into raising the quality of their water services. Many rivers, lakes and estuaries have now been cleaned up and more stringent controls of the oil and shipping industries in the North Sea

PLATE 2.6 Nuclear fuel and waste from Britain and other countries are reprocessed at Sellafield, Cumbria, England, so that they can be used again or safely stored.
(*Brian Harris/Rex Features*)

have reduced pollution levels. However, although water quality in British rivers has improved considerably to 'very good' or 'good' status, three-quarters of rivers in England and Wales in 2009 fell below a new European environmental standard due to pollution from agriculture, over-abstraction of water and poor town planning.

Problems have been experienced with the exploitation of energy resources, such as expense, capacity and availability, and there are environmental concerns about the burning of fossil fuels (coal, oil and gas) and the damage to the countryside caused by new developments. Nuclear expansion had been halted because of government uncertainty about nuclear energy and also because of public opposition to nuclear facilities, the danger of radioactive leaks, the reprocessing of nuclear waste at the THORP and Sellafield plants in north-west England and the dumping of radioactive waste at sea. Yet the previous Labour government embraced plans for a new generation of nuclear power stations, and the repatriation of 40 per cent of foreign nuclear waste has been agreed internationally. However, the coalition government may re-evaluate these proposals for the building of new nuclear stations.

Public concern surrounds the agricultural industry because of its widespread use of fertilizers and pesticides, its methods of animal feeding, the high carbon costs of producing meats such as beef, the effects of intensive farming on the environment, and air emissions caused by flying food imports into Britain from around the world. Many hedgerows, which are important for animal and vegetable life, have been lost as fields have become bigger and farming more mechanized. The quality and standard of food products, particularly those resulting from intensive farming, are of concern and there are worries about standards of hygiene in the food and farming industries. The BSE scare seriously affected the consumption of beef and other meats and led to a drop in demand for traditional foods. The 2000– 1 foot and mouth outbreak raised questions about the quality of British food and intensive methods of farming.

There is also public disquiet about the growth and use of genetically modified (GM) crops to increase yields. The MORI Social Research Institute in February 2003 found that 56 per cent of respondents were opposed and only 14 per cent supported it, although in 2010 the previous Labour government decided to expand the experiment. Despite public scepticism and EU regulations, a number of British farmers and politicians advocate the use of GM crops as animal feed for pigs, poultry and dairy cattle in order to avoid a collapse in the production of chicken, eggs, pork and milk and the loss of agricultural jobs.

On the other hand, the success of organic farming in Britain has been limited and is declining, largely because of the cost of such goods and confusion about their actual quality and benefit. Yet an NOP poll in 2001 reported that 82 per cent of respondents favoured a return to traditional farming methods, even if this meant paying more for food. A *Good Housekeeping* magazine poll in August 2001 found that only one in six people trusted supermarkets to sell safe food; three out of four were more concerned than ever before about the safety of the food they were buying; and although 97 per cent of respondents purchased most of their food from supermarkets, faith in them has suffered and concern is raised about flaws in the regulation and safety checks of Britain's complicated food industry. Although the supermarket chains do provide a service for food consumers, it is alleged that they abuse their buying powers over farmers, which can lead to disputes between retailers and suppliers.

Exercises

Explain and examine the following terms:

UK	Heathrow	Intercity 125	Post Office
weathering	Highland Britain	Lough Neagh	Ben Nevis
arable	Channel Islands	horticulture	BT
CAP	earth movements	the Tube	drought
Shetlands	Powys	postcodes	GM crops

BSE	global warming	CFP	tidal
estuaries	organic food	regionalism	RDAs
devolution	Strait of Dover	glacier	Peak District
emissions	carbon trading	tolls	congestion

Write short essays on the following topics:

1   Does Britain have an energy crisis? If so, why?

2   Examine the impact of Britain's membership of the European Union upon its agricultural and fisheries industries.

3*   What are the reasons for environmental concerns in Britain?

4   Should cars be restricted on Britain's roads and banned from city centres? Give your reasons, for and against

5   Examine the application of the terms 'regionalism' and 'localism' to the UK

Visit **www.routledge.com/textbooks/oakland** for multiple-choice questions, links to related YouTube clips, tips on approaching essay questions, and much, much more.

Further reading

1   Barnett, A. and Scruton, R. (1999) *Town and Country*, London: Vintage

2   Champion, A.G. and Townsend, A.R. (1990) *Contemporary Britain: A Geographical Perspective*, London: Edward Arnold

3   Clapp, B.W. (1994) *An Environmental History of Britain since the Industrial Revolution*, London: Longman

4   Connelly, J. and Smith, G (1999) *Politics and the Environment: From Theory to Practice*, London: Routledge

5   Gray, T. (1995) *UK Environmental Politics in the 1990s*, London: Macmillan

6   Harvey, G. (1998) *The Killing of the Countryside*, London: Vintage

7   Hook, D., Whyte, I. and Winchester, A. (2005) *Society, Landscape and Environment in Upland Britain*, Oxford: Society for Landscape Studies, Supplementary Series 2, Oxbow Books

8   *Regional Trends*, UK National Statistics, London: Office for National Statistics

9   Tulip, K. And Michaels, L. (2004) *A Rough Guide to the UK Farming crisis*, www.corporate watch.org.uk

10   Woodcock, N. (1994) *Geology and Environment in Britain and Ireland*, London: Taylor and Francis

11   *Your Region, Your Choice: Revitalizing the English Regions* (2002), London: The Stationery Office

Websites

Office for National Statistics: www.ons.gov.uk
Department of Energy and Climate Change: www.decc.gov.uk
Department for the Environment, Food and Rural Affairs: www.defra.gov.uk
Department for Transport: www.dft.gov.uk
Transport for London: www.tfl.gov.uk
Office of the Rail Regulator: www.rail-reg.gov.uk
Strategic Rail Authority: www.sta.gov.uk
Office of Telecommunications: www.oftel.gov.uk
Office of Water Services: www.open.gov.uk/ofwat
Office of Gas and Electricity Markets: www.ofgem.gov.uk
Scottish Executive: www.scotland.gov.uk
Northern Ireland Executive: www.nio.gov.uk
Northern Ireland Department for Regional Development: www.drdni.gov.uk
Welsh Assembly Government: www.wales.gov.uk
Countryside Commission: www.countryside.gov.uk
The Green Party: www.greenparty.org.uk
British Geological Survey: www.bgs.ac.uk
The Met Office: www.metoffice.com
The National Archives: www.nationalarchives.gov.uk
MORI Social Research Institute: www.mori.com/environment

3

The people

The British Isles have attracted settlers, invaders and immigrants throughout their history. The contemporary British are consequently composed of people from worldwide origins and are divided into what eventually became the English, Scots, Welsh and (Northern) Irish. These populations have mixed roots derived from diverse settlement and immigration patterns over time. There has also been considerable internal migration throughout the British Isles (particularly in the nineteenth century) as individuals moved between the four nations of England, Scotland, Wales and Ireland. In a similar integration process, the English language, which binds most of the people together linguistically in its various dialect forms, is a mixture of Germanic, Romance and other world languages.

Descent patterns are important distinguishing elements in the ethnicities of the British peoples today. Some individuals may have relatively simple ethnic backgrounds while others may have more complex family origins, resulting at one level from intermarriage between English, Irish, Scottish or Welsh people. For example, opinion polls suggest that one in four adult Britons (English, Scottish or Welsh) claim to have Irish roots or bloodlines in their ancestry (although experts maintain that the true figure is probably one in ten). On the other hand, geneticists argue that most Irish carry English genes in their DNA and that the great majority of the population of the islands carry a common Palaeolithic gene. At a further level, there are immigrant minorities with their own ethnic identities. They may have sometimes intermarried with the indigenous population, maintained their own separate ethnic culture or eventually acquired British identity through naturalization. Their children have often been born in Britain, with many being of mixed parentage, and they may possess several other allegiances in addition to British nationality.

These historical developments have created a contemporary society with multinational, multicultural and multi-ethnic characteristics. However, since assimilation and integration processes are not always successful, controversial questions continue to be asked about the meaning of 'Britishness', the nature of identities and loyalties in the population and the validity of government immigration and asylum policies.

Early settlement to AD 1066

There is no accurate picture of what the early settlement of the present British Isles was actually like and there were long periods when the islands were uninhabited. Historians and archaeologists constantly revise traditional theories about the growth of the country as new evidence comes to light.

The earliest human bones found (1993) in Britain are 500,000 years old (Boxgrove Man, West Sussex). Yet butchered animal bones and stone tools discovered in East Anglia in 2002 indicate hominid activity from 700,000 years ago. The first people were probably Palaeolithic (Old Stone Age) nomads from mainland Europe, who used rudimentary stone implements. It is likely that they travelled to Britain by land when the country was joined to the European land mass. Homo sapiens appeared during the Palaeolithic period, arguably displacing Neanderthals.

Mesolithic (Middle Stone Age) settlers from about 8300 BC arrived in the transitional period between the Palaeolithic and the Neolithic eras and between the end of the last glacial period and the beginnings of agriculture in the Middle East. Neolithic (New Stone Age) arrivals from 4000 BC had more advanced skills in stone carving, began to form settled agricultural communities and to tame wild animals, and the population increased. Some possibly came by sea from central Europe and settled in eastern Britain, while others arrived from Iberian (Spanish-Portuguese) areas and populated Cornwall, Ireland, Wales, the Isle of Man and western Scotland. Their descendants live today in the same western parts. Neolithic groups built large wooden, soil and stone monuments, like Stonehenge and Avebury, and later arrivals (the Beaker Folk) probably introduced a Bronze Age culture.

From about 600 BC there was a movement of so-called Celtic tribes into the islands from western Europe, who have been credited with bringing an Iron Age civilization with them. The Celts were not a unified group, had at least two main languages and were divided into different, scattered tribes, who often fought with one another. Varied Celtic civilizations dominated the islands until they were overcome by warring Belgic tribes (also of Celtic origin) around 200 BC.

The Belgic tribes were subjected to a series of Roman expeditions from 55 BC. The eventual Roman military occupation of the islands (except for Ireland and most of Scotland) lasted from AD 43 until AD 409. The term 'Britain' probably derives from the Greek and Latin names given to England and Wales by the Romans, although it may stem from Celtic originals. It is argued that the Romans did not mix well with the existing population and that their lasting influence was slight. However some Christian practices spread throughout the islands; political and legal institutions were introduced; new agricultural methods and produce were imported; and there is physical evidence of the Roman presence throughout much of England.

After the Roman withdrawal in AD 409, Germanic tribes such as the Angles (from which the name 'England' is supposedly derived), the Saxons and the Jutes from north-western Europe invaded the country. They either mixed with the existing population or pushed it westwards, although the degree of this displacement has been disputed. The country was divided into seven separate and often warring Anglo-Saxon kingdoms in England, with largely Celtic areas in Wales, Scotland and Ireland.

These regions suffered from Scandinavian (Viking) military invasions in the eighth and ninth centuries AD, until the Scandinavians were defeated in England, Scotland and Ireland in the tenth to eleventh centuries. The Scandinavian presence, after initial fleeting raids, was reflected in some permanent settlement, integration of peoples, farming, political institutions and the adaptation of Scandinavian words.

Early English history was completed when the Anglo-Saxons were defeated by French-Norman invaders at the Battle of Hastings in AD 1066 and England was subjected to their rule. The Norman Conquest was a watershed in English history and marked the last successful external military invasion of the country. It influenced the English people and their language (since French was the language of the nobility for the next 300 years) and initiated many social, legal and institutional frameworks, such as a feudal system, which were to characterize future British society.

Yet Celtic civilizations continued in what are now Wales, Scotland and Ireland, which were divided into separate (and often warring) kingdoms, tribes and clans. Anglo-Norman rule of Ireland and Wales was initially patchy and was not successfully imposed upon Scotland. The latter was inhabited (except for Angles in the south) by the original Picts and later Scots (Scotti) from Ireland who colonized western Scotland (AD 200–400), giving their name to present-day Scotland.

Different peoples had thus entered the British Isles from the south-west, the east and the north by 1066. But settlement was often hindered by climatic and geographical obstacles, particularly in the north and west. Many newcomers tended to concentrate initially in southern England and settlement patterns were not uniform over all of Britain at the same time. Despite some intermingling between the various settlers, there were ethnic differences between the English and the people of Ireland, Wales and Scotland, as well as varying identities between groups in all the countries. It is this mixture, increased by later immigration and internal migration, which has produced the present ethnic and national diversity in Britain.

The early settlement and invasion movements substantially affected the developing fabric of British life and formed the first tentative foundations of the modern state. The newcomers often tried to impose their cultures on the existing society, as well as adopting some of the native characteristics. Today there are few British towns which lack any physical evidence of the successive changes. The invaders also influenced social, legal, economic, political, agricultural, cultural and administrative institutions and contributed to the evolving language.

There are no realistic population figures for the early British Isles. The nomadic lifestyle of groups of up to twenty people seems gradually to have ceased and to have been replaced by more permanent farming settlements of a few

TABLE 3.1 Early settlement to AD 1066	
c. 2,500,000 BC	Palaeolithic (Old Stone Age)
c. 8,300 BC	Mesolithic (Middle Stone Age)
c. 4,000 BC	Neolithic (new Stone Age)
c. 2,000 BC	Beaker Folk (Bronze Age)
c. 600 BC	Celts (Iron Age)
c. 200 BC	Belgic tribes
AD 43	The Romans
AD 410	Germanic tribes (Anglo-Saxons)
Eighth to eleventh centuries	The Scandinavians
AD 1066	The Norman Conquest

hundred inhabitants. It is estimated, for example, that the English population during the Roman occupation was one million. By the Norman period, the eleventh-century Domesday Book showed an increase to two million. The Domesday Book was the first systematic attempt to evaluate England's wealth and population, mainly for taxation purposes.

Growth and immigration up to the twentieth century

England, Scotland, Wales and Ireland had developed more clearly defined identities and geographical areas by the twelfth century, although 'tribal' and royalist conflict (rather than national unity) continued in the four nations. Political and military attempts were made by England over successive centuries to unite Wales, Scotland and Ireland under the English Crown. English monarchs tried to conquer or ally themselves with these countries as protection against threats from within the islands and from continental Europe, as well as for increased power and possessions. Internal colonization and political unification of the islands gradually created the British state. This process was accompanied by fierce and bloody struggles between and within the nations, often resulting in lasting tensions and bitterness.

Ireland was invaded by Henry II in 1169. Parts of the country were occupied by Anglo-Norman nobles, but little direct royal authority was initially exercised from England. More extensive later colonization of Ireland by the English and the Scots became a source of conflict between the countries, but it also led to Irish settlements in Scotland, London and west coast ports like Liverpool. Ireland became part of the United Kingdom in 1801 but, after periods of violence and political unrest, was divided in 1921 into the Irish Free State (eventually to become the Republic of Ireland) and Northern Ireland (which remains part of the United Kingdom).

PLATE 3.1 This Northern Ireland parade on 17 March 2009 set off from Belfast City Hall in the centre of the city to celebrate St Patrick's Day. (St Patrick is the patron saint of Ireland.) Strict security was observed, but the armed police on duty joined in with the spirit of the day after years of the Troubles.
(Alan Lewis/Rex Features)

Wales, after Roman control, remained a Celtic country, although influenced by Anglo-Norman and Angevin-Plantagenet England. Between 1282 and 1285 Edward I's military campaign brought Wales under English rule, and he built castles and deployed garrisons there. Apart from a period of freedom in 1402–7, Wales was integrated legally and administratively with England by Acts of Union between 1536 and 1542.

The English also tried to conquer Scotland by military force, but were ultimately repulsed at the Battle of Bannockburn in 1314. Scotland remained independent until the political union between the two countries in 1707, when the creation of Great Britain (England/Wales and Scotland) took place. However, Scotland and England had shared a common monarch since 1603 when James VI of Scotland became James I of England (the dynastic Union of the Two Crowns).

England, Wales and Scotland had meanwhile become predominantly Protestant in religion as a result of the European Reformation and Henry VIII's break with Rome. Ireland remained Catholic and tried to distance itself from England, thus adding religion to colonialism as a foundation for future problems.

PLATE 3.2 Scottish piper in traditional dress, with kilt and sporran, playing the bagpipes, Loch Broom in the Scottish Highlands.
(Chad Ehlers/Stock Connection/Rex Features)

PLATE 3.3 Children celebrate St David's Day (St David being the patron saint of Wales) by dressing up in national costume and waving Welsh dragon flags, Cardiff, 1991.
(Vivien Jones, Rex Features)

Contemporary Britain therefore is not a single, homogeneous country but rather a recent and potentially unstable union of four old nations. Great Britain (1707) is only slightly older than the USA (often regarded as a young country) and the United Kingdom (1801) is younger. Nor did the political unions appreciably alter the relationships between the four nations. The English frequently treated their Celtic neighbours as colonial subjects rather than equal partners and Englishness became a powerful strand in developing concepts of Britishness, because of the dominant role that the English have played in the formation of Britain.

However, despite the tensions and bitterness between the four nations, there was internal migration between them. This mainly involved Irish, Welsh and Scottish people moving to England. Few English emigrated to Wales and Scotland, although there was English and Scottish settlement in Ireland over the centuries.

Immigration from abroad into the British Isles also continued due to such factors as religious and political persecution, trade, business and employment. Immigrants have had a significant impact on British society. They have contributed to financial institutions, commerce, industry and agriculture, and influenced artistic, cultural and political developments, yet immigrant activity and success have also resulted in jealousy, discrimination and violence from the indigenous populations.

In addition to political integration, internal migration and immigration from overseas, Britain's growth and the mixing of its people were also conditioned first by a series of agricultural changes and second by a number of later industrial revolutions. Agricultural developments started with Neolithic settlers and continued with the Saxons in England who cleared the forests, cultivated crops and introduced inventions and equipment which remained in use for centuries. Their open-field system of farming (with strips of land worked by local people) was later replaced by widespread sheep-herding and wool production. Britain expanded agriculturally and commercially from the eleventh century, and also created manufacturing industries.

Immigration was consequently associated with financial, agricultural and industrial skills. Jewish moneylenders entered England with the Norman Conquest, to be followed later by Lombard bankers from northern Italy. This commercial expertise created greater wealth which was influenced by the merchants of the German Hansa League, who set up their trading posts in London and on the east coast of England. Around 1330 saw the arrival of Dutch and Flemish weavers who by the end of the fifteenth century had helped to transform England into a major nation of sheep farmers, cloth producers and textile exporters. Fourteenth-century immigration also introduced specialized knowledge in a variety of manufacturing trades.

Some immigrants stayed only for short periods; others remained and adapted to British society while preserving their cultural and ethnic identities. Newcomers were often encouraged to settle in Britain and the policy of using immigrant expertise continued in later centuries, but foreign workers had no legal rights and early immigrants, such as Jews and Hansa merchants, could be summarily expelled.

Agricultural and commercial developments were reflected in changing population concentrations. From Saxon times to 1800, Britain had an agriculturally based economy with 80 per cent of its people living in villages in the countryside. Settlement was concentrated in the south and east of England, where the rich agricultural regions of East Anglia and Lincolnshire had the greatest population densities. During the fourteenth century, however, the increase in population was halted by plagues and numbers did not start to improve again for another hundred years.

As agricultural production moved into sheep farming and clothing manufactures, larger numbers of people settled around wool ports, such as Bristol on the west coast and coastal towns in East Anglia. Others moved to cloth-producing areas and market towns in the West Country and the Cotswolds. The south Midland and eastern English counties were the most densely peopled, with the total British population at the end of the seventeenth century being estimated at 5.5 million.

Other newcomers continued to arrive from overseas, including gypsies, blacks (associated with the slave trade) and a further wave of Jews, who in 1655 created

Britain's first permanent Jewish community. In the sixteenth and seventeenth centuries, the country attracted a large number of refugees, such as Dutch Protestants and French Huguenots, driven from Europe by warfare, political and religious persecution and employment needs. This talented and urbanized immigration contributed considerably to the national economy and added a new dimension to a largely agricultural population. However, from around 1700, immigration decreased throughout the next two centuries. Britain exported more people than it received, mainly to North America and the expanding colonies.

A second central development in British history was a number of industrial revolutions that took place in the eighteenth and nineteenth centuries. These transformed Britain from an agricultural economy into an industrial and manufacturing country. Processes based on coal-generated steam power were discovered and exploited. Factories and factory towns were needed to mass-produce new manufactured goods. Villages in the coalfields and industrial areas grew rapidly into manufacturing centres. A drift of population away from the countryside began in the late eighteenth century as people sought work in urban factories to escape rural poverty and unemployment. They moved, for example, to textile mills in Lancashire and Yorkshire and to heavy industries and pottery factories in the West Midlands.

The agricultural population changed in the nineteenth century into an industrialized workforce. The 1801 census (the first measurement of population) gave figures of 8.3 million for England, 0.6 million for Wales, 1.6 million for Scotland and an estimated 8 million for Ireland, but between 1801 and 1901 the population of England and Wales expanded to 32.5 million. The numbers in Scotland increased less rapidly to 4.5 million, due to emigration, but in Ireland the population was reduced to 4 million because of famine, mortality and emigration. The greatest concentrations of people were now in London and the industrial areas of the Midlands, south Lancashire, Merseyside, Clydeside, Tyneside, Yorkshire and South Wales.

The industrial revolution reached its height during the early nineteenth century. It did not require foreign labour because there were enough skilled trades among British workers and a ready supply of unskilled labourers from Wales, Scotland, Ireland and the English countryside. Those from North Wales went to the Lancashire textile mills; Highland Scots travelled to the Lowland Clydeside industries; and Irishmen flocked to England and Scotland to work in the manual trades of the industrial infrastructure constructing roads, railways and canals. These migrations created ethnic conflicts (which sometimes grew into violent confrontations in cities such as Liverpool), but also some integration.

Industrialization led to an expansion in commercial markets, which attracted new immigrants who had the business and financial skills to exploit the industrial wealth. Some newcomers joined City of London financial institutions and the import/export trades, to which they contributed their international connections, while others were involved in a range of occupations and trades. Immigration to

Britain might have been greater in the nineteenth century had it not been for the attraction of North America, which received large numbers of newcomers from around the world.

By the end of the nineteenth century Britain was the world's leading industrial nation and among the richest. Although it lost its lead in manufacturing, most of which was in native British hands, as foreign competition grew, its position in international finance, some of which was under immigrant control, was retained.

Immigration from 1900

Although immigrants historically had relatively free access to Britain, they could be easily expelled, having no legal rights to protect them; and entry restrictions were increasingly imposed. But the 1871 census showed that only 157,000 people in the UK out of a population of 37 million had been born outside the British Empire.

Despite these low figures, economic immigrants and asylum seekers caused public and political concern. In the early twentieth century, Jews and Poles escaped persecution in Eastern Europe and settled in the East End of London, which has always attracted newcomers. Demands for immigration control grew and an anti-foreigner feeling spread, fuelled by the nationalism and spy mania caused by the First World War (1914–18). But laws (like the Aliens Act of 1905), which were designed to curtail foreign entry, proved ineffective. By 1911 the number of people in Britain born outside the empire had reached 428,000 (1 per cent of the population).

As a result of the 1930s world recession and the Second World War, refugees first from Nazi-occupied Europe and later from Soviet bloc countries in addition to economic immigrants entered Britain in spite of entry controls. After the war, refugees such as Poles, Latvians and Ukrainians among other nationalities chose to stay in Britain. Later in the twentieth century, other political refugees arrived, such as Hungarians, Czechs, Chileans, Libyans, East African Asians, Iranians, Vietnamese and other Eastern Europeans. Italian, French, German, Irish, Turkish, Cypriot, Chinese, Spanish and Commonwealth economic immigrants increasingly entered the country. These groups (and their descendants) today form sizeable ethnic minorities and are found throughout Britain. Such newcomers have often suffered from discrimination at various times, some more than others.

Public and political concern in the post-war period turned to issues of race and colour, which dominated the immigration debate for the rest of the twentieth century and focused on non-white Commonwealth immigration. Before the Second World War, most Commonwealth immigrants to Britain had come from the largely white Old Commonwealth countries of Canada, Australia and New Zealand, and from South Africa. Yet all Commonwealth citizens (white and non-white) continued to have relatively free access and were not treated as aliens.

From the late 1940s, increasing numbers of people from the non-white New Commonwealth nations of India, Pakistan and the West Indies came to Britain, often at the invitation of government agencies, to fill the manual and lower-paid jobs of an expanding economy. West Indians worked in public transport, catering, the National Health Service and manual trades in London, Birmingham and other large cities. Indians and Pakistanis later arrived to work in the textile and iron industries of Leeds, Bradford and Leicester (which now has a 40 per cent non-white population). By the 1970s, non-white people had become a familiar sight in other British cities such as Glasgow, Sheffield, Huddersfield, Bristol, Manchester, Liverpool, Coventry and Nottingham. There was a dispersal of immigrants throughout Britain, although many tended to settle in the central areas of industrial cities. This concentrated settlement (ghettoization) has grown in recent years and raised concern about the isolation of some ethnic groups from the majority white population and its institutions in northern towns such as Burnley, Blackburn and Oldham.

Non-white communities have increased and work in a broad range of occupations. Some, particularly Indian Asians and the Chinese, have been successful in economic and professional terms. Others (such as Bangladeshis and some West Indians and Pakistanis) have experienced problems with low-paid

PLATE 3.4 Notting Hill Carnival, 2009, a costume parade over two days, beginning 31 August 2009, London. Originally a West Indian street carnival with floats, dancers and steel bands, this annual event now includes other ethnic groups.
(Steve Davey/Rex Features)

jobs, educational disadvantage, unemployment, decaying housing in the inner cities, isolation, alienation and discrimination (including tensions between other non-white ethnic groups). It is argued that Britain possesses a deep-rooted (or institutional) racism based on the legacy of empire and notions of racial superiority, which has hindered the integration of the non-white population into the larger society. Some young non-whites who have been born in Britain feel bitter at their experiences and at their relative lack of educational, employment and social possibilities and advancement. An opposing argument (frequently employed after the 7 July 2005 London bombings) is that ethnic communities should confront their own internal problems (such as generational conflicts, religious extremism and gender issues) and integrate more with the majority population and its institutions.

So many New Commonwealth immigrants were coming to Britain that from 1962 governments treated most Commonwealth newcomers as aliens and followed a two-strand policy on immigration. This consisted, first, of Immigration Acts to restrict the number of all immigrants entering the country and, second, of Race Relations Acts to protect the rights of those immigrants already settled in Britain.

Race Relations Acts since 1976 have made it unlawful to discriminate against individuals on grounds such as race, ethnicity and national origin in areas like education, housing, employment, services and advertising. The Commission for Racial Equality (CRE) was established in 1976; applied the Race Relations Acts; worked for the elimination of discrimination; and promoted equality of opportunity. It was replaced in 2007 by the Equality and Human Rights Commission (EHRC), whose role is to end discrimination and harassment of individuals because of their disability, age, race, gender, sexual orientation, religion or beliefs. Despite their good intentions, both bodies have been criticized for their performances, internal quarrels, bureaucratic methods, unwieldy procedures and lack of clear aims or definitions. Those who suffer alleged discrimination can appeal to race and employment tribunals and may receive help from other anti-discrimination bodies.

There is still criticism of immigration laws and race-relations organizations. Some people argue that one cannot legislate satisfactorily against discrimination and others would like stricter controls on immigrant entry and refugees. The concerns of some white people are made worse by racialist speeches; the growth of nationalist parties like the National Front, the British National Party (BNP) and Combat 18; and racially motivated violence. Non-white citizens, on the other hand, feel that they too easily and unfairly become scapegoats for any problems that may arise. Some have become alienated from British society and reject institutions such as the police, the legal system and political structures. Government policies since the 1940s have not always helped to allay the anxieties of whites or non-whites.

Immigration and race remain problematic. They are complex matters, are exploited for political purposes by both the right and the left, and can be overdramatized. Many non-white immigrants and their British-born children have adapted to the larger society whilst retaining their ethnic identities. Britain does have a relatively stable diversity of cultures and the highest rate of intermarriage and mixed-race relationships in Europe, with one in eight children under five having parents from different ethnic backgrounds. However ghettoization is a problem in some areas; outbreaks of racial tension, violence and harassment do occur; and there are accusations that the police and the courts ignore or underplay race crimes. Some critics are concerned that race, discrimination and immigration problems are not being openly and fairly debated in what they feel is the present climate of 'political correctness' and 'inclusiveness' policies.

The non-white population was initially composed largely of single males. This structure changed as dependants joined settled immigrants, as British-born non-whites developed their own family organizations, and as more people from different ethnic groups intermarried. The emphasis switched to debates about what constitutes a 'multi-ethnic society'. However, the term 'immigrant' has again become prominent as the number of immigrants and asylum seekers has increased and become a focus for public concern and debate.

Apart from people who may be granted right of entry and permanent settlement in Britain, such as the dependants of migrants already settled in the country, all others who wish to enter Britain fall into specific categories. Short-term visitors, such as students, require visas and sometimes work permits. People from EU states have the right to seek work and live in Britain and arguably constitute the largest group of entrants. Non-EU unskilled applicants are no longer accepted, but those with relevant qualifications needed by the employment market may apply to enter under a points system. In addition, but not strictly categorized as immigrants, there are asylum seekers fleeing persecution in their own countries and who must apply for political asylum.

A further category was created after the enlargement of the EU in 2004 to twenty-five members. The government established work permits for new entrants. These are issued to legal migrants seeking work in Britain, initially for at least a year. In 2004, a record 340,000 legal migrants came to fill vacancies in the job market, covering the hospitality and catering industry, transport, the health sector and teaching. Some 130,000 people from East European EU countries registered for work, with Poland, Lithuania and Slovakia providing the largest numbers.

According to the Office for National Statistics, 590,000 people arrived to live in the UK in 2008 (the second-highest figure on record after the 596,000 in 2006) and 505,000 (86 per cent) of these were non-British citizens. The number of people emigrating from the UK for more than twelve months in 2008 was a record high at 427,000, an increase from 341,000 in 2007 and 398,000 in 2006. The rise was influenced by an increase in the number of non-British citizens emigrating from 169,000 in 2007 to 255,000 in 2008. Half of the 86,000 increase were citizens of the Eastern European countries which had joined the EU in 2004 and who were returning home.

These figures mean that net migration (the difference between immigration and emigration) decreased from 233,000 in 2007 to 163,000 as a result of increased emigration. But this was still more than the 90,000 average of the 1990s and is a source of political and public concern. It represents a continuation of high levels of immigration since 2004 and suggests that significant immigration continues, despite restrictive legislation since the 1960s.

Government projections suggest that these figures (allowing for emigration from the country and if sustained) indicate that immigration will fuel an estimated 7.2 million growth in the population over the next twenty-five years. The previous Labour government argued that the nation must compete in the international marketplace and attract those immigrants and migrant workers that the economy needs to compensate for a declining labour force, an ageing population and a shortage of both skilled and unskilled workers. However all the political parties in the 2010 general election campaign admitted that immigration and asylum must be controlled. The Conservatives argued that net immigration must be reduced to 50,000 or lower each year and the Liberal Democrats want a regional points system of control. All agreed that the indigenous unemployed in Britain should undertake education and training to fill job vacancies in order to reduce immigration levels and dependence on welfare benefits.

It is important that the flexible nature of emigration from Britain should be emphasized if the immigration/race debate is to be kept in perspective. Historically, there has usually been a balance of migration, with emigration cancelling out immigration in real terms, but there have also been periods of high emigration. Groups left England and Scotland in the sixteenth and seventeenth centuries to settle in Ireland and North America. Millions in the nineteenth and twentieth centuries emigrated to Australia, New Zealand, South Africa, Canada, other colonies and the USA. Emigration meant that Britain had a net loss of population during the 1970s and 1980s. This trend has been reversed since the late 1990s and more immigrants have entered Britain than emigrants have left: for example, there was a net migration in 2004 of 223,000, a significant increase over previous years despite 360,000 people leaving Britain.

People from India, Pakistan and Africa have traditionally made up the largest proportions of newcomers, with many being dependants of settled immigrants. In addition to New Commonwealth and African immigrants, more entrants have lately come from the Old Commonwealth and the EU.

In recent years, there has also been controversy about the increased numbers of asylum seekers entering Britain and suspicions that many are economic migrants rather than genuinely in humanitarian need. The previous Labour government tried to tighten (ineffectually for some critics) the rules for the admission of asylum seekers and to increase the number of deportations of those who fail in their applications. However, it is estimated that there may be at least 600,000 illegal asylum seekers, migrant workers and immigrants in Britain. The government does not know the exact figure and its drive to remove failed asylum seekers has faltered, although asylum applications fell to a thirteen-year low of 22,000 in 2006. Critics attack the government's policies on asylum, query the accuracy of the statistics and the treatment of asylum seekers.

Opinion polls in the 1990s had suggested that race relations, immigration and asylum were of less concern to Britons than they were from the 1940s to the 1980s. A 1995 MORI poll found that 78 per cent of respondents did not consider themselves to be prejudiced against people of other races. But a 2001 Guardian newspaper poll reported that 70 per cent of readers thought that race relations were not getting better. An Ipsos MORI poll in April 2010 found that race relations and immigration had climbed to second place (33 per cent) in a list of the most important issues facing British society. A Transatlantic Trends (German Marshall Fund) poll in 2009 assessing US and European opinion on immigration showed that the British were by far the most hostile to immigration. Some 53 per cent of respondents thought that immigrants took away jobs from native workers; 54 per cent believed that legal immigrants increased crime; 48 per cent maintained that legal immigrants had no equal rights to social benefits; and 71 per cent felt that governments were mismanaging immigration. However, the Labour government claimed in 2010 that progress had been made since 2000, so that while racial discrimination still exists, disadvantage is now more linked to poverty, class and identity, which increasingly also affects white working-class areas. Some critics and politicians maintain that immigration and asylum regulations need to be reformed and that concerns about ethnic relations have to be faced honestly.

New conditions for naturalization and redefinitions of British citizenship were contained in the Nationality Act of 1981. It was criticized as providing further restrictions on immigration, particularly from the New Commonwealth. Acceptance for settlement does not mean automatic British citizenship. Certain requirements for naturalization have to be fulfilled, together with a period of residence.

More specific requirements for the attainment of British citizenship through naturalization were made in 2002. Applicants must now demonstrate knowledge about life in Britain, reach an acceptable level of English proficiency, attend a citizenship ceremony and swear a citizenship oath and pledge to the Queen and the country. This move has been seen as an attempt to emphasize for immigrants the centrality of Britishness and British values. In 1998 53,900 people were given UK citizenship, rising to a record 164,000 in 2007. In 2008, the number fell to 129,000. Almost 1.2 million foreigners have been given citizenship since 1997.

Ethnic minorities

The next census of the population will take place in 2011, but accurate details will not be known until later. The last (2001) census classified 92.1 per cent (54,154,000) of the British population as white and 7.9 per cent (4,635,000) as belonging to minority ethnic groups (See Table 3.2). 'Minority ethnic' refers only to non-white and mixed groups and excludes people from white minorities. The census shows that the minority ethnic category increased by 53 per cent since the 1991 census; half the ethnic minority population were Asian; and a quarter were described as black.

The non-white minority ethnic groups, some 50 per cent of whom were born in Britain, constitute a relatively small proportion of the British population at 7.9 per cent. Some 50 per cent of them live in London (as opposed to 10 per cent of the white population), where they make up 29 per cent of all residents. By contrast, less than 4 per cent of non-white groups live in the north-east and south-west of England, where ethnic minority groups make up only 2 per cent of the total population.

Prior to the 2001 census, statistics for the 'minority ethnic' category were estimates and the results were underestimated. Respondents to the 2001 census were for the first time able to reply more accurately by reporting what they thought their ethnic identity was. This resulted in a large percentage of those (15

TABLE 3.2 Ethnic minorities in Britain, 2001

	Minority ethnic population	Percentage of total national population	Percentage of ethnic population
Mixed	677,117	1.2	14.6
Asian/Asian British			
Indian	1,053,411	1.8	22.7
Pakistani	747,285	1.3	16.1
Bangladeshi	283,063	0.5	6.1
Other Asian	247,664	0.4	5.3
Black/Black British			
Black Caribbean	565,876	1.0	12.2
Black African	485,277	0.8	10.5
Black other	97,585	0.2	2.1
Chinese	247,403	0.4	5.3
Other	230,615	0.4	5.0
Total ethnic minorities	4,635,296	7.9	100

Source: adapted from Census, April 2001, Office for National Statistics

per cent of ethnic minorities) who described themselves as 'mixed'. A third of this group were from white and black Caribbean backgrounds.

There are also many other ethnic minority communities in Britain, which are usually classified as white. Immigration from the Republic of Ireland continues; the Irish have historically been a large immigrant group and at the 2001 census 691,000 people in Great Britain identified themselves as White Irish (amounting to 1 per cent of Great Britain's population). Movement from Old Commonwealth countries (such as Australia, Canada and South Africa) has increased. There has been arise in the number of immigrants from European Union countries (such as Germany, Spain, Italy and France), and also in newcomers from the USA and Middle East. At the 2001 census, 1.4 million people identified themselves as 'Other White'.

Population movements from 1900

Industrial areas with heavy population densities developed in Britain in the nineteenth century, but in the twentieth considerable internal population shifts occurred which were mainly due to economic and employment changes. There was a drift of people away from industrial Tyneside, Clydeside and South Wales during the 1920s and 1930s trade depressions as coal production, steel manufacture and other heavy industries were badly affected. This movement increased during the second half of the twentieth century, and since the 1950s there has been little population increase in the industrial areas of the Central Lowlands of Scotland, Tyneside, Merseyside, West Yorkshire, South Wales and Northern Ireland, which have seen a decline in their traditional industries and rising unemployment. Instead, people moved away from these regions to the English Midlands with their diversified industries and to London and south-east England where employment opportunities (despite fluctuations) and affluence were greater. Over the same period, there was also considerable immigration into Britain, followed at the end of the twentieth century by increases in the number of asylum seekers. Such groups have tended to settle in urban and inner-city areas throughout the country, although the heaviest concentration has been in London.

The reduction in the rural population and the expansion of urban centres continued into the twentieth century. Yet by the middle of the century there was a reverse movement of people away from the centres of big cities such as London, Manchester, Liverpool, Birmingham and Leeds. This was due to bomb damage during the Second World War, slum clearance and the need to use inner-city land for shops, offices, warehouses and transport utilities. So-called New Towns in rural areas and council housing estates outside the inner cities were specifically created to accommodate the displaced population. Road systems were built with motorways and bypasses to avoid congested areas and rural locations around some cities were designated as Green Belts, in which no building was permitted.

However, Green Belts and other rural locations are now controversially being encroached upon for house construction and other purposes, which can attract fierce local opposition.

Many people choose to live at some distance from their workplaces, often in a city's suburbs, neighbouring towns (commuter towns) or rural areas. This has contributed to a decline in inner-city populations, and one British person in five now lives in the countryside with the rest in towns and cities. Densities are highest in Greater London and south-east England and lowest in rural regions of northern Scotland, the Lake District, Wales and Northern Ireland.

In mid-2008, the population of the United Kingdom was 61,383,000, up by 408,000 on the previous year. Of this total, England had 51,446,000, Wales 2,993,000, Scotland 5,169,000 and Northern Ireland 1,775,000. These figures give a population density for the United Kingdom of some 600 persons per square mile (242 per sq km), well above the European Union average of 117 per sq km. It is twice as densely populated as France, nine times more densely than the US and one hundred times more dense than Australia. England has an average density of some 940 persons per square mile (395 per sq km) and this average does not reveal the higher densities in areas of the country such as London, the West Midlands, West Yorkshire, Greater Manchester, Merseyside, Tyne and Wear, Edinburgh and Cardiff.

The British population grew by 0.3 per cent between 1971 and 1978, which gave it one of the lowest increases in Western Europe, and continued to decline in the 1980s. However, numbers started to increase from the late 1990s partly due to there being a higher number of births than deaths, rising fertility, better life expectancy and increasing immigration. The population is expected to be over 70 million by 2029. To avoid this, more politicians now argue that net migration needs to be cut to up to 50,000 each year. The non-white ethnic minorities are growing fifteen times faster than the white population and are also much younger. It is estimated that the counties of southern and central England will have the highest population growth up to 2011 and the heaviest population losses will occur on Tyneside and Merseyside.

TABLE 3.3 Populations of major British cities, 2001

London	7,172,091	Edinburgh	430,082
Birmingham	970,892	Bristol	420,556
Glasgow	629,501	Manchester	394,269
Liverpool	469,017	Leicester	330,574
Leeds	443,247	Cardiff	292,150
Sheffield	439,866	Belfast	276,459

Source: adapted from Census 2001, Office for National Statistics

Attitudes to national, ethnic and local identities

Immigration to Britain has often been seen as a threat to a presumed British national identity and common social values. However, the peoples of the British Isles have always been culturally and ethnically diverse. There are differences between England, Wales, Scotland and Northern Ireland and contrasting ways of life within each nation at national, regional and local levels. The use of the term 'Britishness' to describe the people of the United Kingdom is consequently problematic. Despite the Labour government's attempts to introduce the concept of Britishness into school citizenship classes and naturalization procedures for new citizens, the term still lacks a precise definition and can mean many things to many people.

The history of the British Isles prior to the eighteenth century, in fact, is not about a single British identity or political entity but about four distinct nations, which have often been hostile towards one another. 'Britishness' since the 1707 union between England/Wales and Scotland was mainly associated with centralized state institutions, such as the monarchy, Parliament, the law and the Protestant churches. Notions of Britishness became more widely used in the nineteenth century following the 1801 Act of Union and later became linked with the Victorian monarchy, the empire and the nation's industrial and military position in the world. These elements weakened as Britain lost its global power; religious faith decreased; respect for Parliament, the law and the monarchy lessened; and people returned partly to their national allegiances.

However, Britons still have a layered identity in which they think of themselves as simultaneously British and either English, Scottish or Welsh. But the use of such terms as 'British' and 'Britain' in this fashion can seem artificial to those members of the population who have retained specific ethnic and cultural identities. Until recently, Britishness was regarded as another name for Englishness, if only by the English. Foreigners often call all British people 'English' and may have difficulty in appreciating these distinctions or the irritation caused to the non-English population by such labelling.

The Scots, Welsh, English and Northern Irish regard their various identities as significant, and it is argued that the 'British' today do not have a strong sense of a 'British' identity. Most Scots think of themselves as primarily Scottish; most of the Welsh as Welsh; Northern Irish identities are complex; and the English apparently increasingly see themselves as more English than British. In this situation, some critics argue that there needs to be a rethinking of what it means to be British in a multinational, multi-ethnic United Kingdom, a changing Europe and an internationalized world.

There has obviously been ethnic and cultural integration in Britain over the centuries, which resulted from foreign invaders, settlers, immigrants, regional conflicts and internal migrations between the four nations. Political unification within the islands gradually took place under the English Crown; UK state power was mainly concentrated in London; the English dominated numerically; and institutional standardization followed English models. The British identification was derived from English norms because of England's historical role.

English nationalism was the most potent of the four nationalisms and the English had no problem with the dual national role. The Scots and Welsh have historically tended to be more aware of the difference between their nationalism and Britishness, resent the English dominance, see themselves as different from the English and regard their cultural feelings as crucial. Their sense of identity is conditioned by the tension between their distinctive histories and a centralized London government. Northern Ireland is often characterized by the tribalism of the Unionist and Nationalist communities and conflicting identities within both.

National identity was historically largely cultural in Wales and more politicized in Scotland. Nevertheless, the British political union was generally accepted, except for Nationalist opposition in Ireland, which resulted in the partition of the island in 1921. Political nationalism increased in the 1960s and 1970s in Scotland and to some extent in Wales, while the Troubles erupted in Northern Ireland. Following the establishment of devolved self-government in 1998–9, calls for full independence in Scotland and Wales have not been strong, except from the Scottish National Party (SNP) and (arguably) the Welsh National Party (Plaid Cymru). It also seems that Scottish, Welsh and Northern Irish devolution have sparked a resurgence of English nationalism.

There are also differences at regional and community levels within the four nations. Since the English, for example, are historically an ethnically mixed people, their local customs, dialects/accents and behaviour vary considerably and can be strongly asserted. Regions such as the north-east have reacted against London influences and supposedly want decentralized political autonomy (although this region actually voted against regional government in a 2004 referendum). The Cornish see themselves as a distinctive cultural element in English society and have an affinity with Celtic and similar ethnic groups in Britain and Europe. The northern English regard themselves as superior to the southern English, and vice versa. English county and city loyalties are still maintained and are shown in sports, politics, food habits, competitions, cultural activities or a specific way of life.

In Wales, there are cultural and political differences between the industrial south (which tends to support the Labour Party) and the rest of the mainly rural country: between Welsh-speaking Wales in the north-west and centre (which partly supports Plaid Cymru) and English-influenced Wales in the east and south-west (where the Conservative Party has some support); between some of the ancient Welsh counties; and between the cities of Cardiff and Swansea.

Welsh people generally are very conscious of their differences from the English, despite the fact that many of them are of mixed English-Welsh ancestry. Their national and cultural identity is grounded in their history, literature, the Welsh language (actively spoken by 19 per cent of the population), sport (such as rugby football) and festivals like the National Eisteddfod (with its Welsh poetry competitions, dancing and music). It is also echoed in close-knit industrial and agricultural communities and in a tradition of social, political and religious dissent from English norms. Today, many Welsh people still feel that they are struggling for their national identity against political power in London and the erosion of their culture and language by English institutions and the English language. Limited devolution has helped to alleviate these feelings and increase a sense of Welsh identity.

Similarly, Scots generally unite in defence of their national distinctiveness because of historical reactions to the English. They are conscious of their traditions, which are reflected in cultural festivals and separate legal, religious and educational systems. There has been resentment against the centralization of political power in London and alleged economic neglect of Scotland (although the UK government provides greater economic subsidies per head of population to Scotland, Wales and Northern Ireland than to England). Devolved government in Edinburgh has removed some of these objections and focused on Scottish identity.

However, Scots are divided by three languages (Gaelic, Scots and English with the former being spoken by 1.5 per cent of the population or 70,000 people), different religions, prejudices and regionalisms. Cultural differences separate Lowlanders and Highlanders, allegiance to ancient Scottish counties is still relatively strong, and rivalries exist between the two major cities of Edinburgh and Glasgow.

In Northern Ireland, the social, cultural and political differences between Roman Catholics and Protestants or Nationalists and Unionists have long been evident and today are often reflected in geographical ghettos. Groups in both communities often feel frustration with the English and hostility towards the British government in London. But many Unionists are loyal to the Crown, regard themselves as British and wish to continue the union with Britain. Many Nationalists feel themselves to be Irish and want to be united with the Republic of Ireland. Devolution in Northern Ireland has not succeeded in eradicating deep-seated differences between the two communities and the peace is still fragile.

To complicate the picture, there are ethnic minorities (white and non-white) within Britain who may use dual or multiple identities. Many call themselves British and also English, Welsh, Irish or Scottish, while still identifying with their countries of origin or descent. Sometimes they employ their ethnic ties to define themselves as Afro-Caribbean, Black British or British Indians. They may also embrace religious identities, such as British Muslims, British Hindus or British Jews.

There is disagreement about whether multiple identities among ethnic minorities are achievable or desirable. Some critics query whether it is possible for an individual belonging to an ethnic minority (whether by birth abroad or by descent in Britain) to feel British. Others argue that British and ethnic minority allegiances can in fact be unproblematically and tolerantly combined, so that for example one can be both British and Pakistani. Yet a *Sunday Times* survey in November 2001 suggested that 68 per cent of Muslims considered being Muslim was more essential than being British (14 per cent). However, a YouGov poll for the *Daily Telegraph* on 23 July 2005 following jihadist bomb attacks in London reported that 77 per cent of Muslim respondents thought the bombings were not justified; 48 per cent felt very loyal to Britain; and 33 per cent felt fairly loyal; while 10 per cent had no opinion.

These features suggest that the contemporary British are a very diverse people with a range of identities. A MORI poll in September 1999 examined responses to different levels of association. Scots were most likely to identify with Scotland (72 per cent) and their region (62 per cent), less with their local community (39 per cent) and only rarely with Britain (18 per cent). The Welsh identified first with Wales (80), then with their region (50) and community (32), and finally with Britain (27). Among the English there was an almost even split between the importance of region (49), Britain (43), local community (42) and England (41).

According to this and other opinion polls, the Welsh, English and Scots seemed increasingly to be defining themselves more in terms of their individual nationalities, rather than as British. At one extreme, a *Sunday Times* poll in 2000 found that schoolchildren saw themselves as English (66 per cent), Scottish (82) or Welsh (79). But there was little desire for a break-up of the United Kingdom.

These findings should be seen in the context of statistics from the Office of National Statistics in 2004 which suggested that a majority of people from non-white ethnic minorities are in fact asserting their Britishness. Feelings about a British identity are increasingly influenced by cultural factors (and civic values) rather than simply ethnic origins and are strongest (87 per cent) among people of mixed race. Some 81 per cent of 'black other', 80 per cent of black Caribbeans and 75 per cent of Indian, Pakistani and Bangladeshi groups have the same response. Such feelings of Britishness are particularly strong among the young and groups in which the majority were born in Britain.

An interesting further result from these 2004 statistics is that almost 98 per cent of white British people (which includes English, Scottish, Welsh and Northern Irish) feel British, which arguably contradicts other poll findings. This high percentage could indicate that while they may have a primary allegiance to their Englishness or Scottishness for example, they, like the non-white minorities, are responding to Britishness in cultural or civic terms rather than simply ethnic origins. Britishness, in this view, can be acquired irrespective of where one is born or one's descent patterns. The problem lies in defining more precisely what these cultural or civic terms actually are. They might involve a blending of multi-ethnic realities and a shared British cultural framework arising out of what are assumed to be traditional British values.

However, another poll in the *23rd Report on British Social Attitudes* in 2007 found that only 44 per cent of respondents described themselves as British, as opposed to 56 per cent in 1998. The decline is arguably explained by the number of people who now describe themselves as English rather than British. There do appear to be very different results from polls on the subject of Britishness which might be due to respondents' uncertainty about the term and fluctuating responses to events.

Foreigners often have either specific notions of what they think the British are like or, in desperation, seek a unified picture of the national character, often based upon stereotypes, quaint traditions or superficial tourist views of Britain. The emphasis in Britain today, however, seems to be a movement away from such images and a focus on positive cultural signs rooted in a multi-ethnic society. Overseas commentators seem to accept that Britain is a 'multicultural' (but not a classless) society although opinion is divided as to whether or not it is also racially tolerant and welcoming to foreigners.

However, a multicultural society does not inevitably lead to greater tolerance and the term 'multiculturalism' has recently been a strongly debated issue in Britain. Most might agree that as an adjective it accurately and factually describes the country's multi-ethnic or multicultural population. However, some critics and politicians from the 1970s onwards adopted it as a political agenda, favouring the separate development of cultural groups and the preservation of their ethnic identities within Britain. Others, including non-white groups, deny the value of such a position, seeing it as 'ethnic tribalism', and argue for assimilation or integration under a British identity. The latter implies an acceptance of basic common values, including those represented by civic, social and political structures, which have primacy over individual cultural identities.

These concerns are central to attempts to define 'Britishness'. Surveys have suggested that there is a popular movement away from the allegedly negative, imperial and English-dominated historical implications of Britishness to a more positive, value-based, inclusive image with which the four nations and their populations can feel comfortable. A Britishness which encompasses opportunity, respect, tolerance, supportiveness, progress and decency is supposedly attractive to the smaller British nations and ethnic minorities.

But these values have to be realized within defining institutional structures. Since there has never been a homogeneous British population, British nationhood has been progressively created by settlers, invaders and immigrants who have brought their individual contributions to a British identity. Critics argue that this experience and a common citizenship allow the British to define Britishness in civic, rather than racial, terms. It exists irrespective of birthplace and is dependent on one's position as a citizen of Britain.

In this view, the success of any country depends on full integration, not multiculturalism. The term 'British' has evolved into one embracing many different types of people and cultures. Britishness becomes a contemporary set of shared values, beliefs, opinions and identities which encompass a way of life and the promotion of inclusiveness. Rather than being divisive, critics maintain that Britishness is the most inclusive and non-discriminatory term to describe the peoples who comprise the United Kingdom. The fact that there have been no serious and sustained threats to break up the UK might suggest that an evolving Britishness still continues as an umbrella identity for most people.

Exercises

Explain and examine the following terms:

nomads	bypass	Anglo-Saxon	industrialization
Cornwall	Stonehenge	asylum seekers	ethnic minorities
Neolithic	East End	Hansa	British National Party
density	Celtic	devolution	Hastings
Merseyside	Domesday Book	immigrant	naturalization
racism	multiculturalism	Iberian	discrimination
census	emigration	Huguenots	Green Belt
Boxgrove Man	EHRC	ghettoization	political correctness
Scotti	Bannockburn	Viking	Palaeolithic

Write short essays on the following topics:

1   Describe in outline the history of early settlement in Britain

2   Is immigration a problem in Britain? If so, why?

3   Examine the changing patterns of population distribution in Britain

4   Is it correct to describe contemporary Britain as a 'multi-ethnic' and 'multinational' society? If so, why?

5*   Critically examine attempts to define 'Britishness'

Visit **www.routledge.com/textbooks/oakland** for multiple-choice questions, links to related YouTube clips, tips on approaching essay questions, and much, much more.

Further reading

1   Aughey, A. (2007) *The Politics of Englishness*, Manchester: Manchester University Press
2   Alibhai-Brown, Y. (2001) *Who Do We Think We Are? Imagining the New Britain*, London: Allen Lane
3   Alibhai-Brown, Y. (2000) *After Multiculturalism*, London: Foreign Policy Centre
4   Bryant, C.G.A. (2006) *The Nations of Britain*, Oxford: Oxford University Press
5   Colley, L. (1996) *Britons: Forging the Nation 1707–1837*, London: Vintage
6   Colls, R. (2002) *Identity of England*, Oxford: Oxford University Press

7 Conway, D. (2007) *A Nation of Immigrants? A Brief Demographic History of Britain*, London: Civitas

8 Davies, N. (2000) *The Isles: A History*, London: Macmillan

9 Donnell A. (2001) *Companion to Contemporary Black British Culture*, London: Routledge

10 Grant, A. and Stringer, K.J. (eds) (1995) *Uniting the Kingdom? – The Making of British History*, London: Routledge

11 Harvie, C. (2004) *Scotland and Nationalism: Scottish Society and Politics, 1707 to the Present*, London: Routledge

12 McKay, S. (2000) *Northern Protestants: An Unsettled People*, Belfast: Blackstaff Press

13 Nairn, T. (2000) *After Britain*, London: Granta Books

14 O'Connor, F. (1993) *In Search of a State: Catholics in Northern Ireland*, Belfast: Blackstaff Press

15 Owusa, K. (1999) *Black British Culture and Society*, London: Routledge

16 Park, A., Johnson, M. Curtice, J., Thomson, K. and Phillips, M. (2007) *British Social Attitudes: The 23rd Report: Perspectives on a Changing Society*, London : SAGE Publications

17 Paxman, J. (2007) *The English: A Portrait of a People*, London: Penguin Books

18 Phillips, M. and Phillips, T. (1999), *Windrush: The Irresistible Rise of Multi-racial Britain*, London: HarperCollins

19 Solomos, J. (2003) *Race and Racism in Britain*, London: Palgrave Macmillan

20 Storry, M. and Childs, P. (eds) (2007) *British Cultural Identities*, London: Routledge

21 Ward, P. (2004) *Britishness since 1870*, London: Routledge

22 Winder, R. (2005) *Bloody Foreigners: The Story of Immigration to Britain*, London: Abacus

Websites

Campaign for the English Regions: www.cfer.org.uk
Devolution: www.britishcouncil.org/devolution/index.htm
Looking into England: www.britishcouncil.org/studies/english
British Studies Now: www.britishcouncil.org/studies/bsn.htm
Scotland Office: www.scottishsecretary.gov.uk
Wales Office: www.walesoffice.gov.uk
Northern Ireland Office: www.nio.gov.uk

4

Politics and government

Most of this chapter deals with central political structures, which involve the whole of the United Kingdom (UK). The final part is concerned with devolved political institutions and local government, which have their own areas of responsibility.

Political history in Britain and Ireland over the past 800 years illustrates the growth of what is now the UK and modern changes in its composition. The weakening of non-democratic monarchical and aristocratic power in England, Scotland, Wales and Ireland led eventually to political and legislative authority being centralized in London in a UK parliament, with a UK government and prime minister. Changing social conditions resulted in the growth of political parties, the extension of the vote to all adults, the development of local government and a twentieth-century devolution (transfer) of some political power to Wales, Scotland and Northern Ireland. These historical processes were accompanied by political, social and religious conflicts as well as by constitutional compromise.

The political structures are still vigorously debated and there is at present considerable public disillusionment with the political process and politicians. The government in London is accused of being too secretive, too centralized, too remote, too media-reactive, too controlling and insufficiently responsive to the needs of the diverse peoples of the United Kingdom. It is argued that the UK Parliament has lost control over the government; that political power has bypassed Parliament and shifted to a presidential prime minister with a prime ministerial office in Downing Street; that unelected appointed bodies (such as quangos or quasi-autonomous non-governmental organizations) and political advisers have become too influential; that the Civil Service has been politicized and lost its independence; that there are serious weaknesses at devolved and local governmental levels; that recent parliamentary expenses scandals have tarnished the reputation of politicians; and that the British political system must be reformed in order to make it more efficient, more accountable to the electorate and more adaptable to modern requirements.

The previous Labour government in 1997 embarked on a process of constitutional and political 'modernization', involving such matters as devolution, reform of the House of Lords (including the creation of a Supreme Court separate from the Lords in 2009) and the introduction of human rights and freedom of information legislation. But these developments have been criticized for creating more problems than they have solved. It is felt that the traditional strengths and structures of British democracy must be retained, where valid, rather than being replaced by inadequate alternatives. In this view, the British constitution and separation of powers must be revitalized, otherwise they could be vulnerable to executive power and political manipulation.

Political history

Early political history in the islands is the story of four geographical areas, now known as England, Wales, Scotland and Northern Ireland, and their turbulent struggles for independent nationhood. It was English political and military expansionism over the centuries that conditioned the development of the other three nations. Ireland was invaded by England in the twelfth century; England and Wales were united by the 1536–42 Acts of Union; the thrones of England and Scotland were dynastically amalgamated in 1603; England/Wales and Scotland were united as Great Britain by the 1707 Acts of Union; the 1801 Act of Union joined Great Britain and Ireland as the United Kingdom; and southern Ireland (later known as the Republic of Ireland) became independent in 1921, leaving Northern Ireland within the UK. In this process, English governmental systems were generally adopted in the modern period for all of the UK until Scotland, Wales and Northern Ireland regained some of their former political identities under devolution in 1998–9.

Decline of the monarchy and the rise of Parliament

Early monarchs or political leaders in the four nations had considerable power, but generally accepted advice and feudal limitations on their authority. However, later English kings, such as King John (1199–1216), ignored these restraints and powerful French-Norman barons opposed John's dictatorial rule by forcing him to sign Magna Carta in 1215. This document protected the aristocracy rather than the ordinary citizen. It was later regarded as a cornerstone of British (not merely English) liberties: it restricted the monarch's powers, forced them to take advice, increased the influence of the aristocracy and stipulated that citizens should not be imprisoned without trial.

Such inroads into royal power encouraged embryonic parliamentary struc-tures. An English Council was formed in 1258 by disaffected nobles under Simon de Montfort, who in 1264 summoned a broader Parliament. These aristocratic and part-time initiatives were followed in 1275 by the Model Parliament of Edward I (1272–1307), which was the first representative English Parliament. Its two Houses (as now) consisted of the Lords/Bishops and the Commons (male commoners). An independent Scottish Parliament was first created in 1326 and Ireland had a similarly well-established Parliament, dating from medieval times.

However, the English Parliament was too large to rule the country effectively. A small Privy Council (royal government outside Parliament) comprising the monarch and court advisers developed. This continued as a powerful influence until it lost authority to increasingly strong parliamentary structures in the late eighteenth and early nineteenth centuries.

But although Parliament gained limited powers against the monarch, there was a return to royal dominance in Tudor England (1485–1603). The nobility had been weakened by wars and internal conflicts (like the Wars of the Roses between Yorkists and Lancastrians). Monarchs controlled Parliament and summoned it only to raise money. Tudor monarchs (of Welsh ancestry) united England and Wales administratively, politically and legally in the sixteenth century. They also intervened in Ireland, with frequent campaigns against Irish insurgents.

Following the Tudors, James VI of Scotland became James I of England in 1603, formed a Stuart dynasty and considered himself to be king of Great Britain. But the two countries were not closely joined politically or culturally. However, the English Parliament now showed more resistance to royal rule by using its weapon of financial control. It refused royal requests for money and later forced the Stuart Charles I to sign the Petition of Rights in 1628, which prevented him from raising taxes without Parliament's consent. Charles ignored these political developments and then failed in his attempt to arrest parliamentary leaders in the House of Commons. The monarch was in future banned from the Commons.

Charles's rejection of parliamentary ideals and belief in his right to rule without opposition provoked anger against the Crown and a Civil War broke out in 1642. The mainly Protestant Parliamentarians under Oliver Cromwell won the military struggle against the Royalists. Charles was beheaded in 1649; the monarchy was abolished; Britain was ruled as a Protectorate by Cromwell and his son Richard (1653–60); and Parliament comprised only the House of Commons. Cromwell asserted the Protestant and parliamentary cause in Scotland and Ireland, which provoked lasting hatred among many people there.

Cromwell's Protectorate became unpopular and most people wanted the restoration of the monarchy. The two Houses of Parliament were re-established and in 1660 they restored the Stuart Charles II to the throne. Initially Charles cooperated with Parliament, but his financial needs, belief in royal authority and support for Catholicism lost him popular and parliamentary backing. Parliament ended his expensive wars and imposed further reforms.

The growth of political parties and constitutional structures

The growing power of the English Parliament against the monarch in the seventeenth century saw the development of more organized political parties. These derived partly from the religious and ideological conflicts of the Civil War. Two groups (Whigs and Tories) became dominant. This is a characteristic feature of British two-party politics, in which political power generally shifts between two main parties. The Whigs were mainly Cromwellian Protestants and gentry, who did not accept the Catholic James II as successor to Charles II and wanted religious

PLATE 4.1 Sir Robert Walpole (1676–1745), first Earl of Oxford, First Lord of the Treasury and Chancellor of the Exchequer, by Christian Friedrich Zincke. Whig politician and statesman who strengthened parliamentary authority and the power of the Chief Minister.
(Roger-Viollet/Rex Features)

freedom for all Protestants. The Tories generally supported royalist beliefs, and helped Charles II to secure James's right to succeed him.

But James's attempt to rule without Parliament and his ignoring of its laws caused a further reduction in royal influence. His manipulations forced the Tories to join the Whigs in inviting the Dutch Protestant William of Orange to intervene. William arrived in England in 1688. James fled to France and William succeeded to the throne as Britain's first constitutional monarch. Since no force was involved, this event is called the Bloodless or Glorious Revolution. Royal powers were further restricted under the Declaration of Rights (1689), which strengthened Parliament. Future monarchs could not reign or act without Parliament's consent and the Act of Settlement (1701) specified that monarchs must be Protestant.

The Glorious Revolution affected the constitution and politics. It effectively created a division of powers between an executive branch (the monarch and Privy Council); a parliamentary legislative branch (the House of Commons, the House of Lords and the monarch); and the judiciary (judges independent of both the monarch and Parliament). Acts of Union joining England/Wales and Scotland followed in 1707; Scotland lost its Parliament; and power was centralized in the London Parliament.

Parliamentary influence grew in the early eighteenth century because the Hanoverian George I lacked interest in British politics. He distrusted the Tories with their Catholic sympathies and appointed Whigs like Robert Walpole to his Privy Council. Walpole became Chief Minister in 1721 and led the Whig majority in the House of Commons, which comprised land and property owners. Walpole increased the parliamentary role and has been called Britain's first prime minister.

PLATE 4.2 George III (1738–1820), King of Great Britain and Ireland 1760–1820, by Allan Ramsay (1713–84). Remembered for his bouts of illness, his attempts to govern personally and in whose reign the American colonies were lost. His reign also coincided with a great expansion of empire and trade, the beginnings of the Industrial Revolution and a strong creative and artistic period.
(© Wallace Collection, London UK/Bridgeman)

But parliamentary authority was not absolute and later monarchs tried to restore royal power. However, George III lost much of his standing after the loss of the American colonies (1775–83). He was obliged to appoint William Pitt the Younger as his Tory chief minister and it was under Pitt that the office of prime minister really developed. Meanwhile, Ireland's Parliament achieved legislative independence in 1782, it represented only the privileged Anglo-Irish minority and the Roman Catholic majority were excluded. In 1801, Ireland was united with Great Britain by the Act of Union to form the UK. The Irish Parliament was abolished and Irish members sat in both Houses of the London Parliament.

The expansion of voting rights

Although parliamentary control grew in the late eighteenth and early nineteenth centuries, there was still no widespread democracy in Britain. Political authority was in the hands of landowners, merchants and aristocrats in Parliament and most people did not possess the vote. Bribery and corruption were common, with the buying of those votes which did exist and the giving away or sale of public offices.

The Tories were against electoral reform, as were the Whigs initially. But the country was rapidly increasing its population and developing industrially and economically. Pressures for political reform became irresistible. The Whigs reformed the parliamentary system and extended voting rights to a small number of the growing middle class in the First Reform Act of 1832. Later Reform Acts in 1867 and 1884 gave the vote to men with property and a certain income. Working-class males were only gradually given the vote in the late nineteenth century and gained some representation in Parliament. All males aged over twenty-one and limited categories of women over thirty received the vote in 1918. Eventually in 1928 all males and females aged twenty-one possessed the vote (with some exceptions) and the age limit was further reduced to eighteen in 1969.

Prior to 1928, most wives and their property had been the legal possessions of their husbands. The traditional role of women of all classes had been confined to that of mother in the home, although some found employment in home industries and factories or as domestic servants, teachers and governesses.

Women's social and political position became marginally better towards the end of the nineteenth century. Elementary education was established and a few institutions of higher education began to admit women in restricted numbers. Some women's organizations had been founded in the mid-nineteenth century to press for greater political, employment and social rights. However, the most famous suffrage movement was that of the Pankhursts in 1903. Their Women's Social and Political Union campaigned for votes for women and an increased female role in society. However, it is argued that a substantial change in women's status in the mid-twentieth century occurred because of a recognition of the essential work that they performed during two World Wars.

The growth of government structures

The elements of modern British government developed haphazardly in the eighteenth and nineteenth centuries. Government ministers were generally, if not always, members of the House of Commons and gradually became responsible to the Commons rather than to the monarch. They shared a collective responsibility for the policies and acts of government, and each had an individual responsibility to Parliament for their own ministry. The prime ministership developed from the monarch's Chief Minister to 'first among equals' and finally the leadership of all ministers. The central force of government became the parliamentary Cabinet of senior ministers, which grew out of the Privy Council. The government was formed from the majority party in the House of Commons. The largest minority party became the official Opposition, which attempted through its policies to become the next government chosen by the people.

Historically, the elected House of Commons gained political and financial power from the unelected monarch and House of Lords and became the main element in Parliament. Subsequent reforms of the Lords (the Parliament Acts of 1911 and 1949) further restricted their authority. Later Acts created non-hereditary titles (life peers), in addition to the hereditary peerages. The House lost most of its hereditary members in 2000 (92), and now has only delaying and amending power over parliamentary legislation, being unable to interfere with financial bills.

The nineteenth century saw the growth of more organized political parties. These were conditioned by changing social and economic factors and reflected the modern struggle between opposing ideologies. The Tories became known as the Conservatives in the early 1830s. They believed in established values and the preservation of traditions; supported business and commerce; had strong links with the Church of England and the professions; and were opposed to radical ideas.

The Whigs, however, were becoming a progressive force and wanted social reform and economic freedom without government restrictions. They developed into the Liberal Party, which promoted some enlightened policies in the nineteenth and early twentieth centuries but declined from 1918 with the emergence of the new Labour Party. Following an alliance with the Social Democratic Party in the 1980s, the two merged and became the Liberal Democrats. This is the third-largest party in UK politics but lacks substantial representation in the House of Commons.

The Labour Party, created in its present form in 1906, became the main opposition party to the Conservatives after the Liberals' decline and continued the traditional two-party system in British politics. It was supported by the trade unions, the working class and some middle-class voters. The first Labour government was formed in 1924 under Ramsay MacDonald. However the party only achieved majority power in 1945 under Clement Attlee, when it embarked on radical programmes of social and economic reform which laid the foundations for a welfare state and economic nationalization.

The contemporary British political framework

Britain has a 'multi-level governance' model (see Figure 4.1) where the different levels have specific functions and influence each other to various degrees. It has a constitution; the monarch is formally head of state; and practical politics operate mainly at national, devolved and local government levels. The UK Parliament with its many government departments has the ultimate say in how the nation is ruled, but the Scottish Parliament, Assemblies in Wales and Northern Ireland and a Greater London Authority have their own forms of limited self-governmental powers, devolved from the UK Parliament. Local government throughout Britain organizes society at smaller community levels. A further tier of government is the European Union (EU), which has increasingly affected British politics. The following pages describe the major constitutional and political elements and local government and devolution appear later in the chapter.

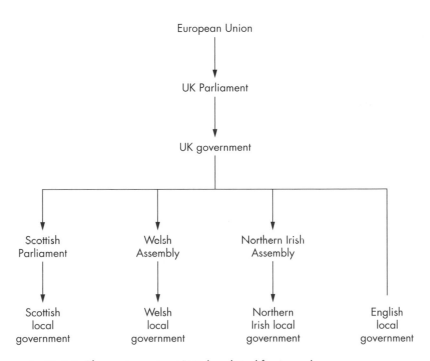

FIGURE 4.1 The contemporary British political framework

Constitution and monarchy

The constitution

The constitutional system has experienced few major upheavals since 1688 and existing principles have been pragmatically adapted to new conditions. However, some significant changes have occurred over the years such as entry to the EU in 1973 and devolution in 1998–9, which have had constitutional implications.

The powers of the state in many countries are defined and laid down in a written document (or constitution) and are often classified as executive, legislative and judicial. These powers relate to distinctive institutions and remain separate. In Britain, however, there is no clear separation of powers, for example between the executive and the legislature.

Britain is sometimes described as a constitutional monarchy, where the monarch reigns as head of state without executive powers under constitutional limitations. Britain is also referred to, more commonly, as a parliamentary system, where the Westminster Parliament (consisting of the House of Commons, the House of Lords and formally the monarch) in London is the legislature and possesses the supreme power to make laws in UK matters.

The executive UK government (sitting mainly in the House of Commons) governs by passing its policies (some of which are applicable to most of Britain) through Parliament as Acts of Parliament and operates through ministries or departments headed by ministers or secretaries of state.

The judicial branch is independent of the legislative and executive branches of government. The judges (judiciary) of the higher courts determine the law and interpret Acts of Parliament. The highest court of appeal for many matters in the UK is now the Supreme Court, created in 2009. This also has jurisdiction to determine devolution disputes concerning Scotland, Wales and Northern Ireland.

These branches, although distinguishable from each other, are not entirely separate; for example, the monarch is formally head of the executive, the legislature and the judiciary. A member of Parliament (MP) in the House of Commons and a peer of the House of Lords may both be in the government of the day.

All the branches are supposed to operate according to the British constitution. But Britain has no written constitution contained in one document. Instead, the constitution consists of distinctive elements, most of which are in written form. These are statute law (Acts of Parliament), common law or judge-made case law, conventions (principles and practices of government which are not legally binding but have the force of law), certain ancient documents such as Magna Carta, and EU law.

The constitutional elements are flexible enough to respond quickly to new conditions. UK law and institutions can be created or changed by the Westminster Parliament through Acts of Parliament. The common law can be extended by the judiciary and conventions can be altered, made or abolished by general agreement.

In constitutional theory, the British people, although historically subjects of the Crown, have political sovereignty to choose the UK government, while Parliament, consisting partly of elected representatives in the Commons, has the legal supremacy to make laws and is the focus of UK sovereignty. Nevertheless, challenges to traditional notions of parliamentary sovereignty have arisen, and the Westminster Parliament is no longer the sole legislative body in Britain. British membership of the European Union means that EU law is now superior to British national law in many areas and British courts are obliged to give it precedence in cases of conflict between the two systems. EU law is directly applicable in Britain and coexists with Acts of Parliament as part of the British constitution. The EU's Council of Ministers consists of heads of government and ministers from the member states and is the EU's supreme law-making or law-initiating body. Some 75 per cent of all Britain's laws are now EU law.

PLATE 4.3 Scotland regained its own Parliament after devolution in 1999. The Parliament building is a new construction completed in 2005 and situated near Holyrood Palace.
(The Travel Library/ Rex Features)

PLATE 4.4 The official opening of the Third Welsh Assembly, Cardiff, 5 June 2007.
(Dimitis Legakis/Rex Features)

Since devolution, Parliament is still able to legislate for the United Kingdom as a whole on reserved matters and for any parts of it separately. However, it has undertaken not to legislate on devolved matters without the agreement of the devolved Parliament and Assemblies. The Scottish Parliament can therefore legislate on devolved matters in which Westminster has no say. Conflicts between the two Parliaments will be resolved by the Supreme Court. The Welsh Assembly has no primary legislative powers, although the Northern Irish Assembly can legislate in devolved matters. Ultimately, however, the UK Parliament still has the constitutional right to abolish the Scottish Parliament, the Welsh and Northern Irish Assemblies and to withdraw from the EU.

Criticisms of the constitutional system

The British constitution was admired in the past for the way in which it combined stability and adaptability with a balance of authority and toleration. However, it has often been criticized. UK governments are able to pass their policies through Parliament because of large majorities in the Commons. This means that there are few effective parliamentary restraints upon a strong government. There has also been concern at the absence of constitutional safeguards for citizens against state power, since historically there have been few legal definitions of civil liberties or human rights in Britain.

These features are seen as potentially dangerous, particularly when UK governments and administrative bodies are arguably too centralized and secretive. It is maintained that Britain is controlled by small groups or bodies which may be unelected and are appointed by government. There have been campaigns for more open government and for more effective protection of individual liberties in the forms of a written constitution (to define and limit the powers of Parliament and government); greater judicial scrutiny of parliamentary legislation; a Freedom of Information Act (to allow the public to examine official documents held for example by Whitehall departments, local councils, the NHS, schools and universities); the creation of a Supreme Court to preserve the independence of the judiciary from Parliament; incorporation of the European Convention on Human Rights into domestic law (enabling British citizens to pursue cases in Britain instead of going to the European Court of Human Rights); and reform of the House of Lords.

In response to these concerns, the previous Labour government created a Freedom of Information Act in 2000 and incorporated the European Convention into British law by the creation of a Human Rights Act, 1998. Both developments have the potential to improve the civil and constitutional rights of British people.

However, the Freedom of Information Act is criticized as lacking teeth, and it can be manipulated by the authorities concerned. The Human Rights Act is having a controversial effect on many levels. It allows the courts to rule in cases

PLATE 4.5 Former Prime Minister Gordon Brown, centre right, chairs a Cabinet meeting in the Cabinet Room, 10 Downing Street, 18 September, 2007.
(Eddie Mulholland/Rex Features)

of alleged breaches of fundamental human rights which are brought to them. While they cannot directly overrule an Act of Parliament they can declare that such an Act is in breach of the Human Rights legislation. In effect, this could force a government to change its legislation and is seen as an encroachment upon parliamentary sovereignty. The courts and the judges have arguably achieved influence by their rulings under the Human Rights Act, but the implications of the Act have yet to be fully worked out. The judiciary has also achieved a greater degree of independence with the establishment of the Supreme Court in 2009.

Despite these movements towards reform, critics still feel that the British parliamentary system is out of date; consider that a written constitution is needed to control executive and administrative bodies; and claim that the UK political system no longer works satisfactorily. They maintain that its traditional bases are inadequate for the organization of a complex society. It is felt that political policies have become too conditioned by party politics at the expense of consensus; that government is too removed from popular and regional concerns and does not reflect contemporary diversity; that it operates on too many unaccountable levels; that national policies lack a democratic and representative basis; and that the constitution can be abused by the executive. However, changes have been made to the apparatus and evolutionary principles may still be adapted to new demands and conditions.

Political and constitutional reform was at the forefront of debate by all political parties during the general election campaign of 2010. This was driven by a parliamentary expenses scandal in which many parliamentarians were criticized for abusing the procedures by which they could claim expenses for carrying out their duties. The system has now been reformed.

The monarchy

The correct constitutional title of the British Parliament is the 'Queen-in-Parliament'. This means that state and government business is carried out in the name of the monarch by the politicians and officials of the system. However, the Crown is only sovereign by the will of Parliament and acceptance by the people.

The monarchy is the oldest secular institution in Britain and there is hereditary succession to the throne, which is reserved only for Protestants. The eldest son of a monarch currently has priority over any older daughters. The monarchy's continuity has been interrupted only by Cromwellian rule (1653–60), although there have been different dynasties such as the Tudors, Stuarts and Hanoverians.

Royal executive power has disappeared, yet the monarch still has formal constitutional roles and is head of state, head of the executive, judiciary and legislature, 'supreme governor' of the Church of England and commander-in-chief of the armed forces. Government ministers and officials are the monarch's servants and many public office-holders swear allegiance to the Crown. The monarchy is thus a permanent fixture in the British system, unlike temporary politicians. It still has a practical and constitutional role to play in the operation of government.

The monarch is expected to be politically neutral; is supposed to reign but not rule; and cannot make laws, impose taxes, spend public money or act unilaterally. The monarch acts only on the advice of government ministers, which cannot be ignored, and Britain is therefore governed by Her Majesty's Government in the name of the Queen. She has a similar role in the devolved governments.

The monarch performs important duties such as the opening and dissolving of the UK Parliament; giving the royal assent (or signature) to bills which have been passed by both Houses of Parliament; appointing government ministers and public officials; granting honours; leading proceedings of the Privy Council; and fulfilling international duties as head of state.

A central power still possessed by the monarch is the choice and appointment of the UK prime minister. By convention, this person is normally the leader of the political party which has a majority in the Commons. However, if there is no clear majority or if the political situation is unclear, the monarch could in theory make a free choice. In practice, advice is given by royal advisers and leading politicians in order to find an acceptable candidate who commands the confidence of the House of Commons.

The monarch has the right to be informed of all aspects of national life by receiving government documents and meeting regularly with the prime minister. The monarch also has the constitutional right to encourage, warn and advise ministers. The impact of royal advice on formal and informal levels may be significant and raises questions about whether such influence should be held by an unelected figure who might either support or undermine elected political leaders.

Much of the cost of the royal family's official duties is met from the civil list (public funds which are approved by Parliament). Following concern over expense, the civil list has now been reduced to a few members of the immediate royal family. Other costs incurred by the monarch as a private individual or as sovereign come either from the privy purse (finance received from the revenues of some royal estates) or from the Crown's own investments, which are very considerable and on which the monarch now pays income tax.

Critics of the monarchy argue that it lacks adaptability, is out of date, undemocratic, expensive, associated with aristocratic privilege and establishment thinking and reflects an English rather than a British identity. It is argued that the monarchy's distance and isolation from ordinary life sustains class divisions and hierarchy within society. It is also suggested that, if the monarch's functions today are merely ceremonial and lack power, it would be more rational to abolish the office and replace it with a less expensive non-executive presidency.

Critics who favour the continuation of the monarchy argue that it is popular, has adapted to modern requirements, and is a symbol of national unity. It is seen as a defender of the constitution and a personification of the state; shows stability and continuity; has more prestige than politicians; is not subject to political manipulations; plays a worthwhile role in national institutions; is neutral; performs ambassadorial functions; and promotes the interests of Britain abroad.

The monarchy in recent years has attracted criticism, although it appears to have coped and kept its appeal despite the difficulties. A MORI poll in 2006 echoed positive findings in a 2004 MORI poll, which found that 71 per cent of respondents wanted to retain the monarchy, while 20 per cent would prefer an elected head of state. After the present Queen, 47 per cent wished to keep the monarchy as it is while 35 per cent wanted it to have a smaller role and fewer members.

Polls also suggest that the monarchy should be modernized to reflect changes in British life. But traditionalists fear that a modernized monarchy would lose that aura of detachment which is seen as its main strength. It would then be associated with change rather than the preservation of existing values. At present, it balances between tradition and modernizing trends.

The Privy Council

The ancient Privy Council is still constitutionally tied to the monarchy. Historically, it developed from a small group of royal advisers into the executive

PLATE 4.6 The Houses of Parliament (Lords and Commons) at the Palace of Westminster on the north bank of the river Thames. The clock tower on the far right contains Big Ben, which is the nickname of the tower bell that strikes the quarter hours.
(Rex Features)

branch of the monarch's government. But its powerful position declined in the eighteenth and nineteenth centuries as its functions were transferred to a parliamentary Cabinet and new ministries. Today, its members (such as Cabinet ministers) advise the monarch on the approval of government business which does not need to pass through Parliament and may serve on influential committees.

There are 400 Privy Councillors, but the body works mostly through small groups. A full council is only summoned on the death of a monarch and the accession of a new one or when constitutional issues are at stake. Should the monarch be indisposed, either counsellors of state or a regent would work through the Privy Council.

Apart from its practical duties and its role as a constitutional forum, the most important tasks of the Privy Council today are performed by its Judicial Committee. It is the final court of appeal from some Commonwealth countries and dependencies. It may be also used by some other bodies in Britain and overseas.

The UK Parliament: role, legislation and elections

Role and composition

The United Kingdom Parliament is housed in London's Palace of Westminster. It comprises the non-elected House of Lords, the elected House of Commons and the monarch. The two Houses contain members from England, Wales, Scotland and Northern Ireland and represent people with varied political traditions. Parliament gathers as a unified body only on ceremonial occasions, such as the state opening of Parliament by the monarch in the House of Lords. Here it listens to the monarch's speech from the throne, which outlines the UK government's forthcoming legislative programme.

In traditional constitutional theory, Parliament has legal sovereignty in all matters and can create, abolish or amend laws and institutions for all or any part(s) of Britain. In practice today, this means the implementation of the sitting government's policies in reserved matters while devolved matters are dealt with by the devolved bodies of Wales, Scotland and Northern Ireland. All three parts of Parliament must normally pass a bill before it can become an Act of Parliament and law. Parliament also votes money to government; examines government policies and administration; scrutinizes EU legislation; and debates political issues.

Parliament is supposed to legislate according to the rule of law, precedent and tradition. Politicians are generally sensitive to these conventions and to public opinion. Formal and informal checks and balances, such as party discipline, the official Opposition, public reaction and pressure groups, normally ensure that Parliament legislates according to its legal responsibility. But critics argue that

PLATE 4.7 State opening of Parliament, 18 November 2009. The Queen delivers her speech from the throne in the House of Lords to the assembled members of the House of Lords and House of Commons.
(Rex Features)

Parliament no longer operates satisfactorily or representatively. Although a MORI poll in 2000 showed that satisfaction with the way Parliament works had (perhaps surprisingly) increased to 43 per cent with dissatisfaction at 29 per cent, satisfaction has dropped with the expenses scandal of 2008–09.

A parliament has a maximum duration of five years, except in emergency situations. But it has often been dissolved earlier and a general election called. A dissolution and the issue of writs for the election are ordered by the monarch on the advice of the prime minister. This power of the prime minister to choose the date of a general election was controversially given up after the 2010 election and a fixed term of five years' duration was substituted. A new 55 per cent majority in the House of Commons was also required for a vote to result in a dissolution of Parliament. If an MP dies, resigns or is given a peerage, a by-election is called only for that member's seat, and Parliament as a whole is not dissolved.

The *House of Lords* at present consists of Lords Temporal and Lords Spiritual. Lords Spiritual are the Archbishops of York and Canterbury and twenty-four senior bishops of the Church of England. The Lords Temporal comprise some ninety-two peers and peeresses with hereditary titles elected by their fellows and about 577 life peers and peeresses, who have been appointed by political parties and an independent Appointments Commission. The earlier Lords of Appeal (law lords) no longer sit in the Lords and their functions have been transferred to the new Supreme Court.

Daily attendance varies from a handful to a few hundred. Peers receive no salary for parliamentary work, but may claim attendance and travelling expenses. The House collectively controls its own procedure, but is often guided by the Lord Speaker who is the presiding officer of the Lords.

There have long been demands that the unrepresentative, unelected House of Lords should be replaced. But deciding on an alternative model is problematic. An elected second chamber could threaten the powers of the House of Commons and result in conflict between the two. An appointed House would consist of unelected members chosen by political parties or an independent Appointments Commission. The previous Labour government abolished the sitting and voting rights of hereditary peers, except for ninety-two of them (whose future is now in doubt). Some life peers continue to be recommended by political parties, while others are appointed by an independent Appointments Commission. Under Labour proposals, it seemed that a future House would have 750 elected members and a reduction (to sixteen) of Lords Spiritual. However, these plans effectively collapsed after Labour lost the 2010 election and the future of the House of Lords is again in doubt.

The current House of Lords nevertheless does its job well as an experienced and less partisan forum than the House of Commons and also takes on a legislative and administrative burden. It has an amending function, which may be used to delay government legislation for up to one year (possibly three months in future) or to persuade governments to have a second look at bills. It is a safeguard against over-hasty legislation by the Commons, is an antidote to powerful governments and has increasingly voted against Commons legislation. This is possible because the Lords are more independently minded than MPs in the Commons and do not suffer rigid party discipline. The House is now more evenly divided in terms of party affiliation and has a number of crossbenchers (or independents sitting across the back of the chamber) who do not belong to any political party. Labour has 221 peers, the Conservatives have 216, the Liberal Democrats have 79 and there are 192 cross-benchers. It is possible that the coalition government elected in 2010 will create more peers in order to strengthen its support in the Lords.

The *House of Commons* has 650 members of Parliament (MPs) who are chosen from all parts of the UK. They are elected by voters (from the age of eighteen) and represent citizens in Parliament. In 2010, 27 came from ethnic minorities and 154 or 22 per cent of them were women. But women face problems in being selected as parliamentary candidates and winning seats in the Commons. MPs are paid expenses and a salary, which is relatively low in comparison with similar jobs outside politics.

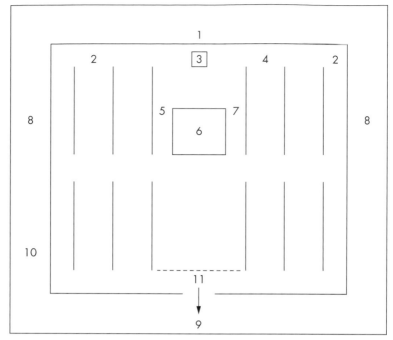

1 Press gallery	5 Government front	8 Galleries for MPs
2 Voting lobbies	bench	9 Public gallery
3 Speaker's chair	6 Dispatch box	10 VIP gallery
4 Civil servants	7 Opposition front bench	11 House of Lords

FIGURE 4.2 The House of Commons

Legislation and procedure

Parliamentary procedure in both Houses of Parliament is based on custom, convention, precedent and detailed rules (standing orders). The House of Commons
meets every weekday afternoon, although business can continue beyond midnight.
Many MPs then spend the weekend in their constituencies attending to business.
They may also follow professions (such as lawyers) on a part-time basis. The
organization and procedures of the Commons have been criticized. It is felt that
the number of hours spent in the House should be reduced and that pay and
resources should be improved. Women MPs feel that it should become a
more women-friendly place instead of the traditional male club. Some changes
were made in sitting hours, but the Commons has reverted to using evening
sessions.

The Speaker is the chief officer of the House of Commons; is chosen by MPs;
interprets the rules of the House; and is assisted by three deputy speakers. The
Speaker is an elected MP who, on election to the Speaker's chair, ceases to be a
political representative and becomes a neutral official (as do the Deputy Speakers).

The Speaker protects the House against any abuse of procedure by controlling debates and votes. Where there is a tied result, the Speaker has the casting vote, but must exercise this choice so that it reflects established conventions. The Speaker is important for the orderly running of the House. MPs can be very combative and often unruly, so that the Speaker is sometimes forced to dismiss or suspend a member from the House.

Debates in both Houses of Parliament usually begin with a motion (or proposal) which is then debated. The matter is decided by a simple majority vote

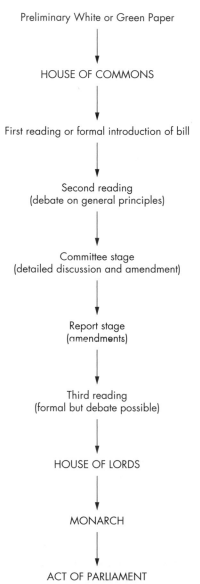

FIGURE 4.3 From Bill to UK Act of Parliament

at the end of discussion. In the Commons, MPs enter either the 'Yes' or 'No' lobbies (corridors running alongside the Commons chamber) to record their vote, but they may also abstain from voting.

The proceedings of both Houses are open to the public and may be viewed from the public and visitors' galleries. Transactions are published daily in *Hansard* (the parliamentary 'newspaper'); debates are televised; and radio broadcasts may be in live or recorded form. This exposure to public scrutiny has increased interest in the parliamentary process, although negative comments are made about low attendance in both Houses and the behaviour of MPs in the Commons.

Before the creation of new UK law (which may take a few days or many months) and changes to existing law a government will usually issue certain documents before the parliamentary law-making process commences. A Green Paper is a consultative document which allows interested parties to state their case before a Bill is introduced into Parliament. A White Paper is not normally consultative but is a preliminary document which details prospective legislation.

A draft law takes the form of a Bill. Most Bills are 'public' because they involve state business and are introduced in either House of Parliament by the government. Other Bills may be 'private' because they relate to matters such as local government, while some are 'private members' Bills' introduced by MPs in their personal capacity. These latter Bills are on a topic of interest to MPs, but are normally defeated for lack of parliamentary time or support. However, some important private members' Bills concerning homosexuality, abortion and sexual offences have survived the obstacles and become law.

Bills must pass through both Houses and receive the royal assent before they become law. The Commons is normally the first step in this process. The Lords, in its turn, can delay a non-financial Bill. It can propose amendments, and if amended the Bill goes back to the Commons for further consideration. This amending function is an important power and has been frequently used in recent years. However, the Lords' role today is to act as a forum for revision, rather than as a rival to the elected Commons. In practice, the Lords' amendments can sometimes lead to the acceptance of changes by the government or to a withdrawal of the Bill.

When the Bill has eventually passed through the Lords, it is sent to the monarch for the royal assent, which has not been refused since the eighteenth century. After this, the Bill becomes an Act of Parliament and enters the statute book as representing the law of the land at that time.

UK Parliament elections

The UK is divided for Westminster parliamentary elections to the House of Commons into 650 constituencies (geographical areas of the country each containing about 66,000 voters – although some have more or fewer). Each returns one MP to the House of Commons at a general election. Constituency boundaries are adjusted to ensure fair representation and to reflect population movements.

General elections are by secret ballot, although voting is not compulsory. British, Commonwealth and Irish Republic citizens may vote if they are resident in Britain, included on a constituency register of voters, aged eighteen or over and not subject to any disqualification. Those not entitled to vote include mentally ill patients detained in hospital or prison, persons who have been convicted of corrupt or illegal election practices, prisoners and members of the House of Lords.

Each elector casts one vote at a polling station set up on election day in a constituency by making a cross on a ballot paper against the name of the candidate for whom the vote is cast. Those unable to vote in person in their local constituency can register postal or proxy votes.

The turnout of voters has often been about 70 per cent at general elections out of an electorate of 43 million, although this proportion has declined in recent elections. At present, the candidate who wins the most votes in a constituency is elected MP for that area. This is known as the simple majority or 'first past the post' system. There is no voting by the various forms of proportional representation (PR), except for EU Parliament and devolved government elections, which have a mixture of first-past-the-post and party-list voting.

Some see the Westminster electoral system as undemocratic and unfair to the smaller parties. The Liberal Democrats campaign for proportional representation (PR), which would create a wider selection of parties in the House of Commons and cater for minority political interests. The two major parties (Labour and Conservative) have preferred the existing system since it gives them a greater chance of achieving power.

It is argued that the British people prefer the stronger government which can result from the first-past-the-post system. PR systems are alleged to have weaknesses, such as party control of lists, coalition or minority government, frequent breakdown, a lack of firm policies, power-bargaining between different parties in order to achieve government status and tension afterwards. But weak and small-majority government can also result from the first-past-the-post system.

The party political system

British elections at parliamentary, devolved and local levels depend upon the party political system, which has existed since the seventeenth century. For UK parliamentary general elections, the parties present their policies in the form of manifestos to the electorate for consideration during the few weeks of campaigning prior to election day. A party candidate (chosen by a specific party) in a constituency is elected to the Westminster Parliament on a combination of party manifesto and the personality of the candidate. But party activity continues

	TABLE 4.1 British governments and prime ministers since 1945	
Date	Government	Prime minister
1945–51	Labour	Clement Attlee
1951–5	Conservative	Winston Churchill
1955–9	Conservative	Anthony Eden (1955–7)
		Harold Macmillan (1957–9)
1959–64	Conservative	Harold Macmillan (1959–63)
		Alec Douglas-Home (1963–4)
1964–6	Labour	Harold Wilson
1966–70	Labour	Harold Wilson
1970–4	Conservative	Edward Heath
1974–(Feb.)	Labour	Harold Wilson
1974–(Oct.)	Labour	Harold Wilson
1974–9	Labour	Harold Wilson (1974–6)
		James Callaghan (1976–9)
1979–83	Conservative	Margaret Thatcher
1983–7	Conservative	Margaret Thatcher
1987–92	Conservative	Margaret Thatcher (1987–90)
		John Major (1990–92)
1992–7	Conservative	John Major
1997–2001	Labour	Tony Blair
2001–5	Labour	Tony Blair
2005–10	Labour	Tony Blair (2005–7)
		Gordon Brown (2007–10)
2010–	Conservative/Liberal Democrat	David Cameron

outside the election period itself, as politicians battle for power and the attention of the electorate at all levels.

Since 1945 there have been nine Labour, eight Conservative and one Conservative/Liberal Democrat government in Britain. Some have had large majorities in the House of Commons, while others have had small ones. Some, such as the Labour government in the 1970s and the Conservatives in the 1990s, had to rely on the support of smaller parties, such as the Liberals and Ulster Unionists, in order to remain in power. Most of the MPs in the House of Commons belong to either the Conservative or the Labour Party. This continues the two-party system in British politics, in which power has alternated between two major parties, except arguably for periods of coalition or minority government, such as that which began in 2010.

The Labour Party has historically been a left-of-centre party with its own right and left wings. It emphasized social justice, equality of opportunity, economic planning and the state ownership of industries and services. It was supported by the trade unions (who had been influential in the party's development), the working class and some of the middle class. Its electoral strongholds are historically in Scotland, South Wales and the Midland and northern English industrial cities.

However, traditional class-based and left-ideological support has changed with increased social and employment mobility. In the 1990s, the Labour Party tried to appeal to middle-class voters in southern England and to take account of changing economic and social conditions. Its then leader (and prime minister), Tony Blair, modernized the party as New Labour by moving to the centre, captured voters from the Conservatives and distanced himself from the trade unions, state ownership and the party's doctrinaire past. As a result, the party achieved landslide victories in the 1997 and 2001 general elections and gained a majority of seats in the 2005 election. But there is a still support for Old Labour ideas in the party and this can lead to tension.

The Conservative Party is a right-of-centre party, which also has right- and left-wing sections. It regards itself as a national party and appeals to people across class barriers. It emphasizes personal, social and economic freedom, the individual ownership of property and shares and law and order. The Conservatives became more socially and economically radical in their eighteen years of government (1979–97), but policy splits in the party (particularly on Europe) have created tensions.

The party's support comes mainly from business interests and the middle and upper classes, but a sizeable number of skilled workers and women also vote Conservative. The party's strongholds are in southern England, with scattered support elsewhere in the country. However, at the 1997 and 2001 general elections, it suffered a heavy defeat, gained no seats in Wales, only one in Scotland and did not greatly increase its support in England. Although improving its performance at the 2005 election, it was still far from being in a position to return to government. Its leader, David Cameron, stressed that it needed to reorganize, strive for unity, modernize, cultivate an image which is more attractive to voters and develop policies which are more in tune with the changing face of British society.

The Liberal Democrats (Lib Dems) were formed in 1988 when the old Liberal Party and the Social Democratic Party merged into one party. Under their present leader, Nick Clegg, they see themselves as an alternative political force to the Labour and Conservative Parties, based on the centre-left of British politics. Their strengths are in local government, constitutional reform and civil liberties.

They are relatively strong in south-west England, Wales and Scotland and increased their number of MPs at the 2001 and 2005 general elections to become the biggest third party in Parliament since 1929. But they lack a clearly defined identity and policies which are recognized by the electorate. The Lib Dems have won some dramatic by-elections and had considerable success in local government elections, but they have not made a large breakthrough either in the Commons or the EU Parliament. Electoral reform to a form of PR might increase their number of MPs.

Smaller parties are also represented in the House of Commons, such as the Scottish National Party; Plaid Cymru (the Welsh National Party); the Ulster Unionists and the Democratic Unionists (Protestant Northern Irish parties); the Social Democratic and Labour Party (moderate Nationalist Roman Catholic Northern Irish party); and Sinn Féin (Republican Northern Irish party). Other small parties like the Green Party, the British National Party (BNP), the United Kingdom Independence Party (UKIP) and fringe groups may also contest a general election. A candidate who fails to gain a certain number of votes in the election loses their deposit (the sum paid when parties register for elections).

Social class and family tradition used to be important factors in British voting behaviour, but these have now been largely replaced by property- and share-owning, job status and other considerations. A more volatile political situation exists as voters switch between Labour, Conservatives and Liberal Democrats and may employ 'tactical voting' in some constituencies to prevent specific opposition party candidates from being elected. General elections are often won by a party which captures 'marginal constituencies' where a slight vote swing can change party representation and 'floating voters' who are not committed to a specific party can influence the result. The changing character of the electorate has moved political parties to the centre ground and forced them to adopt policies which are more representative of people's wishes and needs. But this means that the old ideological divides are no longer so obvious, important or relevant.

The party which wins most seats in the House of Commons at a general election usually forms the new government, even if it has not obtained a majority of the popular vote (the votes actually cast at an election). A party will have to gather more than 33 per cent of the popular vote before winning a large number of seats, and approach 40 per cent in order to expand that representation and form a government with an overall majority (a majority over all the other parties counted together). This majority enables it to carry out its election manifesto policies (the mandate theory).

Election success often depends on whether support is concentrated in geographical areas, for a party gains seats by its local strength. Smaller parties, which do not reach the percentages above and whose support is scattered, gain few seats in the Commons. It is this system of representation that PR supporters wish to change, in order to reflect the popular vote and the appeal of minority parties.

The situation is illustrated by the 2010 general election results (see Table 4.2). On a relatively low turnout of voters of 65.1 per cent, the Conservatives gained 306 seats with 36.1 per cent of the popular vote; Labour received 258 seats with 29.0 per cent of the vote; and the Liberal Democrats had 57 seats with 23 per cent of the vote. No party obtained an overall majority in the Commons;

TABLE 4.2 General election results, May 2010

Party	Percentage of popular vote	Members elected
Conservative	36.1	307
Labour	29.0	258
Liberal Democrat	23.0	57
Democratic Unionist Party (NI)	0.6	8
Scottish National Party	1.7	6
Sinn Féin (NI)	0.6	5
Plaid Cymru (Wales)	0.6	3
Social Democratic and Labour Party (NI)	0.4	3
Green	1.0	1
Alliance Party	0.1	1
Others	1.1	1
Total seats		650
Turnout of voters	65.1%	

Source: Adapted from BBC News, May 2010

no party could form a majority government; and the result was a hung Parliament (the first in Britain since 1974). The main reasons for this result were disillusionment with the record of the serving Labour government and distrust of politicians in general so that no party gained the support of the electorate, which spread its votes.

Either a minority or a coalition government would have to be formed, in which the largest party (Conservatives) would be able to govern only by relying on the informal support of smaller parties in the Commons (minority) on a case-by-case basis or by forming a formal coalition with another party (the Liberal Democrats) or group of parties. Labour could govern only with the support of the Liberals and a number of smaller parties. The Liberal Democrats held the balance of power and offers were made to them by the Conservatives and Labour (including various policies and forms of political or electoral reform). In the event, Labour withdrew from the bargaining and Gordon Brown offered his resignation as prime minister to the Queen. She called on Conservative leader David Cameron to form a government. He became prime minister (the youngest for two hundred years) and formed a coalition government with the Liberal Democrats (the first British coalition since the Second World War). The leader of the Liberal Democrats, Nick Clegg, became deputy prime minister

As part of a revised coalition deal, the two parties agreed on a fixed-term Parliament of five years; a 55 per cent majority of MPs in a House of Commons vote to dissolve Parliament and to trigger a general election; a reduction in the number of MPs from 650 to 600; an equalizing of constituency sizes; and a

referendum on the Alternative Vote (AV) system of preference (but not proportional) voting in elections. It is also possible that some 100 peers may be created in the House of Lords to ensure that controversial legislation would be passed through Parliament.

Public reaction after the election varied between hope for a new, consensus political start and anger by party members who maintained their old tribal identities and opposed the coalition system. Much will depend on how the coalition functions before a judgement can be made as to whether the 2010 election marked a watershed in British political life.

The largest minority party (Labour) became the official Opposition with its own leader and 'shadow government'. It plays an important role in the parliamentary system, which is based on adversarial politics and the two-party tradition of government (even under coalition arrangements). Seating arrangements in the House of Commons reflect this system. Leaders of the coalition government and opposition parties sit on facing 'front benches', with their supporting MPs, or 'backbenchers', sitting behind them. Some parties dislike this confrontational style and advocate more consensus politics. However, traditionally the effectiveness of parliamentary democracy is supposed to rest on the relationship between the government and opposition parties and the observance of procedural conventions.

Opposition parties may try to overthrow a government by defeating it in a vote, though this is usually unsuccessful if the government has a majority and can count on the support of its MPs, allies or coalition colleagues. The opposition parties consequently attempt to influence the formation of national policy by their criticism of pending legislation, by trying to obtain concessions on bills by proposing amendments to them and by increasing support for their policies outside the Commons. They take advantage of any opportunity which might improve their chances at the next general election.

Inside Parliament, party discipline rests with the Whips, who are chosen from among party MPs by the party leaders and who are under the direction of a chief whip. They inform members of forthcoming parliamentary business and maintain the party's voting strength in the Commons by ensuring that their members attend all important debates. MPs receive notice from the whips' office of how important a particular vote is and the information will be underlined up to three times. A 'three-line whip' signifies a crucial vote and failure to attend or comply with party instructions is regarded as a revolt against the party's policy.

The whips also convey backbench opinion to the party leadership. This is important if rebellion and disquiet are to be avoided. Party discipline is very strong in the Commons and less so in the Lords. A government with a large majority should not become complacent, nor antagonize its backbenchers. If it does so, a successful rebellion against the government or abstention from voting by its own side may destroy the majority and the party's policy.

Outside Parliament, control rests with the national and local party organizations, which can be influential. They promote the party at every opportunity, but especially at election time, when constituencies select the party candidates and are in charge of electioneering on behalf of their party. However, national parties are now increasingly imposing candidates upon constituencies, one example being the drawing up of women-only shortlists designed to increase the number of women MPs.

The UK government

The UK government is the executive arm of the political system. It serves the whole of Britain and normally comprises individuals who are members of the successful majority party (or a coalition) at a general election. It is centred on Whitehall in London, where its ministries and the prime minister's official residence, 10 Downing Street, are located. It consists of some 100 ministers who can be chosen from both Houses of Parliament (and coalition parties) and who are appointed by the monarch on the advice of the prime minister. They derive their authority from belonging to the majority party in the Commons (or coalition) and are collectively responsible to Parliament for the administration of national affairs.

The *prime minister* is appointed by the monarch and is usually the leader of the majority party in the Commons. Their power stems from support in Parliament; the authority (or patronage) to choose and dismiss ministers; the leadership of the party in the country; and control over policy-making. The question of authority and ability to choose ministers is more finely balanced when they lead a coalition government with another party. The prime minister sits in the Commons, as do most ministers, where they may be questioned and held accountable for government actions. The prime minister was historically the link between monarch and Parliament. This convention continues in the weekly audience with the monarch, at which the business of the government is discussed.

The prime minister has great power in the British system of government and it is suggested that the office has come to resemble an all-powerful executive presidency, which bypasses Parliament and government departments. It is argued that government policy is decided upon by the Downing Street political machine with its bureaucrats and 'spin doctors'. But there are checks on this power, inside and outside the party and Parliament, which can on occasions bring down a prime minister. However, there is a greater emphasis upon prime ministerial government today, rather than the traditional constitutional notions of Cabinet government. This view of the role may have to be varied now that Britain has coalition government.

The *Cabinet* is a small executive body in the government and usually comprises about twenty senior ministers, who are chosen and presided over by the prime minister. Examples are the Chancellor of the Exchequer (Finance Minister), the Secretary of State for Foreign and Commonwealth Affairs, the Secretary of

State for the Home Department and the Secretary of State for Education who are chosen from both parties in the coalition. The Cabinet originated in meetings that the monarch had with ministers in a royal Cabinet. As the monarch withdrew from active politics with the growth of party politics and Parliament, this developed into a parliamentary body.

Constitutional theory has traditionally argued that government rule is Cabinet rule because the Cabinet collectively initiates and decides government policy at its weekly meetings in 10 Downing Street. Although this notion has weakened, there are still occasions when policy is thrashed out in Cabinet. But, since the prime minister is responsible for Cabinet agendas and controls Cabinet proceedings, the Cabinet can become a 'rubber-stamp' or 'briefing room' for policies which have already been decided by the prime minister or smaller groups. This picture will no doubt change somewhat under a coalition structure, where the deputy prime minister will presumably enter the decision-making process.

Much depends upon the personality of prime ministers and the way in which they avoid potential Cabinet friction. Some are strong and like to take the lead. Others work within the Cabinet structure, allowing ministers to exercise responsibility within their own ministerial fields. Much of our information about the operation of the Cabinet comes from 'leaks' or information divulged by Cabinet ministers. Although the Cabinet meets in private and its discussions are meant to be secret, the public is usually and reliably informed of Cabinet deliberations and disputes by 'leaks' to the media.

The mass and complexity of government business and ministers' concern with their own departments suggest that full debate in Cabinet on every issue is impossible, but it is felt that broad policies should be more vigorously debated. The present system arguably concentrates too much power in the hands of the prime minister; overloads ministers with work; allows crucial decisions to be taken outside the Cabinet; and reduces the notion of collective responsibility. The reality of coalition government may transform the Cabinet into a more collegiate body or alternatively it may suffer from conflicts and party jealousies.

Collective responsibility is that which all ministers, but mainly those in the Cabinet, share for government actions and policy. All must support a government decision in public, even though some may oppose it during private deliberations. If a minister cannot do this, they may feel obliged to resign.

A minister also has an individual responsibility for the work of their government department. They are answerable for any mistakes, wrongdoing or bad administration, whether personally responsible for them or not. In such cases, the minister may resign, although this is not as common today as in the past. This responsibility should also enable Parliament to maintain some control over executive actions because the minister is ultimately answerable to Parliament. However, critics argue that control today has weakened.

Government departments (or ministries) are the chief instruments by which the government implements its policy. A change of government does not necessarily alter the number or functions of departments. Examples are the Departments for Communities and Local Government (DCLG), Business, Innovation and Skills (BIS) and Transport (DfT).

Departments are staffed by the Civil Service, consisting of career administrators (civil servants). They work in London and throughout Britain in government activities and are responsible to the minister of their department for the implementation of government policies. A change of minister or government does not require new civil servants, since they are expected to be politically neutral and to serve the government impartially. Restrictions on political activities and publication are imposed upon them in order to ensure neutrality. There are some 500,000 civil servants in Britain today in central London and throughout the country. Half of these are women, but few of them achieve top ranks in the Service.

The heart of the Civil Service is the Cabinet Office, whose Secretary is the head of the Civil Service. The latter is responsible for the whole Civil Service, organizes Cabinet business and coordinates high-level policy. In each ministry or department the senior official (Permanent Secretary) and their assistants are responsible for assisting their minister in the implementation of government policy. There have been accusations about the efficiency and effectiveness of the Service, and civil servants do not have a good public image. There have been attempts to make the system more cost-effective and to allow a wider category of applicants than the traditional entry of Oxbridge graduates. Posts may now be advertised in order to attract older people from industry, commerce and the professions. Many aspects of departmental work have also been broken down and transferred to executive agencies in London and throughout the country, which have administrative rather than policy-making roles, such as the Driver and Vehicle Licensing Agency (DVLA) in Cardiff and social security offices. There have also been attempts to cut the number of civil servants and to restrict their policy-making role. Critics argue that the Civil Service has been politicized, lost its independence and become a delivery mechanism for targets initiated by unelected consultants, political advisers and 'spin doctors' in Downing Street.

On the other hand, it has been traditionally alleged that the Civil Service imposes a certain mentality upon its members, which affects the implementation of government policies and which ministers are unable to combat. There is supposedly a Civil Service way of doing things and a bias towards the status quo. However, much depends upon ministers and the way in which they manage departments. There may be some areas of concern. Yet the stereotypical image of civil servants is not always reflected in the many who serve their political masters and work with ministers for departmental interests. The Civil Service is highly regarded in other countries for its efficiency and impartiality.

UK parliamentary control of government

British governments (whether coalitions, minorities or single-majorities) have historically tended to govern pragmatically. The emphasis was on whether policies worked and were generally acceptable. Governments were conscious of how far they could go before displeasing their supporters and the electorate, to whom they were accountable at general elections. The combination of adversarial or two-party politics, Cabinet government and party discipline in the Commons seemed to provide a balance between efficient government and public accountability. Yet both Conservative and Labour governments have become more intent on pushing their policies through Parliament. Coalition government may well lead to a more consensus-based government style or forceful compromise between the two parties based on a Commons majority.

Constitutional theory suggested that Parliament should control the executive. However, unless there is a small-majority government, rebellion by government MPs or significant public protest, a government or coalition with an overall majority in the Commons is able to carry its policies through Parliament irrespective of parliamentary attempts to restrain it. The House of Lords has only a delaying and amending power over government legislation, although the Lords have effectively blocked some legislation in recent years. Critics argue for stronger parliamentary control over the executive, which has been described as an elective dictatorship. This may be achieved by moving to a PR electoral system, a more consensual style of politics, a strengthening of Parliament's constraining role and much more independent stances from MPs themselves.

Opposition parties can only oppose in the Commons and hope to persuade the electorate to dismiss the government at the next election. Votes of censure and no confidence are normally inadequate when confronting a government or coalition with a majority. Even rebellious government MPs will usually (if not always) support their parties on such occasions, out of a self-interested desire to preserve their jobs and a need to prevent the collapse of the government and its policies.

Examinations of government programmes can be employed at Question Time in the Commons, when the prime minister (for thirty minutes on Wednesdays) is subjected to oral questions from the Leader of the Opposition and MPs. But the government can prevaricate in its answers and, while reputations can be made and lost at Question Time, it is a rhetorical and political occasion rather than an in-depth analysis of government policy. However, it does have a function in holding the executive's performance up to public scrutiny. The opposition parties can also choose their own topics for formal debate on a limited number of days each session, which can be used to attack the government.

A 1967 attempt to restrain the executive was the creation of the Parliamentary Commissioner for Administration (Ombudsman), who can investigate alleged bad administration by ministers and civil servants. But the office does not have strong watchdog powers and the public have no direct access to it, although its existence does serve as a warning.

In an attempt to improve the situation, standing committees of MPs were established, which examine bills during procedural stages. Such committees have little influence on actual policy. But in 1979 a select committee system was created, which now has 14 committees. They comprise MPs from most parties, who monitor the administration and policy of the main government departments and investigate proposed legislation. MPs previously had problems in scrutinizing government activity adequately and party discipline made it difficult for them to act independently of party policy.

It is often argued that the real work of the House and parliamentary control of the executive is done in the select committees. Their members are now proving to be more independent in questioning civil servants and ministers who are called to give evidence before them (but who may refuse to attend). Select committees can be effective in examining proposed legislation and expenditure and their reports can be damaging to a government's reputation. Although opinions differ about their role, it does seem that they have strengthened Parliament's authority against government and critics would like to see their power enhanced.

Devolved structures

The previous sections have examined political institutions which function at national level. The following sections deal with smaller political units such as devolved structures and local government.

Devolution (self-government or transfer of some political powers short of complete independence from the Westminster Parliament) was first broached in Ireland. Growing nationalist feelings and unrest in the nineteenth century led to calls for Home Rule for Ireland with its own Parliament in Dublin. But early attempts to achieve this failed. Hostilities continued in the twentieth century until Ireland was partitioned in 1921–2 into the Irish Free State (later the Republic of Ireland with its own Parliament) and Northern Ireland. The latter had a devolved Parliament (1921–72) while remaining part of the UK.

Political and cultural nationalism also grew in Wales and Scotland from the 1960s. After failed attempts to give them devolved political power, the previous Labour government created in 1999 (after referendums) an elected Parliament with legislative and tax-varying powers in Scotland and a non-legislative, non-tax-raising elected Assembly in Wales. Northern Ireland achieved an elected Assembly in 1998, which has significant legislative and executive authority, including previous reserved UK powers over policing, security matters, prisons and criminal justice, which were transferred from Westminster in 2010.

Devolution is a tier of decentralized government. It allows these countries (with their executives and first ministers) to decide more of their own affairs, in

devolved matters such as education, health, transport, environment, home affairs
and local government. The Westminster Parliament still has reserved powers over
UK matters such as defence, foreign affairs, social security, taxation, broad
economic policy and immigration. Roles and procedures (except for elections
which tend to employ PR) in local and devolved structures are generally similar
to those at national (UK) level.

The devolution experiment had a shaky start. The Welsh Assembly still lacks
extensive powers: the London Parliament provides its primary legislation and it
had initial political problems. These now seem to have been settled, although the
Welsh generally want more primary legislative authority. The Northern Irish
Assembly was suspended in 2000, 2001 and 2004 largely because of the failure
of the IRA to disarm until 2005, and the province was still under direct rule from
London. However the Assembly was restored in 2007 and the peace process is
holding, although the devolution of policing and security had been a serious
sticking point. The Scottish Parliament initially attracted criticism, being seen

PLATE 4.8 City Hall, headquarters of the elected London Assembly and Greater London
Authority which governs London under devolved powers, on the south bank of the river Thames
and near Tower Bridge.
(Peter MacKinven/View Pictures/Rex Features)

as parochial, ineffective and controlled by London. It is now becoming more independent, has a minority Scottish National Party (SNP) government and first minister and has passed its own legislation on education (student fees) and health issues (care for the elderly), which are significantly different to those in the rest of the UK.

Arguably, devolution still needs to settle down and justify its existence. Critics argue that the devolved structures are inadequate and that the Labour government had not thought through the implications of its policies, particularly in terms of the anomalous position of England.

England has no intermediate devolved tier. It has a network of unelected, appointed Regional Development Agencies (RDAs), which implement UK government politico-economic programmes in the regions, but these areas do not provide elected devolved government. It was intended that they could form the basis for a further regional devolution of power from Westminster, analogous to the devolved structures in Scotland, Wales, Northern Ireland and London. However, a referendum of the people in north-east England in 2004 did not support this policy.

Devolution does not mean independence or separation for Scotland, Wales and Northern Ireland nor a British federal system, although it is argued that a form of 'quasi-federalism' has been created. The Labour government argued that devolution will strengthen the United Kingdom and that legal sovereignty still rests with the UK Parliament at Westminster. In this sense, Britain has a unitary political system and remains a union of England, Scotland, Wales and Northern Ireland (UK).

There was an initial fear that devolution would lead to independence for Scotland and Wales and the breakup of the UK. *British Social Attitudes* (2000–1) reported that while some English thought of themselves as strongly British, many have become more aware of being English in response to devolution. While they do not at present view devolution as an urgent threat to the unity of the United Kingdom, many increasingly would welcome an English Parliament.

Since July 2000, London has been run by an elected, devolved Greater London Authority with its elected mayor (currently Boris Johnson) and assembly. Yet the London mayor does not have the same executive and financial authority of American city mayors, on which the reform was supposedly based. It was hoped that similar mayors would be elected in other British cities, in an attempt to increase devolved powers, but the experiment has not proved attractive in most areas and so there are only a small number of elected mayors. The Liberal Democrats in the Westminster coalition are keen to expand the number of city mayors and to increase the amount of devolved democracy from the UK Parliament.

PLATE 4.9 Elected London Mayor Boris Johnson on the balcony of City Hall, London, 2008
(Richard Saker/Rex Features)

Local government

Britain has had a local government system in one form or another for centuries. It began with the Anglo-Saxon division of England into large counties and small parishes, which were organized by the monarch's local representatives. Local government has grown through the centuries, particularly during the nineteenth century. It now provides local services throughout the UK, such as education, health, fire services, transport, social services, sanitation and housing, through elected councils. In England, it is administered through professional staff and an elected non-professional two-tier system of county and district councils, with some single-tier (unitary) authorities. Scotland and Wales have thirty-two and twenty-two unitary authorities respectively, while Northern Ireland has twenty-six district councils.

Although people count on the services of local government, the system at present is languishing, is subject to centralized control and funding from the London government and no longer by itself provides the full range of traditional local services. Interest in local government is low and opinion polls suggest that dissatisfaction with local councils has increased. Critics argue for a more rigorous, competent and independently financed localism with less bureaucracy, which would be accountable to grassroots interests and free from central government interference and control.

Attitudes to politics

Polls consistently reveal that British politicians and political parties do not rate highly in public opinion. Respondents say that politicians are the least admired group of professionals (apart from journalists) and that they never answer the questions people put to them. In terms of trust, a MORI poll in March 2005 found that 75 per cent of respondents thought that politicians in general did not tell the truth and that 71 per cent felt the same about government ministers. They are criticized and satirized in the media and allegations of sleaze, corruption and unethical behaviour in both Labour and Conservative Parties have led to stricter controls on politicians and their outside interests. The previous Labour government had faced accusations of 'cronyism' (favouring political supporters for public and official positions) since 1997.

The latest scandal in 2008–9 concerned parliamentarians' claims for expenses (within the existing rules) for a range of dubious and often excessive expenses incurred when performing their duties and which most have had to repay. The result has been a sharp decline in the public's trust in politicians and very angry reactions by the public during the 2010 general election campaign. The episode indicated a gulf in basic values between politicians and their constituents. Critics maintain that the politicians do not appear to have learned any lessons from the experience. This has increased the voters' sense of disillusionment with the political process and, in the view of many people, Parliament has become a disgrace.

Commentators describe an increase in political apathy, particularly among the young, and a scepticism about politicians' ability to solve social problems. This atmosphere partly contributed to a 59 per cent turnout at the 2001 general election (the lowest in any general election since 1918) which had only slightly improved to 65.1 per cent by 2010. A Populus poll in March 2005, prior to the 2005 general election, found that 66 per cent of respondents were disappointed with the previous Labour government's performance. Some 11 per cent said that they might not vote at all in the election because of their disillusionment with Labour. Yet disaffected Labour supporters would not vote for another party. During the 2010 general election campaign, many people said in polls and public interviews that they would not vote for any party and were very dissatisfied with politics.

However, MORI opinion research in 2001 showed that interest in politics had actually remained stable in Britain for thirty years; that civic duty and habit were key motivators to voting (less so for the young); and that people had positive attitudes to voting, which they would prefer to be made more convenient by phone/mobile phone, online and by post. The latter is now available, although there have been allegations of and convictions for fraudulent postal voting. The research also found that a low turnout is a result not of declining interest in politics or elections but rather a failure of campaigns to connect with the electorate. This suggests that people want more accurate information, a greater focus on the issues that directly concern them and a sense that politicians are connecting with the public. Such responses have been repeated in surveys and polls since 2001.

People therefore appear to be more interested in the political process and issues than is popularly assumed. Yet the Independent Television Commission's Election 2001 survey found that interest in television election coverage had fallen to its lowest level, with 70 per cent of viewers expressing little or no interest and 25 per cent ignoring all campaign coverage. However, in 2010 the political party leaders for the first time held television debates over three weeks during the general election campaign. The first attracted 9.4 million viewers (an impressive 37 per cent audience share) and was the most watched programme of the day. The second debate attracted 6.5 million viewers across the channels, with very high viewing for digital television. The third and final debate had an average of 8.4 million viewers amounting to a third of audience share, beating *Coronation Street* (a long-running soap) and the UEFA Europa league game between Liverpool and Atletico Madrid.

Despite varied responses to the politicians' performances (which for some concentrated on spin rather than argument), these figures suggest an interest in politics. It seems that there is a disconnection between voters and politicians. None of the political parties, in spite of frequent drifts to the centre ground, individually encompass all the basic views and sense of contemporary reality of the people, who may vary between holding egalitarian economic views and authoritarian social and moral positions. They desire economic freedom and personal liberty but also want state interventionist policies in some social areas such as education, health and law and order. They also want politicians to engage with them and with what they perceive to be the serious issues of the day.

Exercises

Explain and examine the following terms:

Whigs	executive	'three-line whip'
Constitution	Secretary of State	life peers
Magna Carta	conventions	Question Time
Cabinet	manifesto	Oliver Cromwell
Civil servant	devolution	backbenchers
Lords Spiritual	Tories	constitutional monarchy
The Speaker	legislature	'hung Parliament'
Whitehall	sovereignty	select committees
White Paper	secret ballot	sleaze

Write short essays on the following topics:

1   Describe what is meant by the 'two-party system' and whether the result of the 2010 general election will change views on this system.

2*   Does Britain have an adequate parliamentary electoral system. If not, why not?

3   Critically examine the role and power of the prime minister

4   Discuss the position and relevance of the monarch in the British political system

Visit **www.routledge.com/textbooks/oakland** for multiple-choice questions, links to related YouTube clips, tips on approaching essay questions, and much, much more.

Further reading

1   Aughey, A. (2001) *Nationalism, Devolution and the Challenge to the United Kingdom State*, London: Pluto Press

2   Bogdanor, V. (2001) *Devolution in the United Kingdom*, Oxford: Oxford University Press

3   Bogdanor, V. (2009) *The New British Constitution*, London: Hart Publishing

4   Childs, D. (2006) *Britain since 1945: A Political History*, London: Routledge

5   Deacon, R. and Sandry, A. (2007) *Devolution in the United Kingdom (Politics Study Guides)*, Edinburgh: Edinburgh University Press

6 Foley, M. (2000) *The British Presidency*, Manchester: Manchester University Press
7 Foster, C. (2005) *British Government in Crisis*, London: Hart
8 Jones, B., Kavanagh, D., Moran, M. and Norton, P. (2007) *Politics UK*, London: Longman
9 Kavanagh, D. (2000) *British Politics: Continuities and Change*, Oxford: Oxford University Press
10 Leach, R., Coxall, B. and Robins, L. (2006) *British Politics*, Basingstoke: Palgrave Macmillan
11 Ludlam, S. and Smith, M.J. (2000) *New Labour in Government*, London: Macmillan

Websites

UK government: www.open.gov.uk, www.ukonline.gov.uk and www.direct.gov.uk
Houses of Parliament: www.parliament.uk
Monarchy: www.royal.gov.uk
Privy Council Office: www.privy-council.org.uk
Cabinet Office: www.cabinet-office.gov.uk
Prime Minister's Office: www.number-10.gov.uk
Wales Office: www.wales.gov.uk
National Assembly for Wales: www.wales.gov.uk
Scotland Office: www.scottishsecretary.gov.uk
The Scottish Parliament: www.scottish.parliament.uk
Northern Ireland Assembly: www.ni-assembly.gov.uk
Northern Ireland Office: www.nio.gov.uk
You Gov: www.yougov.co.uk
Office for National Statistics: www.ons.gov.uk

5

International relations

Britain's historical position as a colonial, economic and political power on the world stage was in relative decline by the early decades of the twentieth century. Some large colonies, such as Canada and Australia, had already achieved self-governing dominion status. The growth of nationalism and a desire for self-determination among African and Asian nations persuaded Britain to decolonialize further from 1945. The effects of global economic competition, two world wars, the emergence of Cold War politics (dominated by the USA and the former Soviet Union) and domestic economic and social problems forced Britain to recognize its reduced international status.

PLATE 5.1 Queen Elizabeth II greets the Namibian High Commissioner at a reception in Buckingham Palace, 28 April 2009, to mark the sixtieth anniversary of the Commonwealth London Declaration. The 1949 Declaration marked the birth of the modern organization, which was renamed the Commonwealth of Nations.
(Rex Features)

It tried with difficulty to find a new identity and establish different priorities, particularly in relation to Europe. Some of the previous overseas links continue in the form of the Commonwealth (formerly the British Empire), traditional trading partners and the connection with the United States, while other relationships are new. Yet, in spite of these fundamental changes, Britain still experiences uncertainties about its defence policies, potential international influence and appropriate role in global affairs.

Foreign and defence policy

Britain's position in the world today is that of a medium-sized country which faces increasing commercial competition from emerging global powers and ranks economically in sixth place behind the USA, Japan, Germany, France and China. Yet some of its politicians still believe that it can have an international influence and role. The Labour government from 1997 developed a foreign policy which shifted away from traditionally aggressive unilateral action to persuasive partnerships; embarked on coalition military actions around the world; and emphasized ethical and human rights in international and nationalist conflicts. Nevertheless, national self-interest is still evident in attempts at global cooperation and the concerted fight against terrorism.

Critics argue that that such commitments are financially unsustainable and that Britain's foreign policy and self-image do not reflect the reality of its world position. It has engaged in recent wars and peacekeeping duties in the Balkans, Afghanistan, Sierra Leone and Iraq. But, while military action in Iraq (from 2003) was initially supported by a majority of the British public, there was increasing opposition over its aftermath, distrust of the Labour government's justification for the war and scepticism as to whether overseas military involvement would protect Britain's internal security. The ongoing war in Afghanistan attracts public opposition and concern at the loss of British lives and the alleged lack of adequate equipment. It is also felt that the current costs of defence and global commitments could be more profitably directed to solving domestic problems.

Britain's foreign and defence preoccupations reflect its traditional position as a major trading nation and financial centre. It is concerned to maintain stable commercial, economic and political conditions through global connections. Britain is a large exporter of goods and services, has substantial overseas or outward investments and imports much of its food and basic manufacturing requirements. It is dependent upon maintaining global commercial links, although it is increasingly committed to Europe, whose twenty-seven EU member countries are Britain's biggest export and import markets. However, other European countries, the USA, China, India, Japan, South America and Commonwealth nations are also important trading areas.

Britain's *foreign policy* and membership of international organizations is based on the principle that overseas objectives in the contemporary world can be best attained by persuasion, cooperation and actively working with other nations on a regional or global basis. The imperial days of unilateral action are now largely past, although Britain did take such action in the 1982 Falklands War. Its foreign policy can reflect particular biases, with support for one country outweighing that for another.

The USA has often been Britain's closest ally. A 'special relationship' supposedly exists between the two based on a common language, cultural traditions, history and military partnership. Yet this association has varied according to geopolitical circumstances, changing political leadership and opposed policies in the two countries. There have been differences in outlook concerning American entry into the Second World War, Britain's involvement in the Suez invasion (1956), America's role in the Vietnam War, British membership of the EU and American views on Britain's imperial past. Nevertheless, British politicians are concerned to maintain American military and security influence within Europe and NATO and to preserve the Atlantic connection in their own bargaining with EU countries for what they consider to be global stability.

An April 2003 Gallup poll found that 79 per cent of Americans regarded Britain as a close partner of the USA and a MORI research survey of the same date

PLATE 5.2 Former prime minister Gordon Brown, second from left, with other G8 leaders at the G8 summit in L'Aquila, Italy, 9 July 2009.
(Sipa Press/Rex Features)

showed that 73 per cent of British respondents felt the United States was Britain's most reliable ally. However, the latter poll also revealed that when asked which ally was most important to Britain, 34 per cent of British people chose the USA and 42 per cent preferred Europe. A Pew Global Attitudes poll in 2005 found that British favourable opinion of the USA had decreased from 83 per cent in 1999 to 55 per cent in 2005. Only 32 per cent of British respondents thought that American foreign policy considered other nations' interests.

Britain's membership of the EU means that it is to some extent dependent upon EU foreign policy. In 2009 the EU ratified the Lisbon Treaty, which is intended to tighten institutional and policy functions, created a President of the EU Council and High Representative for Foreign Affairs and potentially gave the EU a legal negotiating status on the world stage. But, although the EU is moving towards more unified policies, member states have conflicting interests and Britain also has its own policy priorities. EU foreign policy is still very much in its infancy and many critics doubt its validity and value.

Britain has diplomatic relations with 160 nations and is a member of some 120 international organizations, ranging from bodies for economic cooperation to the United Nations (UN). Support for the UN and the principles of its charter has been part of British foreign policy since 1945, although there has sometimes been scepticism about its effectiveness as a practical and decisive body (for instance, over Iraq resolutions in 2003).

Yet, as a permanent member of the UN Security Council, Britain has a vested interest in supporting the organization. It sees a strong UN as a necessary framework for achieving many of its own foreign policy objectives, such as the peaceful resolution of conflict, arms control, disarmament, peacekeeping operations and the protection of human rights. UN agencies also provide forums for discussing issues in which Britain is involved, such as disaster relief, terrorism, the environment, energy development and world resources. However, Britain, like other nations, may ignore the UN when it sees its own vital interests challenged.

Britain's major *defence* alliance is with the North Atlantic Treaty Organization (NATO). This currently comprises twenty-six members: Belgium, Canada, Denmark, Iceland, Italy, Luxembourg, the Netherlands, Norway, Spain, Portugal, Britain, the USA, Greece, Turkey, Germany, Poland, Hungary, the Czech Republic, France (now again part of NATO's integrated military structures), Bulgaria, Estonia, Latvia, Lithuania, Romania, Slovakia and Slovenia. The justification for NATO's creation was that it provided its members with greater security than any could achieve individually and was a deterrent against aggression by the now-defunct Warsaw Pact countries.

All the major British political parties are in favour of retaining the NATO link and, according to opinion polls, the public would not support any party which tried to take Britain out of the alliance. Membership of NATO also allows Britain to operate militarily on the international stage. Its defence policy is based on

NATO strategies and it assigns most of its armed forces and defence budget to the organization.

Despite changes in Eastern Europe since 1989 and moves to transform NATO into a more flexible, leaner and high-technology military association, the British government has taken such developments cautiously and is concerned to maintain its own military defence with both conventional and nuclear forces. It recognizes that global instability, international terrorism and unstable states would pose increased risks to its own security if it were to reduce its and NATO's armed defence capacity substantially.

However, in 1998 Britain argued that the EU must also have a credible military and security capability to support its political role. The EU is now working towards the creation of its own 'rapid deployment force'. The problem is whether this should be seen as an independent force outside NATO or whether it should operate within NATO frameworks. It could respond to international crises, but without prejudice to NATO (which would continue to be the foundation of collective security). Some critics argue that this development has been inadequately planned and has cooperation problems. It could also weaken NATO and lead to American withdrawal from Europe.

The British government's defence spending (2.4 per cent of GDP in 2010 and a budget for 2010–11 of £36.9 billion) has reduced the number of armed forces personnel, ships, aircraft and equipment, but has increased other priority areas such as capabilities and structures. It aims to depend on leaner, fast-reaction and more flexible forces, although there have been strenuous objections to these policies (such as the reduction in the number of old army regiments) from the military. The primary objectives of defence policy are to ensure the country's security and the NATO commitment and to allow British forces to engage in high-intensity war as well as in peacekeeping roles.

However, although defence spending comes seventh on the list of government expenditure, it is queried whether the money could be better spent in other areas of national life. At the same time, although the British armed forces are increasingly in demand for global commitments, they are undermanned and military equipment is often out of date and in short supply. The military claim that they need more resources as the Afghanistan conflict drags on.

Nuclear weapons, which account for a large part of the defence budget, continue to be fiercely debated. Britain's independent nuclear deterrent consists mainly of long-range American-built Trident missiles carried by a fleet of four submarines (although only one is on patrol at any given time). The previous Labour government committed itself to upgrading the nuclear missile arsenal at a cost of £20 billion. Critics want cheaper alternatives, or the cancellation of the nuclear system (on the grounds that the system was based on Cold War planning which is allegedly no longer applicable). However, it seems that the British nuclear strategy will continue. The major political parties are multilateralist (keeping nuclear weapons until they can be abolished on a global basis).

PLATE 5.3 British soldiers lead French and Afghan troops through central Showai, Helmand Province, Afghanistan, February 2010.
(*Julian Simmonds/Rex Features*)

Britain can operate militarily outside the NATO and European area, although this capacity is increasingly expensive and questioned. Military garrisons are stationed in Germany, Brunei, Cyprus, the Far and Middle East, the Falkland Islands, Diego Garcia, Ascension Island and Gibraltar. The 1982 Falklands War, the 1991 and 2003–4 Gulf Wars and Afghanistan in 2001 showed that Britain was able to respond to global challenges outside the strictly NATO area, although the operations did draw attention to defects and problems in such actions. Iraq and Afghanistan have demonstrated a lack of equipment and manpower. Britain's choices are to retreat from global commitments, greatly scale back defence spending, create one combined military force rather than separate units or cooperate more with countries such as France (now returned to NATO's integrated military structures) across a range of defence activity.

The total strength of the armed forces, which are now all volunteer following the end of conscription in 1962, was 217,130 (including reserves) in 2010. This was made up of 35,030 in the Royal Navy and Royal Marines, 101,330 in the Army and 39,630 in the Royal Air Force. Female personnel in the Army, Navy and Air Force (9 per cent of the total figure) are integral parts of the armed services. Though previously confined to support roles, they may now be employed in some front-line military activities. Reserve forces, such as the Territorial Army

(TA), perform a crucial role, support the regular forces at home and abroad, serve with NATO and coalition ground troops and help to maintain security in Britain.

The strength of the armed forces could be cut by a fifth in coming years, and the Ministry of Defence budget is likely to fall by 2016–17 because of the 2008–09 recession, the rising cost of employing military and civilian personnel and the costs of equipment.

The empire and Commonwealth

The British Empire was gradually built up over four centuries from the sixteenth century, though colonization had in fact begun with the attempted internal domination of the islands by the English from the twelfth century, together with military conquests in Europe. These were followed by trading activities and the establishment of settlements in North and South America. Parts of Africa, Asia and the West Indies were also exploited commercially over time and many became colonies. Emigrants from Britain settled in countries such as the USA, Australia, Canada, South Africa and New Zealand. By the nineteenth century British imperial rule and possessions had embraced a quarter of the world's population.

PLATE 5.4   Queen Elizabeth II (centre, front row) at the opening ceremony of the Commonwealth Heads of Government Meeting in Port of Spain, Trinidad, 27 November 2009.
(Tim Rooke/Rex Features)

In the late nineteenth and early twentieth centuries large colonies such as Canada, Australia, New Zealand and South Africa became self-governing dominions and eventually achieved independence. Many of their peoples were descendants of those settlers who had emigrated from Britain in earlier centuries. They regarded Britain as the 'mother country' and nurtured a shared kinship. However, this relationship has changed as separate national identities in these countries have become firmly established.

In 1931, the British Empire became the British Commonwealth of Nations and independence was gradually granted to other colonies. India and Pakistan became independent in 1947 (leading to the emergence of the modern Commonwealth in 1949), followed by African territories in the 1950s and 1960s and later by many islands of the West Indies. Eventually, most of the remaining colonies became independent. They could choose whether to break all connections with the colonial past or remain within the Commonwealth as independent nations. Most of them decided to stay in the organization, though only a few small British colonies, dependencies and protectorates now remain and are scattered widely, such as the Falklands and Gibraltar.

The present Commonwealth is a voluntary association of some fifty-four independent states (including Britain). It does not have written laws, an elected parliament or one overall political ruler. There is evidence of past colonial rule in many of the countries, such as their educational and legal systems, although few have kept the British form of parliamentary government. Some have adapted it to their own needs, while others are one-party states or have constitutions based on a wide variety of models, with varying records on civil and democratic rights.

The Commonwealth has nearly a third of the world's population and comprises peoples of different religions, races and nationalities, most of whom share a colonial history, with struggles for independence from colonialism. Though the Commonwealth is often described as a family of nations, there are occasional wars, tensions and quarrels between these family members.

The British monarch is its non-political head and has varying constitutional roles in the different countries. A focal point of identification, the monarch has an important unifying and symbolic function which has often kept the Commonwealth together in times of crisis and conflict.

The prime ministers, or heads of state, in Commonwealth countries meet every two years under the auspices of the monarch for Commonwealth meetings or conferences in different parts of the world. Common problems are discussed and sometimes settled, although there seem to have been more arguments than agreements in recent years, with Britain having a minority position on some issues (such as opposing trade sanctions against the former apartheid regime in South Africa).

There is a Commonwealth Secretariat in London which coordinates policy for the Commonwealth, in addition to many Commonwealth societies, institutes, libraries, professional associations and university exchange programmes. Commonwealth citizens still travel to Britain as immigrants, students and visitors, while British emigration to Commonwealth countries continues in reduced amounts. English in its many varieties remains the common language of the Commonwealth and the Commonwealth Games (athletics and other sports) are held every four years. There are many joint British/Commonwealth programmes on both official and voluntary levels in agriculture, engineering, health and education, in which some vestiges of the old relationship between Britain and the Commonwealth are still apparent.

However, British attempts to enter Europe from the 1960s onwards reduced the importance to Britain of the organization. There is no longer the old sense of Commonwealth solidarity and purpose, and the country has little in common with some Commonwealth nations. It is argued that unless member countries feel there are valid reasons for continuing a somewhat moribund association which represents historical accident rather than common purpose, the long-term future of the Commonwealth must be in doubt. Opinion polls show that Europe and the USA are more important to Britons than the Commonwealth. Only 16 per cent of respondents in an April 2003 MORI research survey felt that the Commonwealth was the most important international partnership for Britain.

Britain had preferential trading arrangements with the Commonwealth before it joined the EU in 1973 and the Commonwealth question formed part of the debate on membership. EU entry was seen as ending the close relationship between Britain and the Commonwealth. Yet economic cooperation and trading between the two have continued, and Britain contributes a considerable amount of its overseas aid to Commonwealth countries. However, Britain has a declining share of the Commonwealth trading market and its economic priorities now lie more with the EU and other world partners.

Nevertheless, the previous Labour government felt that the Commonwealth was a success and was committed to raising its profile. Indeed, a number of countries wish to join the organization, not all of whom have been previous British colonies (such as Mozambique). But it is argued that the value of the Commonwealth in the contemporary world must be based on a concrete and realistic role which is distinct from those of other global organizations. For example, it might function as a worldwide political forum which emphasizes accountable government, democratic concerns, anti-corruption reform and civil and human rights.

The European Union (EU)

The ideal of a united Europe with strong economic and political institutions became increasingly attractive to European statesmen after the Second World War (1939–45). There was a desire to create a peaceful and prosperous Europe after the destruction of two World Wars and centuries of antagonism and distrust between the European powers.

The foundations for a more integrated Europe were established in 1957 when six countries (West Germany, France, Belgium, the Netherlands, Luxembourg and Italy) signed the Treaty of Rome and formed the European Economic Community (EEC). Britain did not join then, but instead helped to create the European Free Trade Association (EFTA) in 1959. Not wishing to be restricted by close European relationships in the 1950s, it saw its future in trading links with the Commonwealth and a 'special relationship' with the USA. An old suspicion of Europe also caused many British people to shrink from membership of a European organization, which they thought might result in the loss of their identity and independence.

   However, a European commitment grew among sections of British society in the 1960s, which was influenced by the country's increasing social and economic problems. Yet attempts by Britain to join the EEC were vetoed by the French president, Charles de Gaulle. He was critical of Britain's relationship with the USA (particularly on nuclear weapons policies), queried the extent of British commitment to Europe and arguably did not want Britain as a rival to the leadership of the EEC.

   De Gaulle resigned from the French presidency in 1969, and new British negotiations on membership began in 1970 under the pro-European Conservative

PLATE 5.5 The European Parliament, Brussels. The Parliament also meets in Strasbourg, France, on a rotating basis.
(Etienne Ansotte/Rex Features)

prime minister, Edward Heath. In 1972, Parliament voted in favour of entry, despite widespread doubts and the strong opposition of a politically diverse group of interests among the British people. Britain, together with Denmark and the Republic of Ireland, formally joined the EEC on 1 January 1973, having left EFTA in 1972.

A new Labour government (1974) under Harold Wilson was committed to giving the people a referendum on continued membership. After further renegotiations of the terms of entry, the referendum was held in 1975, the first in British political history. Pro-marketeers won by a margin of two to one (67.2 per cent in favour, 32.8 per cent against).

The EEC was based initially on economic concerns and instituted harmonization programmes such as common coal, steel, agricultural and fisheries policies, the abolition of trade tariffs between member states and development aid to depressed areas within its borders. Britain's poorer regions have benefited considerably from regional funds. In 1986 the member states formed an internal or Single European Market in which goods, services, people and capital could move freely across national frontiers within what was then called the European Community (EC). In 2004, 59 per cent of British exports went to the EU and Britain received 54 per cent of its imports from the EU countries.

Some politicians had always hoped that economic integration would lead to political initiatives and a more integrated Europe. The Maastricht Treaty (1992) was a step in this process as a result of which the European Community became the European Union (EU). The treaty provided for the introduction of a common European currency, the euro, a European Bank and common defence, foreign and social policies. Further treaties have also increased the integration momentum.

There are now twenty-seven EU members with a total population of 501 million people (Britain, Denmark, Germany, Greece, Spain, Belgium, Ireland, Luxembourg, the Netherlands, France, Italy, Portugal, Sweden, Finland, Austria, Cyprus, the Czech Republic, Estonia, Hungary, Latvia, Lithuania, Malta, Poland, Slovakia, Slovenia, Romania and Bulgaria). Since 1994, most of the EU Single Market measures have also been extended to Iceland, Norway and Liechtenstein through the creation of the European Economic Area (EEA). The actual and potential growth of the EU (to include other Eastern European nations and Turkey) has been seen as providing an important political voice in world affairs and a powerful trading area in global economic matters. Today, EU/EEA member states account for 40 per cent of world trade and generate some 30 per cent of nominal gross world product.

The main institutions involved in the running of the EU are the European Council, the Council of Ministers, the European Commission, the European Parliament and the European Court of Justice. In 2009, the Lisbon Treaty came into force, which reformed many aspects of the EU. It created a permanent President of the European Council and a High Representative of the Union for Foreign Affairs and Security Policy.

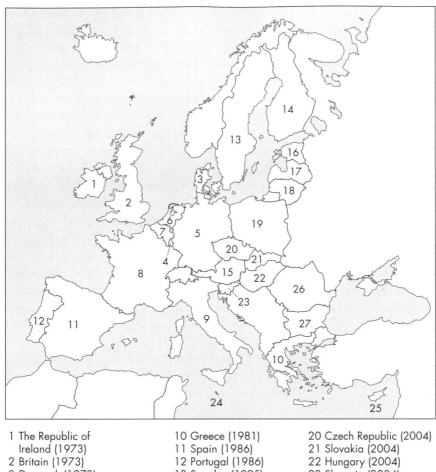

1 The Republic of Ireland (1973)	10 Greece (1981)	20 Czech Republic (2004)
2 Britain (1973)	11 Spain (1986)	21 Slovakia (2004)
3 Denmark (1973)	12 Portugal (1986)	22 Hungary (2004)
4 Luxembourg (1957)	13 Sweden (1995)	23 Slovenia (2004)
5 Germany (1957)	14 Finland (1995)	24 Malta (2004)
6 The Netherlands (1957)	15 Austria (1995)	25 Cyprus (2004)
7 Belgium (1957)	16 Estonia (2004)	26 Romania (2007)
8 France (1957)	17 Latvia (2004)	27 Bulgaria (2007)
9 Italy (1957)	18 Lithuania (2004)	
	19 Poland (2004)	

FIGURE 5.1 The European Union, 2010 (with accession dates)

The European Council consists of government leaders who meet several times a year to discuss and agree on broad areas of policy. The Council of Ministers is the principal policy-implementing and law-initiating body and is normally composed of foreign ministers from the member states.

The Commission (under an appointed president) is the central administrative force of the EU, proposing programmes and policy to the Council of Ministers. It comprises commissioners (with one from Britain) chosen from member states to hold certain portfolios, such as agriculture or competition policy, for a renewable five-year period. Their interests then become those of the EU and not of their national governments. It is argued that the unelected Commission has too much power and should be more democratically accountable.

The European Parliament is directly elected for a five-year term on a party political basis from the EU-wide electorate. It advises the Council of Ministers on Commission proposals, determines the EU budget and exerts some control over the Council and the Commission. It is argued that the Parliament, as the only directly elected body in the EU, should have more power and its veto over EU policy has now been extended. In the 2009 British EU Parliament elections (held mainly under a partial PR arrangement with party lists) the Labour Party did badly compared with the Conservatives. The UK Independence Party (UKIP), which wants British withdrawal from the EU, did very well and came second, while the British National Party (BNP) gained its first seats in the Parliament. Britain has seventy-two seats in the Parliament (see Table 5.1), which was reduced from seventy-eight in 2004 because of EU enlargement.

The Court of Justice comprises appointed judges from the member states. It interprets EU laws and treaties, settles disputes concerning EU law and resolves conflicts between member states and the EU. It is a very influential institution and has built up a solid body of EU case law which is directly applicable in the domestic systems of the member states.

British membership of the EU continues to be difficult. The UK has complained about its contribution to the EU budget (which, although reduced

TABLE 5.1 European Union Parliament: election results (Britain), 2009

Party	Seats	%
Conservatives	25	27.7
United Kingdom Independence Party	13	16.5
Labour	13	15.7
Liberal Democrats	11	13.7
The Green Party	2	8.6
British National Party	2	6.2
Scottish National Party	2	2.1
Plaid Cymru	1	0.8
Northern Ireland		
Sinn Féin	1	26.0
Democratic Unionist Party	1	18.2
Ulster Conservatives & Unionists	1	17.1
Total	72	
Turnout	49 %	

Source: UK Office of the European Parliament, London, 2009

under Margaret Thatcher, is now being reviewed); objected to the agricultural and fisheries policies; and opposed movements towards greater political and economic integration. On the one hand, Eurosceptic critics argue that Britain's sovereignty and independence are threatened by EU developments and want the repatriation of national rights from the EU back to Britain. They, and others, tend to see the EU as a free-trade area in which national legal rights and interests should be firmly retained. Europhile supporters, on the other hand, want economic and political integration (possibly on federal lines), arguing that the EU enables governments to rationalize industrial and agricultural policies and allows European countries to operate effectively in a globalized world and to run external policies which are beyond the capacity of a small or medium-sized country. In this view, membership of the EU means not a handing over of power to Brussels but a net increase in effective power.

All the major political parties are pro-European in the sense of wanting to be in Europe, although there are opposition groups within the Labour and, particularly, Conservative parties. The country is now so closely tied to Europe in economic and institutional ways that withdrawal from the EU would be difficult in practical terms, although it is possible constitutionally.

There are divided views about the pace and direction of future developments. The previous Labour government wanted a strong Europe in which Britain could play a central role; supported the enlargement of the EU; backed the Lisbon Treaty; was in principle in favour of Britain entering the European common currency (euro); and proposed a common defence and foreign policy for the EU. But it was against the concept of a federal 'superstate', favoured the Council of Ministers as the key decision-making body and was against enhancing the powers of the European Parliament.

However, it did not take Britain into the first wave of the euro in 1999. Its policy was to wait until Britain's economy was in line with those of other members, see how the currency developed and then put the issue to a referendum. Polls in recent years have consistently suggested that a majority of Britons are against joining the euro. A MORI poll in February 2005 found that 57 per cent of respondents were against the euro and that 55 per cent would not change their minds if the government strongly urged support. Feelings in Britain about the Lisbon Treaty (a revamped and rejected constitutional treaty) have also been volatile, with many people feeling that Britain should have had a referendum on the issue.

Among other things, the original proposed constitution and the Treaty would give legal identity and authority to the EU; create a legally binding charter of rights; allow for a full-time president and foreign minister; and formally recognize the supremacy of EU law over national law. Although the French and Dutch rejected the Constitution in 2005, the Lisbon Treaty was finally adopted in 2009 when the Republic of Ireland voted 'Yes' in a referendum after earlier rejecting it.

British support for the EU peaked in the 1980s but has since eroded, and Britain is now the least enthusiastic of the EU countries. Some polls in recent years have suggested that only a slender majority of respondents wanted to stay in the EU while a majority wanted a referendum on Britain's continued membership and believed that Britons had not been given enough information about the arguments for and against membership. A 2003 MORI poll found that only 30 per cent of British respondents felt that EU membership was a good thing.

Public support for the EU therefore tends to be lukewarm and indifferent. The turnout for British EU Parliament elections is the lowest in Europe and there is ignorance about, and little trust in, the EU, its benefits and its institutions. A MORI poll in September 2004 found that 32 per cent of respondents felt that the EU needed Britain more than Britain needed the EU; but 32 per cent also felt that Britain and the EU needed each other equally. A BBC/ComRes poll in 2009 found that 55 per cent of Britons wanted to leave the EU; 84 per cent wanted a referendum before transferring new powers to the EU; 55 per cent wanted Britain to leave the EU but to maintain close trading links (41 per cent disagreed); and 51 per cent disagreed that Britain benefited overall from membership in terms of jobs and trade (44 per cent agreed)

However, other polls show more mixed, nuanced and partly positive responses to the EU. Some reveal that 'Europe' is considered to be relatively more important to Britain than the USA and the Commonwealth. Europeanism (rather than an EU institutional entity) seems to be more easily and naturally accepted by people, particularly the young; large numbers of Britons live and work in European countries; people take their holidays in Europe; there is considerable interchange at many levels between Europeans and the British; and increasing numbers of Britons regard themselves as Europeans.

The Republic of Ireland and Northern Ireland

Northern Ireland (also known as 'the six counties', or Ulster after the ancient kingdom in the north-east of the island) is constitutionally a part of the United Kingdom. However, its (and British) history is inseparable from that of the Republic of Ireland. Historically, mainland Britain has been unable to accommodate itself successfully to its next-door neighbours. During the twentieth century, as Britain detached itself from empire and entered the EU, its relationship with Northern Ireland and the Republic of Ireland has been problematic. However, the latter is now more closely involved politically with the UK as a result of the 1998 Good Friday Agreement on Northern Ireland and later legislation.

A basic knowledge of the island's long and troubled history is essential to an understanding of the current role of the Republic and the situation in Northern Ireland itself. Ireland was first controlled by Anglo-Norman England in the twelfth

PLATE 5.6 Steps leading up to the Parliament building, known as Stormont because of its location in the Stormont area of Belfast. The seat of the Northern Ireland Parliament 1921–72 and now home to the Northern Irish Assembly and its power-sharing Executive following devolution in 1998.
(KPA/Zuma/Rex Features)

century. Since then there have been continuous rebellions by the native Irish against English colonial, political and military rule.

The situation worsened in the sixteenth century, when Catholic Ireland refused to accept the Protestant Reformation, despite much religious persecution. The two seeds of future hatred, colonialism and religion, were thus sown early in Irish history. A hundred years later, Oliver Cromwell crushed rebellions in Ireland and continued the earlier 'plantation policy', by which English and Scottish settlers were given land and rights over the native Irish and controlled any Irish revolts. The descendants of the Protestant settlers became a powerful political minority in Ireland as a whole and a majority in Ulster. In 1690, the Protestant William III (William of Orange) crushed Catholic uprisings at the Battle of the Boyne and secured Protestant dominance in Northern Ireland.

Ireland was then mainly an agricultural country, dependent upon its farming produce. But crop (e.g. potato) failures were frequent, and famine in the middle of the nineteenth century caused death and emigration, with the result that the population was reduced by a half by 1901. The people who remained demanded more autonomy over their own affairs. Irish MPs in the Westminster Parliament called persistently for 'home rule' for Ireland (control of internal matters by the

Irish through an assembly in Dublin). The home rule question dominated late nineteenth- and early twentieth-century British politics. It led to periodic out-breaks of violence as the Northern Irish Protestant/Unionist majority feared that an independent and united Ireland would be dominated by the Catholics/nationalists.

Eventually in 1921 Ireland was divided (or partitioned) into two parts as a result of uprisings, violence and eventual political agreement. This attempted solution of the historical problems has been at the root of troubles ever since. The twenty-six counties of southern Ireland became the Irish Free State and a dominion in the Commonwealth. This later developed into the Republic of Ireland, remained neutral in the Second World War and left the Commonwealth in 1949. The six counties in the north became known as Northern Ireland and remained constitutionally part of the United Kingdom. Until 1972, they had a Protestant-dominated Parliament (at Stormont outside Belfast), which was responsible for governing the province.

After the Second World War, Northern Ireland developed agriculturally and industrially. Urban centres expanded and more specifically Catholic districts developed in the towns. But the Protestants, through their ruling party (the Ulster Unionists) in Parliament, maintained an exclusive hold on all areas of life in the province, including employment, the police force, local councils and public services. The minority Catholics suffered systematic discrimination in these areas.

Conflicts arose again in Northern Ireland in 1968–9. Marches were held to demonstrate for civil liberties and were initially non-sectarian. Yet the situation deteriorated, fighting erupted between Protestants and Catholics and violence escalated. The Northern Ireland government asked for the British army to be sent in to restore order. The army was initially welcomed, but was soon attacked by both sides. Relations between Catholics and Protestants worsened and political attitudes became polarized. Violence continued after 1968 with outrages from both sides of the sectarian divide.

On one side of this divide was the Provisional wing of the Irish Republican Army (IRA) and other splinter nationalist groups, which were supported by many republicans and Catholics. The IRA was illegal in both the Republic and Northern Ireland and committed to the unification of Ireland, as was its legal political wing, Provisional Sinn Féin. The IRA wanted to remove the British political and military presence from Northern Ireland. Prior to the Peace Agreement of 1998 they had engaged in a systematic campaign of bombings, shootings and murders.

Protestant paramilitary groups and Unionist parties, such as the Democratic Unionists, were equally committed to their own views. They are loyal to the British Crown and insist that they remain part of the United Kingdom. Protestant paramilitaries, partly in retaliation for IRA activities and partly to emphasize their demands, have also carried out sectarian murders and terrorist acts. British troops and the Ulster Constabulary (now the Police Service of Northern Ireland) were supposed to control the two populations and to curb terrorism, but they were also targets for bullets and bombs and have been accused of perpetrating atrocities themselves.

From 1972, responsibility for Northern Ireland rested with the British government in London (direct rule) after the Northern Ireland Parliament was suspended. There have been various assemblies and executives in Northern Ireland, which were attempts to give the Catholic minority political representation in cooperation with the Protestant majority (power-sharing). Yet these efforts failed, largely because of Protestant intransigence, although most injustices to Catholic civil liberties were gradually removed.

The level of violence in the province fluctuated from 1968 onwards, but emergency legislation and a reduction in legal rights for suspected terrorists continued. Moderates of all political persuasions, who were squeezed out as political polarization grew, were appalled by the outrages and the historical injustices. Outsiders often felt that a rational solution should be possible, but this was to underestimate the deep emotions on both sides, the historical dimension and the extremist elements. There was also little agreement over the cause of the problems, with views encompassing ethnic, religious, political and economic reasons.

British governments have launched initiatives to persuade Northern Irish political parties to discuss the realistic possibilities of power-sharing in Northern Ireland. They have also tried to involve the Irish government and the Anglo-Irish Agreement of 1985 was a joint attempt to resolve the situation. It aimed to solve difficulties (such as border security and extradition arrangements) in order to achieve a devolved power-sharing government for Northern Ireland. The Republic of Ireland had to make some concessions as the price for the agreement, but was given a significant role to play in the resolution of the Northern Irish situation. However, the Republic's cooperation with Britain was seen by Northern Irish Unionists as a step towards reunification of the island and they opposed the agreement. The Republic now sees unification as a long-term aim and the British government insists that no change in Northern Ireland will take place unless a majority of the inhabitants there agree (consent). The population of Northern Ireland consists of Protestants (1,045,500 or 61.5 per cent in 2001) and Catholics (654,500 or 38.5 per cent).

The Downing Street Declaration of 1993 by the Irish and British governments was a further attempt to halt the violence and bring all parties to the conference table to discuss Northern Ireland's future. It largely restated existing positions. However, building on a Protestant paramilitary ceasefire, the Labour government in 1997 set out conditions and a schedule for peace talks between all the political parties. An IRA ceasefire also allowed Sinn Féin (Republican party) into the peace process.

Multi-party talks held in Belfast in April 1998 concluded with the 'Good Friday Agreement'. Legislation was passed in Dublin and London for referendums on the Agreement and provided for elections to a new Northern Ireland Assembly. In May 1998 referendums on the Agreement were held. Northern Ireland voted

71.1 per cent in favour and 28.8 per cent against, while in the Irish Republic the result was 94.3 per cent and 5.6 per cent respectively.

A new Northern Ireland Assembly of 108 members was elected by proportional representation (single transferable vote) in June 1998. A Northern Ireland Act set out the principle of consent to any change in constitutional status in Northern Ireland, provided for its administration and contained arrangements for human rights and equality.

In December 1999, some political power was devolved by the Westminster Parliament to the Northern Ireland Assembly and its Executive. It had legislative and executive authority to make laws and take decisions in Northern Ireland, except for reserved UK powers over policing and justice matters.

Other significant bodies were also created, such as a North–South Ministerial Council, North–South Implementation Bodies, a British–Irish Council and a British–Irish Intergovernmental Conference. These organizations bring together UK and Irish elements. Critics argue that the British–Irish Council is a positive step and a political expression of the mixed ethnic and cultural history of the islands. It comprises the UK and Irish governments, the Northern Ireland Assembly, the Welsh Assembly, the Scottish Parliament, the government of the Isle of Man and the governing bodies of the Channel Islands. It could promote participation in one representative British–Irish body for the first time.

However, in February 2000, following a report from the Independent International Commission on Decommissioning, the Northern Ireland Assembly was suspended due to a lack of progress on the decommissioning of illegally held weapons, mainly by the IRA. Direct rule from London was reimposed. Although periods of devolved power were later restored to the Assembly, obstacles appeared such as Stormont spying allegations against the IRA, a large bank robbery attributed to the IRA and no significant progress on decommissioning. The Peace Agreement was in danger of collapse and the Assembly was suspended between October 2002 and May 2007. During suspension its powers reverted to the Northern Ireland Office.

In 2005, the IRA announced that they would put all their weapons beyond use and ordered their members to stop military action. Critics reacted with scepticism and insisted that action follow these words. The international decommissioning body reported that IRA weapons had been 'put beyond use' and some Unionist paramilitaries moved to disarm. But criminal activities continue to be carried out by Unionist and Nationalist paramilitary organizations, serious sectarian violence broke out again on Belfast streets in 2005 and dissident groups protested against the Good Friday Agreement.

Difficulties remain in the path of achieving the aims of the Agreement. The Protestant Unionists want to remain part of the United Kingdom, oppose union with the Republic of Ireland and argue that any future solution for Northern Ireland must rely on the consent of a majority of the people living there. Sinn Féin and the IRA are committed to a united Ireland and argue that a majority of all people

(Northern Ireland and the Republic of Ireland) must consent to any eventual proposed solution. The 2005 British general election and the 2003 Northern Ireland Assembly election resulted in increased representation for Sinn Féin and the anti-peace agreement Democratic Unionist Party (DUP), with reduced support for the Ulster Unionists and the moderate SDLP. It was feared that these results could lead to more extreme and hardline positions being taken in Northern Ireland.

However, the Assembly met for the first time since suspension between May and November 2006. Following the St Andrews Agreement (2006), an election to the Assembly was held on the 7 March 2007, with the DUP gaining thirty-six seats and Sinn Féin twenty-eight. Following the election of a four-party Executive of 12 ministers, devolution and full powers were restored to the Assembly and Executive in May 2007. A turning point in Northern Ireland came in 2007 when the DUP's Ian Paisley led the new power-sharing Executive with Sinn Féin's Martin McGuinness as his deputy. They managed to work together and the Assembly and Executive functioned, despite outbreaks of violence and bombings by mainly nationalist dissidents and the IRA and Unionist ceasefires held firm. Paisley stood down in 2008 to be succeeded as first minister by the DUP's Peter Robinson. After controversy and conflict, the important powers of policing and security were devolved to the Assembly in April 2010. Despite disputes between the parties, devolution and compromise appear to be working reasonably well in Northern Ireland.

Exercises

Explain and examine the following terms:

Commonwealth	Falklands	Treaty of Rome
decolonialization	Boyne	NATO
direct rule	Stormont	referendum
power-sharing	Trident	special relationship
Sinn Féin	Maastricht	European Commission
EFTA	IRA	pro-marketeer
euro	Unionists	EEA
'consent'	decommissioning	British–Irish Council

Write short essays on the following topics:

1   Should Northern Ireland be united with the Republic of Ireland? Give your reasons.

2   Does the Commonwealth still have a role to play today?

3   Discuss Britain's relationship with the European Union.

4*   Does Britain still have a world role?

Visit **www.routledge.com/textbooks/oakland** for multiple-choice questions, links to related YouTube clips, tips on approaching essay questions, and much, much more.

Further reading

1 Chapters in Black, J. (2000) *Modern British History from 1900*, London: Macmillan
2 Connolly, C. (2003) *Theorizing Ireland*, London: Palgrave Macmillan
3 Dixon, P. (2001) *Northern Ireland: The Politics of War and Peace*, London: Palgrave/ Macmillan
4 Marshall, P.J. (2001) *The Cambridge Illustrated History of the British Empire*, Cambridge: Cambridge University Press
5 Moody, T.W. and Martin, F.X. (2001) *The Course of Irish History*, Cork and Dublin: Mercier Press
6 Srinivasan, K. (2005) *The Rise, Decline and Future of the British Commonwealth*, London: Palgrave Macmillan
7 Tonge, J. (2005) *The New Northern Irish Politics?*, London: Palgrave Macmillan
8 Warner, G. (1994) *British Foreign Policy since 1945*, Oxford: Blackwell
9 Watts, D. and Pilkington, C. (2005) *Britain in the European Union*, Manchester: Manchester University Press
10 Young, J.W. (2000) *Britain and European Unity 1945–1999*, London: Macmillan

Websites

Foreign and Commonwealth Office: www.fco.gov.uk
Department for International Development: www.dfid.gov.uk
The Commonwealth: www.thecommonwealth.org
Ministry of Defence: www.mod.uk
NATO: www.nato.int
European Union: http://europa.eu.int/

6

The legal system

Law and order and the performance of the legal system are of great concern to British people and affect individuals at different levels in their daily lives. In recent years, these issues have been regularly towards the top of public opinion polls about the state of the country. They emphasize worries about the effects of crime, antisocial behaviour, drunkenness and unprovoked violence on the streets, yobbishness and the high incidence of these occurrences among young people. Government and legal structures have attempted to deal with these public concerns, but to little effect according to many people.

Britain does not have a common legal system. Instead, there are three separate elements: those of England and Wales, Scotland and Northern Ireland. These sometimes differ from each other in their procedures and court names. Following devolution, some laws are applicable only to one of the devolved nations although some UK Parliament legislation (e.g. reserved matters) still applies to all of Britain.

To simplify things, this chapter concentrates on the largest element: that of England and Wales, with comparative references to Scotland and Northern Ireland. The Northern Irish legal system is similar to that of England and Wales, but Scotland has historically maintained its independent legal apparatus.

British court cases are divided into civil and criminal law. Civil law involves non-criminal private rights and settles disputes between individuals or organizations. It deals with claims for compensation, financial or otherwise, by a person (claimant) who has suffered loss or damage (such as a breach of contract or a negligent act) at the hands of another (defendant). Civil cases may be decided by negotiation and settlement before trial or by a judge (and sometimes a jury) after trial.

Criminal law protects society by punishing those (the accused or defendants) who commit crimes against the state, such as theft or murder. The state usually prosecutes an individual or group at a trial in order to establish guilt. The result may be a fine or imprisonment. Such punishment is supposed to act as a deterrent to potential offenders, as well as stating society's attitudes on a range of matters.

Legal history

The legal system is one of the oldest and most traditional of British institutions. Its authority and influence are due to its independence from the executive and legislative branches of government. Its role is to interpret and apply the law; serve citizens; control unlawful activities against them and the state; protect civil liberties; and support legitimate government.

However, it has historically been accused of harshness; of supporting vested and political interests; favouring property rather than human rights; maintaining the isolation and mystique of the law; encouraging the delay and expense of legal actions; and being biased against the poor and disadvantaged. It has been criticized for its resistance to reform and the maintenance of professional privileges which can conflict with the public interest.

Some critics feel that the law today has still not adapted to changing conditions, nor understood the needs of contemporary society. Recent miscarriages of justice have embarrassed the police, government and judiciary (judges) and increased public concern about the quality of criminal justice. Similar misgivings are also felt about the expense, delays and functioning of the civil law.

On the other hand, a 'compensation culture' has grown in recent years whereby individuals believe they are entitled to a wide range of remedies for alleged grievances, which are associated with 'human rights'. The employment of the latter can be abused, detract from 'responsibility' and lead to conflicts with other claimed rights. For example, a right to privacy can conflict with the right of expression, both of which are contained in the Human Rights Act, 1998.

The legal system has changed over the centuries in response to changing social structures and philosophies. Contemporary consumer demands, professional pressures and government reforms have forced it to develop, sometimes rapidly and sometimes slowly. Most people in the past were unaffected by the law, but it now involves citizens more directly and to a greater extent. Increased demands are made upon it by individuals, the state and corporate bodies. Concern about crime has emphasized the control role of the criminal law, while increased divorce, family breakdown and a more litigious society have led to a heavier workload for the civil law.

To some extent, the structural differences in the UK legal system are due to the events of history and the internal political development of the British state. Generally, however, English (and gradually British) legal history has been conditioned by two basic concerns: first that the law should be administered by the state in national courts and second that the judges should be independent of royal and political control.

State centralization of the law in England meant that the same laws should be applicable to the whole country. This was achieved by Anglo-Norman monarchs as they rationalized the existing common law and different legal codes. The early courts were therefore mainly based in London, where they dealt with canon (church), criminal, civil and commercial law. But there was an increasing need for courts in local areas outside London to apply the national law. By the end of the twelfth century, London judges travelled throughout England and decided cases locally. In 1327, Edward III appointed magistrates (justices of the peace) in each county who could hold alleged criminals in jail until their later trial by a London judge. The powers of the magistrates were gradually extended and they ran a system of local criminal courts with the London judges. But there was no adequate provision for local civil courts. These were not established until 1846 and a more integrated apparatus of local civil and criminal law was only gradually established at a later stage.

Over the centuries, a growing population, an expanding volume of legal work and increased social and economic complexity necessitated more courts and specialization. But the number of local and London courts in this haphazard historical development resulted in diverse procedures and an overlapping of functions in England and Wales, which hindered implementation of the law. The two periods of major reform to correct this situation were 1873–5, when there was a complete court revision, and 1970–1, when further changes produced the present court system of England and Wales. Similar developments also occurred in Scotland and Ireland.

The second concern was that the judiciary should be independent of the executive and legislative branches of government. Monarchs were responsible for the law in earlier centuries, often interfered in the legal process and could dismiss unsympathetic judges. Judicial independence was achieved in 1701, when the Act of Settlement made judges virtually irremovable from office. This principle has now been relaxed for junior judges, who may be dismissed, and all judges who commit criminal offences are expected to resign. In recent decades under both Labour and Conservative governments, there have been conflicts between judges and politicians, as the judiciary fights to maintain its traditional independence from the executive, its function of interpreting the law and its sentencing powers in individual cases.

Sources of British law

The three main sources of *English/Welsh law* are the common law, statute law and European Union law. The oldest is the *Common Law*, based on the varied local customs of early settlers and invaders. After the Norman Conquest, it became a uniform body of rules, principles and law which was decided and written down by judges in court cases. The same rules still guide judges in their interpretation of statutes and the expansion of the common law.

Common-law decisions form precedents from which judges can find the principles of law to be applied to new cases. Normally today, the creation of new precedents in England and Wales lies with the new Supreme Court, as the highest court of appeal from most courts in the United Kingdom. Its rulings state the current law to be applied by all courts. The tradition of following precedent maintains consistency and continuity, yet it can result in conservative law and fail to take account of changing social conditions.

Statute law was originally made in various forms by the monarch, but the Westminster Parliament gradually became the legislating authority because of its growing power against the monarch. Statutes (Acts of Parliament which create new law) multiplied in the nineteenth and twentieth centuries because rules were needed for a changing, more complex and larger society. Much British law today is in statute form and shows the influence of the state in citizens' lives. Some Acts of the Westminster Parliament are still applicable to England, Wales and often the UK as a whole and are supreme over most other forms of law (except for EU law).

European Union law became part of English (British) law following Britain's entry into the European Economic Community in 1973. EU law takes precedence over British domestic law in many areas and British judges must apply EU law when there is a conflict with Acts of Parliament. EU law and British domestic law therefore now coexist, although over 75 per cent of British law actually originates in the EU.

Scottish law derives from legal principles and rules modelled on both Roman and English law. The sources of Scots law are judge-made law, authoritative legal treatises, EU law and legislation. The first two are the common law of Scotland and are similar to the English common law. Legislation consists of relevant Westminster Acts of Parliament and Scottish Parliament Acts on devolved matters in Scotland.

Northern Irish law has a similar common law tradition to England and Wales. In addition to UK statutes affecting Northern Ireland, the Northern Ireland

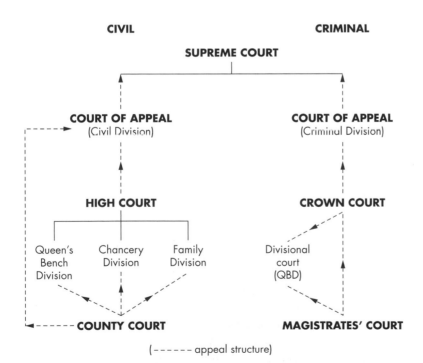

FIGURE 6.1 Civil and criminal courts in England and Wales

Assembly has legislative and executive authority for all devolved matters and can thus make laws in Northern Ireland.

Court structures in England and Wales

The court system is divided into criminal and civil courts (see Figure 6.1) under the central direction of the Ministry of Justice. Increasing numbers of British people have dealings with the different courts at various levels. These are not, therefore, abstract structures remote from the daily realities of British life and their activities are widely reported and commented upon.

Criminal courts

There are two levels of criminal courts. The lower and busiest is the magistrates' court, which deals with summary (less serious) cases and handles over 95 per cent of all criminal matters. The more serious (indictable) criminal offences, like murder, are tried by the higher court, the Crown court.

Magistrates' courts serve local areas in England and Wales. Two types of officials try cases in the courts: justices of the peace (JPs) and district judges.

Most magistrates' courts are presided over by 30,000 lay magistrates (JPs). They are part-time judicial officials chosen from among the general public; hear cases without a jury; receive no salary for their services (only expenses); and have some legal training before sitting in court. Magistrates may be motivated by the desire to perform a public service or the prestige of the position. They sit daily in big cities and less frequently in rural areas. Their office dates from 1327 and illustrates a legal system in which the ordinary person is judged by other citizens, rather than by professionals.

Magistrates are now for an interim period appointed by the Lord Chancellor in the Ministry of Justice, who receives approved names from the Lord Chief Justice (head of the judiciary in England and Wales) who will have been given suitable recommendations by local advisory committees. In the past magistrates were white middle- or upper-class males who were prominent in the local community, such as landowners, doctors, retired military officers and businessmen, but they are now recruited from a wider and more representative range of social, ethnic and gender backgrounds.

The magistrates' court has an average of three JPs when hearing cases, usually composed of both men and women. They decide a case on the facts and pronounce the punishment, if any is to be given. They are advised on points of law by their clerk, who is a legally qualified, full-time official and a professional element in the system. The clerk is restricted to an advisory role and must not be involved in the magistrates' decision-making, but is now able to handle some minor judicial tasks.

Each person accused of a criminal offence (defendant) must usually appear first before a magistrates' court. The court can itself try summary (minor) offences and some indictable(serious)/summary offences ('either-way offences'). The magistrates also decide whether a person should be sent for trial at the higher Crown court in serious cases.

Magistrates have limited powers of punishment. They may impose fines of up to £5,000 for each offence, or send people to prison for six months on each offence up to a maximum of one year. They prefer not to imprison if a fine or other punishment is sufficient and the majority of penalties are fines. In either-way offences, they can send a person to the Crown court for sentencing if they lack sufficient powers.

There is a need for uniform punishments in magistrates' courts. However, sentences vary in different parts of the country. This factor, in addition to alleged bias and the amateur status of JPs, has led to criticism of the system. There have been proposals to replace magistrates with lawyers or other experts. However, these suggestions are criticized by those who oppose the professionalization of the legal process and who argue that such changes would not necessarily result in greater competence or justice.

An important function of the magistrates is to decide cases involving young persons under eighteen in youth courts. Media reports of these cases must not normally identify the accused and there is a range of punishments for those found guilty. Youth courts play a central role, particularly at a time when many crimes are committed by young people aged under sixteen. The previous Labour government tried to encourage tougher treatment for young offenders. Magistrates' courts also handle limited civil matters involving family problems, divorce and road traffic offences.

District Judges in the magistrates' court are qualified lawyers and full-time officials, are paid by the state, usually sit alone to hear and decide cases and work mainly in the large cities. Since the magistrates' system is divided between amateur JPs and the professional district judges, it is sometimes argued that the latter should be used to replace the former on a national basis. But this proposal has been resisted by those who wish to retain the civilian element in the magistrates' courts.

The higher *Crown courts*, such as the Central Criminal Court in London (popularly known as the Old Bailey), are situated in about seventy-eight cities in England and Wales and are centrally administered by the Ministry of Justice.

The Crown court has jurisdiction over all indictable criminal offences and innocence or guilt after a trial is decided by a jury of twelve citizens. After it has reached its decision on the facts of the case, sentence is passed by the judge who is in charge of proceedings throughout the trial.

In *Scotland*, minor criminal cases are tried summarily by lay justices of the peace in district courts (equivalent to English magistrates' courts). Sheriffs' courts deal with more serious offences where the sheriff sits alone to hear summary offences and is helped by a jury (fifteen members) for indictable cases. The most

PLATE 6.1 The Old Bailey central criminal court in the City of London has been the scene of many famous trials in British legal history and is now a Crown court centre. *(Kevin Foy/Rex Features)*

PLATE 6.2 A contemporary Crown court, which contains many of the traditional features such as the dock in which the accused person sits, the judge's chair and bench, jury seats, and prosecution and defence benches.
(*Shout/Rex Features*)

serious cases, such as murder and rape, are handled by the High Court of Justiciary in major urban centres and are heard by a judge and a jury of fifteen lay people. *Northern Irish* criminal courts follow the system in England and Wales with lower magistrates' courts and higher Crown courts (the latter generally with a judge and jury).

Criminal appeal courts

The appeal structure (see Figure 6.1) is supposed to be a safeguard against mistakes and miscarriages of justice, but the number of such cases has increased, resulting in a great deal of publicity and concern. They have been caused by police tampering with or withholding evidence, police pressure to induce confessions, and the unreliability of some forensic evidence. Appeal courts are criticized for their handling of some appeals and an independent authority (the Criminal Cases Review Commission) was created in 1995. It reviews alleged miscarriages of justice and directs some cases back to the appeal courts, which may quash convictions or order new trials.

Appeals to a higher court can be expensive and difficult and permission must usually be granted by a lower court. Appeals may be made against conviction or

PLATE 6.3 The newly established UK Supreme Court (2009) in Parliament Square, London, which took over the role of the House of Lords as the supreme court of appeal for many purposes for most parts of the UK.
(Rex Features)

sentence and can be brought on grounds of fact and law. If successful, the higher court may quash the conviction, reduce the sentence or order a new trial. The prosecution can also appeal against a lenient punishment and a heavier sentence may be substituted.

Crown courts hear appeals from magistrates' courts and both may appeal on matters of law to a divisional court of the Queen's Bench Division. Appeals from the Crown court are made to the Criminal Division of the Court of Appeal. Appeals may then go to the Supreme Court in London as the highest court in England and Wales (and for some cases from Scotland and Northern Ireland). But permission is only granted if a point of law of public importance is involved. Up to five Supreme Court Justices (out of twelve) hear the case and their decision represents the current state of the law.

In *Scotland*, the High Court of Justiciary in Edinburgh tries criminal cases and is the supreme court for criminal appeals. *Northern Ireland* has its own appeal courts, but the Supreme Court in London may also be used.

Civil courts

Civil law proceedings in England and Wales are brought either in the county court (which deals with 90 per cent of civil cases) or in the High Court (see Figure 6.1). Less expensive and complex actions are dealt with in the county court rather than the High Court, and most civil disputes do not reach court at all. Various types of tribunals, such as those dealing with employment and discrimination matters, may also be used by the civil law.

England and Wales are divided into some 250 districts with a *county court* for each district. The county court handles a range of money, property, contract, divorce and family matters and a district judge usually sits alone when hearing and deciding cases.

The *High Court of Justice* has its main centre in London, with branches throughout England and Wales. It is divided into three divisions which specialize in specific matters. The *Queen's Bench Division* has a wide jurisdiction, including contract and negligence cases; the *Chancery Court Division* is concerned with commercial, financial and succession matters; and the *Family Division* deals with domestic issues such as marriage, divorce, property and the custody of children.

In *Scotland*, the sheriff's court deals with most civil actions, because its jurisdiction is not financially limited, although the higher Court of Session may

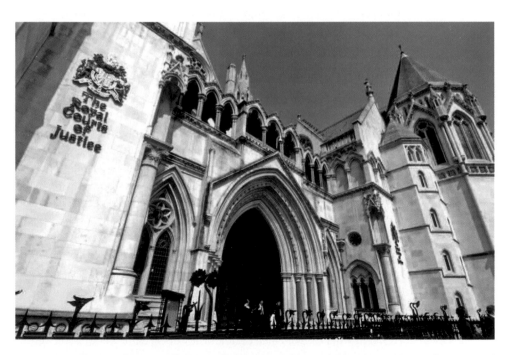

PLATE 6.4 The Royal Courts of Justice, the Strand, London, which contains the High Court and the Courts of Appeal (civil and criminal).
(Alex Segre/Rex Features)

also be used for some cases. The *Northern Irish* High Court handles most civil cases.

Civil appeal courts

The High Court hears appeals from magistrates' courts and county courts. However the main avenue of appeal is to the Court of Appeal (Civil Division), which deals with appeals from all lower civil courts on questions of law and fact. It can reverse or amend decisions, or sometimes order a new trial.

Appeals from the Court of Appeal may be made to the Supreme Court. The appellant must normally have obtained permission from either the Court of Appeal or the Supreme Court. Appeals are usually restricted to points of law where an important legal issue is at stake. In *Scotland* at present, civil appeals are made first to a sheriff-principal, then to the Court of Session and finally to the Supreme Court in London. The *Northern Irish* Court of Appeal hears appeal cases and further appeals may be made to the Supreme Court.

Civil and criminal procedure in England and Wales

Many features of civil and criminal procedure in England and Wales are similar to those in Scotland and Northern Ireland.

Civil procedure

A civil action in the county court or the High Court begins when the claimant serves documents with details of a claim on the defendant. If the defendant defends the action, documents are prepared and circulated to all parties and the case proceeds to trial and judgement. A decision in civil cases is reached on the balance of probabilities. The court also decides the expenses (damages) of the action, which may be considerable, and the loser often pays both personal and the opponent's costs. Civil law procedures have been reorganized, streamlined and simplified since 1999 because of concern about the efficiency of the system, with its delays and expense. Much of the High Court's work has been transferred to the county court. Procedural rules between the two courts have been unified. Active court management is now in place, with judges setting the pace of litigation and cheaper, quicker forms of settlement in other courts have been implemented, such as those dealing with matters in small claims courts. Nevertheless, it is advisable that disputes be settled by negotiation and other avenues rather than by a court trial in order to avoid high costs and any uncertainty about a trial result. Most civil disputes are in fact decided out of court.

Criminal procedure

Crimes are offences against the laws of the state, and it is the state which usually brings a person to trial. Prior to 1985, the police in England and Wales were responsible for prosecuting criminal cases, but the Crown Prosecution Service (CPS) now performs this role. It is independent of the police, financed by the state and staffed by state lawyers. There has been criticism of the performance of the CPS, which has suffered from understaffing and underfunding. The CPS and its head (the Director of Public Prosecutions – DPP) have the final word in deciding whether to proceed with cases. In *Scotland*, prosecution duties rest with the Crown Office and Procurator-Fiscal Service and in *Northern Ireland* with the police and the DPP.

Arrests for most criminal offences are made by the police, although any citizen can make a 'citizen's arrest'. After criticism of the police for their arrest, questioning and charging practices, they now operate under codes of practice, which lay down strict procedures for the protection of suspects. The police cannot usually interrogate people, nor detain them at a police station if they have not been arrested. Once persons have been arrested, had their rights read to them and been charged with an offence, they must be brought before a magistrates' court, normally within twenty-four hours. In serious cases and after arrest, a person can be held for up to ninety-six hours. After this period, the suspect must be released if no charges are brought.

When a person appears before a magistrates' court prior to a trial, the magistrates can grant or refuse bail (freedom from custody). If bail is refused, a person is kept in custody in a remand centre or in prison. If bail is granted, the individual is freed until a later court appearance. The court may require assurances from the accused about conduct while on bail, such as residence in a specific area and reporting to a police station.

Application for bail is a legal right, since the accused has not yet been found guilty of a crime, and there should be strong reasons for refusing it. There is concern that those who are refused bail are, at their later trial, either found not guilty or are punished only by a fine. The system thus holds alleged criminals on remand to await trial and this increases overcrowding in prisons. But there is also great public concern about accused persons who commit further serious offences while free on bail.

Criminal trials in the magistrates' and Crown courts are usually open to the public. However, the media can only report the court proceedings and must not comment upon them while the trial is in progress (the *sub judice* or 'pending litigation' rule).

The accused enters the dock, the charge is read and they plead 'guilty' or 'not guilty'. On a 'guilty' plea, the person may be sentenced after a statement of the facts by the prosecution. However, sentencing can also be deferred to a later date. On a 'not guilty' plea, the trial proceeds in order to establish the person's

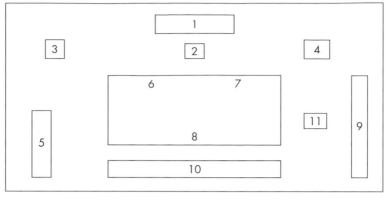

1 Magistrates
2 Clerk to the Justices
3 Defendant
4 Witness
5 The press
6 Defending lawyer
7 Presecuting lawyer
8 Probation officers
9 Witnesses who have
  given evidence
10 The public
11 Court ushers

FIGURE 6.2 A typical magistrates' court in action

innocence or guilt. An individual is innocent until proved guilty and it is the responsibility of the prosecution to prove guilt beyond a reasonable doubt. If proof is not achieved, a 'not guilty' verdict is returned by magistrates in the magistrates' court or by the jury in the Crown court. In *Scotland*, there is an additional possible verdict of 'not proven' (lack of evidence to convict, but judge or jury unconvinced of the innocence of the defendant).

The prosecution and defence of the accused are usually performed by solicitors in magistrates' courts and by barristers and solicitor-advocates in Crown courts, but it is possible to defend oneself. British trials are adversarial contests between defence and prosecution. Each side calls witnesses in support of their case, who may be questioned by the other side. The rules of evidence and procedure in this contest are complicated and must be strictly observed. The accused may remain silent on arrest, charge and trial and need not give evidence. However, the right to silence has now been limited, which means that the police must warn arrestees that their silence may adversely affect their later defence. The prosecution and judge at the trial may comment on silence and it may influence the decision of juries and magistrates.

It is argued that the adversarial nature of criminal trials can result either in the conviction of innocent people or in the guilty escaping conviction. It is suggested that the inquisitorial system of other European countries would be better. This allows the prior questioning of suspects and establishing of facts to be carried out by professional impartial interrogators (or judges) rather than the police.

The judge in the Crown court and the magistrates in the magistrates' court are controlling influences in the battle between defence and prosecution. They

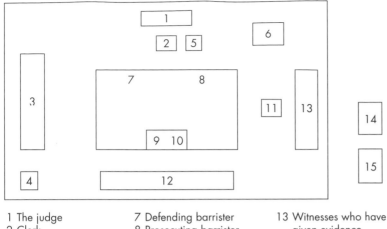

1 The judge
2 Clerk
3 The jury
4 The press
5 Shorthand writer
6 Witness

7 Defending barrister
8 Prosecuting barrister
9 Prison officer
10 The acused
11 Court usher
12 The public

13 Witnesses who have
   given evidence
14 Waiting witnesses
   for prosecution
15 Waiting witnesses
   for defence

FIGURE 6.3 A typical Crown court in action

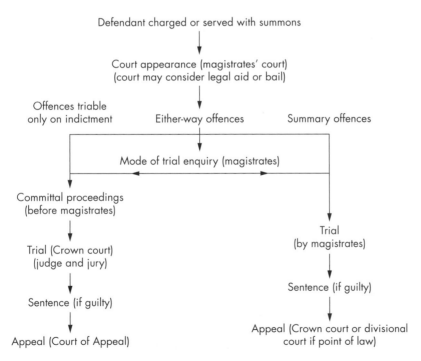

FIGURE 6.4 Criminal procedure

apply the rules of the court and give directions on procedure and evidence, but they should not interfere too actively, nor show bias. After the prosecution and the defence have concluded their cases, the magistrates decide both the verdict and sentence. In the Crown court, the jury delivers the verdict after the judge has given a summing-up and the judge then pronounces sentence (which may be deferred).

The jury

Trial by jury is an ancient and important feature of British justice. It has declined in civil cases (except for libel and fraud), but is the main element in criminal trials in the Crown court for indictable offences. Most British residents are obliged to undertake jury service when summoned.

Before the start of a criminal trial in the Crown court, twelve jurors are chosen from a list of thirty names randomly selected from electoral registers. They listen to the evidence at the trial and give their verdict on the facts, after having been isolated in a room for their deliberations. If a jury cannot reach a decision, it will be discharged and a new one sworn in. The accused can thus be tried twice (double jeopardy) for the same offence (as in appeals which order a new trial or in the re-hearing of cases in the interests of justice where new and compelling evidence appears). Such results are an exception to the principle that a person can only be tried once for the same offence. In most cases, the jury reaches a decision. The judge accepts a majority (rather than a unanimous) verdict after the jury has deliberated for more than two hours, if there are no more than two dissenters (ten to two). The jury does not decide the punishment or sentence, except in some civil cases, where it awards damages.

The jury system is the citizen's link with the legal process. It is supposed to safeguard individual liberty and justice because a common-sense decision on the facts either to punish or acquit is taken by fellow citizens. Yet the system has been criticized because of high acquittal rates, allegedly unsuitable or subjective jurors, the intimidation of and threats against jurors and the need to save time and expense. Some critics wish to replace the jury with 'experts', and the Labour government reduced the right to jury trial in some 'either-way' offences and in some cases of jury intimidation trials may now be heard and decided by a single judge without a jury. However, it seems that the jury system, as an essential feature of British justice, will continue for most relevant cases.

Legal aid and access to legal services

The British legal aid system was created in 1949 and was only the second of its type in the world. It was intended to help eligible persons who could not afford legal representation and advice in criminal and civil matters to have their bills paid by the state. Since then, eligibility for legal aid has been reformed. The granting of legal aid now depends upon the merit of the case and income levels, so that, for example, families with an annual income of more than £27,500 are excluded from civil legal aid. Although criminal legal aid is available for anyone charged with a crime, a guilty person can be ordered to reimburse the aid. Recipients of both civil and criminal legal aid may also be asked to make contributions and meet charges.

Critics argue that legal aid has effectively been reduced and many legal firms (and barristers) have withdrawn from the system because it is unprofitable. In this view, access to legal services is restricted to the poorest members of society (for whom legal aid may be available without contribution) and the richest minority (who are able to pay their own legal fees). Most people on medium incomes will usually have to pay their own civil and criminal expenses in one form or another if they are involved in legal actions.

Since fewer people are now eligible for state help at a time when demand is rising, it is argued that the provision of legal aid should be expanded and liberalized. But increased demand results in a more expensive system (costing £2 billion in 2009) and the Labour government seems to have increased the 'means testing' of legal aid by which any help is tied to income.

A recent reform may help those people who wish to start personal injury civil actions but who cannot afford the cost. Clients can enter into conditional agreements with lawyers, in which payment of legal fees on a percentage basis is only made if the client wins ('no win-no fee'). This scheme may be extended to most civil disputes which involve money or damages (and possibly criminal matters). However, critics argue that such work only appeals to lawyers if there is a reasonable chance of winning; it will not solve the problem of insuring against the cost of losing; and lawyers may impose huge fees.

Law and order

Crime and punishment

Law and order in Britain are serious issues, which are of great concern to people and on which political parties promise action. According to government analyses in 2007, Britain spent more than other industrialized countries on public order and safety (at 2.5 per cent of GDP). But EU statistics in 2009 suggested that it had more violent crime than other European countries. A central problem in evaluating the extent of crime in Britain is that there is significant non-reporting of such offences as assaults, burglary and rape; the level of unsolved crime remains high; and there are conflicting sets of crime statistics and interpretations.

Overall there were 4.5 million crimes recorded by the 43 police forces in England and Wales in 2009. Home Office figures based on police data showed that there was a 7 per cent decrease in overall reported crime (such as falls of 16 per cent in car crime, 11 per cent in criminal damage and 3 per cent in violence against the person). There was also a further fall in the level of gun and knife crime, including a 21 per cent decline in fatal stabbings. Household burglaries fell by 3 per cent, robberies by 5 per cent and fraud and forgery by 9 per cent. But there was a rise in serious sex crimes and violence involving injury, and public perception was that crime was increasing. Media sources suggested that the government and police admitted that public distrust of national statistics and authority meant that some people were unwilling to believe the drop in reported crime.

The 2009 British Crime Survey, which is based on replies from respondents who actually experience crime, agreed with the 7 per cent fall in overall crime. But it said that the level of violence was stable and that a 4 per cent increase in violence where an injury was caused (39,000 offences) was not statistically signficant. It also reported that since Labour came to power in 1997, burglary had fallen by 54 per cent, violence by 41 per cent and vehicle crime by 60 per cent. However, critics point out that the Survey underestimates the extent of crime because it does not cover the under-sixteens, the homeless, students in halls of residence, people in care homes or business crime. It may also fail to obtain real levels of inner-city crime because surveys do not always get responses in these areas.

The big falls in burglary and car theft were partly a result of more homes having window locks and burglar alarms and more vehicles being fitted with immobilisers and central locking. The Association of Chief Police Officers said that the figures showed that the risk of being a victim of crime (22 per cent) was at its lowest level for thirty years. There has also been better reporting of low-level crime, domestic violence and sexual offences, and the number of crimes which affect most people, such as burglary, robbery and vehicle theft, has decreased. However, although robbery represents only 2 per cent of the total, street crime is a politically high-profile issue, and 40 per cent of this type of crime occurs in London.

Other research surveys (such as the Offending, Crime and Justice survey) suggest that 10 per cent of offenders are responsible for 60 per cent of offences and that serious and prolific offenders amount to 1 per cent of the population. However, it is estimated that only one in fifty crimes results in a conviction and that only 23 per cent of all crimes are recorded by the police. Opinion polls regularly suggest that 50 per cent of victims do not report incidents to the police because they lack confidence that the criminals will be caught.

Disturbing aspects of these statistics are the use of knives and firearms in criminal acts, particularly those connected to gang violence and serious organized crime (leading to demands that all police officers should be armed); the increased amount of drug- and alcohol-related crime and violence; and the number of offences committed by young people. Britain has a serious problem with young offenders, the peak age for committing crime is fifteen, and 10 per cent of reported criminal offences are committed by teenagers under sixteen. There is a widespread membership of gangs in this group and adherence to gangster culture (allegedly encouraged by rap music lyrics) in which the carrying and use of guns and knives are prevalent. Binge drinking in town and city centres has also increased and led to more violence on the streets. Critics argue that the previous Labour government's decision to extend drinking hours in pubs, clubs and restaurants from 2005 has only increased the problem.

Respondents to polls think the causes of crime in Britain are a lack of parental discipline and male role models; the breakdown of family and community structures; drugs; alcohol; lenient sentencing by the courts; gangs; unemployment; a lack of school discipline; poverty; television; poor policing; teenage boredom; and a lack of free-time facilities for young people. Tony Blair in 2005 laid the blame on parents and earlier in opposition had tried to ease public concern by promising 'zero tolerance' for crime and being 'tough on crime and the causes of crime'. The Labour government introduced stricter punishment (particularly for young people), curfews and restrictions on persistent offenders, longer jail terms and greater protection for the public. But polls in the 2000s showed that people did not think that the government had delivered on its law and order promises, despite its claim that street crime initiatives were reducing this type of offence.

A person found guilty of a first criminal offence may either receive no punishment or be placed on probation for a period under the supervision of probation officers. Other punishments for adults are fines or imprisonment (for those over twenty-one), which vary according to the severity of the offence and any previous convictions. Stricter sentencing will lead to more prisoners and 18 per cent of convicted persons are imprisoned, a higher rate than in other European countries. In 2009, the UK prison population was 93,574 with 82,000 sentenced and remand prisoners in England and Wales, and 2.5 per cent of these prisoners were under eighteen. The figures have increased since the mid-1990s and are the highest in Europe. Prison overcrowding is a problem and prisons are now at full capacity.

Alternatives to prison are community rehabilitation orders (serving the community in some capacity for a number of hours over a number of months) and suspended prison sentences (dependent upon no further offences being committed for a specified period). A recent experiment is 'tagging' (arm or leg bracelets connected electronically to local police stations) whereby offenders are confined to a specific area and have to observe a curfew. The tag is activated if these conditions are broken. However, tagging has not proved to be a success according to reports in 2005 which suggested that the level of reoffending after and even during tagging is very high. The latest attempt to control yobbish behaviour is the antisocial behaviour order (ASBO), which bans offenders from particular areas or prohibits various forms of thuggish activity. The number of ASBOs reached its height in 2005 before declining, and then started to increase again in 2009.

Young people may be punished by fines (under seventeen), taken into local authority care, confined in a young offenders' institution (Youth Prison) for those between seventeen and twenty, or undergo supervision in the community. Reoffending among young people after a custodial sentence is high, but supervision outside institutions leads less often to re-offending.

The death penalty by hanging for murder was abolished in 1965. The House of Commons has since voted on several occasions against its re-imposition. Earlier polls surprisingly showed that only one in four Britons want the restoration of the death penalty for murder (a much lower figure than previously). However, an Ipsos MORI poll in 2009 revealed that 70 per cent of respondents thought that the UK should still have the death penalty as the maximum possible penalty for at least one of crimes such as paedophilia (31 per cent), terrorism (37), adult murder (51), child murder (62) or child rape (39). The public also seem to support the harsh treatment of criminal offenders and argue that more sympathy and aid should be given to the victims of crime. The government has supported such victims with financial compensation, but its programmes have not satisfied critics or the victims.

Many British people feel that the penalties for criminal offences are inadequate as deterrents to prevent crime. But many prisons are overcrowded, old and decayed, lack humane facilities, are unfitted for a modern penal system and their personnel are understaffed and overworked. Prison conditions have resulted in serious disorder and riots in recent years, low morale among prisoners and prison staff and an increase in suicides by prison inmates. Debates about punishment as opposed to the rehabilitation of offenders continue. Yet proposals to improve the situation usually encounter the problem of expense, although the government is building more courts and prisons. Some prisons and prison services (such as escorting prisoners to court) have now been privatized.

A majority of prisoners are not reformed by their sentences. Some 60 per cent are reconvicted for later offences, and fear of prison or punishment does not seem to act as a deterrent. Critics suggest that jail terms should be cut (with weekend-only prisoners) and that institutions should be humanized and prisoners given a sense of purpose. Alternatives to custodial sentences, such as supervised housing, probation hostels and supervised work projects are also advocated. But others argue that the main concern of the criminal system should be punishment and not rehabilitation.

Law enforcement and the police

The armed forces in Britain are subordinate to the civilian government and are used only for self-defence and emergency situations. An exception has been the deployment since 1969 of the army in Northern Ireland, where they supported the Royal Ulster Constabulary (now the Police Service of Northern Ireland). But there are proposals that the military could help the police to counter organized crime involving drugs, illegal immigration and computer hacking.

PLATE 6.5 Demonstrators against the banks and economic system confront the police in violent clashes in the City of London during the G-20 summit, 1 April 2009, with the Royal Bank of Scotland (RBS) as a focus for protest.
(Matt Somerville/UCF/Rex Features)

The maintenance of law and order rests mainly with the civilian police. The oldest police force is the Metropolitan Police, founded in 1829 by Sir Robert Peel to fight crime in London, and from which the modern forces grew. Today there is no single national police force but instead fifty-two independent forces (forty-three in England and Wales), which undertake law enforcement in county or regional areas, with the Metropolitan Police being responsible for policing London from its headquarters at New Scotland Yard. Regional forces (which may be reduced in England and Wales through mergers) are under the political control of local police committees. Daily authority rests with the head of regional forces (Chief Constable), who has organizational independence and responsibility for the actions of the force.

There were 141,000 policemen and women in Britain in 2009, or about one officer for every 428 people. Although figures have increased in recent years, critics argue that the forces are undermanned and recruitment is difficult. Only a disproportionately small number are from non-white ethnic communities. Many of their members are hostile to or sceptical of the police, although there have been attempts to recruit more of them to the forces, with varying degrees of success. Community Support Officers and part-time special constables provide supplementary help to the regular police in security duties and give a greater street presence.

The police are not allowed to join trade unions or strike, but they do have staff associations to represent their interests. They are subject to the law, and can be sued or prosecuted for any wrongdoing in the course of their work. Individuals can complain about police actions to an Independent Police Complaints Commission which, it is hoped, might provide a stronger role than previous models. However, critics still argue that complaints procedures are unsatisfactory and that democratic control of the police should be strengthened.

The police, with their distinctive helmets and lack of firearms, are often regarded as a typical British institution. They used to embody a presence in the local community by 'walking the beat' and personified fairness, stolidity, friend-liness, helpfulness and incorruptibility. These virtues still exist to a degree and the traditional view is that the police should control the community by consent rather than force and that they should be visible in local areas.

However, in recent years, the police have been taken off foot patrols, put into cars to increase effectiveness and mobility, and more are now armed and trained in riot-control programmes. They have been accused of institutional racism, corruption, brutality, excessive use of force, perverting the course of justice and tampering with evidence in criminal trials. Some of these accusations have been proved. They have lowered the image of the police as well as their morale and have contributed to a loss of public confidence. Additionally, the previous Labour government was concerned to reform the police forces and what it regarded as some of their 'inappropriate' practices.

The police tread a thin line in community activities, strikes and demon-strations. They are in the middle of opposing forces, much is expected of them and uncertain law and politically correct attitudes sometimes hinder their effectiveness. The problems of violent crime, organized criminality, gangs, rela-tions with ethnic communities and an increasingly complex society have made their job more difficult. The police are trying to find ways of adequately and fairly controlling a changing society. They are concerned about their image, but insist that their primary duty is to maintain law and order.

The legal profession

The legal profession in England and Wales is divided into two principal types of lawyer: barristers and solicitors. Each branch has its own vested interests and jurisdiction and fiercely protects its position. This system is criticized because of a duplication of services, delay and expense. But legal services have been reformed to benefit consumers, promote competition and give easier access to the law. Legislation in 2007 suggests further inroads into the profession's traditional self-regulatory role and exclusive representative status, the opening up of legal services and firms to commercial ownership, the sharing of functions with other professionals and better provision for consumer complaints against lawyers.

An independent, lay-dominated Legal Services Board now oversees the regulation of all types of lawyers and their professional bodies in England and Wales. It controls their accountability to clients and society; acts in the interests of the consumers of legal services; and reforms and modernizes the legal services market place. This regulatory function is shared with the regulators of the legal profession, such as the Law Society and the Bar Council, which have responsibility for the everyday regulation of lawyers.

There are 100,000 *solicitors*, who practise mainly in private firms, but also in local and central government, legal centres and industry. They are represented by their professional body, the Law Society but regulation is performed by the separate and independent Solicitors Regulation Authority.

Although the solicitors' profession is a middle-class one it is increasingly attracting members from relatively wide ethnic and gender spectrums of society. Solicitors deal with general legal work, although many now specialize in one area of the law. Their firms (or partnerships) offer services such as conveyancing (the buying and selling of property); probate (wills and succession after death); family matters; criminal and civil litigation; commercial cases; and tax and financial affairs.

The client with a legal problem will first approach a solicitor, who is often able to deal with all aspects of the case. Solicitors were once able only to appear (rights of audience) for their clients in the lower courts (county and magistrates' courts) with cases in higher courts having to be handed to a barrister. This expensive practice has now been reformed and solicitor-advocates can appear in higher courts.

In order to become a solicitor it is usual to have a university degree, not necessarily in law. After passing further professional examinations organized by the Law Society and other colleges, the student serves a practical apprenticeship as a trainee solicitor with an established solicitor for some two years. After this total period of about six years' education and training, the new solicitor is able to practise the law.

There are some 16,000 annual complaints by dissatisfied clients against solicitors. These are handled by the Legal Complaints Service, but due to criticism of this body the function will pass to the Office for Legal Complaints (OLC), launched in 2009 and operative by the end of 2010. It is a consumer-focused organisation and will develop a single independent ombudsman scheme which will deal with complaints by consumers about legal services and all professional providers of legal services including barristers.

There are 10,000 *barristers* in private practice, who have the right to appear before any court in England and Wales. They belong to the Bar, which is an ancient professional legal institution regulated by the Bar Council and four Inns of Court in London (Gray's Inn, Lincoln's Inn, the Middle Temple and the Inner Temple),

PLATE 6.6 The Middle Temple, one of the four Inns of Court in London, where student barristers become members and often work in chambers there on becoming fully qualified.
(Frank Monaco/Rex Features)

where many barristers work in chambers or offices. The Bar Standards Board is an independent body of the Bar Council and responsible for complaints against barristers until the OLC becomes fully operative.

Barristers have two functions: to give specialized advice on legal matters and to act as advocates in the courts. Historically, the general public could not approach a barrister directly, but must have been introduced by a solicitor. This regulation has now been relaxed for some clients.

In order to become a barrister one must usually have a university degree, pass professional examinations and become a member of an Inn of Court. The student must dine in the Inn for a number of terms before being 'called to the Bar', or accepted as a barrister. They must then serve for a one-year period (pupillage) under a practising barrister. After this five-year training period, the new barrister can practise alone.

Barristers are self-employed individuals who practise from chambers (or offices), together with other barristers. The barrister's career starts as a 'junior' handling minor briefs (or cases). They may have difficulty in earning a living or in becoming established in the early years of practice, with the result that many barristers drop out and enter other fields. Should the barrister persist and build up a successful practice as a junior, they may 'take silk' and become a Queen's Counsel (QC). A QC is a senior barrister who can charge higher fees for their work but who is then excluded from appearing in lesser cases. Appointment as a QC may lead to a future position as a judge and it is regarded as a necessary career step for the ambitious.

The *judges* constitute the judiciary, or independent third branch of the constitutional system. There are a relatively small number of judges at various levels of seniority, who are located in most large cities and in the higher courts in London. They are chosen from the ranks of senior barristers, although solicitors are now eligible for some of the lower posts. The highest appointments are made by the Crown on the advice of the prime minister and lower positions on the advice of the Lord Chancellor. This appointments procedure has been criticized because it rests with the Lord Chancellor and the senior judiciary, who consequently hold much power and patronage. In an attempt to combat 'elitism' and 'cronyism', more judgeships are now advertised for open competition and appointments, under present reforms, will be made by an independent Judicial Appointments Commission.

The Lord Chancellor is a political appointee of the sitting government in charge of the Ministry of Justice; effective head of the legal system and profession; and a member of the Cabinet. It has been argued that this office should be abolished because of its political connections, and the process of abolition is under way. Other judgeships are supposedly made on non-political grounds. Senior judges cannot be removed from office until the retirement age of seventy-five, although junior judges can be dismissed for good reason before the retirement age of seventy-two. There have been proposals that complaints against judges and their dismissal should be handled by a complaints board and that judges should be more easily removable from office. However, the existing measures have been designed to ensure the independence of the judiciary and its freedom from political involvement.

Judges are regarded by many as socially and educationally elitist and remote from ordinary life. Their profession is overwhelmingly male. They are seen as people who will not cause embarrassment to the establishment and who tend to support the accepted wisdom and status quo. However, they do rule against government policies and their powers of independence have arguably been increased under the Human Rights Act (1998). They have increasingly argued publicly in the media and elsewhere and have frequently been in dispute with governments about their jurisdiction in areas such as sentences for murder. The judiciary is changing to admit more women, ethnic minorities and people with lower-class and educationally diverse backgrounds. But, although over half of law students are female, there are few women judges (or QCs and senior partners in solicitors' firms).

The judiciary tends to be old in years because judgeships are normally awarded to senior practising lawyers and there is no career structure that people may join early in life. A lawyer's income may be greatly reduced on accepting a judgeship, but the honour and added security are regarded as some compensation.

There are promotional steps within the judiciary from recorder to circuit judge to High Court judge, and thence to the Court of Appeal and the Supreme Court.

The legal professions in *Scotland* and *Northern Ireland* are also divided. Scotland has some 400 practising advocates (barristers) and 8,250 solicitors. Advocates practise as individuals, do not work from chambers and are independent of one another. Scottish solicitors usually operate in partnership with other solicitors. Northern Ireland has 2,300 solicitors and about 450 barristers.

Attitudes to the legal system and crime

Britain historically has not been thought of as a litigious society. People usually avoid the difficulty and cost of legal actions if possible and regard the law and lawyers as a last resort in resolving their problems. Yet recently more Britons have been using the courts in order to gain satisfaction for what they consider to be their 'rights' and a 'compensation culture' has grown, aided by specialist lawyers. Large damages may be awarded in matters ranging from libel cases to complaints about schools, companies, doctors, hospitals and the criminal law system. The Human Rights Act 1998 is also being increasingly used by individuals to assert their claims.

Attitudes about the legal system and crime do vary somewhat over time and some findings contradict others. MORI polls in the early 2000s reported that a majority of people had little confidence in the legal system. Some 47 per cent of respondents in 2000 were dissatisfied with the courts, while 32 per cent were satisfied. A MORI poll in 2003 (see Table 6.1) broadly followed previous polls.

These findings have been reflected in later polls and, except for the police, do not show significant satisfaction with legal institutions. This may reflect greater

TABLE 6.1 Confidence in parts of the criminal justice system in England and Wales (%), 2003

	Very or fairly confident	Not very or not at all confident
Local police	76	22
Police in England and Wales	73	25
Probation service	59	29
Crown Prosecution Service	57	36
Magistrates	55	38
Judges	54	43
Courts	51	44
Prisons	48	43
Youth courts	46	38

Source: MORI, 2003

public familiarity with local police and their performance than with bodies like the courts, judges and prisons. The police at national and local level (perhaps surprisingly given frequent accusations of brutality at demonstrations) are the most admired professional group after doctors and nurses. Lawyers are the least admired.

Yet independent research in 2009 by the Criminal Justice Inspectorate found that 80 per cent of victims and witnesses (those caught up in the immediate realities of crime) were satisfied with their experience of the criminal justice system. Some people are dissatisfied and argue that offenders are not sufficiently punished because of a lack of capacity in the courts and prisons and that the criminal system favours the needs of criminals rather than the victims of crime and the wider public. Other polls have shown support for legal reforms (particularly in the civil courts from 1999) and a MORI poll published by the Home Office in 2009 reported that 85 per cent of respondents supported the Proceeds of Crime Act, 2002 whereby criminals have their assets seized in recompense for their crimes. Over half of the respondents felt that the Act was an effective (or very effective) crime deterrent. But there is still a continuing desire to see more government action on the legal system's remaining delays, risks, penalties, costs, inefficiencies and lack of resources. An Ipsos MORI poll for Channel 4 in 2009 found that 73 per cent of respondents thought that the views of the public were being ignored by politicians and the government when setting maximum sentences and penalties for serious crimes and 76 per cent of respondents believed that there should be more open debate about the penalties for serious crimes, including the death penalty.

An Ipsos MORI poll in April 2010 reported that crime, law and order, violence, vandalism and antisocial behaviour were main concerns for many Britons in third place after the economy and immigration. Yet Home Office and British Crime Survey figures in 2009 showed a decrease in overall crime and revealed that fear of crime and antisocial behaviour, which had not coincided with the underlying fall in the crime rate, was now following the same pattern. The percentage of people who said that they were 'very worried' about violent crime had decreased from 14 to 13 per cent; the percentage of those who were 'very worried' about burglary was down from 11 to 10 per cent; and percentage of those who said that they saw a high level of antisocial behavior in their neighbourhood fell from 17 to 15 per cent.

Six out of seven indicators for antisocial behavior showed falls and only 'noisy neighbours' increased. There was also rising confidence in the police in dealing with antisocial behavior (despite some highly publicized cases of the police not responding adequately or at all); and 51 per cent of respondents said that the police dealt with crime issues that mattered to them locally, compared with 47 per cent in 2008.

However, in spite of the fact that fear of crime is arguably greater than its actuality, other polls in the 2000s reveal that many people (particularly the elderly) are still afraid despite the official crime figures: feel unsafe walking alone after dark; believe that worries about crime affect their everyday life; and think that the police are handicapped in the fight against crime by the criminal justice system. The Crimestoppers Trust reported in September 2001 that three-quarters of British people believed that the country had become a more dangerous place to live in over the preceding ten years.

In a 2000 MORI poll, 44 per cent of interviewees were fairly satisfied and 9 per cent very satisfied with the way their areas were policed. Yet when asked how confident they were that the police would arrive at an emergency within ten minutes, 37 per cent were fairly and 13 per cent very confident. But 44 per cent were not confident.

Some 72 per cent of respondents strongly agreed that people should have the right to defend their property and 24 per cent tended to agree. There has been heated debate on this issue in recent years, with a large majority of people feeling that burglars are treated too leniently by the courts and that homeowners should be able to use force in self-defence proportionate to their fear rather than being judged by the legal test of reasonableness (in response to a perceived threat).

There continue to be mixed messages on crime and its effects in Britain, some of which are exaggerated by media coverage and moral panics. The Labour government insisted that crime was decreasing and that its crime-fighting measures were working. It argued that many people were less worried about crime in 2005 than in 2004 and that fewer people felt that antisocial behaviour was a problem. Yet polls in 2006 suggested that people were in fact very worried about a threatening culture of yobbishness and thuggery on British streets; drugs and drug-related offences; alcohol-fuelled antisocial behaviour; the abusive behaviour of some young people; the breakdown of community cohesion; muggings; and violent crime. All of these may impinge to varying degrees upon people's lives and create a hostile atmosphere. In reaction, people demand zero tolerance for all crime, insisting that the police should be allowed to do their job rather than engage in wasteful form-filling; put more police on the streets to patrol neighbourhoods and reassure people; and give strong punishments to convicted criminals.

Exercises

Explain and examine the following terms:

civil law	claimant	conveyancing
barrister	legal aid	Crown Prosecution Service
indictable	Inns of Court	Common Law
solicitor	Lord Chancellor	Metropolitan Police

jury	Crown court	County court
JP	statute law	bail
'tagging'	summary	District Judge
sub judice	adversarial	either-way offence

Write short essays on the following topics:

1 *   Describe and comment critically on the structure of the legal profession in England and Wales

2   How is the courts system in England and Wales organized?

3   Discuss the role of the police in law enforcement

4   Examine British crime statistics in this chapter and comment on people's fear of crime

Visit **www.routledge.com/textbooks/oakland** for multiple-choice questions, links to related YouTube clips, tips on approaching essay questions, and much, much more.

Further reading

1   Baker, J.H. (2004) *An Introduction to English Legal History*, Oxford: Oxford University Press
2   Berlins, M. and Dyer, C (2000) *The Law Machine*, London: Penguin
3   Clark, B. (2009) *Scottish Legal Systems Essentials*, Dundee: Dundee University Press
4   Cownie, F., Bradney, A. and Burton, M. (2007) *English Legal System in Context*, Oxford: Oxford University Press
5   Emsley, C. (2005) *Crime and Society in England 1750–1900*, London: Pearson Education Limited
6   Griffiths, J. (1997) *The Politics of the Judiciary*, London: Fontana
7   Heale, J. (2009) *One Blood: Inside Britain's New Street Gangs*, London: Pocket Books
8   Martin, E.A. and Law, J. (2009) *A Dictionary of Law*, Oxford: Oxford University Press
9   McShane, J. (2010) *Underworld UK: Knife Crime: The Law of the Blade*, London: Quercus Publishing Plc
10   Muncie, J. and McLaughlin, E. (2002) *The Problem of Crime*, London: Sage Publications
11   Muncie, J. and McLaughlin, E. (2002) *Controlling Crime*, London: Sage Publications
12   Partington, M. (2006) *Introduction to the English Legal System*, Oxford: Oxford University Press
13   Robertson, G. (2006) *Freedom, the Individual and the Law*, London: Penguin
14   Slapper, G. (2009) *The English Legal System*, London: Routledge-Cavendish
15   White, R. (1999) *The English Legal System in Action: Administration of Justice*, Oxford: Oxford University Press

16   White, R. and Wilcock, I. (2007) *The Scottish Legal System*, London: Tottel Publishing/ Bloomsbury Professional

Websites

Lord Chancellor's Department; www.lcd.gov.uk
Law Officers: www.lslo.gov.uk
Home Office: www.homeoffice.gov.uk
Police: www.police.co.uk
New Scotland Yard: www.open.gov.uk/police/mps/home.htm
Amnesty International: www.amnesty.org.uk
Scottish Executive: www.scotland.gov.uk
Northern Ireland Office: www.nio.gov.uk
The Law Society: www.lawsociety.org.uk
The Bar Council: www.barcouncil.org.uk

7

The economy

Fluctuations in the performance of the national economy affect British people directly in their daily lives and are of concern to them. Such changes influence interest and inflation rates, employment and unemployment levels, individual and corporate income, wealth creation, taxation, investment, government pro-grammes, social welfare, political party campaigns and the results of general elections.

Historically, the British economy has been conditioned by agricultural and industrial revolutions; a dramatic growth and later reduction of manufacturing industry; government policies and intervention; the expansion of service indus-tries; and a relative decline in economic performance from the late nineteenth century as competitor nations industrialized. The economy experienced periods of recession and expansion ('boom and bust') in the twentieth century, but grew strongly from 1994 with record levels of people in work and low inflation, unemployment and interest rates. The worst effects of a worldwide recession were avoided in the early 2000s, but from 2005 Britain entered a slowdown in some areas. This coincided with increased global oil prices, high government (public) spending and a fragile consumer market which was affected by higher interest rates and rising inflation.

The economy then suffered the severe global recession of 2007–10 followed by a credit crunch, and there was a fear that the banking and financial system was in danger of collapse. Britain came slowly out of the recession in early 2010, but its recovery was weaker than that of most nations and there were concerns about the resulting £163 billion budget deficit (11 per cent of GDP). In 2010 the Conservative/Liberal Democrat coalition government initiated a £6 billion reduction plan and conceded that public spending cuts would be necessary. Critics also warned of higher direct and indirect taxation to pay off the deficit and a period of prolonged austerity.

Economic history

Britain was a largely rural country until the end of the eighteenth century, and its economy was based on products generated by successive revolutions in agriculture since Neolithic times. However, there had also been industrial and manufacturing developments over the centuries, which were located mainly in the larger towns. Financial and commercial institutions such as banks, insurance houses and trading companies were gradually founded in the City of London and throughout the country to finance and service the expanding and increasingly diversified economy.

The growth of a colonial empire from the sixteenth century contributed to national wealth as Britain capitalized on its worldwide trading connections. Colonies supplied cheap raw materials, which were converted into manufactured goods in Britain and exported. Overseas trade and markets grew quickly because merchants and traders were protected at home and abroad. They exploited the colonial markets and controlled foreign competition. By the nineteenth century Britain had become a dominant military and economic power. Its wealth was based on international trade and the payments it received for its exported products. Governments believed that a country increased its wealth if exports exceeded imports.

This trading system and its financial institutions assisted the Industrial Revolutions, which began in the late eighteenth century. Manufacturing inventions, aided by a rich supply of domestic materials and energy sources such as coal, steel, iron, steam power and water, stimulated mass production and the economy. Manufacturers, who had gained by international trade and a demand for British goods, invested in new industries and technology. Industrial towns

PLATE 7.1 This bridge across the river Severn at Ironbridge, Shropshire, England, was part of the Industrial Revolutions. It represented the first use of iron in industrial architecture and was built by Abraham Darby in 1779.
(David Cole/Rex Features)

expanded; factories were built and a transport system of roads, canals and railways developed. Efficient manufacturing methods produced competitively priced goods for foreign markets and Britain was transformed into an urban and industrialized country.

However, industrialization was opposed by some. For example, the Luddites in the nineteenth century destroyed new machinery in an attempt to halt progress and preserve existing jobs. Industrial and urban development had negative effects, such as long working hours for low wages and bad conditions in mines and factories. Rural areas lost population and there was a decline in traditional home and cottage work. Industrial conditions caused social and moral problems in towns and the countryside and mechanization was often regarded as exploitative and dehumanizing. The situation was worsened by the indifference of many manufacturers, employers and politicians to the human cost of industrialization.

Nevertheless, the industrial changes did transform Britain into a rich and powerful country, despite economic slumps, periods of mass unemployment, the growth of urban slums and significant social and economic hardship in the nineteenth century for many people. Manufacturing output became the chief generator of wealth; production methods and technology advanced; and domestic competition improved the quality of goods and services.

Yet British dominance of world trade did not last. It declined relatively by the end of the nineteenth century as countries such as Germany and the USA rapidly developed their industrial bases and became more competitive. However, British financial expertise continued to be influential in global financial dealings.

The modern economy: policies, structure and performance

It is argued that British economic performance and world status declined further in the twentieth century, although some recent research queries whether decline has been as substantial in comparative terms as is popularly assumed. However, the country was significantly affected by the economic problems created by two world wars; international recessions; global competition; structural changes in the economy; a lack of industrial competitiveness; alternating government policies; and a series of 'boom-and-bust' cycles in which economic growth fluctuated greatly.

Economic policies

Although British governments have historically tended to be somewhat laissez-faire (letting things take their own course) in economic matters, they became much more involved in economic planning from the 1940s and the performance of the economy has been tied to their fiscal, monetary and political policies. All British governments thereafter have variously intervened in economic life in attempts to manage the economy and stimulate demand and growth, particularly as global competition has grown and domestic needs have become more complex.

Conservative governments historically advocated minimum interference in the economy and favoured the workings of the free market, yet they have often intervened out of necessity or changed ideology. Labour governments initially argued that the economy must be centrally planned and its essential sectors should be owned and managed by the state. But they have also changed their policies, which have become more liberal and market-oriented.

Labour governments from 1945 nationalized (transferred to public owner-ship) railways, road transport, water, gas, electricity, shipbuilding, coalmining, the iron and steel industries, airlines, the health service, the Post Office and telecommunications. These industries and services were run by the state through government-appointed boards. They were responsible to Parliament and subsidized by taxation for the benefit of all rather than for private owners or shareholders. But governments were expected to rescue any that had economic problems.

This policy was gradually reversed by the Conservatives. They argued that public industries and services were too expensive and inefficient; had outdated technology and bad industrial relations; suffered from a lack of investment in new equipment; were dependent upon tax subsidies; and were run as state services with too little attention paid to profit-making, consumer demand or market forces. They denationalized some state industries and returned them to private ownership.

Conservative denationalization was later (1979–97) called 'privatization'. Ownership of industries such as British Telecom, British Airways, British Petroleum, British Gas, water and electricity supplies, British Coal and British Rail was transferred from the state to private companies mainly through the sale of shares. These industries are run as profit-making concerns and are regulated in the public interest by independent regulators. The aim was also to liberalize the economy so that restrictions on businesses were removed to allow them to operate freely and competitively. For example, the stock market and public transport were deregulated, resulting in greater diversity in the City of London and private bus companies (although subsidized by local government) compete with one another.

Conservatives believe that privatization improves efficiency, reduces govern-ment spending, increases economic freedom and encourages share ownership. The public bought shares in the new private companies and share-owning by individuals and financial institutions increased, but there was concern about privatization. Private industries became virtual monopolies (although there is now more competition) and there was criticism of the independent regulators' abilities to supervise them. There have been complaints about the private sector's services, business methods, prices and products, although some initial problems have been solved. However, some areas, such as the railway and water systems, are still criticized.

Conservative governments in the 1990s also introduced a Private Finance Initiative (PFI) policy, through which the private sector is encouraged to invest in public sector building projects and services such as schools and hospitals. This was intended to save public money, encourage cooperation on resources between the public and private sectors and, according to some critics, expand the privatization programme.

The Labour government accepted privatization on entering government in 1997 (having dropped nationalization from its party manifesto in 1995). It part-privatized concerns such as National Air Traffic Services and the London Underground, and introduced the private sector into public services such as transport, education and health. Its 'public-private partnerships' (PPPs) allow private companies to invest in large public capital projects.

Policies such as privatization, private finance initiatives (PFIs) and PPP are still attacked by many people and the trade unions, and suggest a continuing adherence to public sector services. MORI polls in the early 2000s found that only 8 per cent of respondents thought that hiring private sector managers to run public services would lead to big improvements. Only 11 per cent believed that using private companies to provide public services would improve them. Large majorities considered that schools, hospitals, trains, public utilities (water and electricity) and pensions should be provided and managed by the public sector. Independent surveys suggest that some private companies have found that PPP and PFI schemes do not generate the expected profits and that the quality of such initiatives is debatable. However, while some projects have collapsed, other private firms such as those involved in the Tube modernization programmes appear to be making a profit.

The major political parties have now accepted free market (or liberal) economics, a closer relationship between the public and private sectors, deregulation and a mobile workforce. But a public or 'social sector market' still exists. The problem is how to manage the liberal economy effectively while satisfying continuing demands for public services, such as the National Health Service and state school education, which are mainly free of charges and funded from public taxation. Following the credit crunch and bank collapses in 2007–09 there have also been demands for stronger regulation of financial institutions.

Economic structure

Government policies have created a mixed economy of public and private sectors. The public sector includes the remaining state-run industries and services which amount to under one-third of the economy. The other two-thirds are in the private sector and this percentage will increase with further privatization (e.g. of the Royal Mail).

Unlike public-sector concerns which are owned by the state, the private sector belongs to people who have a financial stake in a company. It consists of

PLATE 7.2 The production line for the Mini range, BMW, Cowley, Oxford, 2009. The once-flourishing British car industry is now much reduced, with increased foreign ownership and company collapses.
(INS News Agency Ltd/Rex Features)

small businesses owned by individuals, companies whose shares are sold to the public through the Stock Exchange and larger companies whose shares are not offered for sale to the public. Most companies are private and small or medium-sized. They are crucial to the economy and generate 50 per cent of new jobs. Some 10 per cent of the economy is controlled by foreign corporations, which employ 10 per cent of the workforce. Britain (even outside the European common currency, the euro) has been seen as an attractive low-cost country for foreign investment in many areas such as electronic and high-technology equipment, leisure facilities, hotels, finance and cars, although British-based production of the latter has decreased significantly in recent years.

The shareholders are the real owners of those companies in which they invest their money. However, the daily organization of the business is left to a board of directors under a chairperson or managing director. In practice, most shareholders are more interested in receiving profit dividends on their shares from a successful business than in being concerned with its running. Yet shareholder power is occasionally mobilized if the company is performing badly.

National and foreign companies are sometimes involved in takeovers and mergers in the private sector (one example being the American company Kraft Foods' purchase of the traditional and long-established British Cadbury chocolate business in 2010). A takeover occurs when a larger company takes over (or buys) a smaller, often loss-making, firm. Mergers are amalgamations between companies of equal standing. Such battles for control can be fiercely fought and have resulted in certain sections of the economy, such as motor manufacturing, hotels, media concerns and food products, being dominated by a relatively small number of major groups.

Takeovers and mergers can cause concern to the target companies and their workforces. A Competition Commission has been set up to monitor this situation by preventing any one group from forming a monopoly or creating unfair trading conditions. It examines the plans and reports to the Director General of Fair Trading, who, in reporting to the government Secretary of State for Trade and Industry, may rule against the proposed takeover or merger. Some decisions have prevented undesirable developments, though others have allowed near-monopolistic situations, and the Commission's performance has been criticized.

Economic performance

Since the Second World War, Britain has suffered from economic problems caused by domestic and global factors, which have resulted in recessionary and expansionary cycles; high unemployment, inflation and interest rates; balance of trade weaknesses; a fluctuating pound; low growth rates; poor productivity; an often uncompetitive workforce; and industrial relations difficulties. These have sometimes coincided with structural changes in the economy, such as a decline in industrial and manufacturing trades and a growth in service industries. Although Britain's economic performance between 1994 and 2005 was relatively successful, it encountered a serious global recession between 2007 and 2010 and economic problems continue.

The location of British industry, which was dictated by eighteenth- and nineteenth-century industrial revolutions, has been a factor in the nation's manufacturing and industrial decline. Industries were situated in areas where there was access to natural resources and transport systems and where there was often only one major industry. They could be easily damaged in a changing economic climate, unless they managed to diversify their product base. But even regions which had adapted successfully in the past were affected by further deindustrialization, increased global competition and recession from the 1970s to the early 2000s.

Many manufacturing industries failed to adapt to new markets and demands, did not produce goods efficiently and cheaply enough to compete and priced themselves out of the world market. Britain's share of global exports of manufactured goods slumped in the twentieth century due to world competition and a deterioration in its manufacturing industries.

Industrial decline badly affected northern England, the English Midlands, Scotland, Northern Ireland and South Wales. Traditional trades like textiles, steel, shipbuilding, iron and coalmining were greatly reduced. Governments, helped by European Union grants, tried to revitalize depressed areas with financial aid and the creation of new businesses. These policies have gradually had a positive effect in places like Liverpool, Glasgow, Newcastle, Birmingham and Belfast, though other areas are still languishing. Nevertheless, structural change in industry and manufacturing forced adjustments to different markets. New production and research methods led to a growth in specialized industries (such as the high-technology sectors) and the service sector (banking, insurance, catering, leisure, finance and information).

The discovery of North Sea oil and gas in the mid-1970s contributed greatly to the British economy at a time of difficulty and also made the country less dependent upon imported energy. But gas and oil are finite and are now past their peak, and Britain has difficulty in finding alternative sources. It already has to import gas and oil and needs to fill the financial gap with new revenues. It is argued that energy income has been unwisely spent on social targets rather than being used more positively for investment in new industry and in creating a modern economic infrastructure.

Conservative governments (1979–97) addressed the boom-and-bust weak-nesses in the British economy, but opinions on their record differ. They tried to reduce inflation through high interest rates and cuts in public spending. Industry and commerce were expected to restructure themselves, increase their growth rates and productivity, reduce overstaffing and become more efficient under the influence of market forces. Privatization was also gradually applied in many areas of the public sector.

Such measures combined with a world recession resulted in the 1980 British economy falling to very low levels with high interest rates, unemployment and inflation. Although it improved by 1986, it overheated from mid-1988. There were record balance-of-payments deficits, the pound was weak, inflation increased and interest rates were raised. Domestic and international factors forced the country into a very deep recession (1989–93).

In 1990, in an attempt to boost economic strength, Britain joined the European Exchange Rate Mechanism (ERM) which, by linking European cur-rencies, was supposed to stabilize currencies and improve national economies. But, after speculation against the pound in 1992, Britain withdrew from the ERM and allowed the pound to float. The economy recovered outside the ERM. The pound was strong, although this created problems for British exporters and businesses.

In 1993–4, Britain came slowly out of recession, with improved manu-facturing and financial performance and a fall in inflation, unemployment and interest rates. By 1997 the economy was one of the most successful in the world, a situation which the previous Labour government inherited. It continued similar policies to the Conservatives, initially managed the economy prudently and largely avoided traditional boom-and-bust cycles. However, Labour had to spend consid-erably on services like health, education and transport, and government or public

PLATE 7.3 The Lloyd's Building, London. Lloyd's is an association of individuals who provide insurance for a wide range of (often risky) activities, such as oil exploration and shipping.

(Sonny Meddle/Rex Features)

spending was a growing concern. This illustrates the problem of trying to combine a 'market economy' with public services.

Britain in the early 2000s experienced mixed effects from a global economic downturn. Manufacturing was in recession and there was weakness in other sectors. Although consumer spending boosted the economy, consumer confidence was waning. Unemployment, having fallen since 1993, rose again in 2001. Yet interest rates and inflation were low. Britain avoided the worst of an international recession and had above-average growth through 2002.

Britain's growth continued to be strong, though economic forecasts had to be scaled back significantly in 2005. The buoyancy of the economy was affected by heavy government spending; a drop in company profits; increases in oil and energy prices; rising inflation, interest and unemployment rates; a faltering housing market; higher indirect taxation and increased National Insurance contributions for workers; a decline in consumer confidence; and (economists alleged) a loss of control by the Treasury (the government finance ministry) over Britain's public finances. There were other structural problems such as weak trade performance, a declining pound, a fluctuating manufacturing industry, a pensions deficit, low personal savings, a very high level of personal debts and a continuing productivity gap between Britain and the USA, France and Germany. However, by November 2005 the inflation rate had improved, although unemployment rose.

Between 2007 and 2010, the economy weakened and Britain suffered from the worst global recession since the Great Depression of 1929. A credit crunch and crisis-ridden banks suggested that the world's economic structures were on the verge of collapse. Individual consumers had also contributed to the problem by taking out large personal loans and incurring debts they were unable to repay. The British system was rescued by a Labour government bailout of banks such as Northern Rock and Royal Bank of Scotland, which remain partly state-owned. But in 2010 the country was living with the costs of this exercise. The budget deficit (the difference between government spending and the income it receives through taxation and other sources) was £163 billion. Political parties and economists

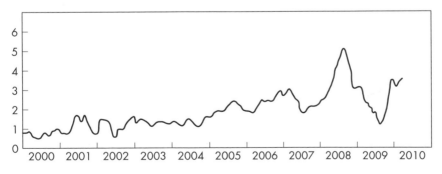

FIGURE 7.1 Inflation rate (% Consumer Price Index), 2000–(est.) 2010
Source: Adapted from ONS, 2010

disagreed on measures to reduce it, but the Conservative/Liberal Democrat government initiated a mixture of quick repayment, cuts in public spending and a higher taxation band of 50 per cent on an income of over £150,000.

Meanwhile, other indicators of economic health were negative. Inflation had varied from 2.5 per cent in 2008 to 3.0 in 2009 and increased to 3.4 in March 2010. The unemployment rate was 8 per cent in April, the highest since September 1996, with youth unemployment (one quarter of the total) at a very high rate.

Britain is the world's sixth largest economy and a significant industrial and manufacturing country, although being challenged by China and India. It is a large exporter of goods and services, despite its reduced share of the global market and manufacturing decline since the 1980s. The gross domestic product (GDP) in 2009 was £22,599 per head of population. GDP comprises the goods, services, capital and income which the country produces. GDP sector share in 2009 was 75 per cent from services and 23.8 per cent from manufacturing and industry, while agriculture contributed 0.5 per cent. These figures illustrate the contemporary importance of the service sector and the corresponding decline of traditional sources of national wealth such as industry, manufacturing and agriculture.

Britain's trading patterns have also changed. In 2009 it ranked as the world's tenth largest exporter and and its chief export partners in 2008 were the USA (13.8 per cent), Germany (11.5), the Netherlands (7.8), France (7.6), Ireland (7.5), Belgium (5.3) and Spain (4.1), with non-EU exports increasing. In 2009 it ranked as the world's seventh largest importer, with its main import partners in 2008 being Germany (13.1 per cent), the USA (8.7), China (7.5), the Netherlands (7.4), France (6.8), Norway (6), Belgium (4.7) and Italy (4.1). Britain's principal exports are manufactured goods, fuels, chemicals, food, beverages and tobacco and its main imports are manufactured products, machinery, fuels and foodstuffs. But it has had a balance of payments problem since 1983, and had a £4.7 billion deficit in 2009 (£1.6 billion with the EU and £3.1 billion with non-EU countries). A trade deficit results when exports do not exceed imports. However, 'invisible exports', such as financial, aviation and insurance services, are not included in this equation and contribute significantly to the economy.

The economy is also affected by fluctuations in the value of the pound. Devaluation (reducing the pound's exchange value) was used earlier by governments as an economic weapon. This boosted exports by making them cheaper on the world market, but raised the cost of imports and dissuaded people from buying foreign goods. Devaluation has not been employed recently. Instead, the pound was allowed to 'float' from 1972 and to find its own market value in competition with other currencies. Although Britain has not joined the European common currency (euro), the pound had performed successfully outside the eurozone (consisting of those EU countries which have adopted the euro). However, its performance and value have significantly weakened under recessionary pressures since 2007.

Social class, the workforce and employment

Social class

Class in Britain has been variously defined by one or more factors, such as material wealth; the ownership of land and property; control of the means of production as against the sellers of labour; education; job or professional status; accent and dialect; birth and breeding; or sometimes by lifestyle.

Over time a British class system evolved which divided the population into upper, middle and working classes. Although in earlier centuries hierarchies were rigidly based on wealth, the ownership of property, aristocratic privilege and political power, a middle class of traders, merchants and skilled craftsmen later made inroads into this system. Industrialization in the nineteenth century further fragmented class divisions. The working class divided into skilled and unskilled workers, while the middle class split into lower, middle and upper sections, depending on job classification or wealth. The upper class was still largely defined by birth, property and inherited money.

It is argued that the spread of education and expansion of wealth to include greater numbers of people in the twentieth century allowed greater social mobility (moving upwards out of the class into which one was born). The working class was more upwardly mobile and the upper class (due to a loss of aristocratic privilege) merged more with the middle class. It was felt that the old rigid class system was breaking down as the proportions of people belonging to the various levels changed over time. Yet clear class divisions still exist, and research from 2005–10 suggests that Britain's rate of social mobility is the lowest among the western nations and its levels of inequality are very high.

Researchers now employ an Office for National Statistics classification (2001) based on occupation:

1   Higher professional and managerial occupations
2   Lower professional and managerial occupations
3   Intermediate occupations
4   Small employers and non-professional self-employed workers
5   Lower supervisory and technical occupations
6   Semi-routine occupations
7   Routine occupations
8   Never worked and long-term unemployed

The last group is also known as the underclass, a term that has been much used in recent years. It consists of people who fall outside the usual class categories and includes the permanently unemployed, some single-parent families, the very poor, the alienated and those with alternative lifestyles. It seems that there is very little social mobility from this group.

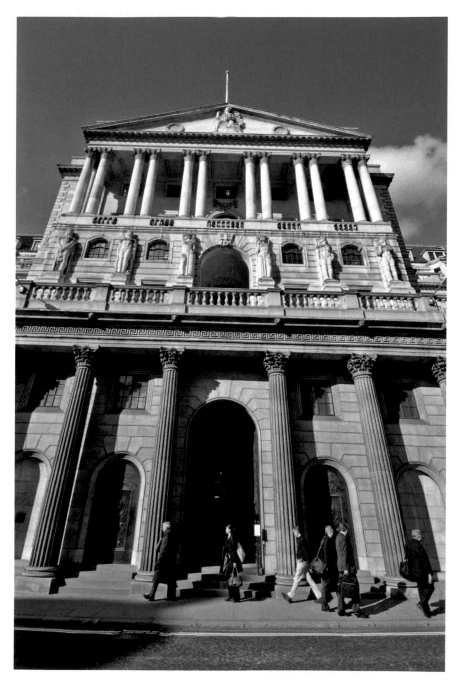

PLATE 7.4 The Bank of England, Britain's independent central bank, which decides interest rates and oversees the economy. It is located in Threadneedle Street in the City of London.

(Geoff Moore/Rex Features)

Research suggests two main social/occupational groupings in contemporary Britain: a 'middle class' made up of classes 1, 2, 3 and possibly 4 and a 'working class' consisting of classes 5, 6, 7 and 8. The British population today largely consists of a middle class (60 per cent) and a working class (40 per cent). Despite a slackening in the social mobility rate, the working class has shrunk historically and there has been more relative upward mobility, with people advancing socially due to economic progress and changes in occupational structures. But such movement can be halted by economic factors such as recession and general decline.

Polls suggest that the British themselves feel they are becoming more middle class and it is argued that many people now have the sort of lifestyle, jobs and incomes which identify them as middle class. It also seems that class is now as much a matter of different social habits and attitudes as it is of occupation and money. The old gaps between the classes have lessened and class today is a more finely graded hierarchy dependent upon a range of characteristics. Yet inequalities of wealth, difficulties of social mobility for the poorest in society, relative poverty, professional differences and questions of prestige remain.

The workforce and employment

The workforce in 2009 was 31.3 million, of whom 28.9 million were in employment (4.2 million as self-employed) and 2.4 million were unemployed. Of these workers, the large majority were employed in the services sector, a smaller percentage in industry (including manufacturing) and declining numbers in agriculture.

Despite twentieth-century occupational changes, the majority of British people, whether part-time or full-time, are employed by an organization. This may be a small private firm, a large company, a public sector industry or service or a multinational corporation. Most people are workers who sell their labour in a market dominated by concerns which own and control production and services. The class-defining boundaries of employees and employers have remained constant, and the top 1 per cent of British society still own more than 18 per cent of marketable wealth, while the top 10 per cent have 56 per cent.

However, the deregulated and mobile economy has created very different work patterns. Manufacturing has declined; service trades have increased; self-employment has risen; managerial and professional fields have expanded; and there are more part-time (7.7 million in 2010), job-sharing and temporary jobs. Manual jobs have decreased in number; non-manual occupations have increased; the working class has been eroded by the increase in salaried jobs; and the workforce has become more mobile, more 'white-collar' and better educated.

Some 70 per cent of working-age women are in employment of various kinds. In 2009 women represented 45 per cent of the total private and public labour force, and they are the principal breadwinners in some 30 per cent of households.

Yet half of female workers are low-paid, part-time, unable to find full-time jobs and often unprotected by trade unions or the law. There may also be more redundancies and job losses generally over the next few years, with the worst employment prospects in a generation. Although women form a 52 per cent majority of the population (30.2 million) and are increasing their numbers in higher education, (where they are a majority of students), the professions and white-collar jobs, they have difficulty progressing to the senior ranks. Yet increasing numbers of new businesses are started by women, particularly in the service sector.

Since the 1960s, women have campaigned for greater equality with men in job opportunities and rates of pay. Legislation has attempted to redress the balance with varying degrees of success. Equal Pay Acts stipulate that men and women who do the same or similar kinds of work should receive the same wages. The Sex Discrimination Act makes it unlawful for the employer to discriminate between men and women when choosing a candidate for most jobs. The Equal Opportunities Commission monitors this legislation and brings cases when there have been breaches of the Acts. Yet the average weekly wage for women is still only some 76 per cent of the average paid to men, particularly in industry and the service sector.

There has been a recent need for more women to enter the workforce at all levels, in order to compensate for a shortage of labour. This situation (if continued in a difficult economic climate) requires improved financial, social and child-care benefits for women to enable them to work, as well as more flexible employment arrangements. Some employers and the government are responding positively in these areas and Britain now seems to be more egalitarian in terms of female

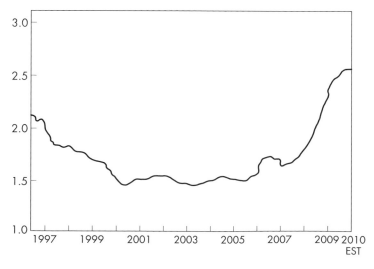

FIGURE 7.2 Unemployment rate (millions), 1997–(est.) 2010
Source: Adapted from The Times, *April 2010*

employment than in the past. However, flexible hours, job-sharing and part-time working (such as work-from-home schemes) for both sexes are increasingly criticized by those in full-time jobs who feel they are being made to bear the brunt of the work being done in the actual workplace.

More jobs were created in the 2000s and unemployment dropped steadily from 1993, although it rose in 2009 to 8 per cent of the workforce in the 2007–10 recession. It remains proportionally high in Northern Ireland, the English Midlands, Merseyside, north-east England, Scotland and South Wales; in localized areas of the big cities and countryside; and among ethnic minorities such as Pakistanis and Bangladeshis. Since the late 1980s it has also affected the normally affluent south of England and included professional and higher-grade workers. Unemployment and jobs were of great concern to respondents in a 2010 Ipsos MORI poll 2010 where they were placed first in a list of the most important issues facing the country.

Job creation is important to the political parties. The previous Labour government introduced (1997) a Welfare to Work programme. Companies willing to create jobs for the unemployed are given subsidies and the unemployed may also be placed in training and employment-related schemes. These train the workforce, in the hope that permanent jobs may be found for them. Young people between the ages of sixteen and eighteen who become unemployed on leaving school do not receive social security benefits and are required to enter a training scheme or further education. The training programmes have been criticized and there is no guarantee that trainees will obtain a job afterwards. However the government argues that their policies have succeeded in getting more people into stable employment, though some critics disagree.

Although the British workforce is now more mobile and flexible, many vacant jobs are low-paid and part-time. Others are in technical and skilled areas, for which the educational system has not adequately provided. The number of traditional apprenticeships has been greatly reduced and technical or vocational education suffers from a lack of investment and facilities. Despite the success of some programmes, Britain lacks adequate vocational education and training schemes for the unemployed and young people in those technical areas which are essential for a modern industrial state. Reports on global competitiveness from bodies such as the World Economic Forum do not rank Britain highly for the quality of its employee training. Firms in the 2000s have experienced skills shortages, with many having unfilled vacancies. It is now recognized that training and education must fit the realistic requirements of the workforce and be something more than disguised unemployment.

Traditional manufacturing industry has been progressively reduced in Britain. Yet an industrial infrastructure will continue to be important and is increasingly emphasized by politicians and the business world. It will not be as labour-intensive as in the past because of technical advances. The high-tech industry and service trades are set to expand. It is also likely that opportunities for professional and skilled workers in managerial, supervisory, personal and financial services will increase. However, maintaining employment levels and a trained workforce will still be problems in this post-industrial society and will entail revisions of the work ethic and concepts of leisure, as well as more flexible employment and child-care arrangements. At present, although the situation is improving and more state aid is being delivered, only a small percentage of working parents can afford to use formal child-care services on a regular basis and most parents have to pay three-quarters of the cost of care themselves.

Financial institutions

Financial institutions play a central role in the economy. In the 1980s, they responded to the deregulated and freer economy created by Conservative govern-ments. Banks, building societies, insurance firms, money markets and the London Stock Exchange expanded, merged and diversified. They entered new fields and reorganized traditional areas of expertise as competition between institutions increased.

They also experienced problems as the economy fluctuated in the late 1980s, the early 1990s, the early 2000s and the deep recession of 2007–10. Nevertheless, despite unemployment in financial businesses, the fluctuating performance of the Stock Market and increased European and international competition, London has retained its status as a global finance centre. However, domestic institutions suffered seriously from the recession and credit crunch. This forced a government rescue of private banks with taxpayers' money, raised questions about the future of the financial system and led to demands for stricter regulation of the finance markets.

Many major financial institutions have their headquarters in London, with branches throughout Britain. The square mile of the *City of London*, with its banks, insurance houses, legal firms and financial dealers' offices, has always been a centre of British and world finance. Its resources have financed royal wars, military and colonial exploration and trading companies. Today it provides financial and investment services for commercial interests in Britain and overseas. Many City institutions were founded in the seventeenth and eighteenth centuries as Britain's prosperity and overseas trade grew, such as the insurance firm Lloyd's (1680s), the London Stock Exchange (1773) and the Bank of England (1694). The City is now facing a serious challenge in financial dealings from the London Docklands commercial redevelopment centred on Canary Wharf.

The *Bank of England* ('the old lady of Threadneedle Street') is the UK's cen-tral bank. Although previously nationalized, it is now independent (1997) of government and has the vital role of setting interest rates to control inflation, while other institutions adjust their interest rates accordingly. It is organized by a governor and directors who are appointed by the government. It is the

PLATE 7.5 Canary Wharf, part of the Docklands redevelopment programme in south-east London, offering a mixture of residential housing, hotels, commercial companies and financial offices. The Canary Wharf Tower (top centre) is 800 feet (244 metres) high with 50 floors. *(Jonathan Player/Rex Features)*

government's banker and the agent for British commercial and foreign central banks, prints money for England and Wales, manages the national debt and gold reserves and supports the pound by buying sterling on foreign currency exchanges.

The main high street banks which provide banking services throughout Britain are the *central clearing banks*, of which the most important are HSBC, Lloyds Banking Group, the Royal Bank of Scotland (including National Westminster) and Barclays. They use a clearing house system based in London to transfer credits and cheques between banks, provide their customers with current and deposit (savings) accounts, loans and financial advice. However, they have been heavily criticized for their role in the 2007–10 credit crunch, for their banking charges to clients, the discrepancy between their savings and loan interest rates, their treatment of customers' complaints and their alleged unwillingness to provide funds for small businesses. They are again making large profits after the recession, are involved in international finance and have expanded their traditional activities. Building societies, many of which have become banks, offer mortgages (loans), banking facilities and Internet banking and provide competition to the high street banks.

In addition to these banks, there are the long-established *merchant banks*, which are mainly located in London. They give advice and finance to commercial and industrial businesses in Britain and overseas; advise companies on takeovers and mergers; provide financial assistance for foreign transactions; and organize a range of financial services for individuals and corporations.

The *London Stock Exchange* is a market for the buying and selling of quoted (listed) stocks and shares in British public companies and a few overseas. Dealings on the Stock Exchange reflect the current market trends and prices for a range of securities, which may go up as well as down. In recent years, the performance of the stock market has fluctuated under domestic and international pressures.

The Stock Exchange was revolutionized in 1986 by new developments, known popularly as the 'Big Bang'. The changes deregulated the financial market and enabled greater freedom of operation. New members were allowed, financial dealers were given greater powers of dealing and competition increased. However, some companies were too ambitious, over-expanded and suffered from the effects of the world stock market crash of 1987. The London market returned to earlier profitability levels only after many redundancies among dealers and the closure of some companies. Since 1997 financial transactions have been organized directly from computer screens in corporate offices by an order-driven system which automates the trading process, rather than traditional dealing on the floor of the Exchange.

The *Foreign Exchange Market* is also based in London. Brokers in corporate or bank offices deal in the buying and selling of foreign currencies. The London market is the largest in the world in terms of average daily turnover of completed transactions. Other money markets arrange deals on the Euromarkets in foreign currencies; trade on financial futures (speculation on future prices of commodities); arrange gold dealings on the London Gold Market; and transact global deals in the commodity, shipping and freight markets.

Lloyd's of London is a famous name in the insurance market and has long been active in the fields of shipping and maritime insurance. However, it has now diversified and insures in many other areas. It operates as a market (or association) where individual underwriters (or insurers) carry on their business. Underwriters normally form groups to give themselves greater security because they have to bear any loss that may occur, but in recent years many have suffered due to heavy insurance losses.

In addition to the Lloyd's market there are many individual insurance companies with headquarters in London and branches throughout the country. They have international connections and huge assets. They play an important role in British financial life because they are the largest investors of capital. Their main activity has traditionally been in life insurance, though many have now diversified into other associated fields such as pensions and property loans. However, their handling of customers' investments (particularly pension mis-selling, insurance problems and the mismanagement of savings schemes) has been heavily criticized in recent years. Investors have lost money and some insurance companies have virtually collapsed.

British financial institutions have traditionally been respected for their honesty and integrity, but, as the money markets have expanded and become freer there have been fraud cases, the collapse of financial organizations and financial scandals. These give the City a bad image and have forced it to institute self-regulatory provisions in order to tighten the controls on financial dealings. Nevertheless consumer confidence and trust in the financial institutions continues to decline and there are often big differences between the promises contained in glossily advertised financial schemes and the actual service provided to customers.

Some critics have argued for stronger independent supervision and regulation of the City's business practices. The Labour government created a watchdog, the Financial Services Authority or FSA, in 2000 and a Financial Ombudsman in 2001 to oversee all financial dealings. However, these institutions were criticized for their lack of adequate control, particularly after the 2007–10 credit crunch and recession. The coalition government has broken up the FSA by handing its regulatory duties to the Bank of England and created a new banking commission to overhaul the City and consider whether the City and banks should be more closely supervised and restricted. A Financial Policy Committee under the Bank of England will have powers to guard the stability of the financial system. Bankers and financiers were not popular with the general public after the credit crunch, continue to receive large bonuses and appear to have little appreciation of taxpayer anger. Their attempts to put their houses in order are not well received and they may face greater government control.

The composition of those who create and control wealth in Britain has changed since the Second World War. Bankers, aristocrats, landowners and industrialists were the richest people in the nineteenth and early twentieth centuries. Today the most affluent are retailers and those who service the consumer society, although holders of inherited wealth are still numerous. Many millionaires are self-made, from lower-middle-class and working-class backgrounds.

There are great inequalities of income and wealth in Britain and many different opinions about what constitutes riches. Some people feel satisfied with their income and others think that the issue is relative and dependent on different factors. Talking about what one earns and about money generally has often been regarded as unseemly in Britain and too closely connected with crude survival. However, this mentality has slowly changed, particularly since the expansion of the business and money markets and ostentatious behaviour and lifestyles are now more common.

Industrial and commercial institutions

The trade unions

Trade unions obtained legal recognition in 1871 after long and bitter struggles. The fight for the right of workers to organize themselves originated in the trade guilds of the fourteenth century and later in social clubs which were formed to give their members protection against sickness and unemployment.

The modern trade unions are associated (if no longer so closely) with the Labour Party and campaign for better pay, working and health conditions for their members. The trade union movement is highly organized, with a membership of 6.5 million people in 2009, although this represents a fall from 12 million in 1978.

Today there are some 167 trade unions and professional associations of workers, which vary considerably in size and influence. They represent not only skilled and unskilled workers in industry but also white-collar workers in a range of businesses, companies and local and central government. Other professional associations such as the Law Society, the Police Federation and the British Medical Association carry out similar representational roles for their members.

Members of trade unions pay annual subscriptions to their unions and frequently to the Labour Party, unless they elect not to pay this latter amount. The funding provides for union activities and services, such as legal, monetary and professional help. The better-off unions are able to give strike pay to members who are taking part in 'official strikes', which are those legally sanctioned by members. Trade unions vary in the amount of funds they receive from members and in their political orientation, which ranges from the left to the right of the political spectrum.

Some unions admit as members only those people who work in a specific job, such as miners or teachers, while others include workers employed in different areas of industry or commerce, such as the Transport and General Workers' Union (T&G). Some unions have joined with others in similar fields to form new unions, such as Unison (public service workers). The largest in Britain in 2009 was Unite, with 2 million members. Workers may choose, without victimization, whether they want to belong to a particular union or none at all.

Some fifty-eight trade unions are affiliated to the Trades Union Congress (TUC), which was founded in 1868, serves as an umbrella organization to coordinate trade union interests and strives to promote worker cooperation. It is able to exert some pressure on government (although this has now decreased) and seeks to extend its contacts in industry and commerce, with employers as well as workers.

The influence of the TUC and trade unions, along with their membership, has declined. This is due to unemployment; changing attitudes to trade unions by workers; the reduction and restructuring of industry; a deregulated economy; a more mobile workforce; and Conservative legislation. Laws were passed to enforce secret voting by union members before strikes can be legally called and for the election of union officials. The number of pickets (union strikers) allowed outside business premises has been reduced, secondary (or sympathy) action by other union members is banned and unions may be fined by the courts if they defy legislation. Such Conservative laws (which the previous Labour government accepted) and the economic climate have forced trade unions to be more realistic in their wage demands. However, pay claims are escalating again and there is increasing, if sporadic, militancy among some union leaders. There are also arrangements for the legal recognition of unions in those workplaces where a majority of workers want them and for consultation with workers on matters such as redundancy.

Legislation has controlled extreme union practices and introduced democratic procedures into union activities. The grassroots membership has become more independent of union bosses and activists, is more determined to represent its own wishes, and is concerned to reform the labour movement. The initiative in industry has shifted to employers and moderate unions, who have been moving away from the traditional 'class war' image of unionism and are accepting new technology and working patterns in an attempt to improve competitiveness and productivity.

Public opinion polls in the past found that, while a large majority of respondents believed that unions were essential to protect workers' interests, a sizeable number felt that unions had too much power in Britain and were dominated by extremists. Half of trade unionists themselves agreed with this latter point of view and half disagreed. The concern over trade unions and their close relationship with Labour governments declined after the 'New' Labour election victory in 1997.

Strike action by unions can be damaging to the economy and has been used as an economic and political weapon in the past. In some cases, strikes are seen as legitimate and gain public support, while others, which are clearly political, are unpopular and are rejected. Britain historically seemed to be prone to industrial disputes, with large numbers of strikes in the 1980s. However, statistics show that fewer working days are now lost in the country each year than in other industrial nations, although the number has increased recently. On average, most manufacturing plants and businesses are free of strikes, and media coverage is often responsible for giving a distorted picture of industrial relations.

Industrial problems should be placed in the context of financial rewards. Britain has a low-wage economy compared with other major European countries, although the Labour government set a minimum wage of £5.80 an hour to help the lowest paid workers over 22, £4.83 for those aged 18–21 and £3.57 for those school leavers aged 16–17. The average gross weekly wage of workers in Great Britain in 2009 was £451 per week or £23,452 a year, though many workers (particularly women) receive less than this. Personal annual income is taxed at 20 per cent up to £37,400, at 40 per cent above this figure and at 50 per cent for those few earning over £250,000. The British tend to believe that they are overtaxed, though the basic and top rates of direct taxation for most people are actually lower than in many other Western countries.

However, direct income tax may have to increase in order to pay for public services, future state pension provision and a deficit of £163 billion following the 2007–10 recession. The previous Labour government also raised indirect or 'stealth' taxes after 1997, such as increased national insurance contributions for workers and employers, and did not increase the bands for income tax allowances. Millions of Britons are now paying increased amounts of various indirect taxes.

Employers' organizations

There are some 101 employers' and managers' associations in Britain, which are mainly associated with companies in the private sector. They aim to promote good industrial relations between businesses and their workforces, try to settle disputes and offer legal and professional advice.

Most are members of the Confederation of British Industry (CBI). This umbrella body represents its members nationally; negotiates on their behalf with government and the TUC; campaigns for greater investment and innovation in industry and technology; and is often more sympathetic to Conservative governments than to Labour ones. However, it can be very critical of Conservative policies. It also acts as a public relations organization, relays the employers' point of view to the public and has considerable economic influence and authority.

Industrial relations

Complaints are often raised about the quality of industrial relations in Britain. Historically, this has tended to be confrontational rather than cooperative and based on notions of 'class warfare' and 'us-and-them' attitudes. Trade union leaders can be extremist and stubborn in pursuing their members' interests. But the performance of management and employers is also criticized. Insensitive managers can be responsible for strikes arising in the first place, and relations between management and workers still leave much to be desired although industrial unrest is not as common as it once was. Opinion polls have suggested that a majority of respondents believe that bad management is more to blame than the unions for poor industrial relations and Britain's economic problems.

The Advisory, Conciliation and Arbitration Service (ACAS)

ACAS is an independent, government-financed organization which was created in 1974 to improve industrial relations. It may provide, if requested, advice, conciliation and arbitration services for the parties involved in a dispute. But ACAS does not have binding powers and the parties may disregard its advice and solutions. Industrial relations in Britain consist of free collective bargaining between employers and workers. It has been argued that arbitration should be made compulsory and that findings should be made binding on the parties concerned. However, strike action is not illegal for most workers if legally called and the government has no power to intervene. Nevertheless, ACAS has performed much valuable work and been responsible for settling many disputes.

ACAS also oversees the operation of employment law and abuses of workers' legal rights. These may involve complaints of unfair and unlawful dismissal under Employment Acts; claims under Equal Pay Acts; grievances under Sex Discrimination Acts; and unlawful discrimination under Race Relations Acts. There is now a large body of employment and regulatory law, which makes conditions of employment much more secure and less arbitrary than they have been in the past, particularly in the cases of women, ethnic minorities and the low-paid. However, there is still concern about the real effectiveness of such legislation.

Consumer protection

In a competitive market, consumers should have a choice of goods and services, the necessary information to make choices and laws to safeguard their purchases. Statutory protection for consumers has grown steadily in Britain, with the Consumer Protection Act of 1987 and the Supply of Goods and Services Act of 1982, and is harmonized with European Union law. Members of the public can complain to tribunals and the courts about unfair trading practices, dangerous and unsafe goods, misrepresentation, bad service, misleading advertising and personal injuries resulting from defective products.

The Office of Fair Trading (OFT) is a government department which oversees the consumer behaviour of trade and industry. It promotes fair trading, protects consumers, suggests legislation to government and has improved consumer awareness. It has drawn up codes of practice with many industrial and commercial organizations, keeps a close watch for any breaches of the codes, and publishes its findings, often to the embarrassment of the manufacturers and companies concerned.

The OFT (and therefore the government) also funds Consumer Direct, which works in partnership with Local Authority Trading Standards Services. It is a telephone and online service offering information and advice on consumer issues.

Organizations which provide help on consumer affairs at the local level are Citizens Advice Bureaux, Consumer Advice Centres and the consumer protection departments of local councils. Private consumer-protection groups, which investigate complaints and grievances and advise consumers on choice of tradesmen, may also exist in some localities, such as those organized by the Trading Standards Institute which is a not-for-profit professional body .

The independent National Consumer Council monitors consumers' attitudes, although its effectiveness is queried. A more active body is Which? (formerly the Consumers' Association). Its magazine of the same name champions the consumer and applies rigorous tests to anything from television sets to insurance and estate agents. *Which?* is the 'buyers' bible' and its reports have raised the standards of commercial products and services in Britain.

Consumer protection at state and private levels has improved over the past forty years. Yet much still needs to be done in this field to achieve minimum standards and adequate protection, such as dealing with unscrupulous builders and others preying on gullible consumers, particularly the elderly; commercial incompetence and the mis-selling of products by financial organizations; bad service in shops and retail outlets; and inferior products flooding a materialist society.

But there are signs that a British reticence to complain about goods and services is breaking down as the amount of litigation and financial claims increase. This attitude is associated with what is seen as a growing complaint and 'compensation culture' in Britain. However, some complaints are clearly frivolous and the previous Labour government tried to curb the worst excesses by introducing new legislation.

Attitudes to the economy

The changing economic climate is reflected in opinion polls, which indicate the public's views at national and personal levels and their attitudes to government actions and policies as politicians respond to crises and unforeseen events. An Ipsos MORI poll in April 2010 reported that the economy remained the most important issue facing the country for respondents. Questions about future public spending cuts, taxation and unemployment during the election campaign were central to people's concerns about an economic recovery.

The period since 2007 has been dominated by a severe recession; a general election campaign in 2010 which was influenced by economic debates; a succession of bad economic statistics and forecasts; serious effects upon businesses and people in their daily lives; and the attempt by politicians to plan economic recovery.

Although Conservative governments traditionally have been trusted to manage the economy efficiently and delivered a booming economy in 1997 to the new Labour government, the electorate was dissatisfied with them in the mid-1990s for political reasons. General elections in 1997, 2001 and 2005 showed that voters were willing to trust the Labour Party to run the economy competently because it had adopted centrist and pragmatic policies and promised not to increase direct taxation. It accepted that the Labour government had managed the economy prudently from 1997, at least initially. The British economy had been the most successful in Europe with relatively strong growth, but suffered a slowdown in 2005 which some economists attributed to government failings. A Deloitte MORI poll in 2005 following the general election of that year found that 50 per cent of respondents did not think the government's policies would improve the economy in the long term compared with 39 per cent who were optimistic. The economy worsened until 2007.

The 2007–10 recession affected British people severely, with unemployment at 2.5 million in April 2010 (an 8 per cent unemployment rate); 35 per cent of 16–17-year-olds and a quarter of those aged 17–24 were jobless. There was high inflation of 3.5 per cent in April 2010 and fears of consequent higher interest rates to follow later in the year. Although some banks had returned to profit after government bailouts, many small businesses and individuals were unable to arrange bank loans or mortgages. Businesses went bankrupt or into administration, homes were repossessed and many people were unable to find jobs. Some one in five working age people (or a record 8.1 million) in Britain were classified as economically inactive because they were either ill, studying or caring for a family. The International Monetary Fund (IMF) estimated that the unemployment rate for 2010 would eventually be 8.3 per cent. Experts warned that even if Britain managed to avoid a second recession, it would experience a slow recovery in which the economy was not creating jobs.

Nevertheless, and despite the recession, a BBC *Newsnight* economy poll in September 2009 found that 53 per cent of respondents thought the economy would improve in the following twelve months, 25 per cent felt it would remain the same and 20 per cent thought it would get worse, with 30 per cent saying they thought their personal financial circumstances would improve, 50 per cent that they would stay the same and 19 per cent that they would get worse.

The recession also raised significant questions about the nature of British society and who was to blame for the credit crunch. In a YouGov/Compass Survey in September 2009, 78 per cent of respondents agreed that the growing gap between rich and poor was bad for society while 6 per cent disagreed. When asked if people on salaries above £1 million helped Britain to prosper economically, 31 per cent agreed while 37 per cent disagreed. When asked if excessive bonuses and pay had fuelled the excessive risk which played a significant role in causing the credit crunch and subsequent recession, 83 per cent agreed while 5 per cent disagreed. Respondents (73 per cent) felt that bonuses above £10, 000 a year should be taxed (10 per cent opposed); 33 per cent thought that individuals would leave the country if very high salaries were curbed (37 per cent disagreed); 68 per cent supported the idea that a tax on transactions by banks and financial companies should be imposed to curb the bonus/risk culture (10 per cent opposed); and 63 per cent supported the proposal that an Independent High Pay Commission should be established to investigate the effects of high pay on the economy and society (14 per cent opposed). The respondents were not asked whether their own levels of personal spending and debt might also have contributed to the credit crunch and recession.

In order to promote recovery from recession by cutting the budget deficit of some £163 billion, a British government would need to cut public spending (and therefore public services on which people depend) or raise taxes (and alienate voters). An alternative to the cutting model might be efficiency savings on management and wastage rather than cuts in front-line services. The Institute for Fiscal Studies (IFS) argued before the 2010 general election that the next government would have to raise more in taxes and implement deeper welfare cuts than any of the three main political parties admitted.

Public opinion had clear priorities. In a Populus poll for *The Times* in September 2009, 81 per cent of respondents agreed that significant cuts in public spending had to be made irrespective of which party won the 2010 election. A YouGov poll for *The Sunday Times* found that 60 per cent of respondents believed the deficit should be cut through cuts in public spending rather than tax increases (21 per cent). An Ipsos MORI/RSA survey found that 21 per cent believed too much money was being spent on public services. Yet 75 per cent said that making public services more efficient could save enough money to help cut government spending without damaging public services. Whether efficiency savings will amount to much actual saving is something the political parties have not elaborated upon. In the event, it seemed that the new coalition government would use a mixture of all these remedies by moving quickly to cut the deficit, increase personal taxation to 50 per cent for income over £150,000 and enforce efficiency savings.

The poll findings above suggest that the economy concerns Britons in those areas which affect them directly and adversely on a personal level, such as unemployment, industrial decline, inflation, interest rates, savings, pensions, public spending, prices, taxation and the provision of public services.

Polls in recent years suggest that, in a mobile and deregulated market, job security (or the ability to get another job if one is lost) is a priority of job seekers, ranked ahead of work satisfaction, promotion and working conditions. Britain also has a reputation as a country of workaholics, where people work the longest hours in Europe (despite an EU maximum working week of 48 hours). This may be out of choice, enjoyment, ambition, coercion or desperation not to lose one's job. However, it seems that a majority of British people are either very or fairly satisfied with their jobs and only a small minority are either fairly or very dissatisfied.

A CBI poll in 2001 showed that flexible working was now a key part of British employment patterns, despite the problems of finding adequate child-care provision: 81 per cent of businesses use part-time workers; 62 per cent operate subcontracting; and 39 per cent use teleworking to allow their employees to work at home for at least some of the time. But there are also negative responses to part-time, flexible or home workers from those full-time employees who have to provide full-time cover in the workplace.

Respondents to polls also still tend to believe that business and economic arrangements in Britain are unfair: the values of managers and workers continue to be opposed in many companies; the country's wealth is unfairly distributed, which favours the owners and the rich at the expense of employees and the poor; the gap between rich and poor is growing; there are no longer 'jobs for life' and businesses do not care about the community, the environment or customers. It is felt that workers should be given more control over and say in the organization of their workplaces (now covered by the Social Chapter of the Maastricht Treaty).

However, a MORI Corporate Image survey in August 2001 showed that public hostility towards profitability and business success had decreased, having risen from 1980 to 1999. In 1999 only 25 per cent of respondents supported corporate profit while 52 per cent were against. In 2001 the figures were 29 per cent and 43 per cent respectively. Stakeholders or shareholders wanted their companies to make a profit but not at the expense of their staff or the community. The public thought that caring for employees should be the top priority for business. The provision of more jobs, the safety of workers and the training of the workforce were also emphasized.

It is often argued that Britain's historical economic ills were due to cultural factors and attitudes. Traditionally, university-educated and upper-class people were reluctant to enter trade and industry; the workforce had a lower productivity rate than those of comparable competitors; there had been insufficient investment in industry and training; management tended to be weak and unprofessional; and there had been too little investment in and encouragement of the technical, scientific and research fields. These views still have some validity. For example, it is felt that Britain lacks adequate technical education and training facilities. This leads to a lack of applicants for vacancies in vital technical trades, manufacturing and industry.

Exercises

Explain and examine the following terms:

diversification	privatization	GDP	invisible exports
merger	Lloyd's	shares	balance of payments
private sector	deficit	TUC	service industries
ACAS	Canary Wharf	HSBC	'market economy'
the City	inflation	*Which?*	mixed economy
devaluation	Stock Exchange	CBI	deregulation
monopoly	PPP	ERM	deindustrialization
textiles	clearing house	Barclays	Bank of England

Write short essays on the following topics:

1   Examine modern British economic policies and performance.

2   Discuss the role of the trade unions in British life.

3* Should the financial institutions in Britain be more closely regulated by government?
    If so, why?

4   To what extent does the performance of the national economy affect individual
    Britons' daily life?

Visit **www.routledge.com/textbooks/oakland** for multiple-choice questions, links
to related YouTube clips, tips on approaching essay questions, and much, much
more.

Further reading

1   Booth, A. (2001) *The British Economy in the Twentieth Century*, London: Palgrave
2   Buxton, T., Chapman, P. and Temple, P. (1997) *Britain's Economic Performance*, London:
    Routledge
3   Cairncross, A. (2006) *Britain's Economic Prospects Reconsidered*, London: Routledge
4   Davies, H. (2006) *The Chancellors' Tales: Managing the British Economy*, Oxford: Polity Press
5   Floud, R. and Johnson, P. (2004) *The Cambridge Economic History of Modern Britain, Vol.
    1 Industrialization, 1700–1860*, Cambridge: Cambridge University Press
6   Gamble, A. (1994) *Britain in Decline: Economic Policy, Political Strategy and the British
    State*, London: Palgrave Macmillan
7   Gregg, P. and Wadsworth, J. (eds) (1999) *The State of Working Britain*, Manchester:
    Manchester University Press
8   Johnson, P., Carnevalli, F. and Strange, J-M (2007) *20th Century Britain:Economic*, Cultural
    and Social Change, London: Longman
9   McIlroy, J. (1995) *Trade Unions in Britain Today*, Manchester: Manchester University Press
10 *The Economist* weekly magazine: www.economist.com

Websites

Department of Trade and Industry: www.dti.gov.uk
HM Treasury: www.hm-treasury.gov.uk
Office for National Statistics: www.ons.uk
British Trade International: www.brittrade.com
Bank of England: www.bankofengland.co.uk
Financial Services Authority: www.fsa.gov.uk
Lloyds of London: www.lloydsoflondon.co.uk
Confederation of British Industry: www.cbi.org.uk
Trades Union Congress: www.tuc.org.uk
Business in the Community: www.bitc.org.uk
The Industrial Society: www.indsoc.co.uk
Populus opinion polls: www.populuslimited.com

8

Social services

State (public) sector provision for social security, health care, personal social services and social housing are very much taken for granted by many Britons today. They also feature prominently in lists of people's concerns and directly affect the daily lives of individuals of all ages. But it was not until the 1940s that the state accepted overall responsibility for providing basic social help for all its citizens. Previously, there had been few such facilities and it was felt that the state was not obliged to supply them. British social services developed considerably from the mid-twentieth century as society and government policies changed. Reflecting this historical context, they are now divided between state (public) and private sectors.

The state provides services and benefits for the sick, retired, disabled, elderly, needy and unemployed. Some are organized through devolved authorities, such as health, housing and social care by the Scottish government and housing, child care and some social security by the Department for Social Development in Northern Ireland. The UK Department of Work and Pensions has reserved powers under devolution and deals with most UK social security matters (welfare and pensions) and the UK Department of Health has responsibility for health care through the National Health Service (NHS) structure and social services for most of the UK except Scotland. The costs of this system are funded mainly by general taxation and partly by a National Insurance Fund to which employers and employees contribute. This means that although many social services, such as health care, are provided free at the point of need, most people will have contributed to them during their working lives through income tax and national insurance contributions.

In the private sector, some social and health services are financed by personal insurance schemes, company occupational plans and by those people who choose to pay for such facilities out of their own income or capital. However, most of these people are also eligible for public sector care if they wish. There are also many long-established voluntary organizations which continue the tradition of charitable help for the needy and depend for their funding upon donations from the public.

Conservative governments (1979–97) introduced reforms in the state sector in order to reduce expenditure, eradicate fraud, improve efficiency, encourage more self-provision and target benefits on those most genuinely in need. Such policies were widely attacked and it was argued that they were based on a market orientation and a return to the old mentality of personal responsibility for social needs.

The previous Labour government since 1997 also tried to reform the very expensive welfare state by encouraging people to insure themselves against unemployment and sickness and to provide for their own pensions and care in old age. It has introduced reforms to help families, reduce poverty and exclusion, and made efforts to return the unemployed to work. But critics argue that the reforms have not been wholly successful and the government has had to increase public spending in these areas (such as the National Health Service) in order to prevent their decay and possible collapse.

Such developments suggest that the state in future may be unable (or unwilling) to meet the financial costs of public social services without increases in personal income tax or alternative funding schemes. People are consequently being encouraged to build their own welfare plans, and government's role in the future may lie in directing aid rather than its funding and provision. This shows the difficulty of reconciling public services demand with a 'free market economy' and of deciding how much dependence there should be upon the state. The Labour government also tried to involve the private sector more in the provision and management of public services, such as Public–Private Partnerships. But there is public and trade union opposition to this policy, which is generally perceived as the privatization of 'free' social services.

Social services history

Historically, state social services were non-existent for most of the British population. The churches, charities, the rural feudal system and town guilds (organizations of skilled craftsmen) did give some protection against poverty, illness and unemployment. But this help was limited in its application and effect. Most people were thrown upon their own, often minimal, resources in order to survive.

In Elizabeth I's reign (1558–1603), a Poor Law was established in England by which the state took over the organization of charity provisions from the church. Similar schemes existed in Wales, Scotland and Ireland. They operated at the local level and parishes were responsible through taxation for their poor, sick and unemployed, providing housing, help and work relief. The Poor Law was the start of state social legislation in Britain, but it was grudging, limited in its effects and discouraged people from relying on it. Poverty and need were considered to be the result of an unwillingness to work and provide for oneself. The state was not expected to have extensive responsibility for social services.

These attitudes persisted, though urban and rural poverty and need continued. Conditions worsened in the eighteenth and nineteenth centuries as industrial revolutions and the population rapidly increased. The urban workforce had to work long hours in often bad conditions in low-quality factories for low wages. Families frequently inhabited slums of overcrowded, back-to-back dwellings which lacked adequate sewerage, heating or ventilation. The situation of many rural agricultural workers was just as bad.

Public health became an inevitable concern and the poor conditions resulted in infectious epidemics in the nineteenth century, such as diphtheria, typhoid, tuberculosis, smallpox and measles. Some diseases remained endemic in the British population into the twentieth century because of bad housing and the lack of adequate health and social facilities.

The old Poor Law was replaced by the Poor Law Amendment Act of 1834 in England and Wales (later in Scotland). This was designed to prevent the alleged abuse of parish social relief and to reduce the high taxes needed to service the system. It created a system of workhouses in which the destitute and needy could work and live. However, these were unpleasant places and people were discouraged from relying upon them. They were dreaded by the poor and accepted only as a last resort. Since nineteenth-century Britain was subject to economic slumps and unemployment, the workhouse system often resulted in misery and the separation of families.

Successive governments until the nineteenth century refused to allow workers to organize themselves into trade unions, through which they might agitate against their working and living conditions. This forced some workers into establishing their own social and self-help clubs in order to provide basic protection for themselves. Although some employers were more benevolent than others and provided good housing and health facilities for their workforces, such examples were few and life continued to be harsh for many in both the towns and the countryside.

The social misery of the nineteenth century persuaded some towns to establish local boards to control public health and initiate health schemes, though a public health apparatus was not created until 1848 and an effective national system was not in place until 1875. Legislation was passed to clean up slum areas, but large-scale clearance was not achieved until the mid-twentieth century. Reforms in housing, health, factory and mine conditions, sanitation and sewerage, town planning and trade unionism were implemented in the nineteenth century. But they were limited in their effects and were seen as paternalistic in their intention.

The social welfare problems of the nineteenth century were considerable, and the state's failure to provide major help against illness, unemployment and poverty made the situation worse. Social reformers, who promoted legislation offering some relief from the more negative effects of industrialization, had to struggle against the apathy and hostility of vested interests in Parliament and the country.

However, small victories had been won and in the early twentieth century it was slowly, if not universally, admitted that the state had social responsibility for the whole of society. Progressive Liberal governments between 1905 and 1922 introduced reform programmes on old age pensions, national insurance, health, employment and trade unionism. These formed the basic structures of the future welfare state. But they affected only a minority of people, and the state was unwilling or unable to introduce further provisions in the early twentieth century. The financial and physical exhaustion resulting from the 1914–18 war and the economic crises of the 1920s and 1930s halted social services expansion.

Yet the underlying need for more state help continued as the population increased. The model for a welfare state appeared in the Beveridge Report of 1942. This recommended that a comprehensive system of social security and free health care for all should be established to overcome suffering and need 'from the cradle to the grave'. It was intended that the system would be largely financed by a national insurance scheme, to which workers would contribute, and out of which they and their families would receive benefits when required. Although Conservative governments passed some of the legislation to implement these proposals, it was the 1945–1951 Labour government that radically altered the social and health systems and created the present welfare state. It was also gradually realized that most of the cost of the system would have to be provided out of general taxation.

Household and demographic structures

The provision of contemporary social services, in both public and private sectors, is conditioned by changes in household structures, demographic factors (such as birth rates and increases in life expectancy), governmental responses to social needs, the availability and cost of services and individuals' personal financial resources.

It is argued that, as new social structures have emerged, the traditional British household either as a nuclear family (two parents and children living together) or

TABLE 8.1 Types of household, Great Britain, 2009 (%)	
One-person household	12
One-family household	
Couple	
No children	25
Dependent children	36
Non-dependent children only	9
Lone parent with children	12
Other households	6
(Includes same-sex couples and civil partners)	
Source: Adapted from Labour Force Survey, Office for National Statistics, 2009	

extended unit is falling apart; failing to provide for its elderly and disabled; suffering from social and moral problems; lacking parenting skills; and looking automatically to the state for support. In 2009, there were 25.2 million households in Great Britain and an increasing trend towards smaller units resulted in the average household size falling to 2.4 people.

Statisticians predict that married couples will in future be outnumbered by those individuals who never marry. The proportion of unmarried men will increase more than that of unmarried women; the rise in cohabiting couples (couples of the same or different genders living together outside marriage) will not compensate for the decrease in married couples; and divorce rates are already declining.

More adults will be living alone in the future. There has been a significant increase over the past twenty years in one-person households with no children. These are people of all ages who may be single by choice, divorced, separated, widows or widowers. There were more than seven million people living alone in the UK in 2007. More than 60 per cent of women and one-third of men aged 75 and over lived alone.

Nevertheless, marriage is still the most common form of partnership for men and women, despite a decrease in popularity of 20 per cent since 1971. There were 275,000 marriages in 2006; 60 per cent were first marriages for both partners (25.3 per cent for women and 21.0 for men); and 52 per cent of men and 50 per cent of women in Great Britain were married.

Two in five marriages were remarriages of one or both parties. Only a quarter of first marriages now have a religious ceremony, while most remarriages are civil. More people are delaying marriage until their late twenties (average age twenty-eight for men and twenty-six for women) for career and other reasons.

The rate of divorce has fluctuated in the past forty years and fell to 148,000 in 2006. This is the lowest number of divorces since 1977, a rate of 12.2 divorces per 1,000 married men/women. Remarriages are at greater risk than first marriages, and people who marry under twenty-one are the most susceptible to divorce. The rate for remarriages among men was more than double that of women (28.4 compared with 13.8) and the most common divorce ages for both women and men were between twenty-five and twenty-nine. Divorce affects a considerable number of children under sixteen. The trauma is increased by the confrontational nature of the divorce system, with conflicts arising over property, financial support and custody of children.

Associated with the declining rate of divorce, there has been, over the past twenty years, a big increase in cohabitation (same-sex couples, couples and civil partners living together outside marriage). In 2006 in Great Britain, 13 per cent of men and women aged 16–59 were cohabiting. This percentage amounts to 1.8 million cohabiting couples in England and Wales and the number is expected to rise to about three million over the next twenty-five years. The proportion of unmarried men cohabiting was 24 per cent and that of unmarried women 25 per cent. Some of these relationships are stable and long-term, and eight out of ten resulting births to couples are registered by both parents, rather than one as previously. Adoption of children by some registered civil partners and same-sex couples is also on the increase.

Non-marital (illegitimate) births arising from cohabitation and to single mothers were 46 per cent of live births in 2009. This figure includes single mothers aged under eighteen. Although the rate of teenage pregnancies in 2009 was the lowest since 1999, the reduction was modest. Consequently, figures in 2010 showed that Britain still had the highest unmarried teenage pregnancy rate in Western Europe. Non-marital births have caused controversy on moral and cost grounds and retain some of the old stigma. However, the legal standing of such children has been improved by removing restrictions in areas such as inheritance.

The British population was some 59.6 million in 2003 and 61.4 million in 2009, representing the greatest population increase in fifty years. Projections suggest that it could reach 65 million by 2050. There were 791,000 live births in 2009; the average UK-born woman has 1.84 children; those from abroad have 2.5 children; and a quarter of babies in 2008 were born to women who came from outside the UK.

On the other hand, between 1971 and 2003 there was an 18 per cent decrease in the number of children aged under sixteen and a 28 per cent increase in the number of people aged sixty-five and over. People aged over sixty-five will exceed the number of children under sixteen in the population by 2013. One in six of the population are now sixty-five, 7 per cent are over seventy-five and there are 1.3 million over-eighty-fives, amounting to 2 per cent of the total population. Life expectancy of men is 75.7 years and women 80.4, so that there are more women among the elderly. However, the number of older people in the population is expected to grow less quickly than in recent years.

The population is growing at a rate of 0.7 per cent every year, which is double the figure for the 1990s. However, childbearing has been delayed in recent years, with women in Britain having their first child on average at twenty-eight, seven years older than in 1971. Some women are delaying childbearing even longer for educational and career reasons, and there has been an increase in the number of single women and married/unmarried couples who choose either to remain childless or to limit their families. Contraception has become more widespread; the voluntary sterilization of both sexes is more common and the number of legal abortions has increased.

A rise in divorce and individualistic lifestyles have led to a threefold growth in the number of one-parent families with dependent children since 1961. It is estimated that some 2 million children are being raised in 1.3 million one-parent units (or 12 per cent of all households). Some 90 per cent of these units are headed by a mother and 10 per cent by a father. Of the women bringing up one-parent families 16 per cent are single, 34 per cent divorced, 22 per cent separated and 17 per cent widowed. Lone fathers tend to be either divorced or widowers. Some of these families (with the highest proportion being in Inner London) often have reduced living standards and are dependent upon social security benefits.

The proportion of married women in employment is now some 70 per cent. More women are returning to work more quickly after the birth of a child and women make up 45 per cent of the workforce. But although Britain has a high percentage of working mothers and wives, provisions for maternity leave and child care are low in European terms.

The various household units have to cope with increased demands upon them, which may entail considerable personal sacrifice. They carry out most of the caring roles in British society, rather than state professionals. Only 6 per cent of people over sixty-five and 7 per cent of disabled adults live in state or private institutions. Most disabled children and adults are cared for by their families and most of the elderly are either cared for by their families or live alone supported by help from the social services. These figures represent a saving to the state without which the cost of state health and welfare care would rise. However, the burden upon families will grow as the population becomes more elderly, state provision is reduced and the numbers of disabled (currently 6 million adults) and disadvantaged increase. There are demands that more state aid should be given to carers, families and local authorities to lighten their burden.

The picture that emerges from these statistics is one of smaller households; more people living alone; an increase in the number of one-parent units and non-marital births; a declining divorce rate; more individuals living longer and contributing to an ageing population; more working mothers and wives; more cohabiting couples; more civil partnerships; and a decline in marriage. These features influence the contemporary state and private provisions for social security, health, social services and housing.

Social services (pensions and welfare)

The social services system is complicated; provides different types of payments such as state pensions and welfare benefits; and is operated by local government and the Department of Work and Pensions in most parts of the UK. British people may receive payments from contributory National Insurance, means-tested benefits, non-contributory benefits, universal benefits and discretionary benefits. Social services payments are the government's most expensive programme (an estimated £196 billion of total government spending in the 2010 budget) and are financed from general taxation and contributions by employers and workers over sixteen to the National Insurance Fund.

This means that social security gives payments to workers who pay contributions to the National Insurance Fund and income tax system; income-related benefits to people who have no income or whose income falls below certain levels and who need assistance; and other non-contributory benefits which are conditional on illness or family needs, such as Disability and Attendance Allowances.

The contributory system gives, for example, relatively low state retirement pensions for employed women at sixty and men at sixty-five (to be equalized to sixty-five for all from 2010 but rising to sixty-eight by 2050); maternity pay for pregnant working women; statutory sick pay for people who are absent from work because of illness or who become incapable of work; and a Jobseeker's Allowance for those who become unemployed (dependent upon people actively seeking work).

Income-related benefits are also provided by the state, usually after means-testing (examination of financial position). For example, *Income Support* depends upon savings and capital and is given at various levels of eligibility to some 5.6 million people in financial need, such as one-parent families, the elderly, long-term sick and unemployed. It covers basic living requirements, although the sums are relatively low. It also includes free prescription medicine, dental treatment, opticians' services and children's school meals. The *Working Families' Tax Credit* is a benefit whereby families with children and at least one parent in low-paid work receive a tax credit through workers' pay packets to increase their earnings. It includes the same extra benefits as Income Support and is dependent upon income, savings and capital. A *Child Tax Credit* is a payment to support families with children and is dependent upon income and the number of children in a family unit. *Housing Benefit* is paid to people on Income Support and other low-income claimants and covers the cost of rented accommodation. A tax-free *Child Benefit* (£15 per week for the eldest child and £10 for other children) is paid to all mothers for each of her children up to the age of eighteen, irrespective of family income.

In the past, people in great need were also able to claim non-contributory single payments, such as the cost of clothes, cookers and children's shoes, in the form of grants or loans, but these have been sharply cut and replaced by a Social Fund, to which people have to apply. The fund is applied restrictively and is criticized as an example of government's alleged reduction of social security aid.

Social welfare benefits do provide a degree of security. They are supposed to be a safety net against urgent needs, but this does not prevent hardship. Some 27 per cent of British people are on different kinds of income-related benefits. It is estimated that in 2007/08, 13.5 million people with 1.8 million children lived in households below the low-income threshold (for example £279 a week for a couple with two dependent children under fourteen). Other models suggest that a quarter of the population exist on the poverty line, which is sometimes measured as 60 per cent of the average national income (about £11,500). But accurate figures of poverty are difficult to gather because of the variable presentation of official statistics; there are different definitions of what constitutes poverty; and poverty today tends to be seen in relative rather than absolute terms.

Social welfare benefits are very expensive and will become more so as the population ages and as the numbers of the sick, poor, disadvantaged and unemployed persist. They are very complicated, with their array of benefits, and subject to fraud, particularly in the cases of Income Support, Disability Allowance and Housing Benefit.

From 1997 the previous Labour government tried to reform the system, attack fraud, cut expense and reduce benefits while still preserving the safety-net commitment and targeting those people with the greatest needs. It was committed to reducing poverty and exclusion, and it succeeded to a limited extent. It is argued, however, that such reforms will mean a real reduction in social security, particularly the social fund, housing benefit, income support, disability allowance and unemployment aid. The young unemployed aged from sixteen upwards are now ineligible for benefits until they reach eighteen and are required to enter training, work or education programmes. Although governments argue that the cost of social security is unsustainable and encourage greater self-provision through work rather than dependency, it is difficult to create a simple and fair system which protects the genuinely needy and also encourages people to become more self-reliant and independent.

Conservative and Labour governments are concerned that people should look after themselves more, without automatic recourse to the state for help, and that they should seek employment more actively. During the general election campaign in 2010 all political parties agreed that it was unacceptable that those who were capable of work should reject it and live off benefits instead as a lifestyle.

The creation of jobs, an embrace of the work ethic and greater personal responsibility are seen as essential in the face of a difficult economic future, social uncertainty and pension difficulties. The value of occupational pensions operated by private companies has effectively been reduced by a movement from final-salary pensions to different forms of subscription. Some firms have gone out of business leaving workers without the pensions to which they have contributed. It is argued that a predicted state and private pension crisis in Britain can be solved only by increased taxation to pay for state pensions at a time when the labour force (which funds retiring workers) is decreasing or by workers working longer and saving more for their retirement (or by a combination of the two).

The National Health Service (NHS)

A Labour government created the National Health Service (NHS) in 1947. It was based on the Beveridge Report recommendations and replaced a private system of payment for health care with one of free treatment for all at the point of need. The medical profession wished to retain private medicine and opposed the establishment of the NHS, but this was countered by the Labour government.

The NHS was originally intended to be completely free for those needing medical help, irrespective of income. This ideal has, to a large extent, been achieved, although most people fund the system through their taxes and National Insurance contributions while working. Hospital and most medical treatment under the NHS is free for British and EU citizens. The NHS provides a range of medical and dental services for the whole country based on hospitals, doctors, dentists, nurses, midwives, ambulance services, blood transfusion and other health facilities.

However, some charges are now made: for example, prescriptions (written notes from a doctor enabling patients to obtain drugs from a chemist) have to be paid for, as is the case with some dental work, dental checks and eye tests. Payments are dependent upon employment status, age and income. Children under sixteen, people on social security benefits and old age pensioners receive free prescriptions. However, NHS dental treatment is in serious trouble and many dentists have left the NHS for private practice.

The NHS and health care was estimated to cost £122 billion of total government spending in the 2010 budget and is the biggest single employer of labour in Western Europe. Yet, despite increased government spending and rising health care costs, state health expenditure in Britain is only 8.8 per cent of the gross domestic product (GDP) and lower than in other major Western countries, which have a higher combination of the public and the private in their health spending.

Although the term NHS usually refers to the UK as a whole, the UK government funds the NHS for the entire country and is responsible for the NHS in England through the Department of Health, while devolved authorities in Scotland, Wales and Northern Ireland handle their own health matters.

The Labour government created two health care levels: primary and secondary care. Primary Care Trusts control two-thirds of NHS budgets at local level; are the first contact for patients; assess local needs; commission care; and include health professionals (such as doctors) and hospitals. Secondary care is acute emergency and specialist care and follows a referral from a doctor or primary care. Both levels work with Strategic Health Authorities to manage and improve local services. The coalition government intends to abolish the PCTs and SHSs, cut bureaucratic costs, give finance and health commissioning duties to GPs (doctors) and make all hospitals independent of Whitehall control.

Doctors

Most people in Britain who require health care will first consult their local NHS-funded doctor, who is a GP or non-specialist general practitioner and of whom there are about 35,000. Doctors have an average of 2,000 registered patients on their panel (or list of names), although they will see only a small percentage of these on a regular basis. The majority of GPs are now members of group practices

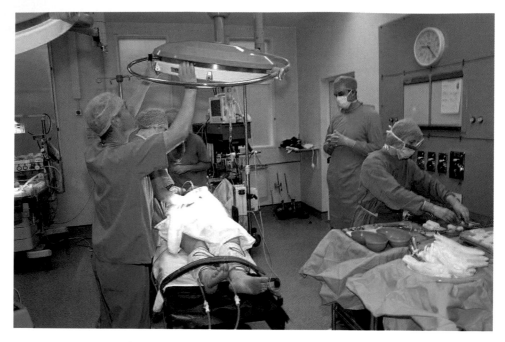

PLATE 8.1 A woman being prepared for a Caesarean section birth in an operating theatre.
(Shout/Rex Features)

where they share larger premises, services and equipment, which also allow for some minor surgery. However, a patient will usually be on the panel of one particular doctor, who will often be a personal choice. An alternative to seeing a doctor is to make use of the NHS Direct service, which allows one to seek advice on the telephone from nurses. There are conflicting reports on this service's effectiveness.

Hospitals

If patients require further treatment or examination, the GP refers them to specialists and consultants, normally at local NHS hospitals or NHS Trusts. NHS Trust hospitals are funded by contracts with the local Primary Care Groups and are 'self-governing' to a large extent. Trusts may apply to become foundation hospitals, which run their own independent budgets and services. Hospitals have about 370,000 beds and provide medical, dental, nursing and midwifery staff. Britain has some very modern hospitals and facilities and more hospitals are being constructed, but it also has many buildings which were erected in the nineteenth century and are in urgent need of modernization and repair. There is a shortage of beds in some hospitals, with wards and hospitals being closed. Waiting times for consultancy visits and admission to hospital for operations as well as for treatment in accident and emergency departments are still a source of concern,

PLATE 8.2 University College Hospital, London, one of the new NHS hospitals being constructed in many parts of Britain.
(Jeff Blackler/Rex Features)

despite a large infusion of government funds into the system and improvements in some areas.

The state of the NHS

The NHS has an ambivalent position in the public mind. On one hand, it is praised for its work as a free service and its achievements. It is considered a success in terms of consumer demand. Today people are in general receiving help when they need it and many who would previously have died or suffered are surviving and being cared for. Standards of living and medicine have risen, better diets have been devised and there is greater health awareness in the population at large.

On the other hand, the NHS is criticized for its alleged inefficiency, inadequate standards, treatment discrepancies throughout the country, scandals and bureaucracy. Its objectives are considered too ambitious for the amount of money spent on it. The media constantly draw attention to shortcomings (such as hygiene problems and infectious disease outbreaks in hospitals) and forecast breakdown. Workers in the NHS, such as doctors, nurses and non-medical staff, complain about low pay, long hours, management weaknesses, levels of staffing (with a shortage of doctors and nurses) and cuts in services. In the past, it was suggested that such problems could be solved simply by injecting more money into the NHS, but increased spending by the Labour government has not eradicated what many critics see as a managerial inability to organize the funds competently at the point where they are needed.

Rising costs and increased demand provoke cries for more finance and resources. The NHS is in many ways a victim of its own success and of the demands that the British place upon it as of right. It is inevitable that a free, consumer-led service will require increasing levels of expenditure, better management of existing resources or alternative funding. Yet despite problems, such as an increasing number of physical assaults upon health professionals in hospitals and surgeries, and undoubted pressures, much of the NHS works well and gives good value for the money spent on it.

There are many suggestions as to how the NHS can be improved, but each can have unfortunate results. Increased government spending on the NHS may lead to an increase in taxation. Charges could be made for some services, but this would go against the principle of free health care, although polls show that many respondents would be prepared to pay for some NHS care if it meant an overall better service. More efficient management of existing funds might make some savings, but possibly not enough. Combining a public service with private insurance would not include poorer people, who would still be dependent upon a free NHS. The previous Labour government involved the private sector more closely in the running of the NHS (through Private Finance Initiatives – PFIs) and paying for patient care in private hospitals. However, many people regard these devices as a form of privatization of the NHS and some private contracts for building hospitals have not been successful.

The previous Labour government was committed to raising NHS spending to European levels, reducing management costs, transferring money to medical care and staff and reorganizing the NHS administration. Yet the public saw little actual improvement and, according to MORI polls in May and July 2005, were disillusioned with Labour's attempts to revitalize the service and very concerned about health facilities. The World Health Organization in August 2001 ranked Britain as twenty-fourth out of 191 countries in terms of the efficiency of its health system, above countries such as Germany, the USA and Denmark. But a 2007 survey from Health Consumer Powerhouse in Brussels said that Britain ranked seventeenth out of twenty-nine European countries on a range of healthcare benchmarks including quality of service, length of waiting times and patient information.

The private medical sector

It is argued that health care should not be a question of who can pay for it but a responsibility of the state. However, the public sector has problems and attempts have been made to involve the private sector in providing health care.

The previous Conservative government encouraged the growth of private health institutions, private medical insurance and partnership between the public and private sectors on a commercial basis. Its Private Finance Initiative allowed new health facilities to be built, maintained and owned by the private sector. These are then leased to the NHS, which provides clinical services and controls planning and clinical decisions. The Conservatives saw the private sector as complementary to the NHS. It would release pressure on state funds; give choice to patients; allow the sharing of medical resources; provide flexible services; result in cost-effective cooperation with the NHS; and allow the treatment of NHS patients at public expense in the private sector.

The Labour government, in a reversal of old Labour ideology, embraced these ideas. It had agreements with private health care providers to enable the NHS to make better use of facilities in private hospitals. Some NHS hospitals share expensive equipment with private hospitals, and NHS patients are treated (at public expense) in the private sector when it represents value for money. However, the scale of private practice in relation to the NHS is small. Much private treatment is confined to minor medical cases and expensive, long-term care is still carried out by the NHS.

A quarter of all operations and healthcare in Britain are paid for privately by patients out of their income, capital or insurance policies. Some 6.9 million individuals and 4.8 million people in company plans are covered by private medical insurance taken out with businesses such as the British United Provident Association (BUPA). Concern about waiting lists and standards of health care in the NHS persuades many to take out such insurance. The insurance policy pays for private care either in private hospitals and clinics or in NHS hospitals which provide 'pay beds' (beds for the use of paying patients, which still exist in NHS hospitals and were a concession in 1946 to those doctors who agreed to join the NHS but who wished to keep a number of private patients). A Consumers' Association report in August 2001 found that 40 per cent of respondents would consider going private to avoid lengthy NHS queues, although 84 per cent did not have medical insurance. Many people today are also likely to be deterred by the rising costs of insurance premiums and private treatment.

The personal social services

The state (public) sector

State (public) social services provide facilities by various agencies in the local community which assist people such as the elderly, the disabled, the mentally ill, families, children and young people. Trained staff, such as district visitors, nurses and social workers, cater for these personal needs. The services are organized by local government and devolved authorities with UK government funding (£33 billion of total government spending in the 2010 budget). While it is argued that social services need extra public money to address problems, local and devolved authorities may privatize parts of the sector to avoid costs.

Increasing pressure is being put upon the social services, families and carers as the elderly population grows and the ranks of the disadvantaged rise. For example, the number of public residential care and nursing homes for the elderly is insufficient for the demand, and some are privatized to save costs, while some private homes close because of cost and reduced profit. In both cases, elderly people may be forced to sell their homes to cover some or all of their expenses. However, in Scotland residential and medical care is free under devolved legislation. Care services for the elderly and infirm in both private and state sectors face severe staff shortage unless higher pay and better training for workers are introduced and the system operates on a better foundation.

The previous Conservative government introduced a 'Care in the Community' programme, which was continued by Labour. The aim is to give financial and material support to families and carers looking after elderly or disabled relatives in the latters' own homes or for children and adults with disabilities in the family home. It also allows psychiatric patients who do not need constant care to be moved into the community under social services supervision and for elderly and disabled people to be cared for in their own homes by the social services. The aim is to prevent the people becoming institutionalized and to give them independence.

But the scheme has had difficulties, such as mentally ill and disabled patients becoming homeless, being housed in inadequate temporary accommodation and neglecting their medication, while elderly people sometimes receive poor attention and help. It is argued that local authorities need more support and that awareness of implementation problems is required if the policy is to be more successful.

The personal social services also cater for people with learning disabilities, give help to families and provide day care facilities for children. Children in need or suffering from family breakdown and dysfunctional parents are also supposed to be protected in residential care accommodation and local authorities facilitate fostering and adoption services. But there have been a number of serious cases in recent years which have focused on physical and sexual abuse in children's care homes as well as child deaths in family homes from neglect and abuse. Local government social services, which are often hard pressed in these cases, have been heavily criticized.

The private social services (voluntary) sector

While there were improvements in state social services in the twentieth century, there is still a shortage of finance and resources to support all the needy in a comprehensive fashion, and their numbers continue to rise. The private sector supplies various care facilities, but these are declining because of costs. It is therefore important that voluntary charities and agencies have remained. These are a complementary welfare service to the state and private facilities and provide an essential element in the total aid pattern. The state system would be unable to cover all needs without them.

Most of the voluntary agencies have charitable status, which means that they receive tax concessions on their income but receive no (or very little) financial support from the state. However, some groups, such as those dealing with drug and alcohol addiction and released prisoners, do receive financial grants from central and local government. There are many thousands of voluntary organizations in Britain, operating at national and local levels and varying considerably in size. Some are small and collect limited amounts of money or donations from the public. Others are very large, have professional staffs and receive millions of pounds from many different sources. Some groups, such as Oxfam (for the relief of famine) and the Save the Children Fund, have now become international organizations.

The following are examples of voluntary agencies. Barnardo's provides help for needy children; the Church of England Children's Society cares for neglected children and is Britain's largest adoption agency; the Cancer Research Fund gathers finance and carries out research into cures for cancer; the People's Dispensary for Sick Animals (PDSA) provides free veterinary aid for people's pets; the Samaritans give telephone help to the suicidal; women's groups have founded refuges for abused women; and Age UK campaigns for the concerns of the elderly.

Housing

Housing in Britain is divided into the public and private sectors. Of the 25 million domestic dwellings, the majority are in the private sector, with 69.8 per cent in 2007 being owner-occupied (after falls in 2006 and 2007) and 12 per cent rented out by private landlords. Some 18 per cent (social housing) are in the public, subsidized sector and are rented by low-income tenants from local government authorities or housing associations (non-profit-making bodies which manage and build homes for rent and sale with the aid of government grants).

In both public and private sectors, 81 per cent of the British population live in houses or bungalows (single-storey houses) and the remainder in flats and maisonettes (19 per cent). Houses have traditionally been divided into detached (22 per cent), semi-detached (32) and terraced housing (27), with the greater prices and prestige being given to detached property.

Public-sector or social housing in England is controlled centrally by the Department of the Environment and by devolved bodies in Wales, Scotland and Northern Ireland. Much of this housing has historically been provided by local authorities with finance from local sources and central government. However,

PLATE 8.3 Detached house on new housing estate, Surrey, England. Detached houses command the highest prices on the British housing market, particularly as here in southern England. But notice the relatively small house plot.
(Rex Features)

PLATE 8.4 Terraced housing, Kensal Rise, London. Terraced housing, where houses are joined together in a row, varies in quality and type throughout Britain. These in London are popular and can be expensive, depending on location and condition.
(*Ray Tang/Rex Features*)

the provision and organization of such properties by local government has declined in recent years and more has been taken over by housing associations.

The previous Conservative government (1979–97) encouraged the growth of home ownership in the housing market as part of its programme to create a property- and share-owning democracy in Britain. In the public sector, the Conservatives were critical of local government housing policies. They wanted local authorities to divest themselves of housing management, and instead work with housing associations and the private sector to increase the supply of low-cost housing for rent without providing it themselves. The government also introduced (1980) a right-to-buy policy by which local government sells off council housing to sitting tenants at below-market prices. This policy has increased the number of homeowners by over 1 million and relieved local authorities of the expense of decoration, upkeep and repair.

The Labour Party, after initially opposing the policy, accepted it, mainly because it proved attractive to tenants. The Labour government ploughed back the revenue from council sales into local government (which previously had not been able to spend it) so that it could provide more low-cost social housing. It therefore returned some control over housing policies to local government and was sceptical of tenants who bought council properties to quickly sell them on

PLATE 8.5 A housing estate, Thamesmead, London. Council or social housing built by local government authorities (here on the south bank of the River Thames) for rent to low-income tenants. Many of these concrete tower blocks have now been demolished.

(Londonstills.com/Rex Features)

for profit on the open market. UK Government spending on housing (and the environment) was £27 billion of total spending in the 2010 budget.

However, the construction of new publicly funded houses has declined in real terms and the private sector is not building enough low-cost or affordable properties. Critics argue that Conservative government housing policies contributed to a serious shortage of cheap rented accommodation in towns and rural areas for low-income groups, single people and the unemployed, at a time when demand was (and is) growing. The biggest increase in this demand is expected to be in the number of one-person households, which is projected to reach 8.5 million by 2021.

Home ownership in the private sector had increased by 10 per cent since 1979. The normal procedure when buying a house or flat is to take out a loan on the security of the property (a mortgage) from a building society, bank or other financial institution. The amount of money advanced on a loan depends mainly on the borrower's salary, and it is usual to borrow three times one's gross annual salary. This long-term loan is usually paid off over a 25-year period and includes interest.

House prices can vary considerably throughout the country, with London and south-east England having the highest and northern England, Scotland and Wales the lowest. Prices increased dramatically at the beginning of the 1970s and much property speculation occurred. Price increases then stabilized for some years, but there was a price boom from 1986 to 1988, followed by high interest rates and an increase in mortgage foreclosures. This means that, when people cannot afford to continue their repayments on the loan, the lending institution takes over the property (repossession) and the occupier becomes homeless. There was also a fall in house prices, a property slump and a growth in negative equity which was only slowly reversed from 1994 as interest rates were reduced and the property market recovered. House prices then increased spectacularly again throughout Britain, and critics argue that properties were overvalued. Interest rates increased to counter the property boom. Lenders gave easy and very high loans, often to borrowers who were unable to repay them. The credit crunch arrived in 2007 bringing a collapse in the housing market and recession due partly to reckless mortgage lending by lending institutions, the accumulation of huge personal debt and (ironically) a chronic oversupply of new properties (particularly buy-to-let flats at high rents). Foreclosures increased. After a period from 2008 when the housing market was close to collapse, there was a growth in sales and prices in 2010 with the end of the recession.

British homes still have variable construction standards. Many older types are old, damp and cold, are frequently badly built and lack central heating and adequate insulation. Yet there has been some improvement in housing quality in recent years and most new houses have a high percentage of the basic amenities. Greater attention has been paid to insulation and energy saving, aided by government grants for older properties. However, as building costs rise and available land becomes scarcer, the trend in new property construction has been towards flats and much smaller, more cramped rooms in houses.

Nevertheless, there are still districts, particularly in the centres of the big cities, where living conditions are bad and the equivalent of contemporary slums. Nearly half of the property in inner-city areas was built before 1919 and, in spite of large-scale slum clearance in the 1950s and 1960s, much existing housing here is in barely habitable shape. Some recently completed high-rise (tower) blocks of council flats and estates in the public sector have had to be demolished because of defective and dangerous structures. According to the National Housing Forum, one in thirteen British homes (or 1.8 million) is unfit for human habitation.

Twentieth-century town renovation and slum clearance policies from the 1930s were largely devoted to the removal of the populations of large city centres to new towns, usually located in the countryside, or to new council estates in the suburbs. Some of the new towns, such as Crawley and Stevenage, have been seen as successes, although they initially had their share of social and planning problems. The same cannot be said of many council estates, which have tended to degenerate very quickly. The bad design of some housing estates, their social deprivation and lack of upkeep are often blamed for the crime and vandalism which affect many of them. Some local councils are now modernizing decaying housing stock rather than spending on new developments, in an attempt to preserve local communities, although the previous Labour government was intent on demolishing old properties, particularly in northern England. Renovation work is also being done by housing associations (with the aid of government grants) and by private builders.

The provision of sufficient affordable and varied housing in Britain, such as one-bedroom properties for young and single persons, has been a problem for many years. People on low (and even medium) wages, whether married or single, are often unable to afford the cost of a mortgage for suitable private property in the current market. Even young professionals such as university graduates with substantial salaries are unable to get mortgages and many end up living with their parents. One of the factors (in addition to high property prices) causing the difficulty for young people in affording first homes, particularly in rural areas within (ever-increasing) commuting distance of London, is the desire of affluent people for homes – or second homes – in the country. It is also difficult for them to obtain council housing because of long waiting lists, which include people with priority over them. The right-to-buy policy has reduced the number of available council houses and flats for low-income groups and the unemployed. Alternatives for many are to board with parents, house-share with others or rent property in the private sector.

In a limited housing market, it is argued that Britons should give up their obsession with home ownership and investigate new ways to meet housing demand, such as shared rentals and part- or shared-ownership arrangements.

The previous Conservative government tried to encourage landlords and other agencies to provide more privately rented accommodation by lessening the effects of rent legislation and introducing new lease structures. But the relaxations have led to accusations of exploitation of tenants by landlords. The Labour government wanted a healthy private rented sector. It tried to improve the rights of leaseholders to purchase their freehold and protect themselves against abuse by unscrupulous landlords. At the same time, there was a growth in the number of purchasers of 'buy-to-rent' properties which, until recently, proved to be attractive investments. The recession led to the virtual collapse of the 'buy-to-rent' market as landlords overextended themselves.

In an attempt to cope with the demand for housing, the Labour government embarked on large-scale building plans in the English south Midlands, the south-east and along the south coast. This policy was criticized since some developments would be built on flood plains with the consequent threat of flooding while others were likely to cause environmental damage and increased traffic congestion. The government also permitted councils to allow high-density housing in urban areas and within Green Belts.

Inadequate housing provision has also partly contributed to the number of homeless people, particularly in London and other large cities, which in turn has

PLATE 8.6 A homeless man begging, Cromwell Road, London. The previous Labour government claimed that the number of homeless people and 'rough sleepers' was reduced during its period of office.
(Denis Cameron/Rex Features)

led to increased social problems. Accurate numbers for the homeless are notoriously difficult to find. Officially, there are some 105,000 homeless people, who need to be housed in temporary accommodation, which is usually inadequate. But figures from charities such as Crisis put the real homeless total for all age groups at about 380,000 (including about 130,000 children), and some of them are visible on the streets and in the doorways of Britain's large cities, particularly London. Others live in squats (unoccupied houses), shelters and temporary accommodation.

The Labour government established programmes and funds to combat 'rough sleeping' (people sleeping in the open) and there was a reduction of one-third in the numbers of rough sleepers by 2000. The causes of homelessness are complex and affect all age groups and types of people, but it is suggested that the problem could be better handled. There are some 700,000 homes (mainly in the Midlands and the north of England but increasingly in southern England) in both the private and public sectors which remain empty and unoccupied for various reasons. Critics argue that these could eradicate the problem of homelessness and the housing shortage if they were properly refurbished and utilized.

Charities such as Shelter and religious organizations like the Salvation Army provide accommodation for the homeless for limited periods and campaign on their behalf. Local organizations, such as Housing Advice Centres and Housing Aid Centres, also provide help. But the problem of housing in Britain is still a major one and a focus of public concern. The high prices of many private houses, the inadequacies of the public sector market and the difficulties of some renting suggest that the problem will remain. The number of new starts for construction in both the public and private sectors collapsed in the 2007–10 recession and continues to stagnate (2010).

Attitudes to the social services

Opinion polls consistently show that a majority of British people are concerned about public health and social services. An Ipsos MORI poll in April 2010 prior to the general election reported that the NHS (including hospitals and health care) was ranked fifth in a list of the most important issues facing Britain. Pensions, social security, welfare benefits and housing were also prominent in the list of concerns. A 2008 British Social Attitudes survey published in 2010 showed that 81 per cent of respondents thought there should be more/much more spending on health. This finding was in line with results in other European countries such as Spain, Norway and Sweden. In the poll, 39 per cent also said the government should increase taxes and spend more on health, education and social services, while 50 per cent thought taxes and spending on these services should be at the same levels as in 2008.

Such opinions apparently show that people in some European countries expect public or state health and social provisions to be readily available. These facilities should be expanded by having more money spent on them without (according to a majority) the need for an increase in personal taxation. Respondents to earlier polls felt there should be increased public spending on the National Health Service and medical resources (such as more doctors and nurses) and did not believe that there had been a great improvement in these areas despite increased funding by the previous Labour government since 2001. They did not consider the NHS as well run as other institutions and there was growing support for a comprehensive, better-funded and more efficient state healthcare service. Yet negative views on the social services may not always accurately portray reality, since the personal experiences of many other individuals in their dealings with the system are often very positive. Doctors and nurses frequently head the lists of professionals with whom Britons are most satisfied, despite recent scandals relating to medical negligence.

However, concern is also felt about the provision of social (council) housing, social security benefits, state pensions, the personal social services and community care. Most people, at least in response to poll questions and despite the above findings, indicate that they would be willing to pay higher taxes in order to ensure better social and health care. There is also some support for the idea that a proportional amount of income tax could be earmarked or ring-fenced as directly applicable to the frontline public services.

The huge budget deficit in 2010 of £163 billion pounds placed social services spending in sharp perspective. Yet it was unclear whether its necessary reduction would be met by cuts in public services, increased taxes, efficiency and wastage savings or a mixture of all three. A 2009 Ipsos MORI poll, published in March 2010, reported that 43 per cent of respondents agreed that spending on public services needed to be cut while 44 disagreed; 62 per cent agreed (while 26 per cent disagreed) that making public services more efficient could save enough money to pay off the budget deficit without damaging the services themselves. The poll also found that 75 per cent of respondents thought that reducing the number of managers in the NHS by a third would save most costs in the health service budget (14 per cent disagreed).

Some 90 per cent of respondents believed more control over health services should be given to doctors and nurses rather than to managers and politicians (7 per cent disagreed); and 80 per cent felt there should be fewer national targets for health services and more devolved local control (14 per cent disagreed).

It is questionable whether the implementation of such proposals and efficiency savings would in fact be sufficient to make sufficiently deep inroads into the budget deficit. The public social services are demand-led and must be serviced by taxation despite the fact that costs rise year on year. Critics suggest that one answer might be to increase the small degrees of privatization that already exist in the public health and social services.

However, the Public Finance Initiative (PFI) and Public–Private Partnership (PPP) schemes favoured by Conservative and Labour governments respectively, which involve the private sector in the provision and organization of public services, are not supported by a majority of the public, who see them as a form of gradual privatization. There is also opposition to other government reforms, such as plans for a controversial reorganization of Primary Care Trusts, which could involve some state health professionals being transferred to the private sector. There has been disquiet about the functions and responsibilities of Foundation Hospitals which, while being state hospitals, are independent, free from government control and open up public medical services to private sector finance and possible control. Critics argue that such developments establish a market for health care which will be extended to the rest of the welfare state.

Earlier polls had confirmed fears about privatization and private control of the social services. A MORI poll in July 2001 found that only one in nine respondents believed extending private sector involvement would improve public services. A later MORI poll in September 2001 found that 64 per cent of respondents felt public services, such as health, should be entirely or mostly provided by the public sector.

On being asked how public services could be improved, 64 per cent of respondents thought better pay and conditions should be given to public sector workers as an aid to recruitment; 43 per cent believed there should be more public sector workers; and 42 per cent considered there should be more investment in new buildings and equipment for public services.

These results show that a majority of British people support the idea of public services funded by taxation. A MORI poll in October 2001 found that only 42 per cent of respondents felt that government policies such as PPP would improve the state of public services. Significantly, all political parties in the 2010 general election campaign committed themselves to support the National Health Service and frontline services. But local councils have still approved the selling of state care homes for the elderly to the private sector.

Exercises

Explain and examine the following terms:

welfare state	chemist	flats	social services
Social Fund	benefits	GP	nuclear family
'pay beds'	rent	Shelter	council housing
workhouses	landlord	Oxfam	Beveridge Report
Poor Law	bungalow	mortgage	Income Support
charities	homeless	cohabitation	building society

Write short essays on the following topics:

1 *   Describe the structure and condition of the National Health Service

2   Does the social security system provide a comprehensive service for the needy in Britain?

3   Discuss the different types of housing in Britain and the method of buying property. What are some of the problems that affect property buying today?

Visit **www.routledge.com/textbooks/oakland** for multiple-choice questions, links to related YouTube clips, tips on approaching essay questions, and much, much more.

Further reading

1   George, V. and Wilding, P. (1999) *British Society and Social Welfare*, London: Palgrave/ Macmillan
2   Glennester, H. (2000) *British Social Policy since 1945*, Oxford: Blackwell
3   Ham, C. (1999) *Health Policy in Britain*, London: Palgrave/Macmillan
4   Harris, B. (2004) *The Origins of the British Welfare State: Social Welfare in England and Wales, 1800–1945*, London: Palgrave/Macmillan
5   Lowe, R. (2004) *The Welfare State in Britain since 1945*, London: Palgrave/Macmillan
6   Ludlam, S. and Smith, M.J. (eds) (2000) *New Labour in Government*, London: Macmillan
7   Mullins, D. and Murie, A. (2005) *Housing Policy in the UK*, London: Palgrave/Macmillan
8   Page, R. and Silburn, R. (eds) (1999) *British Social Welfare in the Twentieth Century*, London: Palgrave/Macmillan
9   Willman, J. (1998) *A Better State of Health*, London: Profile Books

Websites

Department of Work and Pensions: www.dwp.gov.uk
Department of Health: www.doh.gov.uk
Home Office: www.homeoffice.gov.uk
Charity Commission: www.charity-commission.gov.uk
Women's Unit: www.womens-unit.gov.uk
National Assembly for Wales: www.wales.gov.uk
Northern Ireland Executive: www.nics.gov.uk
Scottish Executive: www.scotland.gov.uk

9

Education

British education operates on three levels: schools, higher education and further/ adult education. Schools are divided into state (maintained from public funds) and independent (privately financed) sectors (the latter mainly in England). But there is no common educational organization for the whole country and England/Wales, Northern Ireland and Scotland have somewhat different school systems. To simplify matters, this chapter concentrates on the largest school unit, that of England and Wales, with comparative references to Scotland and Northern Ireland. Further/adult and higher education have similar structures throughout Britain and are mostly state-funded. The individual countries of the United Kingdom have significant degrees of independent self-government in educational matters at all these levels.

The quality of contemporary British state school education is of concern to parents, employers, politicians and students. School inspectors from Ofsted (the Office for Standards in Education) have criticized standards in English, mathematics, technology and writing/reading skills. In recent years, international comparisons by organizations such as the OECD and World Economic Forum have suggested that Britain does not rank highly for the quality of its secondary schools (defined by good passes in national examinations) and that British 13-to-14-year-olds lag behind comparable pupils in most European countries. British pre-school and primary education have also had a poor reputation in international terms, with a lack of high-quality nurseries and low-qualified and underpaid staff and poor working conditions at primary school levels. In 2005, figures from Ofsted reported that almost half of children were leaving state primary schools without the basic skills in reading, writing and arithmetic. It is argued that this results in some functionally illiterate pupils passing on to the secondary level of education. A National Skills Task Force in 2000 reported that 7 million adults (one in five) in Britain were illiterate, although some think tank reports suggest this proportion could now be higher. It is argued that low standards of literacy and numeracy stem in large part from decades of inadequate state school education.

However, the OECD has reported that Britain leads the world in higher education, with the highest proportion (35.6 per cent) of university graduates aged twenty-one, largely because of relatively short (three-year) degree courses. Yet in Britain it is argued that these courses should last two years in order to increase quality and productivity and to cut costs. There is criticism of degree standards and the content of some university courses, varying performances between different universities and the declining quality of students entering university from secondary school.

In spite of these reports, British education should not be seen in a wholly negative light. The previous Labour government in 1997 prioritized education, promised to focus on its quality and to make it a lifelong learning experience. Primary school literacy has improved, but not as much as expected. National school examination and test results have improved in recent years, although some critics attribute this to lower standards. Many schools, teachers and students in the state and independent sectors produce excellent work, as do some universities. It is the failing and underperforming state schools and universities which attract the media headlines. State school education still has weaknesses and the public were dissatisfied with the previous Labour government's progress in raising educational standards or creating an adequate schools structure. Education appears consistently in opinion polls as a main concern of the British public because of its alleged declining quality, political and bureaucratic tinkering with schools and universities, a targets and test culture and a league table mentality.

School history

The complicated nature of British (particularly English) schooling and current educational controversies have their roots in school history. State involvement in education came late and the first attempt to establish a unified system of state-funded elementary schools was made only in 1870 for England and Wales (1872 for Scotland and 1923 for Northern Ireland). Yet it was not until 1944 that the state provided a comprehensive and national apparatus for both primary and secondary state schools, which were free and compulsory.

However, some church schools have long existed. After England, Scotland, Ireland and Wales were gradually converted to Christianity by the fifth and sixth centuries, the church's position in society enabled it to create the first schools. These initially prepared boys for the priesthood, but the church then developed a wider educational role and its structures influenced the later state system.

Other schools were also periodically established by rich individuals or monarchs. These were independent, privately financed institutions and were variously known as high, grammar and public schools. They were later associated with both the modern independent and state educational sectors. But such schools were largely confined to the sons of the rich, aristocratic and influential. Most people received no formal schooling and remained illiterate and innumerate for life.

In later centuries, more children benefited as the church created new schools; local areas developed secular schools; charity schools were provided by wealthy industrialists and philanthropists for working-class boys and girls; and some other poor children attended a variety of schools organized by voluntary societies, women (dames), workhouses and the Ragged School Union. But the minority of children attending such institutions received only a very basic instruction in reading, writing and arithmetic. The majority of children received no adequate education.

By the nineteenth century, Britain (except for Scotland) had a haphazard school structure. Protestant churches had lost their monopoly of education and competed with the Roman Catholic Church and other faiths. Church schools guarded their independence from state and secular interference and provided much of the available schooling. The ancient high, grammar and public schools continued to train the sons of the middle and upper classes for professional and leadership roles in society, but, at a time when the industrial revolutions were proceeding rapidly and the population was growing strongly, the state did not provide a school system which could educate the workforce. Most of the working class still received no formal or sufficient education.

However, local and central government did begin to show some regard for education in the early nineteenth century. Grants were made to local authorities for school use in their areas and in 1833 Parliament funded the construction of school buildings. But it was only in 1870 that the state became more actively involved. An Education Act (the Forster Act) created local school boards in England and Wales which financed and built elementary schools in their areas. Such state schools supplied non-denominational training and the existing religious voluntary (or Church) schools served denominational needs.

By 1880 the state system was providing free and compulsory elementary schooling in most parts of Britain for children between the ages of five and ten (twelve in 1899). The Balfour Act (1902) abolished the school boards, made local government responsible for state education, established some new secondary and technical schools and funded voluntary schools. But, although state schools provided education for children up to the age of fourteen by 1918, this was still limited to basic skills.

Adequate secondary school education remained largely the province of the independent sector and a few state schools. But generally people had to pay for these services. After a period when the old public (private) schools had declined in quality, they revived in the nineteenth century. Their weaknesses, such as the narrow curriculum and indiscipline, had been reformed by progressive head-masters like Thomas Arnold of Rugby, and their reputations increased. The private grammar and high schools, which imitated the classics-based education of the public schools, also expanded. These schools drew their pupils from the sons of the middle and upper classes and were the training ground for the established elite and the professions.

State secondary school education in the early twentieth century was marginally extended to children whose parents could not afford school fees. Scholarships (financial grants) for clever poor children became available; some state funding was provided and more schools were created. But this state help did not appreciably expand secondary education, and by 1920 only 9.2 per cent of 14-year-old children in England and Wales were able to enter secondary schools on a non-fee-paying basis. The school system in the early twentieth century was still inadequate for the demands of society: working- and lower middle-class children lacked extensive education; and hard-pressed governments avoided any further large-scale involvement until 1944.

The 1944 Education Act

In 1944, an Education Act (the Butler Act) reorganized state primary and secondary schools in England and Wales (1947 in Scotland and Northern Ireland) and greatly influenced future generations of schoolchildren. State schooling became free and compulsory up to the age of fifteen and was divided into three stages: primary schools (5–11 years), secondary schools (11–15) and further post-school training. A decentralized system resulted, in which a Ministry of Education drew up policy guidelines and local education authorities (LEAs) decided which forms of schooling would be used in their areas.

Two types of state school resulted from the Act: county and voluntary. Primary and secondary schools were provided by LEAs in each county. Voluntary schools were mainly those elementary schools which had been founded by religious and other groups and which were now partially financed or maintained by LEAs, although many retained a particular religious affiliation. Non-denominational schools thus coexisted with voluntary schools.

Following the 1944 Act, most state secondary schools in England/Wales and Northern Ireland were effectively divided into grammar schools, secondary modern schools and technical schools. Some grammar schools were new, while others were old foundations which now received direct state funding and were known as grant-maintained schools. Placement in this secondary system depended upon an examination result. The eleven-plus examination was adopted by most LEAs, consisted of intelligence tests which covered linguistic, mathematical and general knowledge and was taken in the last year of primary school at the age of eleven. The object was to differentiate between academic and non-academic children, and it introduced the notion of 'selection' based on ability. Those who passed the eleven-plus went to the grammar school, while those who failed went to the secondary modern and technical schools.

Although all schools were supposed to be equal in their educational aims, the grammar schools were equated with a better (more academic) education, a socially respectable role, and qualified children (through national examinations) for good jobs and entry into higher education and the professions. Secondary modern schools emphasized basic schooling, initially without national examinations. The third type of school (technical) educated more vocationally inclined pupils.

The intention of the 1944 Act was to provide universal and free state primary and secondary education. Day-release training at local colleges was also introduced for employed people who wanted further education after fifteen and local authority grants were given to students who wished to enter higher education. It was hoped that such equality of opportunity would expand the educational market, lead to a better-educated society, encourage more working-class children to enter university and achieve greater social mobility.

However, in the 1950s it was felt that these aims were not being achieved under the selective secondary school system. Education became a party-political battlefield. The Labour Party and other critics maintained that the eleven-plus examination was wrong in principle; was socially divisive; had educational and testing weaknesses; resulted in middle-class children predominating in grammar schools and higher education; and thus perpetuated the class system.

Labour governments from 1964 were committed to abolishing the eleven-plus, selection and the secondary school divisions. These would be replaced by non-selective 'comprehensive schools' to which all children would automatically transfer after primary school. These would provide schooling for children of all ability levels and from all social backgrounds in a local area on one school campus.

The battle for the comprehensive and selective systems was fierce. Although more schools became comprehensive under the Conservative government from 1970, it decided against legislative compulsion. Instead, LEAs were able to choose the secondary education which was best suited to local needs. Some decided for comprehensives, while others retained selection and grammar schools.

However, the Labour government in 1976 intended to establish comprehensive schools nationwide. Before this policy could be implemented, the Conservatives came to power in 1979. Thus the state secondary school sector today remains divided between the selective and non-selective options since a minority of LEAs in England/Wales do not have comprehensives and some 164 grammar schools remain. Scottish schools have long been comprehensive. Northern Irish schools are at present divided into grammars and secondary moderns, but the eleven-plus and selective tests for the grammar schools are scheduled for abolition.

The comprehensive/selection debate continues in a different form. School education is still subject to party-political and ideological conflict. Opinion polls suggest that only a minority of parents support comprehensive education while a majority favour a selective and diverse system of schools (including grammars) with entry based on continuous assessment, interviews and choice. It is often argued that the long-running debates about the relative merits of different types of schooling in Britain have not benefited schoolchildren or the educational system. However, reforms to the state school system are still being made by all governments.

The state school sector

State education in the UK is free and compulsory for children between the ages of five and sixteen. The school-leaving age for compulsory education was raised to eighteen in 2008 and will be effective in 2013 for 17-year-olds and 2015 for

18-year-olds. Schools are mainly mixed, although some are single-sex. The vast majority of children (94 per cent) receive free education in state primary and secondary schools, but the state system is complicated by remnants of the 1944 Act and a diversity of school types throughout the country.

In England and Wales, the Department for Education initiates overall policy (with Wales and Northern Ireland having some devolved responsibility and Scotland having its own independent system). Today, state schools broadly consist of non-denominational schools, former grant-maintained schools and voluntary (faith) schools which may be state-controlled or aided, with some being connected to specific religious groups. The LEAs retain decentralized choice to organize school planning in their areas for many of these schools with finance provided by central government and some may be formally responsible for employing staff and school admission procedures. However, LEA control over state schools is declining.

The academic organization of schools has been traditionally left largely to headteachers and staff. Following Conservative and Labour reforms, headteachers now have greater financial responsibility for school budgets, management and academic organization, the appointment of teachers and student admissions. School governors (drawn from among local citizens and parents) have greater

PLATE 9.1 Pupils in a primary school class, Tooting, London. Ethnic minority children can form a majority in state schools in areas of minority group concentration.
(Ilpo Musto/Rex Features)

powers of decision-making, and parents are supposed to have a voice in the running of schools as well as a legal right to choose a particular school for their children (though this is not always successfully achieved). These changes have meant a shift from educational to management roles within state schools and impose increased burdens of time and administration.

State schooling before the age of five is not compulsory in Britain and there is no statutory requirement on the LEAs to provide such education. Yet more parents (particularly those at work) are seeking school provisions for their young children and there is concern about the lack of opportunities. At present, 65 per cent of three- and four-year-olds benefit from a state nursery or pre-school education, while others attend private playgroups. The previous Labour government tried to expand state pre-primary facilities for working parents by establishing Sure Start children's centres which provide basic education, support and child-care opportunities.

Pupils attend primary school (usually divided into infant and junior levels) in the state sector from the age of five and then move to secondary schools normally at eleven until the ages of sixteen to eighteen (school-leaving age eighteen from 2013). Over 87 per cent of state secondary pupils in England and most state secondary pupils in Wales attend comprehensives. There are only a small number of grammar (164) and secondary modern schools left in the state system. The continued existence of these schools depends partly upon local government decisions, partly upon parent power and partly upon Labour government policy. Although the Labour government was ideologically against increasing the number of grammar schools, many critics and parents argue for their retention and expansion. These schools achieve very good national examination results and provide a disciplined academic background.

Comprehensive school pupils are of mixed abilities and come from a variety of social backgrounds in the local area. There is still a good deal of argument about the quality and performance of the system. Some critics argue that disadvantaged students from poor homes receive a poor education. Others maintain that bright academic children suffer, although 'setting' (formerly called 'streaming') divides pupils into different ability and interest classes and examination results can be excellent. Arguably, therefore, a form of 'selection' continues within the comprehensives, although not on entry. There are some very good comprehensive schools, which are not necessarily confined to privileged and affluent areas, but there are also some very weak and failing ones which suffer from a variety of social, economic and educational problems and are usually associated with the deprived inner cities.

In an attempt to encourage diversity in the state comprehensive system, the former Conservative government established secondary level state-funded privately sponsored City Technology Colleges specializing in science, technology and mathematics. The previous Labour government from 1999 also promoted school diversity and standards rather than having only one type of comprehensive

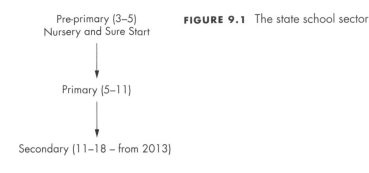

FIGURE 9.1 The state school sector

Pre-primary (3–5)
Nursery and Sure Start

Primary (5–11)

Secondary (11–18 – from 2013)

school and has involved the private sector in school organization. It created a system of publicly funded, part privately sponsored and managed Academies independent of LEA control which replaced failing and underperforming schools and were intended to revitalize deprived areas; some 530 secondary level specialist schools which may concentrate on the sciences, modern foreign languages, sports or the arts; and Beacon Schools which are singled out as best performing schools and are supposed to serve as examples of best practice for other schools. It also intended to increase the number of voluntary schools controlled by faiths (for example, Church of England, Roman Catholic, Methodist, Jewish, Muslim and Sikh). It seems as if selective criteria for entry to some schools (particularly the specialist and faith schools) will be necessary.

The Conservative/Liberal Democrat coalition introduced considerable, but controversial, reforms in 2010. These will allow all existing secondary and primary state schools to apply for Academy status with state budgets and to opt out of LEA control. It will also enable parents, charities and other bodies to set up 'free schools' with state funding for each pupil they attract and which are independent of LEAs. Critics argue that these drives to diversity and choice represent a withdrawal from egalitarian comprehensive principles, creeping privatization and the inevitable creation of a two-tier secondary school system in which some state schools become self-governing independent trusts freed from LEA control. However, serious doubts persist as to who will actually run and control these schools.

Scotland has its own ancient educational system, with schools, colleges and universities which are among the oldest in Europe. Its state school system is comprehensive and non-selective. Children transfer from primary to secondary education at twelve and may continue until eighteen. The Scottish 'public schools' are state and not private institutions (although some eminent independent schools do exist).

In *Northern Ireland* the state schools are mostly divided along religious lines into Catholic and Protestant and are often single-sex. However, there are some tentative movements towards integrated co-educational schools. The comprehensive principle has not been widely adopted and a selective system with an examination at eleven gives entrance to selective grammar schools, which 40 per cent of the age group attend, although the entry tests are to be abolished. Pupils' performances at these schools are generally superior to those of their counterparts in England and Wales, although examination results in the comprehensive schools are comparatively poor.

The independent (fee-paying) school sector

The independent school sector operates mainly in England, is separate from the state school sector and caters for some 7 per cent of all British children, from the ages of four to eighteen at different levels of education. There are 2,500 independent schools of varying size and status with over 615,000 pupils.

The sector is defined by payment for education. Its financing derives from investments and the fees paid by the pupils' parents for their education, which vary considerably between schools and can amount to many thousands of pounds a year. The independent sector is dependent upon its charitable and tax-exempt status to survive. This means that the schools are not taxed on their income if it is used only for educational purposes. A minority of children are scholarship holders, whose expenses are covered by their schools.

So-called public schools (private, not state), such as Eton, Harrow and Winchester, are the most famous of the independent schools and are among the 246 leading schools which are members of the Headmasters' and Headmistresses' Conference. Many independent schools were originally created (often by monarchs) to provide education for the sons of the rich and aristocratic, although some were under public management and offered free schooling to the public. Today, such schools are often boarding establishments, where the pupils live and are educated during term time, although many of them now take day pupils (who do not board).

Independent schools play a significant role in British education and many leading figures have been educated at them. Entry today is competitive, normally by an entrance examination, and is not confined to social class, connections or

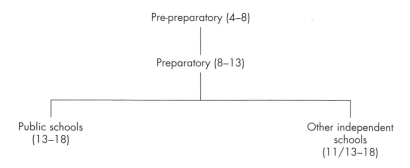

FIGURE 9.2 The independent school sector

PLATE 9.2 Pupils at Eton College, a prestigious independent (public) school near Windsor, England.
(David Hartley/Rex Features)

wealth, although the ability to pay the fees is obviously important for most applicants. Independent preparatory schools (at the primary level) prepare their pupils for independent secondary school entrance and parents who decide to send their children to an independent school will often give them a 'prep school' education first.

Independent schools can vary considerably in quality and reputation. The sector has grown and has an attraction despite its small size and increasing school fees. Insurance schemes for the payment of fees give opportunities for independent education to the less affluent. But some parents make great financial sacrifices so that their children can be independently educated. Opinion polls often suggest that many parents would send their children to an independent school if they could afford it because of the quality of many (if by no means all) of the schools and because such schooling may give social advantages in later life. However, some schools have had to close in recent years because of poor recruitment, bad finances, recessionary factors, competition and the legal demands from government.

The independent sector is criticized for being elitist, socially divisive and based on the ability to pay for education. In this view it perpetuates the class system. The Labour Party in opposition historically argued for the abolition of independent schools and the removal of their tax and charitable status. The previous Labour government's evaluation of the schools concluded that the sector should continue but that its charitable position would be more rigorously defined to include aid to neighbouring state schools, such as the sharing of teaching and sporting facilities. Short of outright government abolition, the independent schools are now firmly established and for many provide choice in what would otherwise be a state monopoly on education.

School organization and examinations

The school day in state and independent schools runs at variable times from about 9.00 a.m. until 4 p.m. and the school year is divided into three terms (autumn, spring and summer), although there have been proposals to reorganize this system. Classes in British schools used to be called 'forms' and in secondary schools were numbered from one to six, but most primary and secondary schools have now

PLATE 9.3 Pupils skipping with a rope in the playground of a secondary (comprehensive) school during a break from classes.
(*Steve Lyne/Rex Features*)

adopted year numbers from one to eleven, which include a two-year 'sixth form' for advanced work. The school year will have to take the new leaving age of eighteen into account from 2013.

A reduced birth rate in recent years led to a decrease in the number of schoolchildren, resulting in the closure of schools. However, numbers have since increased and the average class size for primary schools is 24.5 pupils (one of the highest among European countries) and secondary schools have average classes of 22.4 pupils.

Most teachers are trained at the universities and other colleges. There is a serious shortage of teachers in Britain in many subjects, but especially in mathematics, technology, physics and foreign languages, and there is an increasing use of unqualified teaching assistants to take some of the burden from classroom teachers. Some practising teachers increasingly see the profession as unattractive and leave for better-paid jobs or retire early. Teachers at present are suffering from low morale after battles with the government over pay, conditions, imposed government targets and educational reforms, and from what they perceive as the low status afforded them by government and the general public. The teaching profession has become very stressful and subject to greater pressures, such as physical assaults upon teachers by pupils, increased bureaucracy, pupil indiscipline and a lack of support for teachers from local authorities and the government. The quality of teaching in state schools has also attracted much criticism in recent years and the previous Labour government was committed to raising standards, removing incompetent and underperforming teachers and closing 'failing schools'. However, the recession and financial incentives are now attracting more high-quality and committed applicants into teaching.

The effect of alleged earlier spending cuts in education has been considerable, with GDP public expenditure on education in Britain (6.1 per cent in 2010) being below that of many comparable European countries. This has prevented the building and modernization of schools, especially in inner-city areas. It has also resulted in reduced services and a shortage of books and equipment for pupils, teachers and libraries. The previous Labour government increased spending on schools, but teachers and parents argue that they have not seen visible results from such investment.

Earlier Conservative governments introduced school reforms, which remained under Labour. Tests (sometimes called SATS or standard attainment tests) are set to establish what children should be reasonably expected to know at the ages of seven, eleven and fourteen. The progress of each schoolchild could then be measured against national standards, assessed and reported. However, many teachers are opposed to the extra work involved, have doubted the validity of the tests and feel they are too stressful for pupils. A large number of them have boycotted the tests.

Another radical reform was the creation of a National Curriculum in England and Wales (with similar developments in Northern Ireland but not Scotland).

PLATE 9.4 Pupils and teacher at a secondary (comprehensive) school practise a chemistry experiment.
(Simon Townsley/Rex Features)

The aim was to create a curriculum for primary and secondary levels which was standardized, centrally devised and appropriate to the needs and demands of the contemporary world. In England, for example, it covers all age groups, is structured into Key Stages 1–4 and a two-year sixth form and includes at the secondary stage core subjects such as English, mathematics and science, together with foundation subjects such as design and technology, physical education and information and communications technology, history, geography, music, art, physical education, religious education and modern foreign languages. The latter has become optional rather than compulsory in the later years and a 'citizenship' subject to encourage civic knowledge has been recently added. These reforms have generated controversy, opposition, difficulties of implementation and problems about the content and scope of course material.

The National Curriculum (which is not applicable to independent schools although they follow the subject structure) is tied to a system of examinations at the secondary level. These may be taken at all types of schools in England, Wales and Northern Ireland. The main national examinations are the General Certificate of Secondary Education (GCSE), which is usually taken by 16-year olds; Advanced Subsidiary (AS) qualifications in the first year of the sixth form; and the General Certificate of Education at Advanced Level (GCE A level), which is normally taken at the end of the second year in the sixth form by 18-year olds. Results in all exams at all levels tend to be better in single-sex girls' schools.

The GCSE is taken in a range of subjects, the questions and marking of which are undertaken by independent examination boards whose standards have attracted criticism in recent years. In addition to written examinations, project work and continuous or controlled assessment of pupils by teachers are also taken into account in arriving at a final grade. GCSEs can be taken in any subject(s) according to individual choice, though many candidates will attempt six or seven and the basic subjects required for jobs and further education are English, mathematics (or a science) and a foreign language. The GCSE was intended as a better means of evaluating pupils' abilities than pure examinations and designed to give prospective employers some idea of the candidate's ability. But, although standards continue to improve, a third of students did not achieve high passes and some 8 per cent do not pass a single subject. The minimum standard to be aimed for is five GCSEs at A–C grades.

The GCE A level is associated with more academic children who are aiming for entry to higher education or the professions and who spend two years on their studies in the sixth form or at sixth-form colleges. Good passes are now essential because the competition for both popular and demanding courses at the universities and other colleges has become stiffer. Four AS (Advanced Subsidiary) level subjects are usually taken in the first year in addition to key skills tests, before a concentration on three A2 (A level) subjects, and pupils may combine arts and science subjects. AS subjects can be a lower-level alternative for students who do not wish to go on to A2 levels.

The standards achieved and examination results continue to rise. But there is continuing discussion about the format and content of A levels and the system has been criticized for over-examining students, creating less time for other school activities and leading to teacher overwork. The previous Labour government reviewed the examination structure and decided on a continuation of GCSEs and A levels but also added diploma-type structures for 14–18-year-olds. The aim is to encourage students at various levels to study a choice of academic and vocational subjects for two years, with an emphasis on learning useful skills, whether for entry to work or further study.

Alternative examinations are vocational GCSEs which are mainly taken by young people in full-time education between the ages of sixteen and nineteen and provide a broad-based preparation for a range of occupations and higher education; and National Vocational Qualifications (NVQs), which are job-specific examinations.

Scotland does not have a statutory national curriculum and pupils take the National Qualification (NQ) at the age of sixteen. Those aged between sixteen and eighteen take the reformed Scottish Highers (Higher and Advanced Higher).

GCSE, AS, A level, SATS and alternative examination results by pupils are the basis of school 'league tables', instituted by the previous Conservative government. Examination results and marks at individual schools are published so that parents and pupils can judge a school's performance. League tables have been criticized for their methodology and creating a 'results mentality'. But they are now firmly established and influential and parents use them as a guide to enrol their children in good schools.

Higher education

Should a pupil obtain the required examination results at A level or equivalent, and be successful at possible interviews, they may go on to an institution of higher education such as a university or college. The student, after a prescribed period of study and after passing examinations, will receive a degree and become a graduate of that institution. In the past, only a small proportion of the age group in Britain proceeded to what was an elitist higher education, in contrast to the higher rates in other major nations such as the USA. However, following the creation of new universities and a rapid increase in student numbers from the 1990s (with the ratio of women to men students being three to two) the rate was some 44 per cent of the age group in 2005. The Labour government wished to raise this figure to 50 per cent of students aged between eighteen and thirty by 2010. This target has not been achieved. On the contrary, the government has imposed financial cuts on those universities which have exceeded the recruitment of specified student numbers.

The universities

There were twenty-two British universities in 1960. After a period of expansion in the 1960s and reforms in 1992 when existing institutions such as polytechnics were given university status, there are now some 116 universities (including the Open University and the independent University of Buckingham) and 166 institutions of higher education. In 2009, according to the Higher Education Statistics Agency, there were 1.96 million students at various levels of study in higher education, a 1 per cent drop from 2008 (possibly accounted for by part-timers), despite a 2 per cent increase in full-time students and a 5 per cent rise in EU and non-EU international students.

The universities can be broadly classified into four types. The ancient universities of Oxford and Cambridge, composed of their many colleges, date from the thirteenth century, and until the nineteenth century they were virtually the only English universities and offered no places to women. However, other older universities were founded in Scotland, such as St Andrews (1411), Glasgow (1450), Aberdeen (1494) and Edinburgh (1583). A second group comprises the 'redbrick' or civic universities such as Leeds, Liverpool and Manchester, which were created between 1850 and 1930. The third group consists of universities founded after the Second World War and in the 1960s. Many of the latter, for

PLATE 9.5 Balliol College, one of the largest and oldest (1263) colleges of the University of Oxford. Located in the centre of that city, it has undergraduate and postgraduate students and a high academic reputation.
(Andrew Drysdale/Rex Features)

example Sussex, York and East Anglia, were built in semi-rural areas. The fourth group are the 'new universities' created in 1992 when polytechnics and some other colleges attained university status. Since 1992, many other universities have been created, either based on existing colleges or as new institutions.

Competition to enter universities is now very strong in both popular and demanding subjects, and students who do not do well at A level or equivalent may be unable to find a place. Even students with very high grades do not always succeed. An average of some 17 per cent of students drop out of higher education because of work, financial or other problems. However, the majority aim for a good degree in order to obtain a good job or to continue in higher education by doing further study or research (master's degrees and doctorates). The bachelor's degree (Bachelor of Arts, BA, or Bachelor of Science, BSc) is usually taken in final examinations at the end of the third year of study, although some degree courses do vary in length in different parts of Britain (such as Scotland, with a four-year MA Honours degree). The degree is divided into first-, second- and third-class honours. Some degrees are awarded entirely on the basis of examination results, while others include some continuous assessment over the period of study. Grade inflation, particularly for 'firsts', has encouraged calls to dispense with these classifications and to a possible move to percentage results.

PLATE 9.6 Leeds University in Yorkshire is one of the redbrick or civic universities established in the nineteenth and early twentieth centuries. Founded in 1904, its origins go back to the nineteenth century and it is now a major teaching and research institution. The Parkinson Building, shown, contains the Brotherton Library, one of the largest university libraries in the UK. (*Mark Campbell/Rex Features*)

Universities supposedly have uniform standards, although there are centres of excellence in particular subjects and there has been recent criticism about levels in certain universities and certain subjects. Students can choose from an impressive array of subject areas and teaching is mainly by the lecture system, supported by tutorials (small groups) and seminars. The student–lecturer ratio at British universities has increased – resulting in student protest – because of expanded recruitment and the cutting of government money for teaching. Students live either on campus in university accommodation or in rented property outside the university. Until recently few British students chose universities near their parents' homes, and many seemed to prefer those in the south of England, but financial considerations now persuade many students to live at home or locally.

Universities are independent institutions created by royal charter, enjoy academic freedom, appoint their own staff, award their own degrees and decide which students to admit. But they are in practice dependent upon government money. This derives mainly from finance (dependent upon the number of students recruited and research performance) given by government to Universities Funding Councils for distribution to the universities through university vice-chancellors, who are the chief executive officers of the universities.

Both Conservative and Labour governments have been concerned to make the universities more accountable in the national interest, have taken tight control of their budgets and encouraged them to seek alternative private sources of finance from business and industry. The universities have lost staff and research money; have been forced to adopt more effective management and accounting procedures; must market their resources more efficiently; must attract and recruit students in order to obtain government finance, yet lose funds if they over-recruit; pay greater attention to teaching and research performance, yet have to cope with increased bureaucracy; and must justify their positions financially and educationally.

As a result government intervenes more closely in the running of higher education than in the past. Such policies have provoked considerable opposition from the universities, which argue that the recent large expansion in student numbers has not seen an equivalent rise in funding, salaries or new staff appointments, but they are being forced to adapt rather than continue to lose staff, finance and educational programmes. It is also argued that expansion has led to universities taking poorly qualified students to fill their quotas, who then drop out because of work and other pressures. Some educationalists feel that British universities will decline in quality if they are not better funded. Since governments seem unwilling to do this, critics argue that the universities (or at least those able to do so) should break away from the state, market their own services and attract their own finance.

Other higher education colleges

The 1970s saw the creation of colleges (or institutes) of higher education, often by merging existing colleges with redundant teachers' training colleges or by establishing new institutions. They now offer a wide range of degree, diploma and certificate courses in both science and the arts, and in some cases have specifically taken over the role of training schoolteachers. They were formerly under the control of their local authorities, but the Conservative government granted them independence and some have achieved university status.

A variety of other institutions also offer higher education. Some, like the Royal College of Art, the Cranfield Institute of Technology and various business schools, have university status, while others, such as agricultural, drama and art colleges like the Royal Academy of Dramatic Arts (RADA) and the Royal College of Music, provide comparable courses. All these institutions usually have a strong vocational aspect to their programmes and fill a specialized role in higher education.

Student finance

In the past, British students who gained a place at an institution of higher education were awarded a grant from their local education authorities. The grant was in two parts: first, it covered the tuition fees of a first degree course (paid directly to the institution); and second, it covered, after means-testing of parents' income, maintenance expenses like the cost of rent, food and the books required for a course during term time. This system meant that higher education was largely free for many students.

The Labour government radically changed this situation from 1998 by abolishing the student grant. Instead, students had to pay upfront tuition fees for each year of their course, except in Scotland. Students are now means-tested on their parents' income, with those from less affluent backgrounds (incomes of less than £25,000 a year) generally being exempt from paying the full amount of tuition fees (some 50 per cent). Students must also provide for their own maintenance expenses, usually through loans from the Student Loan Company (ranging from £3,838 to £6,928 a year depending on where they study and live). They start to pay back their loans after graduation on reaching a salary level of £15,000 and upwards. As a result most students now have to finance their own higher education, some are in financial difficulties, and most will finish their studies with an average debt of at least £20,000, and in some cases much higher. But these changes in funding have not resulted in a marked reduction in the number of students applying for university entry, except in the case of mature students.

The Labour government increased tuition fees with effect from 2006–07. This meant that universities were able to charge variable fees up to £3,225 a year by 2009–10 provided they pursued 'fair access' policies by encouraging greater numbers of students from lower-income households. These students will also be eligible for government maintenance grants and financial aid (such as bursaries) from those universities that charge higher tuition fees.

The Open University

The Labour Party broached the idea of the Open University in the 1960s. It would be a non-residential system of 'distance learning' which used television, radio, specially produced books, audio/video cassettes and correspondence courses to teach students of all ages. It was intended to give opportunities (or a 'second chance') to adults who had been unable to enter conventional higher education. It was hoped that OU courses might appeal to working-class students who had left school at the official school-leaving age and wished to broaden their horizons.

The Open University opened in 1969, with its first courses starting in 1971. It now caters for undergraduate, postgraduate and research students in a wide range of subjects. About 7,000 students of all ages and from very different walks of life receive degrees from the Open University each year. First (bachelor's) degrees are awarded on a system of credits for each course completed, and graduates now include some from the European Union, Gibraltar, and Switzerland.

Dedication, stamina and perseverence are necessary to complete the long, part-time courses of the Open University. Students, who are often employed, follow their lessons and lectures at home. Part-time tutors in local areas mark the students' written work and meet them regularly to discuss their progress. There are also special weekend and refresher courses held throughout the year at universities and colleges to enable students to take part in intensive study. The television programmes, websites, books, printed course materials and CD-ROMs/ software associated with the Open University programmes are widely used throughout the world. The Open University is generally considered to be a cost-effective success, has provided valuable alternative educational opportunities for many people and has served as a model for other countries.

Further, adult and lifelong education

An important aspect of British education is the provision of further and adult education, whether by colleges, universities, voluntary bodies, trade unions or other institutions. The present organizations and their offerings originated to some degree in the thirst for knowledge which was felt by working-class people in the nineteenth and early twentieth centuries, particularly after the arrival of elementary state education and growing literacy. Today a wide range of educational opportunities is provided by self-governing state-funded colleges of further education and other institutions. These offer vocational and academic subjects at basic levels for part- and full-time students. Some part-time students over sixteen may study in the evenings or on day release from their employment and their studies are often vocational or work-related, include government training programmes and have close ties with local commerce and industry. Some 5 million full- and part-time students of varying ages are enrolled on a broad spectrum of further education courses.

Adult education is provided by these colleges, the universities, the Workers' Educational Association (WEA), evening institutes, local societies and clubs. Adult courses may be vocational (for employment) or recreational (for pleasure), and cover a variety of activities and programmes.

In the past, a relatively low percentage of the 16–24 age group in Britain were in further and higher education, compared to the much larger percentages in Japan, the USA and Germany. The figures have now improved considerably, with almost three-quarters of 16- to 18-year-olds in Britain remaining in full-time education after this age, either in school or further education colleges. Yet the previous Labour government felt that even more people should be educated or trained further after the age of sixteen. This is particularly true at a time when there is likely to be an increasing shortage of well-qualified people in the future workforce, especially in the vocational, trade and technical fields.

Nevertheless, there has been a recent expansion of continuing education projects and a range of programmes specifically designed for employment purposes and to provide people with access qualifications for further training. The Labour government saw further and adult education as part of a lifelong learning process, which it wanted to prioritize. The aim was to encourage the continuous development of people's skills, knowledge and understanding as well as creating skills and improving employment prospects in a changing labour market.

Attitudes to education

Concerns about the quality of British schools and educational policy at all levels are consistently voiced by Britons and a majority of respondents to public opinion polls. They think that state schools are not run well, that more money should be spent on education generally and that parents' wishes concerning their children's education are not taken seriously by politicians. The previous Labour government responded by giving more funding to the system and changing its structures. However, serious dissatisfaction continued to be voiced in polls leading up to the general election in 2010 and schools are likely to continue as a concern in British life. An Ipsos MORI poll in April 2010 placed education and schools in sixth place in a list of the most important issues facing Britain today.

The amount of public money spent on education in Britain over a period of time is proportionally much less than that spent on health and transport, only marginally more than that on law and order and considerably less than that spent by other European countries and other advanced economies. Some critics therefore question whether the government is totally committed to raising quality, whether education has the same political priority as other areas of expenditure and whether many parents are actually as concerned about the state of schools as they say they are.

There have been continuous and vigorous debates about the performance and goals of British education at all levels since the 1960s, although much of this discussion was (and is) ideological rather than objectively educational. Traditionalist critics, who wanted disciplined learning programmes, felt that state comprehensive schools and 'creative/progressive' methods of child-centred teaching were not producing the kind of people needed for contemporary society. It was argued that pupils lacked the basic skills of numeracy and literacy and were unprepared for employment and the realities of the outside world. Today, employers frequently criticize both schools and higher education for the quality of their products, and only 37 per cent according to SIF UK in 2005, for example, believed that today's graduates leave university with the necessary skills for employment.

The previous Conservative government's reforms from 1986 were based on centralized and consumer-choice policies. They attempted to rectify the educational situation and aimed at producing accountability, improved standards and skills in schools and higher education through more formal learning programmes. The government attempted to reform the teaching profession, improve pupil performance, emphasize science and modern language studies and increase parental choice.

The Labour government from 1997 continued this process by stressing compulsory homework, contracts with parents, 'literacy hours', concentration on the '3 Rs' (reading, writing and arithmetic) and grouping children by ability ('setting'). Progressive 'child-centred' practices were dismissed and funds were provided for school fabric repairs and computers in every school. There was also a move away from having only one type of state secondary school (comprehensive) to embrace diversity and specialism through the expansion of specialist and faith schools and city academies. The government also wanted greater numbers of poorer and working-class students to enter university.

Some critics argue that the school system should not be devoted solely to either elitist standards or market considerations but should provide a choice between (and ideally a mixture of) the academic/liberal tradition, the technical and the vocational. The lack of adequate vocational/technical education and training is creating serious problems for employers, who complain that they are unable to find competently trained staff to fill vacancies. The future of British education will depend in large part on how reforms (such as the new diploma structures) work and how they are perceived by teachers, parents, students and employers. However, successive polls reveal that a majority of respondents say they were dissatisfied with the results of the previous Labour government's 1997 promise to prioritize education.

The schools debate in Britain often reveals polarized points of view and strong reactions to recent Labour and Conservative policies, as revealed in an Ipsos MORI poll for the trade unions NASUWT and Unison in April 2010. When asked if more schools in future should be run by private companies, religious groups, charities or groups of parents rather than LEAs, 44 per cent considered this a bad idea and 24 per cent good. The majority (62 per cent) thought local authorities were best placed to run schools. These replies are in strong contrast to recent Labour measures aimed at diversity in schools and Conservative plans for 'private' state schools.

Similarly, despite the gloomy responses to school education and performance in the last decade, 54 per cent of respondents thought state education was generally good compared with 19 per cent who thought it poor. Some 79 per cent of parents considered their own children's schools good and 65 per cent regarded the schools attended by children of relations and friends as good. If a local authority was failing to deliver good standards of education, respondents considered that the government (37 per cent) and the local authority (26 per cent) were responsible for addressing the failings, even when schools were directly run by other organizations. When asked if individual parents should be asked to pay additional fees for their own children's education to supplement funding from taxes, 18 per cent supported the idea but some 64 per cent opposed it.

Despite the fact that this poll was commissioned by trade unions, respondents' replies indicated a traditional response to schooling and the local direction of education by LEAs. It might also suggest that they wanted certainty, control and stability in their children's schools rather than constant change on the part of central government.

Exercises

Explain and examine the following terms:

public schools	grammar schools	WEA
comprehensives	eleven-plus	tutorial
GCE A level	Open University	scholarships
LEAs	tuition fees	student finance
Eton	GCSE	'prep school'
the Butler Act	degree	vocational
streaming/setting	'3 Rs'	literacy
faith schools	AS levels	specialist schools
Academies	Diplomas	'redbrick universities'

Write short essays on the following topics:

1   Critically examine state secondary education in Britain, analysing its structures, aims and achievements.

2*   Describe the structure of British higher education and its roles.

3   Comment upon the desirability, or otherwise, of the division of British schools into state and independent sectors.

4   Should schoolchildren attend technical, vocational or academic schools, depending on their choices and abilities? Or should they attend one common type of school, which provides compulsory schooling in different areas of study?

Visit **www.routledge.com/textbooks/oakland** for multiple-choice questions, links to related YouTube clips, tips on approaching essay questions, and much, much more.

Further reading

1   Abercrombie, N., Warde, A., Deem, R., Penna, S., Soothill, K., Urry, J. and Walby, S. (2000) *Contemporary British Society*, Oxford: Polity Press, Chapter 14.
2   Chitty, C. (1992) *The Education System Transformed*, London: Baseline Books
3   Chitty, C. and Benyon, J. (2009) *Education Policy in Britain*, London: Palgrave Macmillan
4   Jones, K. (2002) *Education in Britain: 1944 to the Present*, Oxford: Polity Press
5   Lawton, D. (2004) *Education and Labour Party Ideologies 1900–2001 and Beyond*, London: Routledge/Falmer
6   Ryan, A. (1999) *Liberal Anxieties and Liberal Education*, London: Profile Books
7   Tomlinson, S. (2005) *Education in a Post-Welfare Society*, Maidenhead: Open University Press
8   Walden, G. (1996) *We Should Know Better: Solving the Education Crisis*, London: Fourth Estate

Websites

Department for Education: www.education.gov.uk
Independent education: www.isis.org.uk
The Times Higher Education Supplement: www.thes.co.uk
The Times Educational Supplement: www.tes.co.uk
Scottish Executive: www.scotland.gov.uk
National Assembly for Wales: www.wales.gov.uk
Northern Ireland Assembly: www.ni-assembly.gov.uk
Office for Standards in Education: www.ofsted.gov.uk

10

The media

The term 'media' may include any communication system by which people are informed, educated or entertained. In Britain it has historically referred to the print industries (the press or newspapers and magazines) and broadcasting (cable and satellite television, radio and terrestrial or Earth-based television). These systems have overlapped with each other and with other media outlets such as books, theatre, film, records, video and CDs. In their time, they have been profitable businesses and tied to advertising, sponsorship, commerce and industry.

The media have evolved from simple methods of production, distribution and communication to their present sophisticated technologies. Their growth and variety have greatly improved information dispersal, news availability and entertainment opportunities. They cover homes, places of business and leisure activities and their influence is very powerful and an inevitable part of daily life.

However, the Internet, online communication systems, electronic technology and mobile phones have in recent years rapidly come to be the dominant media forces, challenging the more traditional forms. They have become a crucial part of business, education, politics, publishing, news and entertainment. A Nielsen Online survey found there were 48.8 million Internet users in the UK in 2009 or 79.8 per cent of the population. The Internet market has many providers, DSL broadband covers most of the population and cable covers 50 per cent of households. Yet although the market claims to be competitive, there are frequent complaints about broadband and mobile phone services, coverage and performance, with companies promising improvements.

Surveys have shown that traditionally 69 per cent of Britons obtained their daily news from television, 20 per cent from newspapers and 11 per cent from radio. These figures have changed in recent years as newspaper sales and advertising income decline and free online news sites have proved popular. But readers have reacted to newspaper owners' proposals to introduce subscription charges for their news sites. A Techdigest survey in 2009 found that 74 per cent of respondents would find another free site, 8 per cent would use free headlines only and only 5 per cent would pay to continue reading the site. At present, the BBC website is the most popular online source of updated news and is a free service. It also seems that many people are using varied sources of news and information, sometimes simultaneously.

The media continue to provoke debates about what is socially and morally permissible in their content and methods. Questions are asked about the role of advertising and sponsorship; the quality of the services provided at a time of rapidly expanding and diversifying media outlets: the alleged danger of the concentrated ownership of media resources; media influence on politics; legal restraints upon media 'free expression'; the potential abuse of media power and influence; and the ethical responsibility of the media to individuals and society.

The print media

The print media (newspapers and magazines) began to develop in the eighteenth century. Initially, a wide circulation was hindered by transportation and distribution problems, illiteracy and government licensing or censorship restrictions. But over the last 200 years an expanded educational system, the abolition of government control, new print inventions and Britain's small physical size have eliminated these difficulties and created a free, outspoken and often controversial print media.

The growth of literacy after 1870 provided the owners of the print media with an increased market. Newspapers and magazines, which had previously been limited to the middle and upper classes, reached a wider readership. They were used for news and information, but also for profit and entertainment. Media ownership, new types of print media and financially rewarding advertising increased in the competitive atmosphere of the late nineteenth and early twentieth centuries. Owners also realized that political and social influence, as well as the dissemination of combative ideology, could be achieved through control of the means of communication.

National newspapers

National newspapers are those which are mostly published from London (with some regional versions) and are available in all parts of Britain on the same day, including Sundays. Many are delivered direct to the home by local newsagents. The good internal distribution systems of a compact country enabled a national press to develop, and Internet online copies of newspapers (whether free or by subscription) now offer updated news and immediate availability everywhere.

Regional newsletters and newspapers appeared in the sixteenth century and the first titled London newspaper, *Corante* (the *Daily Courant*) was published in 1621. The first British newspapers with a limited national circulation appeared in the early eighteenth century and were followed by others, such as *The Times* (1785), the *Observer* (1791) and the *Sunday Times* (1822). Most of these were 'quality' papers, catering for a relatively small, educated market at a time of mass illiteracy.

In the nineteenth century, the growth and diverse composition of the population conditioned the types of newspaper which were produced. The first 'popular' national papers were deliberately printed on Sundays, among them the

News of the World (1843) and the *People* (1881). They were inexpensive and aimed at the expanding and increasingly literate working class. In 1896, Alfred Harmsworth produced the *Daily Mail*, which was targeted at the lower middle class as an alternative to the 'quality' dailies. Harmsworth then published the *Daily Mirror* in 1903 for the working-class 'popular' market. Both the *Mail* and the *Mirror* were soon selling more than a million copies a day.

The early twentieth century was the era of mass-circulation papers and of owners (described as press barons) like Harmsworth and Arthur Pearson. There was fierce competition between them as they fought for bigger shares of the market. Pearson's *Morning Herald* (later the *Daily Express*) was created in 1900 to compete with the *Daily Mail* for lower middle-class readers.

The *Daily Mirror* was the largest-selling national daily in the early twentieth century. It supported the Labour Party and was designed for quick and easy reading by the industrial and increasingly politicized working class. The *Daily Herald* (1911) also supported the Labour Party, until in 1964 it was sold, renamed the *Sun* and developed different political and news emphases. The competition between the *Sun* and *Mirror* continues today, with each aiming for a bigger share of the mass daily market. Battles are still fought between dominant proprietors, since newspaper ownership is concentrated in a few large publishing groups, such

PLATE 10.1 News International newspaper plant, Wapping, London. News International moved from Fleet Street to Wapping in 1986, which led to violence and confrontation with the print unions. Printing operations moved to Broxbourne, Hertfordshire, in 2010, while the journalists remain at Wapping temporarily. *(Alisdair Macdonald/Rex Features).*

as Rupert Murdoch's News International (which has large media holdings in Britain, Australia and the USA) and Trinity Mirror (see Table 10.1).

The success of the early popular press was due to growing literacy, a desire for knowledge and information (as well as entertainment) on the part of the working class and increased political awareness among workers caused by the rise of the Labour Party. Newspaper owners profited by the huge market, but they also satisfied demand. The price and content of mass papers reflected lower middle- and working-class readerships and tastes. This emphasis attracted a considerable amount of consumer advertising, and owners were able to produce papers cheaply with the aid of modern printing methods and a nationwide distribution network.

The circulation of national papers rose rapidly, with 5.5 million daily sales by 1920. By 1973 these had increased to 17 million. However, newspapers had to cope first with competition from radio and film and later from television. Although they have survived, since the 1970s, there has been a continuing decline in sales and in the number of national and other newspapers as they face pressure from the Internet, mobile phones and digital technology.

Surveys have suggested that some 50 per cent of Britons over fifteen read a national daily paper and 70 per cent read a national Sunday newspaper, but these figures have probably now decreased. The main national newspapers in 2009 had sales of some 9.8 million on weekdays and 9.2 million on Sundays, but it is estimated that on average two people read each paper purchased.

The main national press in Britain today consists of ten main daily morning papers and nine main Sunday papers. It is in effect a London press, because most national newspapers have their bases and printing facilities in the capital, although editions of some nationals are now published outside London, in Europe and the USA. Most of them used to be located in the area around Fleet Street in central London, but all have now moved either to other parts of the capital or offices outside London. The reasons for these moves were high property rents, fierce competition between papers and opposition from trade unions to the introduction of new printing technology. Newspapers and magazines have also had to cope with the expense of newsprint, substantial declines in advertising revenue, rising production and labour costs and competition from other media outlets such as the Internet.

Heavy labour costs were due to the overmanning and restrictive practices of the trade unions. Owners were forced into new ways of increasing productivity while cutting costs. Regional owners outside London (e.g. Nottingham) had in fact pioneered the movement of newspapers and magazines into the new print technology and London newspapers were obliged to follow in order to survive.

The use of computers meant that journalists' 'copy' could be printed directly, without having to use the traditional intermediate and lengthy 'hot-metal' typesetting by printers. This gave owners flexibility in their printing and dis- tribution methods and cheaper production costs. It allowed them to escape from trade union dominance and the concentration of the industry in London. But it also resulted in job losses, trade-union opposition and industrial action, such as mass picketing.

New equipment, improved distribution methods and cuts in labour and production costs have increased the profitability of the print industries. Despite the attraction of other media they still have a considerable presence, although sales are declining. The business is very competitive and papers can suffer from a variety of problems. However, the high risks involved have not prevented the introduction of new newspapers. For example, the quality national daily, the *Independent*, began publication in October 1986 and survives despite circulation losses. Sunday nationals, like the *Independent on Sunday* (1990), have also appeared. But some dailies have been lost.

PLATE 10.2 A selection of national newspapers comprising populars (tabloids), mid-markets and qualities on a news stand, Great Marlborough Street, London, 2008.
(Ray Tang/Rex Features)

Most national papers are usually termed either 'quality' or 'popular' (tabloid) depending on their differences in content. Others are called 'mid-market' and fall between these two extremes (see Table 10.1). The qualities (such as *The Times*) report national and international news in depth and analyse current events and the arts in editorials and articles. Some critics argue, however, that their content has been dumbed down and their features have become overly trendy. The populars (such as the *Sun*) deal with relatively few 'hard news' stories and tend to be superficial in their treatment of events, and critics argue that much of their material is sensationalized. It cannot be said that the populars are instructive, or concerned with raising the critical consciousness of readers. Yet owners and editors argue that their readerships demand particular styles, interests and attitudes. 'Mid-market' papers, such as the *Daily Mail* and *Daily Express*, cater for intermediate groups.

Qualities and populars were also historically distinguished by their format. Populars were tabloid or small-sheet while qualities were broadsheet (large-sheet). This distinction has largely disappeared in recent years as more broadsheets have become tabloid, 'compact' (the *Independent* and *The Times*) or 'Berliner' (the *Guardian*) in format. Only the *Financial Times* and the *Daily Telegraph* are now broadsheets. Some critics argue that the broadsheets have gone downmarket and become more sensationalist and superficial in content.

Total sales of popular papers on weekdays and Sundays exceed those of the qualities. Qualities are more expensive than populars and carry upmarket advertising that generates essential finance. The populars carry less advertising and include more downmarket material. The Internet in 2009 took 23.5 per cent of advertising revenue in Britain; television had 21.9 per cent and the press had about 46.0 per cent.

There is no state control or censorship of the British press, although it is subject to laws of publication and expression and there are forms of self-censorship, by which it supposedly regulates its own conduct. The press is also financially independent of the political parties and receives no funding from government (except for Welsh-language community papers).

It is argued that most newspapers are politically right of centre and sympathize with the Conservative Party. But their positions are arguably usually driven by readers' opinions and their standard biases in fact can vary considerably over time and under the influence of events. For example, the small-circulation leftist *Morning Star* has varied between Stalinist, Euro-Communist and Democratic Left views. Papers may have a political bias and support a specific party, particularly at election times, although this can change. A few, such as those of the Trinity Mirror group, consistently support the Labour Party. Some, such as *The Times* and the *Independent*, consider themselves to be independent. Others, like the *Guardian*, favour a left-of-centre position, while the *Daily Telegraph* supports the Conservative Party. It appears that the British public receive a reasonable variety of political views and coverage from their newspapers.

TABLE 10.1 The main national newspapers (circulation December 2009)			
Name	Founded	Sales	Owned/controlled by
Popular dailies			
Daily Mirror	1903	1,225,502	Trinity Mirror
Sun	1964	2,862,935	News International
Daily Star	1978	784,958	Express Newspapers
Mid-market dailies			
Daily Mail	1986	2,113,134	Associated Newspapers
Daily Express	1900	677,750	Express Newspapers
Quality dailies			
The Times	1785	521,535	News International
Guardian	1821	300,540	Guardian Newspapers
Daily Telegraph	1855	703,249	Telegraph Group
Financial Times	1888	400,837	Financial Times Ltd
Independent	1986	186,940	Independent Newspapers
Popular Sundays			
News of the World	1843	2,791,773	News International
People	1881	532,680	Trinity Mirror
Sunday Mirror	1963	1,113,310	Trinity Mirror
Mid-market Sundays			
Mail on Sunday	1982	2,000,473	Associated Newspapers
Sunday Express	1918	590,596	Express Newspapers
Quality Sundays			
Observer	1791	351,019	Guardian Newspapers
Sunday Times	1822	1,113,195	News International
Sunday Telegraph	1961	525,088	Telegraph Group
Independent on Sunday	1990	155,460	Independent Newspapers

Source: Adapted from Audit Bureau of Circulations, December 2009

The press is dependent for its survival upon circulation/sales figures; upon the advertising it can attract; and upon financial help from its owners. A paper may face difficulties and fail if advertisers remove their business, and all the media have experienced difficulties in attracting advertising revenue. A high circulation does not necessarily guarantee the required advertising and consequent survival, because advertisers now tend to place their mass-appeal consumer products on television, where they will benefit from a larger audience. Most popular papers are in constant competition with their rivals to increase their sales. They attempt to do this by gimmicks such as bingo games and competitions, or by calculated (often sensationalist) editorial policies designed to attract a mass readership.

Many newspapers now have colour pages and daily and weekend supplements covering a range of interests which attempt to attract the newspaper-reading public and appeal to advertisers. Owners, however, may refuse to rescue those papers which make continuous losses. A number of newspapers in the twentieth century ceased publication because of reduced circulation, loss of advertising revenue, refusals of further financial aid or a combination of all three factors.

Despite a fall in hard-copy circulation, most national newspapers now have online Internet versions, which are often free (at least in outline format). They also offer subscription access to special features and longer articles. This rapidly expanding service provides an additional medium for information, communication and advertising revenue as well as continuously updated news. It may be that subscriptions may be required in future for all free services.

Regional and ethnic newspapers

Some 1,300 regional and local newspapers are published in towns and cities throughout Britain. They largely focus on local or regional news, but also contain national and international features; are supported financially by regional advertising; and may be daily morning or evening papers, Sundays or weeklies. Some nine out of ten adults read one or more of the different regional or local papers every week, and 75 per cent of local and regional newspapers operate an Internet website. However, ABC figures for December 2009 show declines in circulation for the majority of newspaper groups and a reduction in the number of individual titles.

Excluding the national newspaper industry, London and South East England have one dominant evening paper (the *London Evening Standard*) with increased daily sales of 1.4 million in February 2010. In January 2009, the *Standard* was purchased by Alexander Lebedev; in October 2009 it became a free newspaper (see below); and has a new business model including an e-edition with free subscription, mobile phone platform links and digital services, which may be a template for other newspapers. There are also about a hundred local weeklies, dailies and evening papers of various sizes and types which appear in the Greater London districts.

Quality daily regional (and national) papers, such as *The Scotsman* (Edinburgh), the *Glasgow Herald*, the *Western Mail* (Cardiff), and the *Yorkshire Post* (Leeds), have good reputations and sales outside their specific regions. Other high-selling Scottish papers are the *Daily Record*, the popular *Sunday Mail* (Glasgow) and the *Sunday Post* (Dundee). Northern Irish papers include the Belfast-based *Belfast Telegraph* and the *News Letter*.

There has been a growth of 'free newspapers' throughout Britain, such as the daily *Metro* with a circulation of 450,000 in London (now widely available throughout the country in shops, train stations and at street stalls with a circulation of 1.2 million). Some 650 free papers, such as the *Manchester Metro News* and the *Glaswegian*, are published weekly on a local basis and are financed by local advertising, to such an extent that news is often outweighed by the advertisements. It is estimated that they have a weekly circulation of some 29 million. These are often delivered direct to homes, as well as being widely available elsewhere, and are free to the consumer. However, like the national papers, the regional, free and local press has been severely affected by the recent downturn in advertising revenue, on which it is dependent for survival.

Britain's ethnic communities also produce some 106 newspapers and magazines, which are increasing in number, are available nationally in the larger cities and are improving in quality. Some, such as Muslim magazines, are becoming more mainstream in an effect to appeal to a younger Muslim and wider non-Muslim audience. There is a wide range of publications for Jewish, Asian, Afro-Caribbean, Chinese and Arabic readers, published on a daily or (more commonly) periodic basis, such as the *Asian Times* and Afro-Caribbean papers such as the *Gleaner* (founded in 1951), the *Voice*, *New Nation* and *Caribbean Times*.

Some of the ethnic papers are resilient and enthusiastic, some quickly disappear and all are short of money. Many have poor publishing sites and sales. They struggle to attract advertising from the private sector and rely on their income from the cover price and from local and national government advertising.

Periodicals and magazines

There are some 8,500 different periodicals and magazines in Britain, which are of a weekly, monthly or quarterly nature and are dependent upon sales and advertising to survive. They are aimed at different markets and levels of sophistication and either cover trades, professions and business (read by 95 per cent of occupational groups) or are consumer titles dealing with sports, hobbies and interests (read by 80 per cent of adults).

Although the number of periodicals has expanded, it is still difficult to break into the established consumer market with a new product. Some attempts, which manage to find a gap in the market, succeed, but most usually fail. Others, which are initially successful, may also become victims of new fashions and trends.

The teenage and youth magazine market is fiercely fought for but has suffered large sales losses recently. This is attributed to greater Internet and mobile phone usage. The men's general interest magazine market (some with a specifically 'laddish' appeal) is similarly volatile. Women's periodicals, such as *Take a Break*, *Woman* and *Woman's Own*, have large and wide circulations. But the best-selling publications are the weekly *Radio Times* and *What's on TV*, which contain feature stories and scheduled programmes for BBC and independent television and radio.

Other magazines cover interests such as computers, rural pastimes, gardening, railways, cooking, a wide variety of sports, architecture and do-it-yourself skills.

Among the serious weekly journals are the *New Statesman and Society* (a left-wing political and social affairs magazine); *The Economist* (dealing with economic and political matters); the *Spectator* (a conservative journal); and *New Scientist*. *The Times* publishes influential weekly magazines, such as the *Educational Supplement*, the *Higher* (education supplement) and the *Literary Supplement*. The lighter side of the market is catered for by periodicals like *Private Eye*, which satirizes the shortcomings of British society.

The broadcast media

The contemporary broadcast media are still divided into what has traditionally been thought of as two sectors. The 'public sector' is the British Broadcasting Corporation (BBC) financed by the television licence fee (payable by anyone who owns a television set). The 'independent sector' consists of commercial stations or channels, which are funded mainly by advertising revenue. Both sectors cover radio, terrestrial (Earth-based) television and cable/satellite television.

Since 2003, the Office of Communications (Ofcom) has replaced the roles and duties of former regulators in both public and independent sectors and is now the single regulator for the broadcast media. But although the BBC is subject to Ofcom regulation on programme standards and economic management, the BBC Trust is responsible for managing its public service remit. Opinions differ as to the future of the BBC in its present role and the continuance of its funding by the licence fee.

Historically, radio was the first broadcast medium to appear in Britain. Experimental transmissions were made at the end of the nineteenth century and were developed further in the early twentieth century. After a period of limited availability, national radio was established in 1922 when the British Broadcasting Company was formed under John Reith.

In 1927 Reith became the first Director-General of the British Broadcasting Corporation (BBC) and set the tone and style for its development. Funded by the licence fee, it had a monopoly on national broadcasting and a paternalistic image. Reith insisted that it should be independent of government and commercial interests, strive for quality and be a 'public service broadcaster' (defined as having a solemn duty to inform, educate and entertain). On this basis, the BBC built a reputation for impartial news reporting and excellent programmes.

The BBC's broadcasting monopoly in radio and television (which started in 1936 for a limited audience) led to pressure from commercial and political interests to widen the scope of broadcasting. As a result, independent television financed by advertising and under the supervision of the Independent Television Authority (ITA) was created in 1954 and the first programmes were shown in

1955. The BBC's monopoly on radio broadcasting was also ended in 1972 and independent radio stations were established throughout the country, funded by advertising.

A duopoly (two organizations) then covered broadcasting: the public service of the BBC and the independent service of the ITA. The latter was expanded as cable, satellite and other broadcasting services developed. The ITA then evolved into the IBA (Independent Broadcasting Authority), which was succeeded by the ITC (Independent Television Commission) and the Radio Authority. These were replaced in 2003 by Ofcom. British broadcasting has thus been conditioned by significant change and the competition between the BBC and independent organizations.

Substantial reforms to British broadcasting were made by Conservative governments in the 1980s and 1990s, which created more radio and television channels. A deregulation policy was supposed to promote competition among broadcasters and more choice for consumers. This process is being continued today as broadcasting services expand and are digitalized. Yet digitalization has proceeded slowly because of initial technical problems, geographical availability and a limited consumer take-up due to scepticism of the new digital offerings. However, digitalization will potentially create many more radio and television channels as analogue systems are phased out in most British households by 2012.

These and earlier changes have been controversial and criticized for their apparent emphasis on competition and commercialism, rather than quality. A larger number of television and radio channels may not lead to greater real choice, but rather to inferior programmes of the same trivial type as broadcasters chase bigger audiences. There is a finite number of people available to watch television or listen to radio, advertisers' budgets cannot be stretched to cover all available broadcast offerings and so advertisers use those programmes which attract large audiences and therefore profits. Television in 1995 accounted for 28 per cent of total advertising spending, but this had dropped to 25 per cent by 2003 and to 21.9 per cent by 2009.

The public service ethos, embodied in the BBC, is also now a statutory requirement for all terrestrial independent channels, although opinions differ as to its application. Ofcom is concerned to maintain the quality of programmes by the terrestrial public service broadcasters (the BBC, ITV1, Channel 4, Five and SC4 – see below). Under recent legislation they must provide a minimum level of different types of programming. Ofcom has found that standards are dropping, that there is too much reliance on programmes with popular appeal and that the audience share for public service broadcasters is falling. Critics have echoed this view and condemned the 'dumbing down' of British broadcasting in general and television in particular and the proliferation of inferior offerings.

The BBC

The BBC is based at Broadcasting House in London but has centres throughout the country which provide regional networks for radio and television. It was created by Royal Charter and has a Trust which is responsible for supervising its programmes and their suitability. Trustees are appointed by the Crown on the advice of government ministers and supposedly constitute an independent element within the organization of the BBC. Daily operations are controlled by the Director-General, chosen by the Trust.

The BBC is financed by a grant from Parliament, which comes from the sale of television licences (£3.5 billion in 2008–09). These are payable by anyone who owns a television set and are relatively low in international terms (£142.50 annually for a colour set in 2009). The Corporation also generates a considerable income from selling its programmes abroad and from the sale of a programme guide (*Radio Times*), books, magazines, videos and DVDs.

The BBC has recently come under pressure from government and commercial pressures to reform itself. It has struggled to maintain its position as a public service broadcaster, funded by the licence fee, at a time of fierce competition with independent broadcasters. Internal reorganization and cost-cutting has led to a slimmer, more efficient organization. But it has had to develop alternative forms of funding, such as subscription and pay services, and is obliged to include independent productions in 25 per cent of its television schedules. Although its charter has been extended, it is likely that the retention of the licence fee could again be re-evaluated at the next application, thus posing questions about the future role of the BBC.

The BBC's external services, which consist of radio broadcasts in English (the World Service) and forty-two other languages abroad, were founded in 1932 and are funded by the Foreign Office. These have a reputation for objective news reporting and programmes. The BBC also began transmitting commercially funded television programmes in 1991 by cable to Europe and by satellite links to Africa and Asia, such as BBC World (news) now merged with the World Service and BBC Prime (entertainment).

The BBC is not a state organization in the sense of being controlled by the government. However, it is not as independent of political pressures as many in Britain and overseas assume. Its charter has to be renewed by Parliament and by its terms government can, and does, intervene in the showing of programmes which are alleged to be controversial or against the public interest. The BBC Trustees, though independent, are in fact government appointees. Governments can also exert pressure upon the BBC when the licence fee comes up for renewal by Parliament. The BBC does try to be neutral in political matters, to such an extent that all political parties have periodically complained (as with the previous Labour government over the conduct of the Iraq war) that it is prejudiced against them, being either too liberal/critical or too conservative/establishment-minded.

The major parties have equal rights to broadcast on the BBC and independent television.

Historically, the BBC (with its monopoly on radio) was affected by the invention of television, which changed British entertainment and news habits. The BBC now has two main terrestrial television channels (BBC1 and BBC2). BBC1 is a mass-appeal channel with an audience share of 20.7 per cent in 2010. Its programmes consist of news, plays and drama series, comedy, quiz shows, variety performances, sport and documentaries. BBC2, with an audience share of 6.8 per cent, tends to show more serious items such as news analysis and discussion, documentaries, adaptations of novels into plays and series, operas, concerts and some sport. It is also provides Open University programmes.

The Labour government from 2001 expanded BBC television services by the creation of two satellite channels, BBC3 (contemporary entertainment, comedy, music and drama) and BBC4 (culture and the arts), as well as a children's channel. Audience figures for these channels have initially been low.

BBC Radio performs an important service, although some of its audiences have fluctuated recently. There are five national stations; thirty-nine local stations serving many districts in England; and regional and community services in Scotland, Wales and Northern Ireland. They all have to compete for listeners with independent stations but offer an alternative in news, debate and local information to pop-based local and national independent stations. The national channels specialize in different tastes. Radio 1 caters for pop music; Radio 2 has light music, news, and comedy; Radio 3 provides classical and modern serious music, talks, discussions and plays; Radio 4 concentrates on news reports, analysis, talks and plays; and Radio Five Live (established 1990) has sport and news programmes. The BBC national and local radio audience share amounted to 55 per cent in 2009 (as opposed to independent radio with 42.4 per cent).

Independent broadcasting (The Office of Communications – Ofcom)

Ofcom does not make or produce programmes itself. Its government-appointed board regulates the independent television and radio companies (including cable and satellite services). It grants licences to the transmitting companies which commission many of the programmes shown on three advertising-financed terrestrial television channels (ITV1, Channel 4 and Five).

The ITV network is the biggest commercial television network in the UK. It comprises fifteen regional licences and provides television to viewers across Britain. The licences cooperate with each other, commission and schedule television programmes and undertake to provide regional programming. Since 2004, eleven of the licences in England and Wales have been owned by ITV plc following the merger of Carlton Communications and Granada plc. Smaller companies own the rest in Scotland, Northern Ireland and the Channel Islands.

ITV plc also owns the digital channels ITV2, ITV3 and ITV4 in addition to new media and interactive services via the Internet, mobile phones and broadband.

The licences granted to ITV1 companies are renewable every ten years and the companies have to compete with any other interested applicants. They receive nothing from the television licence fee, which applies only to the BBC. The companies are thus dependent upon the finance they receive from advertising and the sales of programmes, videos, DVDs, books, records and other publications.

ITV1 (with 17.6 per cent of audience share in 2010) is the oldest independent television channel and once seemed only to provide popular programmes of a light-entertainment and sometimes trivial type. Although its quality has improved and it now has a high standard of news reporting, drama productions and documentaries, critics argue that the hunt for audience ratings is once again producing inferior mass entertainment programmes.

Channel 4 (with 7.1 per cent of audience share) was established in 1982 to create a commercial alternative to BBC2. It is a public corporation, which is funded by selling its own advertising time. It was intended to offer something different and challenging in an appeal to minority tastes and provides programmes in Welsh in Wales (S4C). Channel 4 initially had serious problems with advertising and the quality of its programmes (commissioned or bought from independent producers), but has now developed a considerable reputation for its news and documentary productions, art programmes and films.

Five (with 4.3 per cent of audience share) became operative in 1997 after a ten-year licence was awarded to Channel 5 Broadcasting Limited. It is funded by advertising, subscription and sponsorship; covers 80 per cent of the population; but had a shaky start in terms of the attraction of its programmes. Some of its programmes still attract criticism but it has increased its financial base.

It was argued that the former ITC did not always keep a close watch on independent broadcasting developments and lacked clear regulatory powers and consistent policies. There had been controversy over its system of awarding ITV1 licences, which often went to the highest bidder with little apparent regard to quality and production efficiency. Ofcom is an attempt to improve on this structure.

Television and its associated technological developments have become very attractive in Britain and a rich source of entertainment profits. At one stage, it was thought that cable television by subscription would considerably expand these possibilities. Cable television (with the main provider being Virgin Media) is growing steadily through digital technology (with its increased number of channels) and is potentially available to 12.5 million homes largely in urban and suburban areas, with 4.2 million subscribers in 2010. But it has been challenged by DVD and satellite.

Television broadcasting by satellite through subscription was established in Britain in 1989 by British Sky Broadcasting (BSkyB). It is the biggest UK satellite television programmer (2010) with ten million subscribers. Its channels provide news, light entertainment, sport and feature films. The choice of satellite channels is expanding steadily through digital technology with over 420 radio and television satellite servers providing programming in Britain. One in three homes in the UK and Ireland use the Sky service. However, it still lags behind terrestrial ITV1 and BBC1 in audience viewing share.

Ofcom also controls independent radio (three national stations and 150 local and regional stations throughout the country). All are funded by advertising, and revenue figures suggest that radio is the fastest-growing medium in Britain.

The national radio stations were created by Conservative governments to expand radio broadcasting. The first licence was awarded in 1991 to Classic FM (popular classical music and news bulletins); the second in 1992 to Virgin 1215 (rock music); and the third in 1995 to Talk Radio UK (speech-based service).

Local independent radio once seemed to provide mainly pop music, news flashes and some programmes of local interest, but expansion has occurred at city, local and community levels because broadcasting has been deregulated by the government in an attempt to increase the variety of radio and include more tastes and interests. Local and national independent stations accounted for 42.4 per cent of total radio audience share in 2009.

The role and influence of television

Television is an influential and dominant force in modern Britain, as well as a popular entertainment activity. Over 98 per cent of the population have television sets in their homes, 95 per cent of these are colour sets and over 50 per cent of homes have two sets or more. Some people prefer to rent their sets instead of owning them because rented sets are repaired and maintained free of charge.

Reports in 2001 suggested that radio (independent and BBC) was more popular than television, indicating that some people were deserting the latter because of its alleged superficiality and declining quality. Nevertheless, despite recent years when figures have moved up and down, average television viewing time (2009) seems to have increased slightly to 26 hours per week, and about 94 per cent of individuals watched TV at least once a week. Analysts suggest that these increased figures were due not to improved programme quality but to money worries which prevented people from spending money outside the home and because the data was collected in the winter months when people tended to stay indoors.

A large number of the programmes shown on television are made in Britain, although there are also many imported American series of high quality which prove popular. A few programmes come from other English-speaking countries, such as Australia, New Zealand and Canada. However, there are relatively few foreign-language productions on British television and these are either dubbed or subtitled.

The range of programmes shown is very considerable, but they also vary very widely in quality. Although some British television has a high reputation abroad, it does attract substantial criticism in Britain, either because of the low standard of some programmes, a lack of variety, the tameness of content or because programmes are frequently repeated. News reports, documentaries and current affairs analyses are generally of a high standard, as are some dramatic, educational, sporting, natural history and cultural productions. But there is also a wide selection of series, soap operas, films, quizzes and variety shows which are of doubtful quality, although they clearly appeal to significant sections of the viewing public.

Reality TV, dance and singing talent shows, confrontational and confessional programmes and genres such as makeover, decorating and property have led to charges of a 'dumbing down' of British television. Many of these programmes are calculated to appeal to a mass audience, in search of high ratings and involve exploitation, voyeurism and aggression, celebrity worship, a desire for instant fame, public emotional display and self-absorption. Independent television companies need such successful offerings to attract advertising and profit. It is also necessary for the BBC to produce commercial offerings to demonstrate its mass appeal.

Competition between the BBC and independent television is strong and the battle of the ratings (the number of people watching individual programmes) indicates their popularity (or otherwise). But competition can mean that similar programmes are shown at the same time on the major channels, in order to appeal to specific markets and attract the biggest share of the audience. It is also argued that competition has reduced the quality of programmes overall and resulted in an appeal to the lowest common denominator in taste. The BBC in particular is criticized for its increasing commercialism and failure to provide quality arts, drama and news programmes. It is argued that the BBC must maintain its public service obligations to quality and creativity in order to justify the annual licence fee.

Voices have been raised about the alleged levels of sex, vulgarity, violence and bad language on British television, even before the 'watershed' of 9 p.m. in the evenings when young children may be watching. There have been scandals about the on-screen and radio behaviour of some television personalities and a yobbish atmosphere. Some groups and individuals have attempted to reform and influence the kind of programmes that are shown. Academic research had long denied a crossover influence, but some critics now suggest that individuals can in fact be morally harmed by the content of particular television programmes, images, behaviour and speech which can be rapidly imitated, particularly by children.

The previous Conservative government considered that violence, sex and obscenity on television did affect viewers and could encourage copycat behaviour. It was concerned to 'clean up' television. A Broadcasting Standards Complaints Commission had previously monitored programmes, examined complaints, established codes of conduct for the broadcasting organizations and tightened its rules concerning the invasion of privacy by broadcasters. The Commission's role has now been taken over by Ofcom. The sale and rent of 'video nasties' (videos which portray extreme forms of violence and brutality) have been banned and rules for the sale and hire of videos have been tightened. However, polls and surveys, such as the annual *British Social Attitudes*, have frequently suggested that Britons are becoming more permissive about the portrayal of sex and different lifestyles in the media if this is relevant to a plot, and even more liberal if it occurs outside a family context on adult channels, video and cinema. The downloading of explicit material from the Internet is also becoming much more prevalent.

There continues to be an 'entertainments' expansion in Britain where broadcasters fight to attract viewers and advertising revenue. Yet critics question whether this means more genuine choice or declining quality. Digital broadcasting will increase the number of television channels and has transformed some media into interactive forces which combine the Internet and personalized programming in a single package. However, broadcasters risk losing audiences and revenue as more people switch to DVD and the Internet as alternatives to television programmes. ONS reported that in 2009, 18.3 million households in the UK (70 per cent) had Internet access and 63 per cent of all UK households had a broadband connection.

Media ownership and freedom of expression

The financial and ownership structures of the British media industry are complex and have traditionally involved a range of media outlets, which include the press, radio and television. Sometimes an individual company would own a number of print products, such as newspapers and magazines, and would specialize in this area.

However, this kind of ownership is declining. Today it is more common for newspapers to be owned and controlled by corporations which are concerned with wide media interests, such as films, radio, television, magazines, the Internet and satellite and cable companies. Other newspaper- and media-owning groups have diversified their interests even further, and may be involved in a variety of non-media activities. In Britain, only a few newspapers, such as the *Guardian* and the *Morning Star*, have avoided being controlled by multinational and multimedia commercial concerns.

This involvement of large enterprises in the media, and the resulting concentration of ownership in a few hands, such as newspapers and other media interests controlled by News International and Trinity Mirror, has caused concern. Although these concentrations do not amount to a monopoly situation, there have been frequent enquiries into the questions of ownership and control. Some critics argue that the state should provide public subsidies to the media industries in order to prevent them being taken over by big-business groups. But this suggestion has not been adopted, and it is felt that there are potential dangers in allowing the state to gain any direct or indirect financial influence over the media.

Today the law is supposed to guard against the risks inherent in greatly concentrated ownership of the means of communication. The purchase of further newspapers by an existing owner is controlled by law and newspaper owners' shareholdings in independent radio and television stations are restricted. Further restrictions, such as independent directors of newspapers, guarantees of editorial independence from owners' interference, and trustee arrangements to allow newspapers to maintain their character and traditions, are usually imposed. These arrangements are intended to prevent monopolies and undue influence on the part of owners. However, such safeguards do not always work satisfactorily in practice and takeovers of ITV1 television companies by rival companies and multi-media corporations are now permitted within limits.

The question of free expression in the media continues to be of concern. Critics argue that the media do not have sufficient freedom to comment on matters of public interest. But the freedom of the media, as of individuals, to express themselves, is not absolute. Regulations are placed upon the general freedom in order to safeguard the legitimate interests of other individuals, organizations and the state, so that a balance between competing interests may be achieved.

There are several legal restraints upon media freedom of expression. The *sub judice* rule means that the media may not comment on court proceedings and must restrict themselves to reporting the court facts. The rule is intended to protect the individuals concerned, and if a media organization breaks the rule it may be found guilty of contempt of court and fined. Contempt of court proceedings may also be used by judges to obtain journalists' sources of information, or to prevent the media from publishing certain court details and documents. Some journalists have refused to disclose their sources and have gone to prison as a result.

The obtaining and publishing of state and official information is controlled tightly by the Official Secrets Act and by D-notices (directives to the media concerning information which should not be divulged). The media are also liable to court proceedings for libel and obscenity offences. Libel is the making of accusations which are proved to be false or harmful to a person's reputation. Obscenity covers any action that offends against public morality. In such cases, the media organization and all the individuals involved may be held responsible. There are current debates about whether the English libel laws and their application should be restricted because they may inhibit freedom of expression.

New legislation by the previous Labour government has had considerable media implications. The Human Rights Act (1998) is a two-edged sword in terms of free expression. On the one hand, it supposedly allows the media greater freedom of expression to comment on matters of public importance. On the other, it allows individuals to complain and seek compensation if they feel that their individual rights and privacy have been infringed (for example, by the media). Legislation was passed in 2006 which made incitement to religious hatred a criminal offence in England and Wales. Although much will depend upon actual court decisions, this arguably restricted the media's and artists' rights of expression to comment critically on religion and religious belief. The question becomes one of distinguishing between genuine critical comment and deliberate criminal behaviour, particularly if the test for a successful charge of incitement rests on the subjective or personal assessment of the complainant. While a BBC poll in 2009 found that a majority of Britons considered religion should be respected and valued in public life, other research found that they opposed domineering religion.

These restrictions prevent absolute media freedom of expression. It is argued that there is a need for reform if responsible investigative journalism and the media are to do their job adequately. Britain is a secretive society, and it was thought that the Labour government's Freedom of Information Act (2000) might break down some of the secrecy and executive control. But, while the media have been able to use the Act successfully in some cases, it is suggested that it is not working satisfactorily and that official bodies avoid giving the information requested.

On the other hand, the media can act irresponsibly, invade individual privacy, behave in unethical ways and sensationalize events for their own purposes. The media have won some libel cases brought against them and gained important

PLATE 10.3 Photographers lined up to record the wedding of Prince Charles to Camilla Parker Bowles, Windsor, 9 April 2005.
(*Nils Jorgensen/Rex Features*)

victories for open information. Yet they have also lost other cases because of their methods. Some irresponsible media practices do cause concern and the government could impose statutory restrictions on invasions of privacy unless the media reform themselves. However, it is generally felt that freedom of expression could be less restricted than it is at present.

A restraining self-regulatory media institution, the independent Press Complaints Commission (PCC), was created in 1990. It is financed by newspaper owners and its role is to guard the freedom and independence of the press, maintain standards of journalism and judge complaints by the public against newspapers. Some critics argue that the PCC is not fighting as hard as it might for press freedom, while others maintain that it is not strict enough with newspapers when complaints against them are proved. A fear that the government might legislate against media abuses has led to a tightening of the PCC's rules about privacy invasion, harassment by photographers and protection of children. Newspaper owners have also created an ombudsman system for each newspaper, through which public complaints can be made and investigated. It remains to be seen whether the PCC, editorial control and the ombudsman system will be truly effective.

It is sometimes argued that the concentrated ownership patterns of the media might limit freedom of journalistic expression by allowing owners undue influence over what is included in their products. Former journalists have claimed that there is proprietorial interference in some (if by no means all) of the media, which is not being curbed by either editorial guarantees or legal and government restrictions. On the other hand, editors and journalists can be very independently minded people who will usually object strongly to any attempts at interference. Owners, in practice, seem to be careful not to tread on too many toes, because there are always competing media sources which are willing to publish the facts.

A further concern about limitations on media freedom has been the extent to which advertisers might dictate policy and content when they place their products. The question of advertisers' influence is complex and might today be more applicable to the mass-consumer market of radio and television than the press. Advertisers dealing with the press are more concerned with the type or status of readers than with their numbers. Arguably, the media have not succumbed in a substantial degree to the direct manipulations of the advertising agencies, in spite of the media's dependence upon advertising revenue.

Attitudes to the media

Apart from the issues discussed above, opinion polls suggest that the media are not a source of great concern to most British people, who tend to accept them for what they are without any great illusions. Respondents are reasonably satisfied with the BBC and independent broadcasters as sources of news. However, most are generally very sceptical of the press and journalists, mistrustful of the content of newspapers and do not believe that they present all sides of a question fairly.

It is difficult to evaluate absolutely whether the media play a dominant part in influencing public opinion on political and other matters. The left-wing view assumes that they do and consequently disapproves of the alleged right-wing bias in the British media. But, while some people may have their attitudes directly shaped in these ways, it is argued that many readers and viewers have already made up their own minds and react against any blatant attempts at indoctrination. On certain occasions (such as general elections), the media may have an important effect on public opinion. But it is also likely that the media may merely follow popular trends and reflect changing political and social views among the public.

Many people learn to read between the lines of newspapers and broadcasts and are conditioned early in life 'not to believe everything you read in the papers', or hear 'on the telly'. Since television in particular is often accused of being either right-wing or left-wing, depending on which government is in power, it would seem that the British people are receiving enough information from all sides of the political spectrum. In practice, most people make up their own minds, object to having politics and other concerns 'thrust down their throats' and many take a sceptical (and often cynical) attitude to such matters.

Given such attitudes, it is interesting to note that a MORI/British Council poll in 1999 found that only 28 per cent of overseas respondents (5 per cent for Germany) believed that the British media as a whole cannot be relied on to tell the truth. The British media were regarded as being more truthful than their counterparts in most of the overseas countries surveyed in the poll. The British themselves would not necessarily agree with these findings. Yet, according to a BBC/Reuters/Media Center poll in 2006 trust in the media as a whole had (perhaps surprisingly), increased in Britain from 29 per cent to 47 per cent in the period 2002–06.

Exercises

Explain and examine the following terms:

media	circulation	newsagents	'compacts'
press	tabloid	'free newspapers'	'hot metal'
advertising	broadsheet	*Private Eye*	libel
Fleet Street	*Sun*	ownership	*sub judice*
The Times	John Reith	Rupert Murdoch	BBC 2
licence	Ofcom	World Service	dubbing
PCC	mid-market	Channel 4	duopoly
terrestrial	digital	Virgin Media	Classic FM

> Write short essays on the following topics:
>
> 1*　Describe and comment critically on the structure of British broadcasting.
>
> 2　Examine the problems of media freedom of expression.
>
> 3　Discuss the division of British national newspapers into 'populars' and 'qualities'.

Visit **www.routledge.com/textbooks/oakland** for multiple-choice questions, links to related YouTube clips, tips on approaching essay questions, and much, much more.

Further reading

1　Bignell, J., Lacey, S. and Macmurraugh-Cavanagh, M.K. (2000) *British Television Drama: Past, Present and Future*, London: Macmillan/Palgrave

2　Branston, G. And Stafford, R. (2006) *The Media Student's Book*, London: Routledge

3　Briggs, A. and Cobley, O. (2002) *The Media: An Introduction*, London: Pearson Longman

4　Curran, J. and Gurevitch, M. (2005) *Mass Media and Society*, London: Bloomsbury Academic

5　Curran, J. and Seaton, J. (2009) *Power without Responsibility: The Press and Broadcasting in Britain*, Routledge: London

6　Franklin, B. (2001) *British Television Policy: A Reader*, London: Routledge

7　O'Sullivan, T., Dutton, B. and Rayner, P. (2003) *Studying the Media: An Introduction*, London: Bloomsbury Academic

8　Seaton, J., Petley, J. and Gaber, I. (2005) *Culture Wars: The Media and the British Left*, Edinburgh: Edinburgh University Press

9　Stokes, J. and Reading, A. (eds) (1999) *The Media in Britain: Current Debates and Developments*, London: Palgrave/Macmillan

10　Wedell, G. and Luckham, B. (2001) *Television at the Crossroads*, London: Macmillan/Palgrave

Websites

Department of Culture, Media and Sport: www.culture.gov.uk
British Broadcasting Corporation (BBC): www.bbc.co.uk
ITV (Channel 3): www.itv.com
Channel Four: www.channel4.com
Five: www.channel5.co.uk
Office of Communications (Ofcom): www.ofcom.gov.uk
The Press Association: www.pad.press.net

Press Complaints Commission (PCC): www.pcc.org.uk
The Times: www.the-times.co.uk
The *Guardian*: www.guardian.co.uk
The *Daily Telegraph*: www.telegraph.co.uk

11

Religion

British religious history since the earliest conversions from paganism (possibly around AD 300) has been predominantly Christian. Following the Protestant Reformation in the sixteenth century and the gradual creation of the Church of England, religion was subsequently characterized by conflict between Roman Catholics and Protestants and by quarrels among different Protestant traditions, which led to division into separate Nonconformist churches and sects. But this history has also included at various times the appearance of non-Christian faiths, such as Judaism, and groups with humanist and special beliefs. Today, Britain still possesses a diversity of religious denominations (170), which have been added to over the years (particularly in the twentieth century) by immigrants and their religions, such as Islam, Hinduism, Buddhism and Sikhism.

Despite these features, commentators have long argued that there is a continuing decline in religious observance and that the country seems to be largely secular in terms of the low figures (estimated at 13 per cent) for all types (Christian and non-Christian) of regular weekly attendance at religious services. Secularization (the movement from sacred to worldly concerns and the Enlightenment's scientific challenge to belief in God) is allegedly affecting most faiths, particularly Christianity. This has led to a decline in the attraction of organized religion represented by mainstream or traditional faiths.

However, critics argue that the apparent decline of religion in modern British society refers primarily to affiliation to or identification with the Church of England. Religious observance in other faiths, such as Roman Catholicism, Islam and Ultra-Orthodox Judaism, is actually increasing while that in others such as Hinduism and Sikhism seems to be relatively stable. It is suggested that adherence to religion is declining in some areas, but changing its character in others.

In these arguments, a distinction has to be made between attendance at religious services and non-practising religious belief in the population. Religion still arguably remains a factor in national life, whether for believers or as a background to the national culture. It is reflected in an active adherence to specific denominations, in a nominal identification with different faiths and in a general ethical and moral code of behaviour. Formal adherence to a religious faith is proportionally greater in Wales, Scotland and (particularly) Northern Ireland than in England.

Religious history

There is little evidence of organized religion in very early British history, beyond archaeological discoveries which suggest the existence of various forms of pagan belief. Some Christian influences had reached Britain during the Roman occupation, but opinions differ as to how widespread or permanent these were.

Missionaries and monks in Ireland, who represented a Gaelic variant of the Roman Catholicism brought from Rome, had converted some of the pagan Irish kings to Christianity possibly as early as AD 300. This process continued, and much of Ireland was converted from around AD 432 by St Patrick and other monks. Irish missionaries spread Christianity to Wales, Scotland and northern England, establishing religious centres, such as that of St Columba on the Scottish island of Iona. Opinions differ as to the extent of the Gaelic Church's influence in England.

In AD 596–7 the Anglo-Saxons of Kent in southern England were further influenced by the Catholic faith through St Augustine and other monks, who had been sent from Rome by Pope Gregory and who founded the ecclesiastical capital of Canterbury in AD 597. The spread of Christianity was encouraged by Anglo-Saxon kings, who thought the hierarchical example of the Christian church would support their royal authority. The church also provided educated advisers and administrators through whom the kings were able to control their kingdoms more efficiently. The connection between church and state was consequently established at an early stage in English history.

Southern English Christianity was based on the beliefs and practices of the Church of Rome. Although the faith of Ireland, Wales, Scotland and northern England was also founded on Roman doctrines, it had a more Gaelic identification. Conflicts and divisions arose between the two branches of Christianity, but these were eventually resolved in AD 664 at the Synod (meeting) of Whitby, where all the churches agreed to accept the Catholic form of worship and practice.

Christianity became a central and influential force in society. The church was based on a hierarchy of monks, priests, bishops and archbishops. It was a part not only of religious culture but also of the administration, government and law. However, it was increasingly accused of worldliness and materialism and thought to be corrupt and concerned with politics rather than religion. Nevertheless, monarchs maintained their allegiance to the Catholic Church and the Pope in spiritual matters, some with more conviction than others.

However, the relationship between England and Rome became difficult and by the sixteenth century was at breaking point. English monarchs were jealous of the wealth and power of the church and resented the influence of Rome in national affairs. Henry VIII argued in 1529 that as King of England he, not the Pope, was the supreme legal authority in the country and that the church and courts owed their allegiance to him.

In 1534 Henry broke away from Rome and declared himself head of the church in England. The immediate reason for this breach was the Pope's refusal to accept Henry's divorce from his queen, Katherine of Aragon, who had not produced a male heir to the throne. But Henry also wanted to curb the church's power and wealth. In 1536 he dissolved many monasteries and confiscated much of the church's property.

Although Henry had established a national church, that church was still Roman Catholic in its faith and practices. Henry did not regard himself as a Protestant, nor did he consider the English church to be part of the Protestant Reformation, which was affecting religious life in continental Europe. Indeed, Henry had defended the papacy against Martin Luther in 1521. The Pope rewarded him with the title of Fidei Defensor (Defender of the Faith), which British monarchs still bear today and which can be seen on most British coins.

Nevertheless, the influence of the European Reformation caused the English, Scottish and Welsh churches to move away from Rome's doctrines. This development in England increased under Edward VI (1547–53), when practices and beliefs became more Protestant. John Knox in Scotland also accelerated the process by founding the separate Protestant Church of Scotland in 1560. Meanwhile, Ireland remained mostly Catholic.

Conflicts between Catholics and Protestants began, which often involved violent persecution. Henry VIII's daughter, the Catholic Mary Tudor, tried to restore the Catholic faith during her reign (1553–8), but did not succeed. Her half-sister, the Protestant Elizabeth I (1558–1603), established the Protestant status of the Church of England by the terms of her Church Settlement. The Church's doctrine was stated in the Thirty-Nine Articles of Faith (1571) and its forms of worship were contained in the Book of Common Prayer (both revised in later centuries). English replaced Latin in church documents and services and priests were later able to marry. The English church now occupied an intermediate position between Catholicism and the Protestant churches of Europe.

However, the creation of the Protestant Church of England did not put an end to the religious arguments which were to affect Britain in later centuries. Many Protestants in the sixteenth and seventeenth centuries felt that the church had not distanced itself sufficiently from Rome, and some left to form their own religious organizations. Initially called Dissenters because they disagreed with the majority view, they were later known as Nonconformists and today are members of the Free Churches. Tension between adherents of various forms of Protestantism also occurred in the Civil War (1642–51) between Parliamentarians and Royalists, which led to the Protectorate of Oliver Cromwell.

The collapse of Cromwell's narrowly puritan regime after his death, and the restoration of the Stuart monarchy under Charles II in 1660, did bring some religious moderation. Yet minority religions still suffered. The Roman Catholic Church had undergone persecution and exclusion after the Reformation, and Jews and Nonconformists also experienced discrimination. These religious groups were excluded from the universities, the House of Commons and public office. It was not until the early nineteenth century that most restrictions placed on them were formally removed. Meanwhile, the Church of England solidified its dominant position in 1688, when the Protestant William III succeeded James II, the last English king to sympathize openly with the Catholic cause.

But further quarrels affected religious life in the eighteenth century, as groups reacted to rationalist developments in the Church of England. For example, the Methodists (founded 1739) stressed the emotional aspects of salvation and religion. They tried to work within the Church of England, but opposition to their views eventually forced them to separate. Nevertheless, an Evangelical wing within the Church was strongly affected by Methodism. The Evangelicals based their faith on a literal interpretation of the Bible and a humanitarian idealism. They accomplished many industrial and social reforms in nineteenth-century Britain. Today, the 'Low Church' wing of the Church of England is influenced by Evangelicalism.

Other groups reacted to the Church of England in the eighteenth and nineteenth centuries and founded a variety of Nonconformist sects, such as the Baptists. Nonconformism was (and is) particularly strong in Wales. On the other hand, the Oxford or Tractarian Movement, which developed in the 1830s, emphasized the Church of England's connections with Roman Catholicism. It followed Catholic doctrines and used elaborate ritual in its church services. It influenced succeeding generations and today is represented by the Anglo-Catholic or 'High Church' wing of the Church of England.

By the end of the nineteenth century the various Christian and non-Christian churches, such as Judaism, were scattered throughout Britain. In the twentieth century, immigrants added further religious diversity. Muslim mosques, Sikh and Hindu temples, and West Indian churches, such as the Pentecostalists, are common in areas with large ethnic communities.

In Britain today the growth of Christian and non-Christian religious observance and vitality is found outside the big traditional Christian churches. The Evangelical movement continues to grow as a branch of Christianity and is characterized by a close relationship among members and a personal feeling between them and God, Christ and the Holy Spirit. It has basic Christian beliefs, but expresses them in different ways; breaks down the barriers of more traditional worship; places little reliance on church furniture; and has many different meeting places. The growth of fundamentalist faiths, 'enthusiastic' Christian churches and some 500 cults or religious movements has also increased the number of people active in religious life. Meanwhile non-Christian faiths, such as Islam, have expanded significantly.

There is religious freedom in contemporary Britain, a person may belong to any religion or none and religious discrimination is unlawful. There is no religious bar to the holding of public office, except that the monarch must be a member of the Church of England. None of the churches is tied to a political party and there are no religious parties as such in Parliament. In 2006, the Labour government legislated to make incitement to religious hatred a criminal offence in

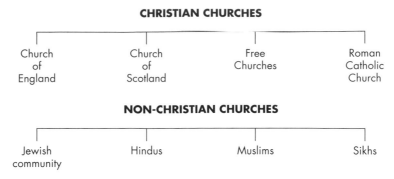

FIGURE 11.1 The main contemporary religious groups

England and Wales. There was strong opposition from secularists and those who argued that it was not a criminal offence to robustly criticise religion. The eventual Act was limited to threatening words or behaviour and much will depend on how the courts interpret 'incitement to religious hatred' in a given case.

The Christian tradition

Christianity in Britain is represented mainly by the Church of England (Anglican) and the Roman Catholic Church (which are the largest denominations), the Church of Scotland and the Free Churches. It is estimated that the Church of England attracts about a fifth of religiously active Britons and the Roman Catholic Church does only marginally better. It is argued that these two churches built too many buildings for too few people in the nineteenth century. They have since used resources to subsidize churches that should have been closed, and poorly attended services contribute to further decline. Surveys suggest that the traditional or mainstream Christian churches have lost their ability to attract the young and need a more contemporary image; some 42 per cent of members of existing congregations consist of retired people and the average age of churchgoers is over seventy. People aged under fifty-five tend to opt for more evangelical forms of worship.

The Church of England

The Church of England is the established or national church in England. This means that its legal position in the state is confirmed by the Elizabethan Church Settlement and Parliament. The monarch is the head of the Church; its archbishops, bishops and deans are appointed by the monarch on the advice of the prime minister; and Parliament has a voice in its organization and rituals. But it is not a state church because it receives no public financial aid, apart from salaries

PLATE 11.1 West Newton Church, Sandringham, Norfolk, a characteristic church of the Church of England. This one, however, is on the royal estate at Sandringham and is attended by members of the royal family when they are in residence.
(Albanpix Ltd/Rex Features)

for non-clerical positions and help with church schools. The Church therefore has a special relationship with the state, although there are calls for its disestablishment (cutting connections between Church and state) so that it has autonomy over its own affairs.

The Church is based on an episcopal hierarchy, or rule by bishops. The two Archbishops of Canterbury and York, together with twenty-four senior bishops, sit in the House of Lords, take part in its proceedings and are the Church's link with Parliament. Organizationally, the Church is divided into the two provinces of Canterbury and York, each under the control of an archbishop. The Archbishop of Canterbury (called the Primate of All England) is the senior of the two and the professional head of the Church. The two provinces are subdivided into forty-four dioceses, each under the control of a bishop. Most bishoprics are very old and have situated in ancient cathedral towns such as York, Chichester, Lincoln, Durham and Salisbury.

The dioceses are divided into some 13,000 parishes, each centred on a parish church. Most parishes, except for those in rural areas, have a priest (called either a vicar or a rector) in charge and a large parish may have additional assistant priests (curates). The priest occupies rent-free accommodation in a vicarage, but has only a small salary, paid out of diocesan funds.

The main financial resources of the church come from its substantial property and investment holdings, and it is the third largest landowner in Britain (after the Crown and the Forestry Commission). The assets of the church, which have been estimated at £400 million, are administered by the Church Commissioners. This wealth has to finance many very expensive demands, such as pensions for the clergy and administrators, the maintenance of churches and cathedrals and activities in Britain and abroad. In recent years the finances of the church have been depleted because of investment failures and growing demands upon its capital.

The Church of England is considered to be a 'broad church' in which a variety of beliefs and practices coexist. Priests have freedom as to how they conduct their church services. These can vary from the elaborate ritual of High Church worship to the simple, functional presentation of Low Church services. The High Church or Anglo-Catholic wing (some 20 per cent of church membership) lays stress on church tradition and the historical influence of Roman Catholic practices and teaching. The Low Church or Evangelical wing (some 80 per cent of church membership) bases its faith and practice on simplicity and often on a literal interpretation of the Bible and is suspicious of Roman Catholic influences.

The two wings of the church do not always cooperate happily and there is considerable variation in styles of worship. Some priests have introduced internet services, contemporary music and theatre into their worship in order to appeal

PLATE 11.2 Westminster Abbey, London. A large Gothic church in Westminster where most English monarchs since William I (the Conqueror) have been crowned. Many eminent people are buried or commemorated here.
(Andy Drysdale/Rex Features)

to younger congregations and more modern concerns or to provide alternatives for those unable or unwilling to attend the local church. Today priests have to deal with a wide variety of problems and pressures in their work, particularly in deprived and inner-city areas, and their role cannot easily be restricted to a purely religious one.

The membership of the Church of England is difficult to determine because the church does not have adequate registers of members. Membership is assumed when a person (usually a baby) is baptized into the church. However, only 40 per cent of the English population have been baptized. This membership may be confirmed at 'confirmation' at the age of fourteen or fifteen. It is estimated that only a fifth of those baptized are confirmed and that 1.2 million people are formal members of the church according to electoral registers.

Church of England statistics suggested that in 2007 the average weekly total attendance (adults, children and young people) at Sunday services was 978,000. This figure was a decrease from 983,000 in 2006, suggesting that the Church is now the second-largest Christian faith after Roman Catholicism. The number of priests also continues to decline (due to retirement and lack of recruitment). However, many other Britons may nominally identify themselves with the Church of England, even though they are not formal members.

Lay members of the parish are associated with church organization at the local level through parochial church councils. These send representatives to the local diocesan councils (or synods), where matters of common concern are discussed. Cases may then be sent to the General Synod, which is the national governing body of the Church. It has spiritual, legislative and administrative functions and makes decisions on subjects such as the ordination of women priests and the consecration of women bishops.

Women in the past served as deacons (an office below that of priest) and in women's religious orders but could not be ordained as priests in the Church. Debate and conflict still surround this question, although the General Synod approved the ordination of women and the first women were ordained in 1994. There are now 1,262 full-time women priests (compared with 7,720 male clergy) and a small number have reached senior positions. The debate split the Church into factions, drove some members and clergy into the Roman Catholic Church, and there is significant hostility to the idea of women priests in many parishes and from a number of male priests. Current debate in this area is concerned with the agreed proposal that women should be appointed bishops in the Church.

Another area of conflict is the question of whether priests should be openly gay or in practising gay relationships. At present, non-practising gays may become priests, but the issue raises fierce controversy. Splits have appeared in many parishes and the Church is finding it difficult to maintain an acceptable policy.

The Church of England is sometimes referred to as the 'Anglican Church', in the sense that it is part of a worldwide communion of churches whose practices and beliefs are very similar, and many of which descend from the Church of

England. This Anglican Communion comprises some 90 million people in the British Isles (with Anglican churches in Wales, Scotland and Northern Ireland) and abroad, such as the Protestant Episcopal Church in the USA and others in Africa, South-East Asia, South America and Canada. Some of these churches have women priests and bishops, while others do not. But the question of whether to accept practising gays as priests or bishops is also being debated in the Communion, with the danger of schism between conservative (African) and liberal provinces (North American). The Lambeth Conference (a meeting of Anglican bishops from all over the world) is held every ten years in London and is presided over by the Archbishop of Canterbury. It has great prestige and its deliberations on doctrine, relations with other churches and attitudes to political and social questions can be influential.

Today, much of the Church membership is middle- and upper-class, rural-based and ageing, and it is identified with the ruling establishment and authority. There is conflict within the Church between traditionalists, who wish to maintain old forms and beliefs, and modernists, who want a more engaged and adventurous Church to attract a contemporary congregation.

In recent years, the Church of England has been more willing to enter into controversial arguments about social and political problems in contemporary Britain, such as the condition of people living in the inner cities, and has been critical of government policies. This brought it into conflict with the earlier Conservative government, and its popularity among politicians is not high. It tended to avoid such issues in the past and was described as 'the Conservative Party at prayer' because of its safe, establishment image. It is still widely felt that the Church, like the monarchy, should not involve itself in such questions and historically it has favoured compromise. However, some critics argue that the Church is mediocre, riven with squabbles, uncertain of its future and lacks both authority and charm. In this view, it will need to modernize its attitudes, organization and values if it is to continue as a vital force in British life.

The Church of Scotland

The Church of Scotland (commonly known as the Kirk) is the second established Protestant Church in Britain and the largest in Scotland. Its position as the official national Church in Scotland has been confirmed by successive legislation from 1707, which has asserted its freedom in spiritual matters and independence of all parliamentary supervision. The Church is separate from the Church of England, has its own organizational structures and decides its own doctrines and practices.

It was created in 1560 by John Knox, who was opposed to episcopal rule by bishops and considered that the Church of England had not moved sufficiently far from Roman Catholicism. The Scottish Church followed the teachings of Calvin, a leading exponent of the European Reformation, and developed a rather severe form of Presbyterian Protestantism. Presbyterianism means government by ordained ministers and elected elders (who are lay members of the Church).

The Church has a democratic structure. Individual churches are governed locally by a Kirk Session, which consists of the minister and elders. Ministers (who include women) have equality with one another. The General Assembly is the supreme organizational body of the Church and comprises elected ministers and elders. It meets every year under the presidency of an elected Moderator, who serves for one year and is the leader of the Church during the period of office.

The official membership of the Church in 2008 was 489,000. This amounts to 10 per cent of the Scottish population, although 42 per cent of Scots identified themselves as Church of Scotland by religion in the 2001 Census. The membership is declining and ageing. The Church has financial problems, is experiencing difficulties with the acceptance of homosexuality in general and among its ministers and has struggled to maintain its relevance to the younger generations.

The Roman Catholic Church

The Roman Catholic Church in Britain experienced much persecution and discrimination for centuries after the Reformation and had difficulties in surviving. Although its hierarchy was restored and the worst suspicions about it abated by 1829–32, reservations about it still continued in some quarters.

Today Catholicism is widely practised throughout Britain and enjoys complete religious freedom, except for the fact that no monarch can become a Catholic. There are seven Roman Catholic provinces in Great Britain (four in England, two in Scotland and one in Wales), each under the supervision of an archbishop; thirty dioceses each under the control of a bishop; and over 3,000 parishes. The head of the Church in England is the Cardinal Archbishop of Westminster and the senior lay Catholic is the Duke of Norfolk. In Northern Ireland, there is one province with seven dioceses, some of which overlap with dioceses in the Irish Republic.

It is estimated that there were five million nominal members of the Roman Catholic faith in England and Wales in 2009 (under 10 per cent of the population), although the number of active participants is about 1.9 million. But regular weekly observance is just over a million, which makes it the single largest Christian Church in Britain. Its membership is centred on the urban working class, settlers of Irish descent (particularly in Liverpool), a few prominent upper-class families and some middle-class people. In recent years the Church has been strengthened by the arrival of Polish immigrants and increasingly by other migrants from EU countries.

The Church continues to emphasize the important role of education for its children and requires its members to try to raise their children in the Catholic faith. There are many voluntary schools which cater (if not exclusively today) for Catholic pupils and are sometimes partly staffed by members of religious orders,

PLATE 11.3 Requiem mass at Westminster Cathedral (Roman Catholic), London. This mass was in memory of Pope John Paul II, 3 April 2005. The cathedral is the centre of England's Roman Catholic faith and the seat of its premier Catholic cleric, the Cardinal Archbishop of Westminster. *(Rex Features)*

like the Jesuits and Marists. These and other orders also carry out social work such as nursing and hospital duties, child care and looking after the elderly.

The Free Churches

The Free Churches are composed of those Nonconformist Protestant denominations which are not established like the Churches of England and Scotland. Some broke away from the Church of England after the Reformation and others departed later. In general, they dissented from some of the Church's theological beliefs; refused to accept episcopal rule or hierarchical structures; and most have ordained women ministers. Their history has also been one of schism and separation among themselves, which has resulted in the formation of many different sects.

Their egalitarian beliefs are reflected in the historical association between political and religious dissent, which were important in the formation of the Labour Party and the radical wing of the old Liberal Party. They have developed their own convictions and practices, which are often mirrored in their simple church services, worship and buildings. The Free Churches tend to be strongest in northern England, Wales, Northern Ireland and Scotland and most of their membership has historically derived from the working class. The main Free Churches today are the Methodists, Baptists, the United Reformed Church, Pentecostalists and the Salvation Army.

The *Methodist Church* is the largest of the Free Churches, and Great Britain's fourth largest Christian denomination with 267,257 adult members in 2007 and a community of 800,000 people who have an active connection with the Church. It was established in 1784 by John Wesley after Church of England opposition to his evangelical views obliged him to separate and form his own organization. This had a major impact and influence upon the growing English working class (1760–1820). Further arguments and division occurred within the Methodist Church in the nineteenth century, but most of the doctrinal and administrative disputes were settled in 1932. Today the Methodist Church in Britain is based on the 1932 union of most of the separate Methodist sects, but independent Methodist churches still exist in Britain and abroad, and there is a total worldwide membership of 15 million. Attempts were made in the 1960s and 1970s to unify the Methodists and the Church of England, but the proposals failed. In practice, however, some ministers of these denominations share their churches and services and renewed ideas about unification have again been aired lately.

The *Baptist* English founders (with roots in post-Reformation sixteenth-century Netherlands) wished to purify the Church of England, and baptism by water was their cleansing symbol. The Baptists are today grouped in associations of churches. Most of these belong to the Baptist Union of Great Britain (covering England and Wales), which was formed in 1812 and has a membership of 145,000 people with 2,150 churches. There are also independent Baptist unions in Scotland and Ireland (bringing the total number of Baptists to some 240,000), in addition to a worldwide Baptist fellowship of some 37 million members, making this the fifth largest Christian Church in the world.

The *United Reformed Church (URC)* is a union between old churches. The ancient Congregational Church in England and Wales had its roots in sixteenth-century Puritanism. It gradually merged with the Calvinist-influenced Presbyterian Church in England, Wales and Scotland, the Churches of Christ and other sects in 1972, 1981 and 2000 to form the URC. It is one of the smallest Christian denominations in Britain with 100,000 members, 1,600 congregations and 800 ministers. It believes in Christian unity and ecumenicism worldwide, and a multicultural perspective achieved through Trinitarian creeds and the Bible as the Word of God. It is centred on local churches (congregations) through which all members collectively make decisions.

The *Salvation Army* is an international Christian evangelical movement. It emphasises saving souls through a practical Christianity and social concern and its message is based on the Bible. It was founded in Britain by William Booth in 1865; now has some 55,000 active members; has spread to 118 other countries and has a worldwide strength of 2.5 million. The Salvation Army is an efficient organization and has centres nationwide to help the homeless, the elderly, the abused, the poor, the sick and the needy. Its uniformed members may be frequently seen on the streets of British towns and cities playing and singing religious music, collecting money, preaching and selling their magazine the *War Cry*.

Other Christian churches

Although active membership of the large Christian churches is declining, there are a considerable number of smaller Free Church denominations throughout Britain. The dissenting tradition has led groups in very varied directions and they all value their independence and origins. For example, the Religious Society of Friends (Quakers) was founded in the seventeenth century. It is a Christian group but has no ministers and its worship meetings are somewhat unconventional. Their individual beliefs can range widely and may include influences from other religions, although their faith is highly organized. The Quakers' pacifism and social work are influential and their membership has increased since the early twentieth century to about 18,000 in Britain with 305,000 worldwide.

There has been a significant recent increase in 'enthusiastic' Christian churches. These are defined as independent Christian groups, which number half a million members and are characterized by their Pentecostal or charismatic nature. They emphasize the miraculous and spiritual side of the New Testament rather than dogma, sin and salvation. Among them are churches, like the Assemblies of God and the Elim Pentecostal Church, which have many members of Afro-Caribbean descent. Fundamentalist evangelical groups have also been increasing. There are many other religious sects in Britain, such as the Seventh Day Adventists with a defined Christian ambience, and others such as Jehovah's Witnesses, the Mormon Church, Christian Scientists and Spiritualists which are Christian variants often deriving from the USA. Immigrants to Britain over the centuries have established their own Christian denominations in the country (mainly in the large cities), of which the largest today is the Greek Orthodox Church.

This diversity of Christian groups produces a very varied religious life in Britain today, but one which is an important reality for significant numbers of people. Some of it illustrates a growth area in religious observance, marked by frustration or disenchantment with the heavy, formal and traditional style of the larger mainstream churches and a desire to embrace a more vital, less orthodox and more spontaneous form of Christianity and personal religious experience.

The non-Christian tradition

The non-Christian tradition in Britain is mainly associated with immigrants into the country over the centuries, such as the Jews and, more recently (from the nineteenth and particularly twentieth centuries), Muslims, Sikhs and Hindus, among others.

The Jewish community

The first Jews possibly came with the Norman Conquest and were involved in finance and commerce, although some critics argue that they arrived with the Romans. The present community dates from the mid-seventeenth century, following its earlier expulsion in the thirteenth century. It now has some 267,000 members and is estimated to be the second largest Jewish population in Europe. The community is composed of the original Sephardim (from Spain, Portugal and north Africa) and the subsequent majority Ashkenazim (from Germany and central Europe).

In religious terms, the community is divided into the majority Orthodox faith (of which the main spokesman is the Chief Rabbi) and minority Reform and Liberal groups. The focus of religious life is the 300 local synagogues and Jewish schools are attended by one in three Jewish schoolchildren. The Board of Deputies of British Jews is the umbrella representative body and voice for all the country's Jews. The majority of Jews live in London, where the East End has traditionally been a place of initial Jewish settlement, while others live mainly in urban areas outside London.

The community has declined in the past twenty years. This is due to a disenchantment with religion and a growing secularism; an increase in civil and

PLATE 11.4 Interior of Bayswater Synagogue, west London, with parchment Torah containing the first five books of the Hebrew Bible.
(Jonathan Hordle/Rex Features)

mixed marriages; emigration by a considerable number of young Jews; a relatively low birth rate; and an ageing population of active practitioners. However, it is estimated that the growth of the Ultra-Orthodox community may eventually lead to it outnumbering the more secular Jewish communities. For some British Jews, their Jewishness is a matter of birth and they tend to assimilate more with the wider society. For others, it involves deep religious beliefs and practice, and this fundamentalism is increasing. But the majority also have a larger global identity with Jewish history and experiences.

Other non-Christian religions

Immigration into Britain, particularly during the last sixty years, has resulted in a substantial growth of other non-Christian religions, such as Islam, Sikhism and Hinduism. The number of practitioners is growing because of relatively high birth rates in these groups and because of conversion to such faiths by young working-class non-whites and middle-class whites.

There were some 1.6 million Muslims recorded in the 2001 Census and most live in England and Wales, where they form 3 per cent of the population. Religious observance is higher than in the general population and some 665,000 regularly

PLATE 11.5 Muslims attending Regent's Park Mosque in west London for Friday prayers, 15 July 2005.
(Andy Paradise/Rex Features)

PLATE 11.6 A Hindu wedding ceremony
(Richard Gardner/Rex Features)

attend mosques, of which there are some 1,500 in the UK. Estimates in 2010 suggest that the total Muslim population might be 2.4 million because of high birth rates. Most have origins in Pakistan and Bangladesh, but there are other groups from India, the Arab countries, Cyprus, the Middle East and Eastern Europe. The Islamic Cultural Centre and its Central Mosque in London are the largest Muslim institutions in the West. The Muslim Council of Britain, formed in 1997, is the umbrella representative body for most British Muslims.

There are also active Sikh (336,000 in 2001) and Hindu (558,000 in 2001) religious adherents in Britain. Most of these come from India with a minority from East Africa and have many temples located around the country in areas of Asian settlement, with 200 Sikh and 143 Hindu temples. Later estimates suggest growths to 500,000 (2005) for Sikhs and 1.5 million (2007) for Hindus. Various forms of Buddhism are also represented in the population, with about 152,000 active participants in 2001. All these faiths have their own representative bodies and most members tend to live in England.

It is estimated that non-Christian religions may amount to some 2 million active, observing or practising members and represent a significant growth area when compared to the Christian churches. Yet these communities constitute a relatively small proportion of the total British population, 72 per cent of which remains nominally Christian despite the growth in the number of agnostics, atheists and those who claim no denominational identity. Non-Christian groups have altered the religious face of British society and influenced employment conditions, since allowances have to be made for them to follow their religious observances and customs.

They have also become vocal in expressing their opinions on a range of matters, such as protests about British foreign policy in the Middle East, Iraq and Afghanistan; a Muslim demand for their own schools supported by state funds; Muslim outrage against Salman Rushdie's novel *The Satanic Verses*, parts of which are considered to be blasphemous; and Muslim claims that British law discriminates against their religion.

Cooperation among the faiths

The earlier intolerance and bigotry of Christian denominations in Britain have gradually mellowed after centuries of hostility, restrictions and repression. There is now considerable cooperation between the churches, although this stops short of ecumenism (full unity). Discussions continue between the Roman Catholic Church and other Christian churches about closer ties and an Anglican–Roman Catholic Commission explores points of possible unity. The old enmity between Protestants and Catholics has been reduced, though tension continues in parts of Scotland and most demonstrably in Northern Ireland.

On other levels of cooperation, Churches Together in Britain and Ireland has representatives from the main Christian churches and works towards common action and Christian unity. The Free Church Federal Council does a similar job for the Free Churches. The Anglican and the main Free Churches also participate in the World Council of Churches, which attempts to promote worldwide cooperation and studies common problems. The Council of Christians and Jews works for better understanding among its members and the Council for Churches of Britain and Ireland has established a Committee for Relations with People of Other (non-Christian) Faiths. A recent creation, the Inter Faith Network for the UK, consists of some 100 organizations and promotes good relations between the country's different faiths. The growth of inter-faith and multi-faith bodies since 2000 indicates both a desire and a need for such cooperation in order to solve some of Britain's current problems.

Such attempts at possible cooperation are seen by some as positive actions, which might break down barriers and hostility and promote a more inclusive Britain. Others see them as signs of weakness since denominations are forced to cooperate because of declining memberships and their lack of real influence in the contemporary world. Movement towards Christian unity may also be threatened by the ordination of women priests and bishops in the Church of England, since the Roman Catholic Church is opposed and there are rifts in Anglicanism worldwide.

Many church people at the grassroots level argue that the churches must adapt more to the requirements of modern life, or else decline in membership and influence. Religious life in Britain has become more evangelical and cooperative in order to reflect a diverse contemporary society and values. However, some traditionalists wish to preserve the historical elements of religious belief and practice and the tension between them and modernists in all religious groups is likely to continue.

Religion in schools

Non-denominational Christian religious education is legally compulsory in state primary and secondary schools in England and Wales. The school day is supposed to start with an act of collective worship and religious lessons should be provided which concentrate on Christianity as the main religious tradition of the country but also include the other main faiths. However, if a pupil (or parent) has strong objections, the pupil need not take part in either the service or the lessons. Religious services and teaching are not compulsory in Scotland.

In practice, few schools hold daily religious assemblies. Customs differ for the religious lessons, particularly in areas with large ethnic communities. The lessons can take many different forms and may not be tied to specific Christian themes. Frequent proposals are made that the legal compulsion in religious education should be removed, but it is still enshrined in legislation. Some people see religious education and collective worship as a way to raise moral standards and encourage social values, while others disagree. Many schools are unable to meet their religious legal obligations and question the point of doing so.

Religion-based schools at primary and secondary levels ('faith schools') have long existed in Britain and are now largely funded by the state. Most of them are Christian and emphasize the particular faith of the school, such as the Church of England, Roman Catholicism and Methodism. The Labour government wished to increase the number of faith schools because of their academic records and discipline, as well as its wish to reflect social and religious diversity. The Church of England and the Methodists want to open more such schools, and the first state-funded Islamic secondary school for girls opened in 2001. Independent religious schools (such as a few Muslim schools) are not funded by the state.

These developments are controversial. It is argued that single-faith schools will institutionalize segregation; lead to a 'balkanization' of British society rather than an embrace of pluralism; increase intolerance from inside and outside the schools; and that pupils will grow up ignorant of other religious and social values. Experience in Northern Ireland illustrates the potential dangers of segregated religious schooling, although there has been a recent increase in the number of integrated schools in the province.

Religious identification

Declining membership of some Christian churches and reduced regular attendance at religious services in the twentieth century have continued. But expansion has occurred in some Free Churches, new or independent religious movements and, in particular, some of the non-Christian denominations. It is argued that there has not necessarily been an overall religious decline in the UK but rather that patterns of religious membership and observance have changed in recent years under different conditions, such as immigration, new non-religious organizations and old traditions.

Historically, it has been difficult to obtain precise information about religious membership and belief in Britain since denominations have their own methods of assessing membership and attendance figures. Estimates based on internal registers, public opinion polls, research surveys and Census results at different times can vary in their findings.

The Census takes place every ten years. More religious information for England, Wales and Scotland (Great Britain) became available from the 2001 Census, which for the first time contained a question on religious identification and a choice from a number of specified religions. Response to the primary question was voluntary, but 92 per cent answered. Some 77.2 per cent reported that they identified with a religion or faith, 15.1 per cent said that they had no religion and 7.8 per cent either did not state a religion or entered a non-specified faith.

Of those respondents who identified with a religion in the 2001 Census, 71.6 per cent (42 million people) regarded themselves as Christians, making Christianity the main religion in the UK. This group included the Churches of England and Scotland, the Church in Wales, Protestant and other Christian denominations (Free Churches) and the Roman Catholic Church.

A religious question has been asked in Northern Ireland since 1926, although the 2001 Census query was different from that for Great Britain. The results showed that some 86 per cent identified themselves with a religion; 53 per cent identified with the Protestant community; 44 per cent with the Catholic; and 3 per cent had no or another religious identity.

In Great Britain, those who claimed a non-Christian religion (5.4 per cent) were Muslim at 1.6 million (2.7 per cent), Hindu at 559,000 (1.0 per cent), Sikh at 336,000 (0.6 per cent), Jewish at 267,000 (0.5 per cent), Buddhist at 152,000 (0.3 per cent) and other religion at 179,000 (0.3 per cent). Some 9.1 million respondents (15.5 per cent) had no religion.

However, the influential *British Social Attitudes* survey produced significant changes in 2007 when compared to its 2000 Survey. It reported that 45.7 per cent of respondents had no religion or denomination. The remaining respondents claimed identification with Christian religions such as the Church of England (20.9 per cent), Roman Catholic (9.0 per cent), Presbyterian/Church of Scotland (2.8 per cent), Methodist (1.9 per cent), 'other Protestant' (2.7), Christian (no denomination) 10.3 per cent and 'other Christian' (0.4 per cent). Non-Christian respondents claimed religious identification as Muslim (3.3 per cent), Hindu (1.4 per cent), Jewish (0.4 per cent), Sikh (0.4 per cent) and 'other non-Christian religion' (0.4 per cent).

These figures suggested a 7 per cent reduction in Church of England membership and an increased number of people without a religion since 2000.

Secularization appeared to be increasing, but growth and pluralism were indicated in non-Christian religions. The statistics might indicate that secularism has not advanced as much as is commonly thought. However, 'identification' does not necessarily translate into regular observance, formal membership of a denomination or allegiance to a given set of religious doctrines, practices and beliefs.

Despite these identification figures, in 2000 the *British Social Attitudes Survey*, found that only 13 per cent of those belonging to all faiths actually attended a service once a week; 54 per cent never attended or practically never; 10 per cent attended at least twice a year; and 6 per cent at least once a year. These figures had remained constant over an eight-year period. But while church attendance outside special occasions such as weddings, funerals and baptisms was low, the degree of decline, though continuing, had been (surprisingly) slight. The figures suggest a large overall decline in church membership, but a smaller decline in actual church attendance. This conclusion would correlate with findings from 2000–10. It seems that the majority of British people very rarely actually enter a religious building for observational or religious purposes, apart from occasional 'rites of passage' visits.

Attitudes to religion and morality

There are three opposed positions on religious life in modern Britain. The first suggests falling levels of involvement with the main Christian churches and a general decline in religious faith. Increasing secularization indicates that religious institutions and consciousness are losing their social and public significance. The second position suggests a religious renewal in some churches and an actual growth in others because of religious pluralism and a diversity of faiths. The third position is that while formal membership of denominations and observance may no longer be popular in Britain, polls suggest that people still have religious beliefs or feelings on a personal level, which may include belief in a God, sin, a soul, heaven, life after death, the devil and hell or a more general sense of spirituality. In this view, religion has become privatized and fragmented.

When respondents to the *British Social Attitudes Survey 2000–1* survey were asked about belief in a God, it was found that there had been little change from 1991–8. The figures suggested that 52 per cent believed in a God, 22 per cent did not know and 25 per cent did not believe. Over time, this meant that there had been only a small decline in belief in a God (whether as a personal god or a vague entity).

It is argued that such results, which vary between polls, mean that people in modern Britain are becoming more individualistic and less dependent upon church authorities. They consequently adopt a more personal approach towards religion and no longer automatically follow the lead of organized religion. The statistics suggest that a distinction can be made between formal religious observance of an institutional or organized kind and the private, individual sphere of religious or moral feeling. Despite the appearance of a secular state, religion in its various forms is still a factor in national life. Radio, television and the press concern themselves with religious and moral topics on a regular basis. Religious broadcasting on radio and television attracts large audience figures and a demand for more, despite the attempts of some broadcasters (such as the BBC) to cut religious programming.

On an institutional level and despite secularist opposition, religion is also reflected in traditions, ceremonies, and public or national morality. Religious denominations are relatively prominent in British life and are active in education, voluntary social work and community care. Religious leaders of all faiths publicly debate doctrine, social matters, political concerns and the moral questions of the day, not always necessarily within narrow church limits. They may frequently come into conflict with politicians on issues such as Iraq and poverty in Britain. Yet some large churches appear incapable of countering further institutional decline and, given their ageing congregations, this process seems likely to continue.

At the level where public or civic behaviour impinges upon morality and according to a Leeds University survey in 1997, many Britons do not trust other people and now see life as less predictable, more time-pressured, less secure, more materialistic and fast-moving, and their society as riddled with mistrust, cynicism and greed. Lacking traditional faith in conventional religion, more people appear to put their trust in materialism, physical appearance, fashion, trends, the celebrity circus and individualism.

Nevertheless, there also seems to be a longing for spirituality, otherworldly comfort and explanation, particularly among the 18–30 age group. This search can lead in different directions. Some people believe in mysticism, alternative spiritual disciplines, New Age practices, the paranormal, telepathy, second sight and astrology, as well as belonging to smaller religious groups such as Spiritualism, Paganism, Wicca, Rastafarianism, Jain, Bahá'í and Zoroastrianism. It is argued that this need for spirituality is not being provided by the established or mainstream churches.

Such religious concerns seem also to influence matters of personal morality and civic responsibility. Although there are differences of emphasis between younger and older generations and between men and women, many Britons have strong views about right and wrong. Yet these are not necessarily tied to the teaching of any particular denomination. Polls suggest that a majority of people think, for example, that the following are morally wrong: hard drugs like heroin, scenes of explicit violence on television, adultery, pornography on the Internet, and scientific experiments on human beings and animals.

However, the British have become more tolerant, for example, of sex in films, homosexuality, cohabitation outside marriage, soft drugs such as cannabis, alternative lifestyles and euthanasia (allowing a doctor to end a patient's life) if the person in question is suffering from a painful incurable illness. A majority also feel that it is worse to convict an innocent person (miscarriage of justice) than to let a guilty individual go free.

In terms of civic responsibility, polls suggest that attitudes to authority remain relatively conventional in some areas. A majority of respondents feel that children should be taught in the home environment to respect honesty, good manners and other people. Negative attitudes to 'yob culture', antisocial behaviour and teenage excess have increased. Feelings have hardened towards those individuals who reject society as it is presently constituted, who demonstrate and protest and who encourage disobedience in children. Most respondents agree that schools should teach children to obey authority. But the number of people who consider that the law should be obeyed without exception has fallen and more now believe that one should follow one's conscience, even if this means breaking the law.

These mixed views indicate that many Britons now embrace an authoritarian position on some questions of morals and social behaviour. 'Moral traditionalism', old values, a sense of 'what is right' and civic responsibility are still supported. But there is often a greater adherence to concepts of personal and social morality than to those dictated by official, religious and legal restraints. This is also reflected in people's considerable concerns about drugs, law and order, violent crime, unprovoked violence and vandalism, and their preference for strong action to be taken in these areas. On other matters, there seems to be a growing liberalism.

Exercises

Explain and examine the following terms:

Canterbury	Henry VIII	'Low Church'	confirmation
bigotry	Iona	Free Churches	General Synod
St Patrick	Episcopal	Church Settlement	John Knox
Whitby	Quakers	vicar	Salvation Army
baptism	ecumenism	denomination	evangelism

Write short essays on the following topics:

1   What does the term 'Christianity' mean in terms of British religious history?

2   Discuss religious membership and observance in contemporary British life.

3*   Critically examine the role of the Church of England

4   Examine the public opinion polls in this chapter. What do they tell us about British society?

Visit **www.routledge.com/textbooks/oakland** for multiple-choice questions, links to related YouTube clips, tips on approaching essay questions, and much, much more.

Further reading

1   Alderman, G. (1998) *Modern British Jewry*, Oxford: Clarendon Press
2   Bebbington, D. (1988) *Evangelism in Modern Britain: A History from the 1730s to the 1980s*, London: Routledge
3   Brown, C. (2009) *The Death of Christian Britain*, London: Routledge
4   Brown, C. (2006) *Religion and Society in Twentieth-Century Britain*, London: Longman
5   Bruce, S. (1995) *Religion in Modern Britain*, Oxford: Oxford University Press
6   Davie, G. (1997) *Religion in Britain since 1945: Believing without Belonging*, Oxford: Blackwell Publishers
7   Furlong, M. (2002) *C of E: The State It's In*, London: Hodder and Stoughton
8   Morris, R.M. (ed.) (2009) *Church and State in 21st Century Britain: The Future of Church Establishment*, London: Palgrave Macmillan
9   *Religion in England and Wales: Findings from the 2001 Home Office Citizenship Survey* (2004), London: Home Office Research Study 274
10 *Religion in the UK Directory, 2001–3* (2001) Religious Resource and Research Centre at the University of Derby and the Inter Faith Network of the UK
11 Sewell, D. (2001) *Catholics: Britain's Largest Minority*, London: Viking
12 *UK Christian Handbook, Religious Trends,7* (2008) Intervarsity Press

Websites

The Church of England: www.church-of-england.org
Church of Scotland: www.cofs.org.uk/3colcos.htm
Roman Catholic Church: www.tasc.ac.uk/cc and www.catholic.org.uk
United Synagogue: www.brijnet.org.uk
Judaism: www.jewish.co.uk
Islam: www.muslimdirectory.co.uk
Q-News (Muslim): www.q-news.com
Churches Together in Britain and Ireland: www.ctbi.org.uk
Inter Faith Network for the UK: www.interfaith.org.uk
Office of the Deputy Prime Minister/Inner Cities Religious Council: www.neighbourhood.gov.uk/faith_communities.asp
Church of England Internet parish: www.i-church.org
Office for National Statistics: www.statistics.gov.uk

12

Leisure, sport and the arts

The diversity of life in contemporary Britain is reflected in the ways the British organize their leisure, sporting and artistic interests. These features reveal a series of very different cultural habits rather than one unified image, are divided between participatory and spectator pastimes and include various degrees of active and passive engagement. Some are associated with national identities and others with minority participation. In many cases, they are connected to social class, the national economy, disposable income, the expense involved in the pursuit of activities and pressures on leisure time.

According to the authors of *We British* (Jacobs and Worcester 1990: 124), the substantial variety of available leisure, arts and sporting activities disproves the criticism that Britain is a country of philistines who prefer second-rate entertainment to the best. Yet there are frequent complaints about a 'dumbing down' of British cultural life in television programmes, films, the arts, literature, popular music and education, as well as reduced standards in sports and a declining participation in exercise, which is arguably linked to an increase in adult and child obesity. Such criticism is not new. It was common in the nineteenth century at a time when the working class was growing rapidly, and the contrasts between high and low cultures had also been commented upon by writers and artists in earlier centuries.

Public opinion polls in the 1990s and 2000s showed that Britain's cultural life was thriving, although there had been decreases in some activities and increases in others. However, the recession of 2007–10 had serious effects on individuals and businesses. People cut down on leisure activities; stayed at home rather than going out to socialize; 'staycations' (38 per cent of the population holidaying in Britain in 2009 rather than abroad) became popular; and there was less available or disposable income to spend.

Yet research by Aegis Media UK in 2009 found that while attitudes were less positive than in 2008, 44 per cent of respondents reported that the recession had not had a large effect on their daily lives, although they were budgeting carefully and avoiding debt. Adult leisure activities in most consumer categories were affected and 17.3 million respondents said they spent less than usual in pubs, bars and restaurants, on leisure days out, on home entertainment (such as purchases of DVDs/CDs/console games) and on holidays, newspapers and magazines. It seemed that items perceived as 'luxuries' were most affected.

The Office for National Statistics (ONS) 2009 statistics on family spending found that the second highest category of spending after transport was recreation and culture at £60 a week, or some 19 per cent of weekly spending. This increased in 2010 to £62.50, ahead of transport, and became Britain's biggest single expense for the first time. There had been greater rates of increase in family expenditure historically from 1977 until 2006 and the pattern of expenditure had changed over time because of both greater disposable income and rising costs.

The category of recreation and culture includes television sets, computers, newspapers, books, electronic equipment, leisure activities (such as trips to the cinema, theatre and football matches) and package holidays. On average, £13.60 a week was spent on package holidays abroad, compared to £1.10 a week on package holidays in the UK. Spending on alcoholic drinks in 2009 had remained unchanged at 3 per cent of the average weekly household budget, possibly because supermarkets have greatly cut alcohol prices in competition with each other.

Despite the recession and other socio-economic problems such as inequality of income and status, the statistics indicate that Britain is a more affluent society and able to spend a larger part of personal income on both motoring and leisure activities. Large numbers of Britons participate in a wide variety of available pastimes, sometimes with surprising priorities. For example, reading and visits to the library compare relatively favourably with the most popular habits, such as watching television or playing music.

The authors of *We British* (1990: 133) reached conclusions which are still arguably valid today, although some observers of British life might disagree:

> we can report that the nation is in no telly-induced trance. Its tastes mix watching and doing, 'high' and 'low' cultures, with a richness that con-tradicts the stereotypes of the British as divided between mindless lager louts and equally money-grubbing consumers. The mix we have found will not please everybody. Not enough football for some, not enough opera for others. But that is what we should expect in the culture of a whole nation.

Theoretical models of 'leisure pursuits' and their social implications have been formulated by academics. On one level, and since much leisure time in Britain is now spent within the home, there would seem to be a growing separation from the wider social context and a movement into individual and small group activity. On another level, the actual provision or production of most leisure needs is increasingly commercialized or profit-oriented and part of the consumer market in which producers try to attract and maximize consumers. Yet access to leisure, sports and arts activities is unevenly distributed in the population, because it is dependent upon purchasing power, opportunity and availability. Exclusionary factors operate against some participation, whether they are a lack of disposable income, the cost of expensive equipment, the price of tickets, shortage of time in busy and frenetic lives or a lack of resources and opportunities for people living in deprived areas such as council estates and some rural locations.

The creative and cultural industries which service the 'leisure market' (such as cinema, theatre, publishing, museums, the performing arts and popular and orchestral music) are an important part of Britain's social and economic life. These industries generate substantial annual revenue and export earnings and employ large numbers of people.

The government Department for Culture, Media and Sport (DCMS) also spends considerable amounts of public money on supporting the arts and cultural life in Britain. Some areas of expenditure are museums, galleries and libraries; historic buildings in England; the arts in England and tourism in the UK. Sometimes this aid can prove controversial and be criticized. Other organizations, public and private, also give substantial funding to leisure activities, sports and the arts.

Leisure activities

Leisure activities in earlier centuries, apart from some high cultural interests exclusive to the metropolitan elite, were largely conditioned by the rural and agricultural nature of British life. Villages were isolated and transport was either poor or non-existent. People were consequently restricted to their villages and obliged to create their own entertainments. Some of these participatory activities were home-based, while others were enjoyed by the whole community. They might be added to by itinerant players, who travelled the countryside and provided a range of alternative spectator entertainments, such as drama performances, sports and musical events.

Improved transport and road conditions from the eighteenth century onwards enabled the rural population to travel to neighbouring towns where they took advantage of a variety of amusements and wider social opportunities. Spectator and participatory activities increased with the industrialization of the nineteenth century, as more of the population moved to the towns and cities and as theatre, concerts, music halls and sports developed and became available to more people. The establishment of railway systems and the formation of bus companies initiated the pattern of cheap one-day trips around the country and to the seaside, which were to grow into the mass charter and package tours of contemporary Britain. The arrival of radio, films and television in the early twentieth century resulted in a hugely expanded professional entertainments industry. The variety of offerings and levels of participation again increased dramatically from the 1960s and coincided with more leisure time, higher disposable income and the weakening of barriers between 'high' and 'low' culture. In all these changes, the mixture of participatory, spectator, home-based and wider social leisure activities has continued.

Many contemporary pursuits have their roots in the cultural and social behaviour of the past, including boxing, wrestling, cricket, football and a wide range of athletic sports. Dancing, amateur theatre and musical events were essential parts of rural life for all classes and were often associated with the changing agricultural seasons. The traditions of hunting, shooting and fishing have long been widely practised in British country life (not only by the aristocracy), as well as blood sports such as dog and cock fighting and bear baiting, which are now illegal. However, serious betting and gambling on brutal illegal dog fights between specially bred dogs does continue in secluded locations.

A feature of contemporary Britain is the continuing attempt to stop some kinds of rural activities like angling and foxhunting on the grounds that they are cruel to animals. Activists have become more violent in their objections to and campaigns against what they see as the cruelty of many rural traditions as well as in their opposition to the use of animals in commercial and medical experiments. For example, a MORI poll in 1997 showed that two-thirds of respondents favoured a complete ban on foxhunting with horses and dogs. The countryside lobby opposed such action, but foxhunting was banned first in Scotland and then in England and Wales in 2005. However, a MORI poll in February 2005 found that the actual support for a foxhunting ban had fallen to about a half, with an increase in the number of respondents who said they were neutral on the issue. It may be that the issue will be reopened in Parliament with a free vote for MPs in the near future.

In addition to cultural and sporting pastimes, the British enjoy a variety of other leisure activities since many more opportunities are now available to them and, despite their long working hours and busy lives, more people have more free time. The problem is how to organize and prioritize their activities. Most workers have at least four weeks' holiday a year, in addition to public holidays such as Christmas, Easter and Bank Holidays, although Britain has fewer public holidays than most other European countries. The growing number of pensioners (some, if by no means all, of whom are reasonably affluent) has created an economically rewarding leisure market which benefits the elderly and commercial service companies. Increased unemployment also means that some groups of people have more enforced spare time (if not always the finances to enjoy it in full).

Consumer patterns associated with leisure activities are also changing in Britain. These coincide with part-time and shift working and higher disposable incomes, particularly among young people and especially at prosperous times. There is a demand for pubs, clubs, cinemas, shops, restaurants and a range of leisure services to be open and available for longer periods during the week and at weekends.

However, the recession has clearly affected unemployment and spending. In more normal times, the most common leisure pastimes are social or home-based according to a DCMS survey on Culture, Leisure and Sport in 2006–07. These include watching television, videos and DVDs, visiting or entertaining friends and family, listening to music, the radio, tapes and records, eating out in restaurants, sport/exercise, reading books and magazines, days out away from home, shopping, going to pubs (public houses), bars or clubs, Internet/e-mailing, DIY (do-it-yourself) home improvements, gardening, going to the cinema, attending the theatre, concerts or cinema and playing computer games. According to public opinion polls, these activities reflect consistent patterns of behaviour over recent years.

However, although men and women have much in common in these activities, there are differences. Men are more likely to take part in physical activities, such as sport and exercise, than women, while women are more likely than men to shop, participate in cultural activities, read and attend the theatre or classical music concerts. Nevertheless, both women (at 73 per cent) and men (56 per cent) scored relatively high in having reading as a leisure activity in the DCMS survey.

The most popular non-sporting leisure activity for all people aged sixteen and over (women 85 per cent and men 84 per cent) is watching television (for 30 hours a week in 2010). This figure is 2.5 hours more than in 2009, despite an apparent dissatisfaction by some people with the quality of the programmes shown on British television, together with the growing challenge from DVDs and alternative pursuits. DVDs, however, tend to appeal more to the middle-aged and elderly who prefer them to both television and the cinema. It is suggested that

PLATE 12.1 Drinking outside the White Horse pub, Soho, London. Soho has long been a popular area for pubs, clubs, exotic entertainment, restaurants and theatre which have appealed to a wide variety of people of all classes. Its image has often been bohemian, eccentric and raffish.

(Kevin Foy/Rex Features)

film producers are increasingly catering for immediate DVD production rather than first using the traditional intermediate step of cinema screenings.

Television remains a popular entertainment medium. The rise in viewing hours may be due to more people staying at home in the recession and the greater choice offered by digital television following the transition from analogue. Some 93 per cent of homes now have digital television (according to the Broadcasters' Audience Research Board, 2010), giving a greater choice of channels, as well as interactive alternatives and high definition (HD) screens.

The British now occupy some two-thirds of their spare time using electronic equipment. A large amount of money is spent on items such as television sets (owned by some 98 per cent of households with 10 million subscriptions to satellite television and 4.2 million to cable television in 2010), radio equipment (listened to for some ten hours a week), video recorders, computers, compact disc players (CDs), DVD equipment and DVDs. There were 48.8 million Internet users in 2009 and 58 per cent of adults had accessed it at some time. By 2010, increasing numbers of homes and businesses were using high-speed broadband connections and more people were using the Internet in preference to television.

In these examples, the home has become the chief place for family and individual entertainment and poses competition to other activities outside the home, such as the cinema, sport and the theatre. Leisure activities for both males and females exclusively within the home include listening to the radio or music; watching television; studying; reading books and newspapers; relaxing; conversation; entertaining; and hobbies.

Despite the competition from television, the cinema and other electronic media, reading is still an important leisure activity for over half of men and women in Britain (with 40 per cent not reading books). There is a large variety of books and magazines to cater for all tastes and interests. In 2005, Britain led the world in the number of new books (206,000) published and the e-book market (together with equipment such as the Kindle and iPad) is rapidly increasing. The best-selling books are romances, thrillers, modern popular novels, detective stories, science fiction and works of adventure and history. Classic literature is not widely read, although sales of older novels can benefit from adaptations on television. The tie-in of books (of all types) with videos, DVDs and television series is now a very lucrative business.

There were 4,125 public libraries in the UK in 2009, although this marked a decline in the number of buildings since the great days of the public library tradition. They provide books, music CDs, talking books and DVDs on loan (for a small fee) to the public, together with information, computer and Internet facilities. A further 573 mobile libraries take books out to communities and rural areas. However, according to the DCMS, annual library visits have declined from 302 million to 280 million and the decrease in book loans is sharper, although e-book marketing has recently helped to promote a surge in library membership.

Bodies such as the Reading Agency are more optimistic and argue that public libraries are popular and well used. They argue that in fact more people visit libraries than go to football matches, tourist attractions, museums, galleries, the cinema and the theatre. According to the DCMS, there were 328 million visits to public libraries in 2007–08, with 46 per cent of the adult English population visiting at least one library in 2006–07 and half of these visiting once a month or more often.

Libraries in Great Britain are very well used, especially by young children if appropriate arrangements are made for them. Writers who organize library events report that there is still a thirst for and curiosity about reading and books, with 34 million people (60 per cent of the population) in 2003 being members of local libraries. In total, 361 million books and 42 million other library articles were borrowed in 2003. Only readers in Finland, Denmark and the Netherlands borrow more library books per head of population.

Do-it-yourself hobbies (DIY), such as house painting, decorating and gardening, are very popular and home repairs and improvements amount to a large item in the total household budget. Until the recession, the number of restaurants had increased, and the practice of eating out is popular, with expenditure on

PLATE 12.2 The Dog and Fox, a celebrated pub in Wimbledon village in the London borough of Merton. It is reputed to be the oldest pub in Wimbledon and an inn has been on this site since the reign of Henry VIII. Today it has a large bar and a separate dining area.
(Stephen Behan/Rex Features)

restaurants and hotels being a significant part of the household budget. There are a variety of 'ethnic' restaurants (particularly Indian, Chinese, Italian and French, but many more types) in most British high streets and fast-food outlets serving pizza, hamburgers, kebabs, chicken and fish and chips. The quality of food in British restaurants has continued to improve, as has the variety and number of available cuisines. Chefs have gained wide television exposure and raised an awareness of food among the general public.

Visiting the pub is still a very important part of British life and leisure. Some seven out of ten adults visit pubs and one-third go once or more a week. But the pub, as a social institution, has changed over the years, although it still caters for a wide range of different groups and tastes. The pub is said to be Britain's most envied and imperfectly imitated institution, where people can gather on neutral ground and socialize on their own terms. However, falling custom, the recession, the ban on smoking in public places in 2005, rising property prices, takeovers by chain ownership and restaurants, an obsession with trendiness, faddishness and quick profits have led to a decline in Britain's unique pub heritage. The UK's 56,000 pubs are disappearing at the rate of more than forty a month (March 2010), with many being turned into gentrified eateries, clubs or bars in an attempt to emulate 'café society'. At worst, the premises are converted into huge palaces dedicated to vertical drinking with little of the traditional pub ambience. More people are also drinking at home and buying cheap cut-price alcohol from supermarkets.

Pub licensing hours, which apply to opening times for the sale of alcohol, were liberalized in 2005 and pubs can open for extended drinking hours in the evening or into the early morning. Most pubs provide food in addition to drinks, and some, in more prosperous urban and rural areas, have restaurants attached. Attempts in 2006 to allow smoking in pubs which do not offer food were defeated in Parliament.

In recent years, there has been a mushrooming of wine bars, café bars, discos and clubs with extended opening hours. The growth and popularity of the club scene with its music, drink and appeal to the young offers considerable competition to the traditional pub trade, although people move between different venues during an evening. Such developments (together with extended pub opening hours and the availability of cheap alcohol) have also led to an epidemic of 'binge-drinking' (drinking to excess) in city and town centres and an upsurge in antisocial behaviour on the streets, which is causing great concern and provoking calls for the system of licensing to be tightened.

British nightlife for most young people is varied and vibrant, with nightclubs, large-scale rock gigs at arenas and sports grounds, music festivals and outdoor 'rave' parties. British bands and DJs are much admired throughout the world. Use of so-called recreational drugs such as cannabis, Ecstasy (despite well-publicized deaths from its usage) and cocaine has become so widespread that there have been calls for decriminalization of some hard and soft drugs. There is

PLATE 12.3 The resort of Benidorm on Spain's Costa Blanca has long been a favourite destination for British tourists. It opened up mass tourism and the package holiday phenomenon to the British.
(*Geoffrey Robinson/Rex Features*)

also a thriving lesbian and gay scene, more developed than in some other European countries.

Holidays and where to spend them have also become an important part of British life and have been accompanied by increased leisure time and money for the majority of the people. They represent the second major leisure cost (after pub drinking). Some Britons take their holidays in Britain itself (38 per cent of total holidays in 2009), with the south-west English coastal resorts and Scotland being very popular in summer. But larger numbers now also go abroad in both winter or summer, and the great days of the British (particularly seaside) resorts have declined. The number of long holidays taken abroad by the British amounted to 40 per cent of total holidays in 2009, with Spain, France, Ireland, the USA, Italy and Greece being the main attractions for holidaymakers, who buy relatively cheap package tours. Yet the British seem to have become more adventurous and many are now travelling widely outside Europe to Asia and Africa on a variety of holidays. The 2007–10 recession has altered these patterns to some degree, with more people taking their holidays in Britain.

Many people prefer to organize their own holidays and make use of the good air and sea communications between Britain and Europe. In Britain itself, different forms of holiday exist, from the traditional 'bed and breakfast' at a seaside boarding house to hotels, caravan sites and camping (the latter at 10 per cent of total holidays). Increased car ownership has allowed greater travel possibilities, with day trips in Britain, for example, amounting to 51 per cent of total holidays in 2009. Today, more than seven out of ten households have the use of at least one car and 27 per cent have two or more.

Sport

There is a wide variety of sport in Britain today, catering for large numbers of spectators and participants (the latter at different levels of competence). Some are minority or class-based sports (such as yachting and rugby league respectively), while others (like football) appeal to majority tastes. The number of British people participating in sports increased in the 1990s. This coincided with a greater awareness of health needs and the importance of exercise, particularly at a time when many Britons are overweight and increasing numbers are obese. Expenditure on playing and watching sports, and buying sports equipment, amount to a considerable part of the household budget. But it is argued that Britain has inadequate sporting facilities and leisure centres in both the public and private sectors and that sports participation has again declined in recent years. However, it is recognized that the creation of new and increased facilities can lead to greater national sporting success, as with the British cycling team at the Beijing Olympics (2008) and the awarding of the 2012 Olympic Games to London.

The 2007 *British Social Attitudes* reported that 49 per cent of adults over eighteen had attended a sports event at least once a year as a spectator. Fewer numbers had attended on a more regular basis. A *Social Trends* poll in 2006/7 reported that 40 per cent of adults had participated in moderately active sport for at least thirty minutes in the week of interview and 22 per cent had managed three separate days in that week. There appeared to have been a decrease in participation in outdoor and indoor sports or forms of exercise for both men and women compared with earlier years. Opinion polls in the early 2000s varied somewhat but most suggested consistently that the most popular participatory sporting activity for both men and women was walking (including rambling and hiking). Billiards/snooker/pool were the next most popular for men, followed by cycling, indoor swimming, football and golf. Keep fit/yoga was the next most popular sport for women, followed by indoor swimming, cycling and snooker/pool/billiards. Fishing was the most popular country sport. But most of these percentages have declined over the decade, despite government efforts to increase the exercise rates and to counter obesity. At the beginning of the 2000s, gyms and

PLATE 12.4 A Football Association Premier League football match between Arsenal and Wolverhampton Wanderers at Arsenal's home ground, the Emirates Stadium, London. Nicklas Bendtner (in the red shirt) heads the winning goal for Arsenal, 3 April 2010.
(Offside/Rex Features)

indoor activities were very popular, but membership has gradually declined because of gym costs, a lack of time and the recession.

Amateur and professional football (soccer) is played throughout most of the year and also at international level. It is the most watched and popular sport in Britain and today transcends its earlier working-class associations. The professional game has developed into a large, family-oriented organization but has suffered from stadium tragedies, hooliganism, high ticket prices, declining attendances and financial crises. However, enforced changes in recent years such as all-seater stadiums, greater security, improved facilities and lucrative tie-ins with television coverage (such as Sky Sport and ITV1) have improved this situation. Many of the top professional football clubs in the English Premier League have become public companies quoted on the Stock Exchange, have foreign owners and players and football is now big business.

Yet there is a widening gulf between the top clubs (such as Chelsea, Arsenal, Liverpool and Manchester United) and others in the lower divisions and the bottom half of the Premier League. Some 80 per cent of England's soccer clubs in 2001 were losing money despite television income, which goes largely to the twenty clubs in the Premiership. Most football clubs (even at the top end of the Premiership) are in a precarious financial position despite increased income, with only a few making a profit, many losing control over their costs, suffering

PLATE 12.5 Wembley has been the home of English football since 1923 and the new stadium, built on the foundations of the old, was opened in spring 2007. It holds 90,000 spectators and hosts other events such as rugby, American football and pop concerts.
(Charles Bowman/Robert Harding/Rex Features)

accumulating debt and some going into administration (a form of bankruptcy). It is argued that this situation is due to poor club organization, bad business sense, huge salaries for players, inflated transfer fees and a lack of success on the pitch and in European competition. Football success brings European and world competition and huge financial rewards.

Rugby football is a popular sport and is widely watched and played. Two forms of the game are played. Rugby union was once confined to amateur clubs and was an exclusively middle-class and public school-influenced game, but it became professional in 1995 (at least for the top clubs), now covers a wider social spectrum and received a boost when England won the World Cup in 2003. England's fortunes and performance have declined since then, although Scotland, Wales and Ireland have sporadically improved. Rugby league is played by professional teams, mainly in the north of England and still tends to be a working-class sport in terms of participation and support. Both types of rugby are also played internationally.

Cricket is a summer sport in Britain, but the England team also plays in the winter months in Commonwealth countries. It is both an amateur and professional game. The senior game is professional and largely confined to the English

PLATE 12.6 A traditional cricket match between two villages, Chagford and Feniton, at Chagford, Devon, June 2008.
(Christopher Jones/Rex Features)

(and one Welsh) county sides which play in the County Championship. Attendance at county cricket matches continues to decline, although one-day 20–20 games attract large spectator numbers and financial backing. It is felt that the contemporary game has lost some of its attractiveness as it has moved in overly professional and money-dominated directions. It was in danger of becoming a minority sport. But it regained popularity in the summer of 2005 when England gained victory over the visiting Australians in the Ashes Test Match series and the short game has achieved success internationally, with England becoming 20–20 world champions in 2010.

There are many other sports which reflect the diversity of interests in British life. Among these are golf, horse racing, hunting, riding, fishing, shooting, tennis, hockey, bowls, darts, snooker, athletics, swimming, sailing, mountaineering, walking, ice sports, motorcar and motorcycle racing and rally driving. American football and basketball are increasingly popular owing to television exposure and are played in Britain. These sports may be either amateur or professional, and spectator- or participator-based, with car and motorcycle competitions, greyhound racing and horse racing being the most watched on television and on the few remaining circuits. Donington Park in the English East Midlands lost its chance to stage Formula One (F1) motor races in 2009 because of a failure to modernize the circuit.

PLATE 12.7 Surfing on the Cornish coast (here Polzeath, Hayle Bay) has attracted growing numbers of participants, nationally and from abroad.
(David Hughes/Robert Harding/Rex Features)

The professional sporting industry is now very lucrative, and is closely associated with sponsorship schemes, television income, brand merchandizing and non-sport sales. Gambling or betting on sporting and other events has always been a popular, if somewhat disreputable, pastime in Britain, and is now much more in the open and acceptable. Most gambling (through betting shops or bookmakers and increasingly online) is associated with horse and greyhound racing but can involve other sports. Weekly football pools (betting on match results) are popular and can result in large financial wins, although the traditional appeal and involvement seem to have diminished.

The new-found acceptability of gambling in Britain was reflected in the establishment of a National Lottery in 1994. It is similar to lotteries in other European countries and considerable amounts of money can be won. Some of its income has also funded artistic, community, leisure and sports activities which are in need of finance to survive. It is also helping to finance the London Olympics in 2012 and British Olympic athletes. But falling ticket sales and profits have recently meant that the lottery could no longer guarantee financial support for all its 'good causes'.

A National Centre for Social Research survey in June 2000 found that 72 per cent of British adults gamble at least once a year (if only on the annual Grand National horse race at Aintree in Liverpool). The National Lottery came top (65 per cent) followed by scratch cards (22 per cent), fruit machines (14 per cent), horse racing (13 per cent), private bets with friends or workmates (11 per cent), football pools (9 per cent), bingo (7 per cent) and casino gambling (3 per cent). The previous Labour government had also controversially opened up the possibility for more casinos in some big cities, although there has been little progress due to local and national protests.

Many sports have contributed to institutionalized features of British life and provide a certain degree of national identity. For example, Wimbledon is tennis;

the Football Association Cup Final is football in England (at Wembley Stadium); St Andrews is golf in Scotland; Twickenham in England, Murrayfield in Scotland, and the Millennium Stadium in Cardiff, Wales are rugby union; Lords Cricket Ground in London is cricket; the Derby at Epsom is flat horse racing, the Grand National in Liverpool is steeplechasing; Henley Regatta is rowing; Cowes Week off the Isle of Wight is yachting; Ascot is horse racing; and the British Grand Prix is Formula One motor racing at Brand's Hatch and other circuits. Some of these sports may appeal only to certain sections of the population, while others may still be equated more with wealth and social position.

Although tobacco sponsorship of most sporting events was banned by the previous Labour government, some people feel that the professionalization and commercialization of sport in Britain has tended to weaken the traditional sporting image of the amateur, of fairness and the old emphasis upon playing the game for its own sake. Yet these values still exist to some degree, in spite of greater financial rewards for professional sport, the influences of sponsorship and advertising and more cases of unethical behaviour in all sports. Football and cricket players, in particular, have been accused of increasingly boorish and aggressive behaviour on the field.

British governments have only recently taken an active political interest in sport. They are now more concerned to promote sport at all levels and there are Ministers for Sport in England, Scotland, Wales and Northern Ireland, who are supposed to coordinate sporting activities throughout the country. The previous Labour government was concerned to improve sporting facilities in Britain by setting up sports councils, colleges, funds and action zones, operating on a regional basis. However, nationally funded provisions for sport in Britain are still inadequate and there is a lack of professional coaches, capital investment and sporting facilities compared with other countries. Local authority sports and leisure centres, particularly in inner-city areas, continue to be sold off, despite the previous Labour government's attempt to focus more money on playing fields and open spaces in deprived areas.

The notion of 'a healthy mind in a healthy body' has long been a principle of British education. All schools are supposed to provide physical recreation and a reasonable range of sports is usually available to schoolchildren. Schools may play soccer, rugby, field hockey or netball during the winter months, while cricket, tennis, swimming and athletics take place during the summer. Some schools may be better provided with sporting facilities than others and offer a wider range of activities. There have also been government attempts to increase fitness in children and to reduce childhood obesity

However, there are frequent complaints from parents that physical education classes, team games and competitive sports are declining in state schools and that there is a lack of professionally trained PE teachers. School reorganization and the creation of large comprehensives have reduced the amount of inter-school competition, which used to be a feature of education; some left-wing councils are opposed to competitive activities; there is a shortage of playing fields (which continue to be sold off); and a lack of adequate equipment and coaching facilities. The position is particularly acute in the inner-city areas and is of concern to those parents who feel their children are being denied much-needed physical exercise. They maintain that the state school system is failing to provide sporting provision for children, with some turning to the independent sector, which is usually well-provided with sports facilities. As part of its attempt to make independent schools justify their charitable status the previous Labour government insisted that they should share sporting facilities with local state schools.

The Labour government had also promised more aid in an attempt to improve the availability and standards of state school sports. In a reversal of previous ideology, it has tried to address the lack of sporting facilities and recent achievement in Britain by embracing the notion of competition between schoolchildren and creating databases of sporting facilities, since none were available at school or local government level. Nevertheless, 70 per cent of the most talented youngsters drop out of sport between the ages of fourteen and seventeen, as opposed to 20 per cent in countries such as France. But better facilities in themselves may not be enough and critics maintain that some schools and local areas are in fact reasonably good in terms of provision. It is argued that more people of all ages should be encouraged to take up sport and that there should be greater cooperation between schools and local communities in the use of facilities and coaching.

The arts

The 'arts' once had a somewhat precious and exclusive image associated with notions of high ('highbrow') culture, which were usually the province of the urban and privileged metropolitan middle and upper classes or the landed aristocracy. This attitude has lessened to some degree since the Second World War under the impetus of increased educational opportunities and the gradual relaxation of social barriers. The growth of mass and popular culture has increased the potential audience for a wider range of cultural activities, and the availability and scope of different varieties of the arts has spread to greater numbers of people. These activities may be amateur or professional and continue the mixture of participatory, spectator- and home-based entertainment.

It is argued that the genuine vitality and innovation of the arts in Britain arise from the millions of people across the country who are engaged in amateur music, art and theatre rather than from the professional and commercial arts world. Virtually every town, suburb and village has an amateur group, whether it be a choir, music section, orchestra, string quartet, pipe band, brass band, choral group, opera circle or dramatic club. In addition, there are some 500 professional arts and cultural festivals held each year throughout Britain, many of which are of a very high standard and appeal to diverse tastes. These range from the Glastonbury (pop and rock) Festival to the Glyndebourne Opera Festival in East Sussex.

The funding of the mainstream arts in Britain is precarious and involves the private and public sectors. The public sector is divided between local authorities and the regional Arts Councils. Local authorities raise money from the council (property) tax to fund artistic activities in their areas, but the amounts spent vary considerably between different areas of the country and local authorities are attacked for either spending too much or too little on cultural activities.

Members of the regional Arts Councils in England, Scotland, Wales and Northern Ireland are appointed by the Secretary of State for Culture, Media and Sport. They are responsible for dividing up an annual government grant to the arts and the finance has to be shared among theatres, orchestras, opera and ballet companies, art galleries, museums and a variety of other cultural organizations. The division of limited funds has inevitably attracted much criticism. It means that many artistic institutions are often dependent upon the private sector and individuals to supply donations, sponsorship and funding, in addition to their state and local government money, in order to survive and provide a service. However, some cultural organizations, such as the Royal Opera and museums, have also received much-needed finance from the National Lottery.

British theatre can be lively and innovative and has a deserved international reputation. There are some 300 commercial or professional theatres, in addition to a large number of amateur dramatic clubs, fringe and pub theatres throughout the country. London and its suburbs have about 100 theatres, but the dominant influence is the capital's 'West End'. The majority of West End theatres are commercial in that they are organized for profit and receive no public funds. They provide a range of entertainment offerings from musicals to plays and comedies.

However, some of the other London theatres are subsidized by grants supplied by the Arts Council, among them the National Theatre, the Royal Shakespeare Company (as well as at Stratford-upon-Avon) and the English Stage Company. These cater for a variety of plays from the classics to modern drama. The subsidized theatres in both London and the regions constantly plead for more state financial aid, which the government is loath to give. The government subsidy is considerably less than that given to most comparable theatres in continental Europe. But there is a feeling in some quarters that these theatres should be more competitive and commercially minded like those in the West End, although Arts Council grants have been recently increased.

Many of the theatres in the regions outside London are repertory theatres, which means that they provide a number of plays in a given season and have a resident theatre company and organization. They present a specific number of classical and innovative plays and a variety of other artistic offerings in a season. The repertory companies have traditionally been the training ground for British actors and actresses, but there is concern that they may further decline.

PLATE 12.8 West End commercial theatres on Shaftesbury Avenue, regarded as the centre of London's theatreland.
(Alex Segre/Rex Features)

Most theatres in London and elsewhere have had difficult times in recent years in attracting audiences and in remaining solvent, although the West End theatres bring considerable financial rewards for the British economy. They have had to cope with increased competition from alternative and new entertainment activities. New commercial theatres in some cities are proving popular and are taking audiences away from the established repertory companies. These commercial theatres provide a wide range of popular entertainment, shows and drama, as well as plays prior to a London run. There are now signs that audience figures for all types of theatres are picking up again.

Opera in Britain occupies a similar position to that of the theatres and is divided into subsidized, commercial and amateur companies. The Royal Opera operates from the reburbished facilities of the Covent Garden Theatre in London. It provides London seasons and occasional regional tours while the English National Opera Company supplies a similar service from its base at the London Coliseum. There is a range of other opera companies, both in London and the regions, such as the English Touring Opera, the Welsh National Opera and Scottish Opera. There are also several light opera groups, and ballet companies such as the Ballet Rambert, the London Festival Ballet, the Scottish Theatre Ballet and the Royal Ballet, the latter of which operates in London and Birmingham. A number of contemporary dance companies have also been formed in recent years.

Britain has many quality orchestras, although most of them are based in London, such as the London Symphony Orchestra, the London Philharmonic and the BBC Symphony Orchestra. There are regional symphony orchestras of high quality, such as the Hallé in Manchester, the City of Birmingham Symphony, the Ulster Orchestra, the BBC National Orchestra of Wales and the Royal Scottish National Orchestra along with a number of chamber groups in London and the regions. Most of the opera, ballet and orchestra activities have their greatest appeal in London and still cater only for a minority of the people. More popular forms, such as brass bands, choral singing and light music once had a large following, but audiences and participation have recently declined. The more exclusive entertainments are heavily dependent upon Arts Council subsidies, local government grants and private donations. The country's operatic, dance and classical music offerings can compete against international rivals.

According to the DCMS *National Survey of Culture, Leisure and Sport,* 2006–07, the top six items in the top ten arts events attended by different household groups in descending order were theatre performances (including play/drama and other forms of theatre), followed by carnival and street arts; live music events (excluding jazz and classical music performances); exhibitions of art, photography or sculpture; craft exhibitions; and classical music performances. Less well attended were culturally specific festivals; jazz performances; events connected with books and writing; and opera and operetta. Other polls have similar attendance results, although they may include a wider range of arts events and different names for the events. For example, cinema may appear first in popularity, followed in descending order by theatre performances, pop and rock concerts, plays, art galleries or art exhibitions, classical music concerts, jazz performances, ballet, opera and contemporary dance. These examples suggest a reasonable response to the arts and a relatively impressive spread of artistic forms.

The history of the cinema in Britain has shown a big decline since its early days as a very popular form of mass entertainment and from 1946 when annual visits reached a total of 1.6 billion. The domestic film industry had virtually ceased to exist, because of a lack of investment and government help, although British films with British actors continued to be made abroad and in Britain with foreign financial backing. Although some government and National Lottery finance has recently been provided to support British film-making, relatively few British films are being made in Britain, many films made in Britain are either foreign or co-productions and the film industry has been criticized for making too many indifferent films.

In 1960 there were over 3,000 cinemas in Britain, but many have now either gone out of business or changed to other activities such as dancing and bingo. However, new screens have been built since 1996 and today there are 2,954 cinema screens situated either in single buildings or in multiplexes with five or more screens. Annual audience figures dropped from some 501 million in 1960 to 193 million in 1970. This decline was hastened by the arrival of television and continued as new forms of home entertainment, such as videos, DVDs and the Internet increased. Annual admissions had sunk to 55 million by 1984. There was then an increase to 142 million in 2000 and to 176 million in 2002 followed by a decrease to 167 million in 2003. There was a slight increase in admissions in 2009 to 173.5 million and combined box office takings in the UK and Ireland exceeded £1bn for the first time.

Some improvement in audience figures since 1984 has been encouraged by cheaper tickets, a wider range of films (beyond the usual blockbuster fare), responses to competition, an increasing appeal to younger people and the pro-vision of an alternative leisure activity within more modern surroundings. The latest figures suggest that increased audience figures are due in part to the success of British-based films aimed at the younger generation (such as the Harry Potter films). Yet more than 30 per cent of the population do not go to the cinema and 47 per cent of those aged over thirty-five never go at all.

British popular music increased hugely and influentially in Britain, led the world from the 1960s and was both an economic and cultural phenomenon. Since the Beatles and early Rolling Stones, the domestic market for music sales has multiplied more than sixfold. However, in recent years, there has been a staleness in the popular field which has affected mainstream genres, hip hop, rap, avant-garde and 'ethnic' music alike. Some critics attribute this to commercial manipulation, overly packaged offerings and standardized bands, and others to a lack of substantial and consistent talent. Old-guard pop stars complain about the inadequacy of contemporary British pop music with its bland, vacuous material and ephemeral boy and girl bands, which have difficulty breaking into the global (and particularly the American) market.

But British popular and rock music still has a domestic and international following, is again slowly becoming attractive to the home and overseas youth market and constitutes a considerable industry. Music was worth £2 billion a year in 2003 (down in value from 2000) and the industry employed some 125,000 people. UK record sales in 2003 saw an increase to 236 million pop albums, but a decrease to 36 million pop singles. The increase in albums and the decline in singles has been marked in recent years. Sales of classical albums have tended to increase steadily. However, all these sales have been negatively affected by widespread piracy and the downloading of music from Internet sources, the development of equipment which bypasses the traditional record product (and CDs) and the recession.

However, in 2009 according to the British Phonographic Industry, the music industry grew in value for the first time in six years as record companies saw a rise in income from music sales to £929 million. Vinyl records and cassette tapes also saw a resurgence in popularity and an increase in sales of 5 per cent in 2009. But this improvement, which came from breakthrough artists, digital sales and advertising, was relatively small; the competition from illegal downloads continues; record companies and government have to seriously address the technological

PLATE 12.9 The Millennium Walkway (from the north to the south bank of the river Thames) and Tate Modern, a very successful gallery and exhibition hall created in 2000 from a disused power station, which specializes in contemporary art.
(Andy Lauwers/Rex Features)

problems; and the music business remains volatile. However, music still represents a sizeable amount of British exports in the form of recordings, concert tours, clothing and books. Polls suggest that 81 per cent of Britons aged between sixteen and twenty-four spend their leisure time listening to music at least once a week and more people attend live music performances than football matches.

There is a wide range of museums and art galleries in Britain (some 1,860), which provide for a variety of tastes. Most of them are financed and controlled by local authorities, although some are commercial ventures and others, such as national institutions like the British Museum and the National Gallery in London, are the province of the Secretary of State for Culture. Entry to most of the public museums and art galleries is now free of charge, after a period when entrance fees were levied by some institutions. But museums and art galleries are finding it difficult to operate on limited funds and are dependent upon local government grants, Arts Council subsidies and National Lottery donations. Museum and art gallery attendance in England rose to 34.7 million in 2003–4 and there were proportional increases in Wales, Scotland and Northern Ireland.

As with sport, certain arts activities and their associated buildings have become virtual institutions, such as the West End, repertory companies, the Last Night of the Proms, the Albert Hall, the Royal Festival Hall, the National Theatre, the Tate Gallery (now called Tate Britain), the National Gallery and the Royal Shakespeare Theatre at Stratford-upon-Avon. These have been added to in recent years by buildings such as Tate Modern, which is associated with often controversial prizes such as the Turner Prize. They reflect Britain's lively (and internationally important) contemporary art scene.

Exercises

Explain and examine the following terms:

Do-It-Yourself (DIY)	the pub	rugby football
package tour	National Lottery	sponsorship
bear baiting	casinos	'bed and breakfast' (B&B)
'high culture'	cricket	the Arts Council
'West End'	brass bands	repertory theatres
football pools	ethnic restaurants	multiplexes
binge-drinking	vinyl	digital

Write short essays on the following topics:

1   What impressions do you gain of the British people, based on their leisure, sporting and artistic activities?

2*   How would you account for the fluctuations in cinema attendance in Britain in the twentieth and twenty-first centuries?

Visit **www.routledge.com/textbooks/oakland** for multiple-choice questions, links to related YouTube clips, tips on approaching essay questions, and much, much more.

Further reading

1 Bennett, A. (2000) *Popular Music and Youth Culture: Music, Identity and Place*, London: Palgrave/Macmillan
2 Christopher, D. (2006) *British Culture: An Introduction*, London: Routledge
3 Fowler, D. (2005) *Youth Culture in the Twentieth Century*, London: Palgrave/Macmillan
4 Gray, C. (2000) *The Politics of the Arts in Britain*, London: Palgrave Macmillan
5 Hill, J. (2002) *Sport, Leisure and Culture in Twentieth-Century Britain*, London: Palgrave/Macmillan
6 Holt, R. and Mason, T. (2000) *Sport in Britain 1945–2000*, Oxford: Blackwell
7 Jacobs, E. and Worcester, R. (1990) *We British: Britain under the Moriscope*, London: Weidenfeld and Nicolson
8 Monk, C. and Sargeant, A. (2002) *British Historical Cinema*, London: Routledge
9 Polley, M. (1998) *Moving the Goalposts: A History of Sport and Society Since 1945*, London: Routledge
10 Rowell, G. (1984) *The Repertory Movement: A History of Regional Theatre in Britain*, Cambridge: Cambridge University Press
11 Silva, T., Elizabeth, B. And Selwood, S. eds. (2006) *Cultural Trends: Culture, Taste and Social Division in Contemporary Britain*, Cultural Trends, 15 (2/3) London: Routledge

Websites

Department for Culture, Media and Sport: www.culture.gov.uk
UK Sport: www.uksport.gov.uk
Sport England: www.english.sports.gov.uk
The FA Premiership: www.fa-premier.com
Rugby Football Union: www.rfu.com
Artsonline: www.artsonline.com
The Arts Council (England): www.artscouncil.org.uk
Arts Council of Wales: www.ccc-acw.org.uk
Scottish Arts Council: www.sac.or.uk
Arts Council of Northern Ireland: www.artscouncil-ni.org
National Lottery Commission: www.natlotcomm.gov.uk
BBC: www.bbc.co.uk
ITC: www.itc.org.uk

Index